THE MODERN GIRL

Feminine Modernities, the Body, and Commodities in the 1920s

With her short skirt, bobbed hair, and penchant for smoking, drinking, dancing, and jazz, the "Modern Girl" was a fixture of 1920s Canadian consumer culture. She appeared in art, film, fashion, and advertising, as well as on the streets of towns from coast to coast. In *The Modern Girl*, Jane Nicholas argues that this feminine image was central to the creation of what it meant to be modern and female in Canada.

Using a wide range of visual and textual evidence, Nicholas discusses both the frequent public debates about female appearance and the realities of feminine self-presentation. She argues that women played an active and thoughtful role in their embrace of modern consumer culture, even when it was at the risk of serious social, economic, and cultural penalties. The first book to fully examine the Modern Girl's place in Canadian culture, *The Modern Girl* will be essential reading for all those interested in the history of gender, sexuality, and the body in the early twentieth century.

(Studies in Gender and History)

JANE NICHOLAS is an associate professor in the Department of Women's Studies at Lakehead University.

STUDIES IN GENDER AND HISTORY

General Editors: Franca Iacovetta and Karen Dubinsky

JANE NICHOLAS

The Modern Girl

Feminine Modernities, the Body, and Commodities in the 1920s

UNIVERSITY OF TORONTO PRESS
Toronto Buffalo London

© University of Toronto Press 2015
Toronto Buffalo London
www.utppublishing.com
Printed in the U.S.A.

ISBN 978-1-4426-4828-9 (cloth)
ISBN 978-1-4426-2604-1 (paper)

Printed on acid-free, 100% post-consumer recycled paper with vegetable-based inks

Library and Archives Canada Cataloguing in Publication

Nicholas, Janes, 1977–, author
The modern girl : feminine modernities, the body, and commodities in the 1920s /
Jane Nicholas.

(Studies in gender and history)
Includes bibliographical references and index.
ISBN 978-1-4426-4828-9 (bound)   ISBN 978-1-4426-2604-1 (pbk.)

1. Feminine beauty (Aesthetics) – Canada – History – 20th century.   2. Women in popular
culture – Canada – History – 20th century.   3. Beauty, Personal – Social aspects – Canada
– History – 20th century.   4. Women – Canada – Social conditions – 20th century.
5. Women – Canada – Economic conditions – 20th century.   6. Canada – Social
conditions – 1918–1930.   I. Title.   II. Series: Studies in gender and history.

HQ1220.C3N52 2015   305.4097109'042   C2014-907290-2

University of Toronto Press acknowledges the financial assistance to its publishing
program of the Canada Council for the Arts and the Ontario Arts Council, an agency
of the Government of Ontario.

 Canada Council   Conseil des Arts
for the Arts   du Canada

 ONTARIO ARTS COUNCIL
CONSEIL DES ARTS DE L'ONTARIO
an Ontario government agency
un organisme du gouvernement de l'Ontario

This book has been published with the help of a grant from the Federation for the
Humanities and Social Sciences, through the Awards to Scholarly Publications Program,
using funds provided by the Social Sciences and Humanities Research Council of Canada.

University of Toronto Press acknowledges the financial support of the Government of
Canada through the Canada Book Fund for its publishing activities.

For Karl and Sebastian

Contents

Illustrations

Acknowledgments

Typing these acknowledgments is a bit of an emotional archaeological dig as I peel back the layers of my own history that have shaped this project. It is a real pleasure to be able to publicly thank many of the people who supported this project and me.

The initial work took place at the University of Waterloo. I am profoundly grateful that I had the good fortune to work with Wendy Mitchinson. Her guidance, insight, and generosity are nothing short of exceptional. As part of the Tri-University program, my years at Waterloo also allowed me to work with Cynthia Comacchio whose scholarly support and advice were essential. Jamie Snell, Sandra Burt, Suzanne Zeller, and Keith Walden generously provided advice and feedback. Daniel Bender's brief time in Waterloo distinctly shaped my thinking of history. James Walker mentored me as a teacher and taught me much about historical practice and pedagogy. As an historian, I became part of a wide community of supportive scholars, including Renee Bondy, Tracy Penny Light, Kirrily Freeman, Jason Churchill, Patrizia Gentile, Elise Chenier, Christina Burr, and Cheryl Krasnick Warsh.

All of my colleagues at Lakehead University have provided much support or motivation. Everyone thanked here helped through crises and stages of grieving that took me away from writing, as they reminded me of the significance of friendship and community. For their encouragement, and collegiality I thank Patricia Jasen, Victor Smith, Kristin Burnett, and Peter Raffo as well as my colleagues in the Department of Women's Studies, Pamela Wakewich, Jenny Roth, and Lori Chambers. Lori read the entire manuscript, provided valuable insights, and (perhaps most importantly) encouraged me to send it off. One of the great benefits of working at Lakehead University has been joining the collegial and exciting academic community that crosses faculties and disciplines. For their friendship and support, I thank Monica Flegel, Judith Leggatt, Batia Stolar, Doug Ivison, David Richards, Adam van Tuyl, Gillian Siddall, Rhonda Koster, Rachel Warburton, and Tony Puddephatt. My good friend and colleague Helen Smith was a source of inspiration. As an undergraduate student I became enthralled with Canadian women's history because of her classes and she enthusiastically welcomed me back as a colleague. She died while this book was in progress, and I miss her terribly.

Archivists and librarians at the National Archives of Canada, the Archives of Ontario, the University of Toronto Archives, the City of Toronto Archives, the City of Vancouver Archives, the University of Waterloo Library and Archives, the Lakehead University Library and Archives, the Thunder Bay Museum, Dance Collection Danse, and the Canadian National Exhibition Archives helped with the research portion of this project. In particular, I want to acknowledge Linda Cobon at the CNE and Miriam Adams and Amy Bowring at Dance Collection Danse whose help was extraordinary. A number of individuals assisted in trying to locate paintings for me including Charles Hill, Brian Foss, David and Laura Kilgour, Jan Huk, and Glenn Allison. Thanks to the corporations, archivists, historians, and lawyers that provided permission to reprint the images or assisted me in tracking down the appropriate copyright holders. I have a new respect for the complications of copyright law and I have tried to be diligent in finding the correct copyright holders. Unfortunately, some of my requests to reproduce images were denied leaving visual "holes" in the manuscript.

At the University of Toronto Press, Len Husband and the Gender and History series editors Franca Iacovetta and Karen Dubinsky have supported this project along the road to publication. Len is a patient and understanding editor and working with him has been a pleasure. I have benefitted greatly from Franca's and Karen's ethusiasm and support as well as their scholarship. The anonymous readers were generous and rigorous, and I appreciated their feedback. My thanks to Frances Mundy for expertly guiding the book through the last stages of publication and to Anne Fullerton for her excellent work as copy editor. Thanks to Barbara Kamienski for the index. Portions of chapters 2 and 4 were published in *Consuming Modernity* edited by Cheryl Krasnick Warsh and Dan Malleck and *Historie Sociale/Social History*, respectively. I thank the editors for the permission to reprint that material and for their invaluable feedback and encouragement on the earlier drafts.

My parents Peter and Barbara Nicholas and brother Daniel Nicholas might not quite understand my persistence in asking such complicated although seemingly banal questions, or my compulsive desire to seek out the answers, but they have always supported me. My mother died of cancer during the last stages of this book and I was reminded again of women's resiliency and the significance of commodities like face cream and eyebrow pencils in providing comfort and a sense of normalcy in the wake of the devastation of cancer's full-blown attack on the body. I picked up the phone to call her when I first saw the cover of this book only to remember she was gone.

In the end, after all that has happened, it might seem strange to dedicate a book on the Modern Girl to a boy and his father, but through all of this I have come to embrace contradiction. So, to Sebastian and Karl for all the patience, love, time, and support it took to get to this moment.

THE MODERN GIRL

Feminine Modernities, the Body, and Commodities
in the 1920s

0.1 Sylvia Horn, Sylvia Horn Fonds, Dance Collection Danse, Toronto, Ontario. Courtesy of Dance Collection Danse.

Introduction:
The Canadian Modern Girl

The young dancer in the photograph is posed carefully in a small studio in Fort William, Ontario in the late 1920s. She was Sylvia Horn, the daughter of white, middle-class parents living in the neighbouring town of Port Arthur, Ontario. It is impossible to know how exactly the photograph would have been read by her contemporaries. For some, her pose, dress, and bobbed hair would have been disturbing, perhaps almost scandalous. We can see her entire leg, and her chest is covered with light catching sequins that draw the eye. Would viewers have associated her image with the powerful discourses on future mothers of the nation and the desire to maintain the standards and standing of the white, middle class seen to be imperilled by a dangerous, sexually-charged, popular consumer culture? Would others have experienced pangs of jealousy at her ability to meet the demands of the idealized body: long, thin, lithe, young, and white? Perhaps some were drawn to the associations with internationally known modern dancers like Isadora Duncan, Maud Allan, or Ruth St. Denis, whose movements brought shape to some of the fundamental feelings of modernity: dislocation, alienation, desire for the Other, pleasure, and freedom. Horn's body itself, however, could be read as an allegory for the debates, discussions, pleasures, and anxieties of the Modern Girl and her place in Canadian culture in the 1920s, as she is precariously balanced and stretched in all directions. Another question looms: How does a young woman from a small town in Northern Ontario end up looking like the iconic image of the 1920s: the Modern Girl?

The photograph of Sylvia Horn opens a host of questions on the making and meanings of feminine modernities in English Canada and the significance of the modern, female body to the project of modernity. The answers to those questions formulate the basis of the argument here that the Modern Girl did important cultural work in creating, maintaining, and contesting what it meant to be modern and female, and at the heart of those discussions were issues of class, gender, race, sexuality, and age. The Modern Girl – although simultaneously popular and problematic – was the embodiment of feminine modernities in Canada, which were themselves defined by popular culture and consumerism.[1] She was defined by her mass-market clothing, including the requisite short skirt and cosmetics. She consumed goods from clothing to cigarettes and eschewed established visual cues of gender, class, and ethnicity. Situating feminine modernities at the centre of the study allows for an exploration of how the modern body itself was tied up in feminine performances of disciplining and caring for the body; how, as Penny Tinkler and Cheryl Krasnick Warsh have argued, "modernity was cast as a feminine experience;" and how a pleasure-seeking popular culture was deemed a feminine threat – something challenging traditional values.[2] The unevenness of Canadian women's representation of feminine modernities however, is important to note, as it was complicated by discourses of race, age, and class. Place is also significant, but in this study I have chosen to emphasize the mobility of representations and discourses of the Modern Girl, largely dislocated from the particularities of local contexts. This allows me to emphasize wider cultural patterns, but roots the study more amorphously in English Canada. As such, the evidence here is (unevenly) from cities scattered over the map.

Taking the Modern Girl as a central organizing figure or a heuristic device, I study facets of feminine modernities – consumerism, appearance, the making of the modern body, popular culture, and common contemporary representations – to reveal how women were represented as modern objects and also represented themselves as modern subjects.[3] Primarily, my interests lie in what might be summarized as discourses of beauty, and my focus here of feminine modernities is organized around the production and performance of the modern female body, rather than how women made domestic settings modern or were fashioned as modern mothers.[4] It is not, I would argue, possible to neatly separate these discussions from those of nationalism and nation building. While beauty may seem to be distant from political considerations, I argue here that the Modern Girl did important political work in defining Canadianness on both a political and racial level. Thus, while I recognize that there were multiple levels and ways of being modern, my focus is that the shaping of the modern female body was central to propagating, understanding, debating, and performing modernity. These met around the broad group of the Modern Girl, which included different variations: the more extreme flapper, the modern working woman, the beauty contestant, the mannequin, and the film starlet. Despite significant differences, especially in class, these Modern Girls were brought together by their imbrications with metropolitan life, consumer culture, and new body projects.

The Modern Girl was not the first representation of womanhood meant to define a generation. She was preceded by Charles Dana Gibson's creation of the quintessential "American Girl" – the Gibson Girl – and sometimes overlapped or was compared with other fictional female icons, in particular the New Woman, the sexually charged "It Girl," and the vamp.[5] Like these other representations, the Modern Girl was caught up in a complex web of meaning about femininity, sexuality, age, and nation. Part of the variation in Modern Girls was due to her integration into various national contexts. As a result, stereotypically distinct Canadian Modern Girls – depicted rosy-cheeked in winter settings – existed alongside other more global variations like the middle-class flapper who appropriated working-class habits and behaviour and some of the culture of the Harlem Renaissance to make herself modern.[6] In short, I consider the Modern Girl a historical actor in her own right. Producing a modern body was both intimate and personal and distant and public, and at the heart of many debates discussed in detail here in chapters 4, 5, and 6, class was a fundamental factor. Modern femininities certainly crossed class lines – which was a source of concern and debate – but propelling them to a good degree were young, working women. By the 1920s this included most young women, since many engaged in paid labour between schooling and marriage. This makes the Modern Girl more than a central character to histories of work, especially the cultural history of the 1920s. Although young women's associations with consumerism has sometimes been viewed by labour historians as the reason for the decline in labour activism, if not the breaking down of working-class collective identities in the 1920s, this is an assessment rooted in the assumption of young women as pawns of industry, unthinking dupes of advertisers, and generally the conduits for a corrosive culture.[7] Placing young, working women in the context of cultural change gives us a chance to take their bodies, work, consumption, and performances seriously.

Feminine modernities and the inequities of power that accompanied them rested on a new visual economy, emerging in the late-nineteenth-century urban, industrial West and intensifying in the early decades of

the twentieth century, that placed women's bodies at its centre.[8] Technological innovations from photography to electricity to printing to transportation provided for the quick and plentiful circulation of images. If
people "imagined community" in the early decades of the twentieth century, they did so to a great extent because of visual depictions.[9] While the
representations of women's bodies for aesthetic, allegorical, or figurative
purposes were hardly new, modern visual culture intensified, proliferat-
ed, and simultaneously flattened representations of women, creating
common types broadly employed. Images were more than the paper
they were printed on. The new visual economy was intimately tied to
wider historical processes, especially consumerism and changes in class
and gender brought on by the urban, industrial environment. As such,
exploring women's bodies leads us beyond the body proper to discussions about culture itself. The Modern Girl continued the trend of sym-
bolizing the desires and fears of the nation in a young woman's body, but
in the context of a consumer culture that increasingly sexualized the female body for the pleasure of visual consumption. One of the markers of
modernity was visuality and women's ubiquitous presence as objects
to be looked at, coinciding with both commercial culture and quasi-
nationalist aims, as was the case with beauty contests (discussed here in
chapter 4). For women, modern visuality meant an intensification of
self-display that was translated into quests for mobility, freedom, and an
independent sexual identity propelled in part by an increasingly sophisticated advertising industry, but also women's desires and demands.[10]
The Modern Girl's body was produced through a variety of new disciplinary strategies, which embraced the possibilities for pleasure in caring for
the body and performing it as modern. At the nexus of contemporary
consumer culture, the Modern Girl often bore the brunt of developing
standards for the body – a modern, female, sexed body – as well as subsequent debates about women's proper place and their relationship with
community, society and nation.

Overall, the argument that follows attempts to shed light on the role
representations of femininity played in defining the meanings and limits
of modernity in Canada in the 1920s. As such it builds upon discussions
in women's and gender history that have focused on women's experiences as workers, social reformers, and mothers in the period, and
women's bodies as sites of medicalization, as well as discourse analyses
on gender, class and sexuality.[11] It adds to these studies by focusing especially on gendered modernity through popular and consumer culture, building upon feminist analysis on the history of consumerism.[12]

Invoking gender and women's history recognizes that, despite significant differences in perspectives on theory and practice, feminist histories share a concern with inequities in women's lives.[13] In particular to
this study, Strong-Boag's social history of girls and women was a land-
mark study in focusing on the private aspects of female lives in the interwar period and connecting them to wider national changes as well as
continuities.[14] Ultimately, Strong-Boag challenged the idea of the "new
day" – the promise of social progress for women in the period following
major achievements like women's suffrage. Well ahead of many serious
discussions on the body and beauty, Strong-Boag also outlined the
changes in consumer culture and shifts in the expectations of women's
beauty. My investigation picks up on this thread from *The New Day Recalled*
and makes it central, using analytical tools that have developed in cultural historiography over the last two decades or so. In some ways, then,
this is a complementary study to Strong-Boag's, with a cultural orientation that extends from international discussions on the flapper and the
Modern Girl like those sparked by Billie Melman, Nancy Cott, and more
recently, The Modern Girl around the World Research Group.[15]

Since the late 1980s when many of these studies began to emerge,
cultural analysis has become *de rigueur*. Questions of the politics of
women's bodies and scholarly work on consumer culture have become
popular and prolific fields influenced by sociology, cultural studies, and
women's studies, among others. These shifts were part of a wider one
often labelled "the linguistic turn" to reveal the influence of post-
structuralism. Extending to even earlier debates, but really taken up in
the Canadian historiography of the 1990s, the linguistic turn introduced
discourse analysis and gender (often in opposition to women's) history.[16]
Born out of these changes was a spate of studies reassessing Canadian
history by asking questions about gender and gender conflicts, the latter
defined by the contributors to one important collection as encompass-
ing conflicts between men and women, but also conflicts of class, race,
ethnicity, and culture among women.[17] In *Toronto's Girl Problem* Carolyn
Strange noted that historians have not given ample attention to the
"enormous cultural relevance" of working girls in their own time, and as
a result their history has largely "fallen between the cracks of conventional historical inquiry."[18] Strange's focus was on the tensions between
moral and social reformers (especially white, middle-class women) concerned with young, single women in Toronto and their lives as working
girls and pleasure-seekers. Given Strange's evidence base (court documents, state investigations, and moral reformers' advice to working girls),

it is not surprising that the study focuses far more on dangers than pleasures. Discussions of bodies, fashion, and beauty remained more stifled,
something not unique to the findings in Strange's study. My study builds
directly from Strong-Boag's and Strange's to uncover the cultural work
of women's bodies, in regard to their messages consumed about the appearance of women's bodies, and also their cultural work in defining
what it meant to be modern.

The Modern Girl is also indebted to a wider range of scholarship on
women's bodies developed since the 1980s. "The body" has been a focus
point and a methodological point of entry for a variety of studies, including analytical studies of clothing, bodily practices, and beauty.[19] While
English-Canadian historians did not accumulate the critical mass of body
history other countries did, there are a number of significant studies that
take the body as a point of departure.[20] Studying "the body" has proved
to be both a promising and frustrating area. Where are bodies in the
historical record? How do we separate "the body" from other analytical
categories like gender and race; – can "the body" stand alone as its own
analytical category? Is it a useful avenue to investigate? I think that it is
for a number of reasons, all of them related to the messiness of the category itself. In the expanded 2005 version of "The Body as Method?"
Canning concludes "bodies sometimes do different work at the same
historical moment."[21] The instability between material and discursive
bodies is something that Canning sees as useful when mobilized in specific, historically-rooted studies. The body here provides an entry point
because it was so commonly and richly invoked by commentators and
people of the twenties to discuss modernity, and to provide evidence of a
host of concerns and pleasures that accompanied modernity. When
women engaged in processes of making their bodies modern and feminine, they opened them to becoming allegories, sites of intervention and
debate, although as Modern Girls themselves they likely focused on making themselves beautiful, young, and desirable. The body here serves as
a central site for the collection of meaning from wider historical processes such as consumption, to delicate, ephemeral individual acts such
as wearing a bathing suit, to the ways in which people represented themselves and others based on what they saw (or thought they saw) of the
bodies before them. Theorist Elizabeth Grosz's work, which challenges
us to think beyond the dichotomy between real bodies and their representation, also serves to challenge the idea that we must choose between
materiality and discourse. She writes, "I will deny that there is the 'real,'
material body on one hand and its various cultural and historical repre-

sentations on the other. It is my claim throughout this book that these representations and cultural inscriptions quite literally constitute bodies and help to produce them as such." As Kathleen Canning points out, Grosz's work opens up the possibility for understanding the "shifting attention to the assignment of meaning to bodies by subjects."[22] While I see this as a contribution to Canadian *women's* history, my thinking has been influenced by Joan Wallach Scott's formulation of gender as constituted and constitutive in regard to both the body and the discourses that serve to inform it as well as wider, seemingly natural structures.[23]

A significant part of the wider project of feminist theory has been to uncover the masculine bias in the ideological positioning of things as natural. From this wide spectrum, I've taken up this project to frame feminine modernities in the English-Canadian context as another important aspect of the wider narrative of modernity in Canada, which has had (either implicitly or explicitly) a masculine timbre. It also engages with critiques that dismiss the significance of beauty and the performances of the female body as superficial, insignificant, or evidence of women's inability to stand firm against the tides of popular culture. Although it is important to keep in mind feminist critiques of modern femininity as objectification, this is only part of the story.[24] Women were not simply dupes of the media or a modern visual culture that enslaved them to consumerism and told them to hate their bodies. Rather, women, however unequally, were active participants in defining what it meant to be modern and female. [25] Modern women's bodies were not separate from images – they occupied them. Women took on tasks to perform modernity, and as in the case of beauty contests, self-selected and self-presented as Modern Girls in ways that allowed them to make and show their choices in being modern. To be seen and to see, to embody an image, and to produce an image of oneself for public consumption were foundational components of feminine modernities.[26] That one understood bodies in types – and worked to reproduce a type, for example – was a necessity in the crowded urban environment of the modern city.[27] Moreover, as these chapters unfold, the inequalities of gender, race, class and age are never distant from the analysis, as the category of woman was deeply fractured in early twentieth century Canadian society. Feminine modernities were objectifying and patriarchal, but not always wholly oppressive, as some women found ways to express pleasure in fashioning female subjectivities by accessing (and only sometimes successfully) the promised rewards of meeting the standards of the object-image, such as beauty contestants.[28] A woman's ability to do so, however, was based on a system that delineated race, age, and class privileges. In light of this, for example, beauty was a politicized discourse that shaped the boundaries of who was and who wasn't beautiful (and the attendant privileges that afforded), as well as who was "ordinary" and who was "exotic."[29] The fractures were significant, particularly class, race, age and (hetero) sexuality, which defined the uneven terrain of who could claim status as modern and feminine.

Caught up in commercial culture, the Modern Girl occupied space in similar ways to her precursors like the middle-class department store shopper. Yet, the Modern Girl was distinct from the reformist and Progressive drives of one of her predecessors: the New Woman. Interested in improving women's lives, the New Woman carved out important public space, especially for those who matched her white, middle-class status, and challenged conventional attitudes about various issues like education, paid work, and health. Although the timeline for the New Woman overlaps with the Modern Girl, and in many ways the Modern Girl can be understood as the metaphorical daughter of the New Woman, hard and fast divisions between politics and frivolous consumption are not entirely useful.[30] New Women were consumers and Modern Girls engaged in politics – even in the more traditional sense of the word as historians of France and South East Asia have demonstrated.[31] My delineation of Modern Girls from New Women, however, is based largely on age and class – young women endeavouring to make themselves modern and working girls. The Modern Girl represents a more deliberately ambiguous class position and an appropriation of working class ideas and values, especially regarding commercial amusements and attention-getting dress in the pursuit of pleasure and opportunity.

If one attribute in particular held together the different types of Modern Girls, it was a focus on youth as indicated by the troubling word "girl." While "girl," when used to refer to women, has taken on a rightfully problematic status, following recent scholarship I use "Modern Girl" here to refer to women who were represented or represented themselves as particularly modern.[32] In order to differentiate between Modern Girls and the actual life stage of "girls" I've capitalized Girl when referring to a modern incarnation of womanhood. Yet the word "girl" is a difficult term, and one that second-wave feminists have long sought to refer strictly to female children to avoid condescension and patronization. Third-wave feminisms and popular culture more generally, however, have reclaimed and revised the word (to sometimes troublesome effect), and from Girl Power to Grrls, the word has taken on alternative meanings. The Modern Girl does not meet strict life course definitions of girlhood, as many women who took on the trappings and performance of the Modern Girl were more correctly fitted into categories of adolescence or womanhood. But if the New Woman elbowed her way into a hostile public sphere with notions of improving it, the Modern Girl had a different – some might argue less mature, more self-centred – goal of experiencing pleasure. Even her name "*Girl*" was a sign of her allegedly apolitical and fancy-free lifestyle that fit with the increasingly dominant white, middle-class expectations for childhood and adolescence. In this way, my use of Girl differentiates her from the New Woman, but that is not to say pleasure was not riddled with anxiety or caught up in contemporary politics. Indeed, the Modern Girl opens up the space to explore a deeply personal politic that was at the centre of many public debates: the politics of beauty and the body. For women, the demands of feminine modernities transformed how they were to think about, take care of, and even see their bodies. While much of the evidence of this is prescriptive in nature, and it is difficult to know how women absorbed the messages from magazines, advertisers and beauty culturists, there was a complex connection between "image" and "reality." Images were an important and intensifying part of modern women's reality, and were essential to the production of modern femininity. At the same time, meeting – to whatever degree – the ideal of the Modern Girl meant reproducing an image as one's lived experience.

Modernities, Antimodernism, and Canadian History

Modernity was both a time period and a consciousness of the particularities of being modern. From the 1870s onwards, the trend to urbanization was first realized in many Canadian cities, especially those in the eastern half of the country like Montreal and Toronto. The nation-wide shift from predominantly rural to urban occured in the mid-1920s. Cities themselves changed with towering skyscrapers built to house white-collar workers of massive, consolidated industries, and were accompanied by sprawling factories with regulated workdays and wages for their blue-collar workers. These changes were the result of massive shifts in industrialization and the breaking down of craft and artisanal industries in favour of mass-produced factory-made goods with access increased by new technologies like the railway. Advancements in production required consumers and the rise of consumption, and in turn further changed cities with massive advertising campaigns, department stores and other

changes in retail culture, including the expansion of credit, which facilitated mass consumerism by way of catalogue shopping across the country from the late 1880s.[33]

Modernity was also a shift in consciousness with new ideas and values:
a faith in progress, technologies, and science. Change was the word. As
Keith Walden writes, "the rapid succession of images, spectacles, and
social environments inevitably shaped internal consciousness ... life
seemed more a matter of becoming rather than being."[34] Different patterns in immigration brought New Canadians to cities from places beyond the British Isles, and class tensions exploded. These wide patterns
of change, which occurred slowly and unevenly, prompted varied responses: delight in the new offerings of the city; disruptions and death;
overcrowding, filth, and disease – impulses to cure social and cultural ills.

Many theoretical perspectives on modernity focus almost exclusively
on men's mobility, their place in urban settings, and their ability to gaze
freely. Walter Benjamin tells us that Charles Baudelaire imagined modernity as a city with the flâneur wandering, looking around and slipping
in and out of the anonymous crowd, while he took in the experience of
the urban environment. With the privileged position of anonymous observer, the flâneur could make sense of the disconcerting, disjointed, and
even trivial experiences of the city as well as take in the breadth of the
spectacle of people and things on display and for sale.[35] As recent scholarship demonstrates, however, such perspectives account only for portions
of modern experience. While the masculine metaphor for modernity is
informative, it creates a partial picture of what it meant to be modern and
of the contours of modernity itself. Who, after all, was he watching? The
flâneur was only a spectator of the circulation of goods and bodies for
sale, which differentiated him, as a type, from late-nineteenth-century
female modern types like the middle-class department store shopper or
the prostitute, whose power to witness and describe modern life were
heavily circumscribed, but not absent.[36] The New Woman also carved out
public space. In this mix of types – flâneur, shopper, prostitute, New
Woman – urban modernity was embodied by gendered representations, and until recently, the observer has been given more historical attention and agency than the observed. But nineteenth-century Paris (the
world of Baudelaire and the point of fascination for Benjamin) is distant
from the English-Canadian urban experience of the 1920s: geographi-
cally, temporally, culturally, politically, and socially. It is also similar in
the gendering of urban modernity; the discourse of pleasure, fear, and
anxiety; the troubling and unresolved issues of class and sexuality; the

rise of conspicuous consumption; the ongoing panic over shifting gender relations; and concern over race relations crystallized around a type – a trope of urban femininity that embodied these issues on the English-Canadian landscape: the Modern Girl.

Two related points here are important in situating Canadian Modern Girls historiographically and historically. First, as Cecilia Morgan notes, antimodernism has received more attention from Canadian historians than modernity.[37] Second, the dominant narrative of interwar culture has been shaped by postwar cultural nationalism and its related high artistic pursuits. Studies of modernity in the Canadian historiography have tended to focus on conservative reactions to popular and consumer culture and their alleged threat to Canada and Canadians.[38] Taken together, these two points have given the period a particular tone – one that is distinctly masculine in character and rooted in a particular vision of Canadianness that is rugged, engaged with nature, and fighting against the tides of a cheap popular culture. For example, in trying to define a national Canadian culture, English-Canadian cultural elites championed the Group of Seven whose masculinist, antimodern vision of the nation represented Canadian Art and Culture and as an unofficial vision for the country itself.[39] Within this formulation, art, literature, music (apart from jazz), poetry, and perhaps even good-quality, moral Canadian-made films counted as culture, and the literature on the 1920s has sought to recover much of this self-conscious cultivation of the high arts. Yet, at the heart of the desire for a completely "Canadian" culture was a nationalism that mythologized as much as it endorsed. English-Canadians were enmeshed in a North American culture that can be exemplified by the cross-border trade of films, magazines, and literature.[40] Underlying the project of cultural nationalism and the ways it has been emphasized and, at times, reinscribed as the main cultural movement in the historiography is what Andreas Huyssen calls "the great divide." He asserts that traditional conceptions of modernism rejected popular, consumer culture exactly because it was deemed feminine. As a result, "the great divide" between high artistic culture and low popular culture is an artificial gendered construction propagated and maintained by a variety of practices. Huyssen makes it clear that this feminine culture was distinguished from high masculine forms as well as from folk culture like those of the antimodern impulse.[41] Applied to Canadian historiography and history, Huyssen's discussion of the divide helps to explain the predominance of antimodernism and cultural nationalism in the historiography because of their masculinist orientation. Further, as Daniel Coleman's recent work has demonstrated, the grand narrative of Canadian history, which this falls into, is also one defined by race.[42] Thus, the story of "colony-to-nation," especially in the 1920s, has been defined by a white, middle-class conservative narrative of self-conscious cultural nation-building.

By the 1920s Canada had become modern, and the First World War brought to a head other changes and anxieties that would define the decade.[43] In the aftermath of the First World War, Canadians were frequently told that the world had permanently changed, and these changes were complex for Canadian girls and women. Two key aspects of the early feminist movement in Canada – the vote and prohibition – had been achieved, although the latter wouldn't last the decade. Social and cultural changes accompanied political and legal ones. Psychologists, physicians and educators worked to define new standards of health, education and well-being and in doing so carved out new categories like adolescence and helped to shift ideas on women's involvement in sport and physical activities. While women's participation in the First World War was limited, their volunteer and paid work as nurses, factory workers, and fundraisers helped change perceptions on the relations between the sexes, women's place in the public, and their duty to the country.[44] Cracks in Victorian morality, which had appeared before World War I, had fallen open by the end of it. For youth who came of age in the wake of the war, a revolution in morals was at the core of their generation. The challenge of the "new" morality was not simply looser attitudes towards sexual experimentation with potential repercussions for the individual. The future health of the nation was also deemed to be at stake.[45] Discussions of such broad changes were difficult. Honing in on particular women's bodies localized and familiarized the discussion. Women's bodies had a longer history of representing the nation and being caught up in allegorizing its health and rooting changes. More importantly, women were seen as more easily modernized than men and seemed more precocious, more in danger, and simply more modern. As a result, English-Canadians were preoccupied with how modern life was changing women: their place in public as reformers, workers, and shoppers all seemed to challenge the residual ideal of Victorian womanhood. Women, however, were not a single category. Some saw their place in the public as a necessity to challenge the decaying influence of modern life where cities were both literally and allegorically dirty. Predominantly white and middle-class social reformers turned their maternal gaze towards single working girls "adrift" in the city. Working girls sometimes revelled in the delights of the city, experiencing the full cast of new commercial amusements, while others certainly found the city harsh and dangerous. Emphasis on material conditions and personal histories, however, were often eschewed by a focus on types – the central theme for this study.

Though none of these experiences were uniquely Canadian, an increasing body of international scholarship has started to explore the simultaneous appearance of the global Modern Girl in the 1920s. What is universally shared (albeit unevenly) is the process of modernization, the upheaval of the First World War, and the intensified influence of consumer culture, including novels, magazines, advertising, and movies. Studies on French, British, Danish, Japanese, Indian, Australian, Chinese, and American women, for example, reveal the contours and different influences in the wider global patterns of change and how these shifted in particular national contexts.[46] The Canadian Modern Girl's contentiousness, if not rejection of having existed at all has been documented in the historiography. It is, perhaps, most apparent from the lack of serious consideration she's been given to date, and to interpretations that stress the continuities (often cast as similarities in work and domestic patterns of marriage and motherhood) between her life and her mother's over any change. As Brigitte Søland's work on Danish modern women in the twenties reminds us, emphasis on continuity is contested by women's own memories of their youth and does not adequately address changes in dominant constructs of femininity, the body, leisure, and heterosociability.[47] The Modern Girl may seem too frivolous, too insignificant, too feminine, too American, and too elusive to count in the serious business of Canadian history. She may well be (in part) all of those things, but that is exactly why she is significant.[48] Making a modern, female body placed women at the centre of wider cultural changes related to consumerism, the relations between the sexes, racial and class politics, and the significant role gender played in defining modernities. Some historians have also suggested that advertising created the sexualized image of women and the Modern Girl in the 1920s. David Monod, however, points to a more complex relationship, driven by the appearance of independent modern women. He writes, "These images [of female consumers] were not created by a handful of patriarchal advertising agents and department store executives; they were a product of the reciprocal relationship between buyer and seller that lay at the heart of a consumer society."[49] To reduce women's consumer identities to patriarchal authority is to minimize their agency in forming modern sexed identities and to reduce them to unthinking children in the world of smart men. Nevertheless, this is not a claim of victory over patriarchy. Women were paid less as workers, treated paternalistically as both workers and consumers, and were victims of structures and people who saw their modern identities in terms of sexual availability and took advantage of them. Their ability to forge modern identities in spite of these proscriptions, and to become a cultural force in defining Canadian modernities and continue to do so in spite of ridicule and violence speaks to their collective strength, not their weakness.[50] As Peter Baskerville has recently argued in regard to middle-class women, they were far more powerful players in the world of late-nineteenth-century urban capital than historians have subsequently given them credit for.[51]

In the end, *The Modern Girl* is an attempt to cross not only a high/low artistic divide but also to take consumerism and the production of the modern body seriously as a foil against better studied masculine elements of modernity. This study also seeks to de-code some of the feminine threat of popular culture, and to explore the gender anxieties of the 1920s. Antimodernism was, after all, a reaction to something, and its assertion of masculinity – a hardy, virile, land-loving, rugged masculinity – was a reaction to the threat of feminine modernities. This threat was symbolized in part by Modern Girls' alleged political and sexual independence: their ability to vote and their public desiring of non-white men, for example. If we take the centre to be the production of high culture in the context of supporting nationalistic aims, then perhaps the Modern Girl looks like a neat aside to the "real" story. But the centre is not only defined by its periphery, it is enmeshed with it. While Canadian culture was promoted as one born in a rugged Northland, true to a higher national spirit, and free from the obscenity and cynicism that seemed to mar American culture, underneath the discourse were simmering tensions of race, class, and gender extended throughout modern consumer culture. The Group of Seven and other cultural elites were cultural gatekeepers who refined and attempted to shore up white, masculine privilege in the face of the feminine threat. The Modern Girl in Canada both chafed against and shored up these nationalistic aims. Her existence must then be discussed as part of – not separate from – the discourses of nation, art, and masculinisation.

Finding the Modern Girl

The Modern Girl is about particular representations of bodies and changes in expectations of women's lives, but also about how femininity and modernity were ultimately assembled and re-assembled through a variety of discursive practices (texts that encompass both the written and the visual) that shaped understandings of modernity itself. That the Modern Girl was represented in a variety of ways in advertisements, artistic renderings, and corporeal performances leads to a necessary instability and multiplicity – thus the plurality of feminine modernities. The Modern Girl was made of texts, but this does not mean there were no flesh and blood people who embodied, embraced, and contested her. Through embracing the textual it is important to acknowledge that those people have largely passed, that the Modern Girl's existence was primarily constituted of ephemeral and largely undocumented "naturalized" performances; furthermore, even those flesh and blood people of the 1920s were enmeshed with the texts of her production, making it impossible to cleave text from experience.

Documentation on the Modern Girl is both prolific and paltry. She exists in thousands of advertisements and fashion spreads, but very few voices of Canadian women who transformed themselves in any way into Modern Girls are available. This is, perhaps, unsurprising given that the essence of this discussion is ephemeral performances, and these are difficult, if not impossible, to capture and archive in the traditional sense. The evidence of her is, perhaps, as fragile, elusive, and superficial as the Modern Girl herself. The documentation collected here ranges from newspapers, magazines, advertisements, photographs, and limited archival sources, including one oral history. Archival holdings proved to be limited in tracing the Modern Girl. How could a Modern Girl possibly narrate her performances of self that seemed so naturalized, obvious, and essential in caring for and producing the modern body? In any case, to suggest a dichotomy between lived experiences and prescriptive sources is to suggest an authentic self free from the representations, commodities, and performances that produced the Modern Girl. This dichotomy is one that I seek to complicate.

Advertisements provide an important body of evidence for this analysis. By the 1920s, advertisers were in tune with the fact that the benefits of commodities sold products rather than the products themselves. Incorporating tactics like participatory techniques in which readers are encouraged to visualize themselves in the story, advertisers tapped into modern anxieties about an increasingly disjointed, impersonal, quick-paced world that was increasingly "rationalized" and "bureaucratized." The result was, as Roland Marchand describes it, the recognition of a widespread inferiority complex and lack of other means of seeking advice. The mass media then was fully tapped into the desires and discontents of modernity.[52] What had changed were the advertising techniques to harness and direct female consumers' attention and dollars, and the increasing pressure to participate in a gendered visual economy premised on particular ways of appearing. Increasingly sophisticated advertising techniques did more than sell commodities. As Liz Conor argues, "the new class of advertisers began to understand the importance of capitalizing on women's metropolitan presence and directing their gaze, not only to products but back to themselves and their potential to be visually transformed through the use of goods."[53] Advertisements also provided advice on new, modern ways of appearing, ideas of bodily care, and ways to behave both in public and in private, the latter of which typically revolved around careful self-surveillance and scrutiny. Subjectivity was caught up in commodities and objects, which were themselves gendered and embodied by the Modern Girl.

Overall, the evidence that makes up the bulk of this text is drawn from Canadian magazines and newspapers that were heterogeneous in their content and often carried advertisements virtually indistinguishable from American ones. Despite the popularity of American magazines, my focus here remains largely on Canadian magazines and newspapers in order to get a better sense of the Modern Girl's fit within the Canadian landscape, although it must be noted that syndicated columns, advertisements, and even stories were often of American origin and simply reprinted in Canadian magazines.[54] Such a complication in delineating "Canadian content," however, is important in keeping the global element of the Modern Girl in mind. Magazines and newspapers have been well-studied documents in Canadian history.[55] What I hope to add to the discussion is an intertextual reading focusing on the representation of women's bodies as markers of modernity, images to be emulated, and vehicles for understanding deeper cultural transformations. Here, advertising, letters to the editor, editorials, regular columns, articles and short stories are all used to get a sense of feminine modernities. By taking these sources seriously as part of a significant discourse on women's bodies, consumerism, and modernity, I also hope to explore the superficial and artificial as legitimate subjects.

It is a truism that the historian has to be careful moving from prescriptive sources to lived experience. The close reading of magazines has provided insight into the changing nature of gender and consumer culture.[56] The fact that these sources may be deemed "prescriptive" does not mean, however, that we are doomed to study only what has been sometimes dismissed as secondary to the real business of Canadian history. There is, as Liz Conor points out in regard to the Australian Modern Girl in the 1920s, a decisive connection between images of women and female identities in the modern visual economy.[57] Self-perception and presentation cannot be understood as neatly separated from the production, circulation and consumption of modern representations of women.

This is a story firmly rooted in historical evidence, but a story nonetheless of the meanings of the Modern Girl in Canada in the 1920s and, in turn, what she might add to understanding feminine modernities. She's gone and what we have are pieces of stories made up of images, advertisements, and critical accounts. This fragmentary nature is, in part, intended to help us rethink our previous stories about women, girls, modernity, and commodities in a way that takes them seriously. I do think there is a risk in discounting or dismissing feminine modernities, but whether I've gone too far, or not far enough, is up to readers and other storytellers to decide. As Carolyn Steedman argues, "The point of a story is to present itself momentarily as complete, so that it can be said: it does for now, it will do; it is an account that will last a while."[58] If the Modern Girl has taught me any lesson at all, it is that she defies simple categorization or explanation. And if, as I suggest here, she was at the centre of feminine modernities in Canada in the twenties, she existed by working her way back and forth between establishing a core, revelling in its margins, and being outcast from the centre. She was and is transient, elusive, artificial, ubiquitous, and ephemeral, and in some ways, must remain so. Her ornamental status – how her body was produced and represented as modern – is a key aspect of feminine modernities, and it is this fragment that I focus on in the following chapters. Ornament, artifice, and superficiality were also important aspects and had much deeper implications for Canadian culture and even the nation. Valerie, the beauty columnist for *Saturday Night* related the following real-life story to her readers in 1920:

A woman of decided views said at a meeting recently held: "We must give up our face creams and our rouge, and make a serious business of life."

"Just look at her," whispered a frivolous young thing. "She would be a great deal nicer if she'd put a little powder on her nose or on that shiny spot on her forehead."

Such is the charitable remark which usually follows a declaration of "principle" on the part of the woman who knows what the other woman should give up. If anyone had suggested that the speaker should deny herself tea, she would have been highly indignant, because tea is essential to her comfort. It is important to another woman to know that her nose is not a beacon and that her skin is somewhat protected from the winds and the weather. So, in one way, it is a matter of comfort to be considered, after all, in this question of essentials.[59]

Chapter 1 addresses the "question of essentials," more fully exploring the landscape of modern consumer culture and the production of a female body. In particular, it focuses on the dominant body projects women were expected to take on and the underlying politics of fashion and beauty. It explores how the body was segmented and how those pieces were individually commodified. Such specific commodification relied heavily on changing ways of seeing and performing the body, as well as different disciplinary codes. As chapter 1 reveals, the legs of the Modern Girl took on particular significance in the webs of feminine modernities and consumerism.

While chapter 1 highlights the complicated and confusing terrain of producing a Modern Girl's body, chapter 2 analyses how modern beauty experts in popular Canadian magazines helped women both negotiate and, at times, contest those body projects. Through the popular advice columns by the beauty experts Mab (*Chatelaine*) and Valerie (*Saturday Night*), the section analyses how experts' advice on techniques of appearing encouraged the production of modern, female bodies in Canada in the 1920s through a modern consumer magic, and shored up the discourse that goods were a necessary investment to being modern and beautiful. While critical of these discourses, I also explore the possibilities for pleasure in caring for and producing a modern body. This chapter also discusses when beauty columnists contested the dominant discourse of beauty, and reveals some of the fractures in the politics of beauty.

Chapter 3 builds from the modern body projects to show how they were embroidered into discourses of the city and the nation in which these seemingly neutral practices were in fact embedded within white nation-building projects. White Modern Girls were offered a number of different racial masquerades as part of producing a modern body. Far from neutral forays into different clothing and make-up looks, these performances reaffirmed the privilege of whiteness and did so in ways that had deep implications for the nation, since who could be represented as modern was significant. In this chapter, I also tease out some of the deeper meanings of a racialized modernity for the women whose bodies represented it, as well as explore the racialized frame for heterosexual expressions of modern women's erotic initiatives.

The fourth chapter brings facets from the first three chapters together (body projects, expert advice on appearing modern, consumerism, and nationhood) in reading modern beauty contests as performances of modern femininities by flesh and blood Canadian women. This chapter offers a glimpse (although a seriously mediated one) of actual Canadian women's embodiment and performance of modern femininity for public consumption. It is also suggestive of the sort of cultural conflict over lower middle-class and working-class girls' participation in popular culture in a way that sometimes blurred those class lines.

Chapter 5 hones in on the relationship between high and low culture and how the Modern Girl and modern femininities transgressed these boundaries. Specifically, it analyses the reaction to three nude paintings hung at the Canadian National Exhibition in 1927. It also maps out some of the complicated terrain of so-called ordinary peoples' responses to her, revealing how deeper changes in modernity – exemplified by the Modern Girl – were anxiety-inducing and contentious on a number of levels, but especially in regard to working-class cultural influence summed up by the threat of popular culture. In addition, this chapter addresses the important question of the maintenance of patriarchy. While the Modern Girl challenged masculine modernities, she did not fundamentally upset the patriarchal structure of society. As such, women continued to live and be represented in unequal and sometimes damaging ways.

The sixth and final chapter focuses on women's bodies, cars, and films in bringing together ideas of modernity, consumer culture, and femininity. In returning to feminine modernities, consumerism, and beauty contests, it shows how these complicated processes reinforced each other and, more importantly, gendered seemingly gender-neutral goods and concepts, therefore suggesting a deeply gendered nature of modernity interwoven into and represented by bodies, goods, and performances.

To return to the image that opened this discussion, *The Modern Girl* addresses questions about how the dancer in the photograph produced and performed her body as female and modern. Here, I also seek answers to deeper questions on the fundamental nature of feminine modernities. The dancer posing in a small, Northern Ontario town had the ability to become and perform as a Modern Girl, but that look was also transposed into other locations, and because of the circulation of modern commodities and images (in magazines, on film and in advertisements) her image was pervasive. But it was never just an image: embodied, performed, and allegorized it stood for much more. Her body functioned as a symbol by which cultural shifts in relation to gender, age, and race could be summarized. Her image also marked out some of the complicated territory of feminine modernities in Canada – the threat and delight of popular culture and the gendering of goods and experiences themselves.

1 Making a Modern Girl's Body: Commodities, Performance, and Discipline

The stunning front cover of the 1 February 1924 issue of *Maclean's* magazine depicts a Modern Girl in a winter setting smiling warmly at the viewer. This was a common cover girl for *Maclean's*. Two years earlier, *Maclean's* published a scandal-seeking (and often-cited) article, "Is the Flapper a Menace?" While the article raised concern over the so-called promiscuous behaviour of the flapper, in the introduction it was noted, "This is not an indictment of Canadian girlhood *en masse*. It is no crime to be a flapper, and we have every belief that – in the majority of cases – our Canadian young women are wholesome and sound."[1] In the essay, author G.S. Pringle concluded that the fashion and style of the flapper were not to blame for certain undesirable behaviours of some young women. Yet, cleaving the look of the Modern Girl from how she was interpreted was and is difficult, because commodities created the modern female body, and in a myriad of ways imbricated her into the web of modernity: as a self-disciplining subject, a spectacular object for visual consumption, and as a consumer of goods (from magazines to cosmetics). Her appearance on the cover of the 1924 *Maclean's* reveals these connections, and when juxtaposed with the earlier article, suggests a complex embodied cultural politic.

By the 1920s, there was a cultural expectation that women would look a certain way to be deemed modern, female, and beautiful – and the quest for beauty was a powerful discourse, not easily ignored. It seemed that women were bound to be beautiful and simultaneously judged (on a number of grounds including morality, sexual availability, class status, and desirability) for either meeting the standards of beauty or not. Judgment was the constant. My focus here is on the representations that encouraged particular ways of disciplining the body as modern and female through the use of specific commodities and practices including skin care, dress, and self-surveillance in order to explore aspects of this powerful discourse of beauty that was fundamental to shaping the identity and body of the Modern Girl.

In the 1920s, the Modern Girl became the standard representation of modern beauty, and this embodiment of normative femininity was situated at the heart of commercial culture, commodities, disciplinary practices, and technologies of the self. These developments were not new to the twenties, although the decade witnessed an intensification of them. The Modern Girl did not simply appear as modern, but produced and performed as such through a whole host of commercial goods including clothing and make-up. These commercial and homemade preparations along with clothing and other bodily interventions produced a body that was identifiable as female and modern. As a result, the Modern Girl's body was situated at an important junction of production of the self, disciplinary practices, and modern subjectivity. If consumer goods continued to be a source of desire for working-class women and a source of anxiety for middle-class women seeking to regulate working "girls" behaviour, I might be tempted to conclude that cosmetics and the related disciplining of the female body were potentially democratising, if equally patriarchal. But it's too easy to suggest that the Modern Girl was simply a middling-class fantasy thrust upon women of all classes. If working women's purchasing power was circumscribed by poverty and low wages, then concerns about working women's investment in consumerism and making their bodies modern also reveals the centrality of their participation. As subsequent chapters reveal, it was often working Girls' bodies that were the source for debates on modern femininities.

In this chapter, I explore messages of feminine modernities from consumer culture, especially advertisers. These are best described as the dominant consumer messages on women's bodies of the decade. They might also be described with adjectives like artificial, transient, superficial, and commoditised. Such words, however, should not be moored to judgments like unimportant, parochial, or trivial, since they represent important aspects of modernity itself. In some accounts, however, these words have come to represent women's shallow relationship to the public, their susceptibility to advertising "men," their passivity, their excess, and perhaps even their insignificance.[2] To discount this type of feminine modernity is to discount the significant role of women's visibility in modern life. This also goes for essential aspects of modern life – especially commodity culture – and its place in shaping and demarcating the

1.1 *Maclean's* Cover of the Canadian Modern Girl, *Maclean's*, 1 February 1924.
Used with the permission of *Maclean's* Magazine.

Modern Girl's body. As Donica Belisle argues, studying consumption can also highlight identities not easily uncovered in the historical record. She writes, "when scholars dismiss consumption, they inadvertently dismiss non-bourgeois and female consumer subjectivities."[3] It was her artifice and connection to commodities that made her the Modern Girl, and it was her appearance that represented so many other facets of modern life, especially when tuned into the shifting class and gender dynamics of the period. As Kathy Peiss warns, we should not dismiss her as "too frivolous, body-conscious and self-absorbed."[4] The Modern Girl can tell us much about refashioning the body in connection to modern discourses of gender and sexuality (especially as middle-class women imitated her look creating some of the class hybridity in the Modern Girl). But she is also political, with clear investment (as the debates about her reveal) in the health of the nation, generational conflict (defined in particular by the rupture of WWI) and contemporary politics of race and nation (discussed in chapter 3).

The relationship between artifice, commodities, and modernity relied heavily on self-surveillance as a type of modern spectatorship that fused anxiety and pleasure. Consuming was not only about purchasing, but also about seeing, longing for goods, and understanding the body in very particular ways. The latter certainly rendered the body as something in need of constant monitoring and attention, as well as something capable of quick and alarming change. Acts of production, however, needed to be constantly repeated in order to be maintained. Consuming was also about adopting particular ideas on the necessity of monitoring and changes, which crossed class, race, and gender differences in the period. While certainly connected to literal purchasing power and access to capital, desire and longing were not exclusive to it. It must be noted that the dominant look of the Modern Girl was white and young, although her exact class position remained more amorphous. In part, this is because of changes to the nature of women's work as their subsequent relationship to consumer style. The discourses of beauty naturalized and universalized a look that could be copied in different or cheaper forms.

This chapter takes messages of consumerism as a significant aspect of modern femininities. As such, it enters into conversation with scholars who have called for more historical attention to consumerism. Influenced by mid-twentieth century critical theory indebted to Marxism, many scholars dismissed consumption:[5] until the 1990s, its study was treated with suspicion due, in part, to the dismissal of the Frankfurt school of consumption as mere manipulation and false consciousness. Second-wave feminists also tended to see women's engagement with beauty industries as oppressive. In the 1980s and 1990s, cultural studies influenced by post-structuralism explored the complicated terrain of pleasure in and the making of subjectivities through acts of consumption and display. The scholarship also began to recognize the power and value in seriously considering women's engagement with consumer culture.[6]

In the scope of Canadian historiography, Cynthia Wright's 1992 essay in *Gender Conflicts* was an influential publication in asking historians to reconsider questions of gender and consumerism.[7] Wright notes that though many Canadian women's political and social roles remained circumscribed into the 1920s, their power as consumers flourished. Women's roles as consumers meant they were responsible for purchasing everything from flour to face powder, while being the target of an increasingly intensified consumer message which circulated through a variety of media and spaces, including advertisers, movies, and department stores. Consumer culture was not simply defined by transactions of time and labour for money that, in turn, were exchanged for a particular good, thing, or ephemeral experience. As Victoria de Grazia reminds us, consumption is more than an act of purchasing a good, as it is also about the processes of commodification, spectatorship, and desire for both things and images.[8]

The beauty practices involved in making the female body were hardly liberating, but nor were they simple, taken up by an unthinking female consumer. While women's participation in consumer culture was proscribed by class and race that perpetuated multiple inequities (including who could be seen as modern), women nevertheless mindfully fashioned their bodies through commodities by making deliberate choices about what to buy, wear, and use, and how to fashion, present, and perform their identities. In doing so, they made themselves modern with all the dangers, pleasures, and desires that accompanied it. This chapter adds to these discussions by analysing the dominant messages of beauty and the body, sketching out the ideals of modern, female bodies, including expectations of discipline, display, pleasure and appearance. Consumer culture was not simply about buying things, it was also about using products in ways that changed the body and simultaneously represented it as modern.

Framing the Modern Girl

It was not only advertisers and businesses hoping to sell goods and increase profits that invented the Modern Girl. Her appearance reflected a more complicated origin tied into shifting social and cultural values of the early twentieth century. To understand her origins, it's important to look to wider shifts in class and gender of the period. One of the first references to flappers came, tellingly, in a description of the spontaneous street celebrations in Toronto with the rumour of Armistice. The *Globe* reported a conversation between two individuals: "'Well, Washington deserves a bump if this is not true,' commented a flapper to her friend." The same reporter in a jubilant tone described peering down from a skyscraper witnessing business men and male and female factory workers celebrating downtown:

> From the top of the Royal Bank Building, the highest office building in the British Empire, one could see five or six different processions going on simultaneously. Those in line carried whistles, bells, motor horns, dishpans, confetti, bugles, paper trumpets and all sorts of instruments. The word 'abandon' best describes the spirit of the crowd. Old men and young boys, dignified-looking members of the Church and the professions mingled with the grimy-faced sons of toil and street urchins who were rushing about in every direction shouting the tidings. Girls threw confetti and convention was completely ignored. All were equal at that moment ...[9]

The newspaper's description of a cacophonous crowd of mixed classes and genders foreshadowed the combined sense of newness, pleasure, abandon and anxiety that would mark the decade. Old men, young boys, street urchins, and girls were figures that drew attention by and through the Modern Girl, but it was changes in the Girl herself that symbolized much of modern life because, quite simply, she was so modern.

By the 1910s, urban working-class girls with their demands for leisure and fun (often facilitated though commercial amusements) and their interests in clothing and beautifying goods were an undeniable presence in Canadian cities. In the late nineteenth century, middle-class reformers' concerns over working girls' morality were expressed in relation to their alleged "love of finery." As Mariana Valverde notes, at this time English-Canadian "young working women were increasingly seen as committing sins of consumption."[10] By the 1920s, however, the culture of consumption had at least cracked such narratives. A *Chatelaine* article from 1929 continued the anecdote of the naive (new to the city) working girl lured into the depths of prostitution by the promise of a movie ticket, or by responding to an advert for chorus girls, or with vague promises of parties. The author Anne Elizabeth Wilson pointed to problems in the girls' families, but also laid the blame on social agencies that pushed "the sugar-coated pill of righteousness." Wilson subtly advocated that working girls should not be ridiculed for their love of finery, describing urban working-class girls' "desire for dainty things" as "natural" and rural girls' desire for luxury as something that did not make her "a mental defective nor one deaf to decency." Wilson concluded by telling her readers that she was recently in the store room of a social agency that was filled with a "pretty assortment of dainty feminine 'undies.'" Wilson quoted the store woman as having said: "Those clothes will do more to keep the girls straight than any amount of supervision we can give them." Wilson concurred. In order to understand this shift and the Modern Girl's existence in Canada in the 1920s, it is necessary to sketch out the dramatic social, economic, and cultural shifts from the late nineteenth century. The Modern Girl existed as part of consumer society, which had its own complex development in nineteenth-century changes in industrialization and urbanization.

Consumption was an important element of industrialization, which produced goods for purchase and consolidated people in urban centres. In pre-confederation Canada, industrialization was apparent in small regions in the early decades of the nineteenth century. Spreading slowly and unevenly, by the latter decades of the century industrialization had changed the landscape socially, culturally and ecologically.[11] Although regional and local differences provide exceptions, the general pattern reveals a shift towards urban living, factory work, or other industrial work for wages (rather than barter, home production, or payment in commodities).

Industrialization reshaped patterns of settlement and forged modern communities out of a dense mix of people. The 1921 census revealed that patterns of urbanization apparent in the 1881 census were intensifying, with Toronto and Montreal leading the way with more than a half million inhabitants. Winnipeg, Vancouver, Hamilton, and Ottawa, each with over 100,000, followed. The trend continued through the decade with cities increasing by almost twenty thousand (Ottawa) to two hundred thousand (Montreal).[12] Industrial economic growth was haphazard, leaving mid-to-late nineteenth century Canadian cities struggling to address issues of "spaces and services" such as placement of factories, adequate housing, utilities, transportation, water and sewage, and recreational spaces.[13] It was a much different experience for workers living in the city than their wealthier counterparts. Montreal provided a dramatic example, as its geography was sharply divided by class. The "city below

the hill" lacked proper water and sewage facilities, and residents disproportionately experienced disease, crime, poverty, and premature death.
Social movements to clean up cities like the "city beautiful" movement
and urban reform movements pushing for playgrounds, water treatment, and planned housing, along with social and moral reform movements which focused on temperance and social purity, largely neglected
economic roots to social problems in cities.[14]

Middle class anxieties over urbanization were directed towards immigration and the "proper" development of the Canadian nation. By the
late nineteenth century, Anglo-Saxons no longer dominated immigration to Canada. The 1921 census revealed increasing numbers of
Canadians from southern and eastern Europe as well as an increase in
Asian Canadians. Despite the fact that an overwhelming majority reported British or French ancestry, many white Canadians were concerned
about the country's racial health as evidenced by ongoing discussions
of eugenics and the necessary preservation of white Canada.[15] Racist
concerns dovetailed with changes over traditional small-town and rural
associations. Urban concentrations of people broke down traditional
networks of kin and community, replacing familiarity and character with
anonymity and personality.[16] Community responses predominantly from
white, middle-class folks in cities like Toronto focused on eliminating
vice and instilling morality to the point that the urban slum was viewed
as a moral, not economic problem. As Mariana Valverde and Margaret
Little have demonstrated, vice and morality were not neutral descriptors,
but rather powerful discourses reflecting middle-class, white, Protestant
values. However well-meaning they were intended to be, the negative
impact on immigrants, the poor, working-class mothers, and others were
profound. Poor Winnipeggers, for example, found themselves subjected
to night-time public health inspections of their homes, while single
mothers in Ontario found themselves giving up personal items and relationships in order to receive small, but still much-needed government
allowances.[17] Other dangers of the city – including crime from pick-
pocketing to prostitution – were responded to with an increasingly sophisticated system of doctors, probation officers, social workers, and
other "experts" schooled in modern scientific practices to address the
problems. Increasingly, specialization delineated "types" and groups by
gender and age, while class and racial stereotypes created structures
with built-in biases. As Tamara Myers' study of juvenile delinquency in
Montreal aptly demonstrates, *the jeunes filles modernes* were instrumental
to the development of Quebec's juvenile justice system. Standing in for

the alleged social and moral bankruptcy of the modern age, probation officers, social workers, and other members of the juvenile justice system filled the gap, and provided a venue of appeal for parents of wayward daughters in search of delight or escape. A free and easy lifestyle was an appealing and popular narrative, and yet the behaviour it exalted could still be socially proscribed. The individual penalties of being young, female, urban, and pleasure-seeking (social, economic, sexual, cultural, familial, and personal) have been documented in various cities in Canada.[18]

Modern cities, then, were complicated and complex spaces as newly urban Canadians attempted to address a variety of issues from infrastructure to moral regulation. With concern for the future of the nation in terms of future mothers and still imaginary children, young women's bodies were subject to much scrutiny. In the twenties, the anxiousness over women alone in the city had shifted to one of acceptance, though there were still persistent concerns about her leisure, health, and role in reproducing the nation.[19] As birth rates of white, middle-class Anglo-Saxon women fell and immigration increased, the bodies of working women became subjects of national scrutiny and pro-natalist policies as a means of ensuring the racial health (whiteness) of Canada. Though racial fears continued and intensified, the reform impetus driven by white, middle-class women in the 1920s did not. Whether this was the result of achievements, a generational shift, exhaustion, or a combination of the three, the imperative point is that the 1920s saw a decline in the influence of these organized movements.

Changes in urbanization and industrialization reverberated into homes by way of shifts in production and consumption. Urban life did not lend itself to home-based production, and most families required the paid and unpaid labour of all members. For working families, this left little time to engage in time-consuming production, and cramped urban spaces made domestic production difficult. Changes in production and consumption were gendered, and the culture of consumption did not neutrally present utilitarian messages of goods' values. Victorian domestic ideology placed an emphasis on women in the home, but modern life also required their presence in the public as consumers. The nineteenth-century department store was constructed as part of the private sphere to appeal to middle-class female shoppers.[20] Moreover, in the case of immigrants, consumer goods were marked with a particular social status that worked to define people as of a particular class or level of Canadianness. While this did not replace homemade goods like

clothing, it did mean that patterns for home-sewn fashions were advertised as being able to mimic mass-produced ones, placing the emphasis on store-bought, and revealing the unfashionable backwardness of
home-produced clothing.[21]

Despite serious class inequities, a lack of welfare state, and widespread
labour abuses, working families were part of rising standards of living
across Canada. As Belisle observes, increases in domestic production in
the last two decades of the nineteenth century are indicative of this
trend, as are rising rates of home ownership. Further, Monod argues
that it was manufacturers' frustration with worker's high wages in the
1870s and 1880s that pushed them into marketing their products directly.[22] Changes in patterns of work, increased regulation of working
hours, child labour, and the recognition of the necessity of leisure time,
helped to ensure support of various commercial amusements.[23] In addition, early twentieth-century changes in industrialization, like scientific
management with new work organizational structures and streamlined
production, increased production thresholds and flooded consumer
markets with cheaper goods.

By the 1920s, consumer culture would have been impossible to escape
with indentations of new media, mass circulation magazines, and advertising in magazines, newspapers, and on the street that flooded the cultural landscape. A significant shaping of consumer culture came through
advertising, which appropriated and developed the long-standing repre-
sentational use of women's bodies. In the consumer economy they became incorporated into messages of beauty, luxury, and youth used to
sell a host of goods as well as more ephemeral ideas on style. As Mike
Featherstone argues, the body became both a means to pleasure and
fulfilment as well as a message – largely housed in images – of how people should look and act.[24] Such messages were persuasive, especially as
advertisers deliberately developed adverts to encourage people to imagine themselves within a particular consumer scene and "to identify with
portrayals of themselves as they aspired to be, rather than as they 'really
were.'"[25] Women's roles as consumers, and their responsibilities for
household budgets and household spending, made the messages of consumerism especially acute. This was also the result of wider shifts in class
and gender that took place in the late nineteenth century, and especially
in the first two decades of the twentieth. Women – especially young working women – could be consumers (to the varying degrees their pay packets allowed) because they were also an integral part of the workforce as
wage earners.

Unlike in Britain, for example, the First World War did more to level the Canadian population by sex, which had a higher proportion of men than women since the first census in 1851.[26] Increasing numbers of women were engaged in paid employment, and 1921 census takers noted a significant different since 1911, with further declines in women in domestic service, but a tripling of women in office work (to approximately 90,000), and an increase of women under the category of "transportation" who worked as telephone operators.[27] Legislation passed in 1921 that pushed married women to stay in the home seriously disadvantaged them, and the result was that single women dominated public work.[28]

Young women working in the city were a literal reality as well as an oft-repeated cultural trope used to embody the seemingly rapid shifts in modern, urban life. Beginning in the 1880s, young women flocked to cities in search of work outside of domestic service. The "girl problem" in large Canadian cities like Toronto, Montreal, and Vancouver formed a particular class-based discourse that dictated working conditions, but also leisure time and dress as points of public concern. By the 1920s most young women would experience a period of paid work between leaving school and marriage, but the jobs open to them were restricted to "pink collar" ghettos, with low wages and much competition.[29] Significantly, however, changes in work in line with the rise of consumer style flattened some visual indicators of class. In the 1920s, lower-level white collar jobs opened to working class women, and department stores – the beacons of modern consumerism – hired women of the working and middle classes to staff stores. As Suzanne Morton argues in regard to Halifax in the 1920s, "New opportunities in employment may have confused women's sense of class identity, but clarified their self-perception as women."[30] Consumer messages certainly eschewed a sense of class stratification in democratizing messages that appealed to women as women.

Yet, race, class, and gender still delineated work. By the 1920s, domestic work was the least favoured because of lower wages, a lack of freedom, and the many potential dangers of working in someone's home. As white, working-class women increasingly favoured factory work, the domestic service was defined by racialized and immigrant women. African-Canadian women, for example, were discriminated against in hirings, leaving fewer options for employment outside of service. In the 1920s, the Salvation Army sponsored an immigration scheme that brought 80,000 women from the British Isles to work as domestics. Women from countries restricted by Canada's racist immigration policy now found an opening.[31] White, middle-class women found more preferable jobs in the recently "pinked" clerical sector, which had almost tripled in the percentage of female clerks from 1891 to 1921. Optimism about women's work in the post-World War I period ignored economic inequalities and abuse. Middle- and working-class feminists fought against sex discrimination and class oppression, but were often met with a powerful conservative and misogynist response.[32] Female workers themselves advocated for better conditions often to find their efforts frustrated by stereotypes of class and gender, as female strikers against Bell Telephone found in 1907.[33]

Despite women's increasing public presence in the paid labour force, their wages remained severely depressed because of patriarchal assumptions of a male breadwinner and the belief that women were working for so-called pin money. We know for certain this was untrue. Both middle- and working-class women found themselves managing budgets of sometimes-scare resources with many demands. Consumer culture framed desire and pitched democratization through goods, but seriously faltered in delivering either. Women from various streams found their desires frustrated, limited by economic circumstances, or denied outright. They found ways to lessen these feelings through shoplifting, letter writing to the stores, and doing without, but also reworking limited funds to satisfy consumer desires.[34]

Purchasing goods involved delicate budgeting. In 1912, for example, journalist Maud Petit went "undercover" as a factory worker. She informed readers that she had to skip meals in order to afford the types of clothing other working girls regularly wore. Mary Kinnear's study on working women in Manitoba reveal young women working in manufacturing consistently faced shortfalls in their budgets (some as high as $17 a year).[35] Evidence from other locales also suggests that working class women went without lunches to facilitate the purchase of cosmetics.

In Canada, predominantly middle-class moral reformers worried that movie tickets and consumer goods were used in a complex system of treating, dangerously close to prostitution. W.I. Thomas, in an influential American study published in the twenties, worried that working girls' craze for consuming and lax morals were leading them to prostitution. He wrote, "the beginning of delinquency in girls is usually an impulse to get amusement, adventure, pretty clothes, favourable notice, distinction, freedom in the larger world which presents so many allurements and comparisons." Prostitution and delinquency remained serious issues for the women accused and their families. The wider association between working women, consumerism, and the veneer of sexual favours, however, is itself problematic as it discursively undercuts working women's claim on leisure and the increasingly heterosocial opportunities for commercial amusement, as well as their prerogative to consume. Moreover, the perspective of moral reformers and experts like Thomas reflects assumptions of working class women's (in)ability to have fun, self-regulate, and meet middle-class expectations of respectability (or even want to). The subtext of treating, however, also subtly suggests that women who made themselves desirable in looks and performances could use limited social capital to stretch their budgets to include commercial amusements like visits to movie houses or the CNE.[36]

By the 1920s, the consumer landscape in English-Canada had intensified with the expansion of existing department stores, increasing the numbers of chain stores. A few points are indicative: Eaton's, Canada's largest retail chain, increased mail-order services by opening a walk-in order office handled by salespeople, and had forty-seven stores and a national presence by the close of the decade, including smaller centres like Red Deer, Alberta and Port Arthur, Ontario. Construction of other department stores increased over the course of the decade and retailers introduced instalment buying as credit became more widespread. The mobility of Canadians, due in large part to very high increases in car ownership in the 1920s, meant that lower priced chain stores were draws to the city, especially during the economic recession in the early years of the decade. Here the changing nature of women's work was revealed as well. Department stores relied on women to sell to other women. As Monod argues, however, the shop-girl was more than a breadwinner or symbol for conservatives, "she was a bell-wether of style."[37]

Magazines and Advertisers

By the 1920s "style" was a discourse meshing personal appearance and behaviour and modern marketing. Goods like cigarettes, for example, were not sold for their utility, but rather as a means for women to produce stylish, sophisticated, and erotic identities.[38] The association between goods and identities represented one modern advertising strategy popular in the twenties. In particular, working women's associations with consumer style, youth culture, and commercial culture made young women central to wider changes in advertising and magazine culture.[39] *Maclean's*, for instance, began as *The Busy Man's Magazine* in 1905, but changed to its current masthead in 1911.[40] Advertisements, stories, and short fiction in the magazine in the 1920s were directed towards female readers. These changes came about with the recognition of the feminization of shopping – from working shop girls to leisurely middle-class consumers, women were at the heart of these widespread cultural transformations.[41]

Women's place as modern consumers grew out of a longer tradition of women being in charge of domestic matters; however, the intensity of the consumer message addressed to them was also born from wider changes in magazine culture extending from the 1890s. Magazines and advertisers certainly worked to groom consumers.[42] Technological changes in producing images along with changes in the costs of paper and printing helped give rise to a new style of magazine that carried an increasing number of images and advertisements. Shifts in journalistic styles produced a more sensationalist approach to news. These were related to shifts in middle-class magazines' conception of culture that increasingly blurred the lines between an established middle-class conservative culture that emphasized civilising, and a new rising popular culture with a focus on leisure and fun.[43] Increasingly slick advertising techniques focused on the visual as opposed to the textual, which was made possible by the development of half-tone engraving technology. By the 1920s, modern advertising was increasingly sophisticated in the means and methods of spreading the message and in the way it was harnessed by national companies. Lessons from the wartime propaganda machines also propelled the industry forward.[44] By the end of World War I, the logic of advertising had decisively swung from focusing on the utilitarian nature of the good for a wide swathe of readers, to targeting the "nonrational yearnings" of individual consumers.[45]

Although both men and women were appealed to as consumers, for women the direct pressure to consume and change their bodies was stronger. Part of this relates to differences in the cosmetic industry, and its advertising techniques and intensity. By 1929, the beauty industry's investment in advertising bested both the food and automobile industries.[46] In the first two decades of the twentieth century, the cosmetic industry blossomed into a national and international mass market with sophisticated production, branding, and advertising, which shifted beauty culture from the local and homemade to the mass-produced and marketed. It must be emphasized that this was a *shift*, as women continued to create their own treatments when commercial preparations could not be found or afforded. Nonetheless, by the twenties powerful mass-produced images carried in newspapers and magazines in North America and beyond deeply influenced discourses of the practices of feminine beauty.[47]

That advertisers co-opted the language of feminism should give us some sense of its *perceived* power in the period. Feminists were always a fractured and diverse group, and in early twentieth-century Canada, class, race, ethnicity, region, and place (urban versus rural) marked out significant differences in organizations, goals, and achievements.[48] The 1890s saw women's groups consolidating into formal organizations like the National Council of Women with affiliated Provincial and Local Councils, which was religiously diverse but still largely Protestant in orientation. The largest group remained the Women's Christian Temperance Union. Women's Institutes drew heavily from rural, agricultural women. From the late nineteenth century, many women organized to improve their lives and the perceived social ills of modernity. For women of the Women's Christian Temperance Union (predominantly but not exclusively of the white, middle class), alcohol was the source of problems ranging from poverty to abuse. The method of achieving temperance varied, but support grew for female suffrage in the early decades of the twentieth century.[49] In the wake of some of the key successes of the so-called first wave of feminism in Canada (suffrage and prohibition), the language of feminism was appropriated by advertisers who sold body-binding goods, painful depilatories, and addiction in the form of smoking, all the while using the language of feminine freedom.[50] Freedom, especially in regard to the highly addictive habit of smoking, was a double-edged sword. And the appropriation of the language of freedom, choice, and even voting (in more obvious incarnations) says more about the power of industrial capitalism to re-package dominant messages for mass consumption than the popular influence of feminism.[51]

Feminist historians have been rightly suspicious of the appropriation of the language of feminism, but changes in consumer culture – especially fashion – did offer benefits. To a lesser extent than in the United States, dress reform was still an issue and certainly women were hampered by nineteenth and earlier twentieth-century fashions (the hobble skirt leaps to mind) that could be unhealthy, dangerous and restrictive. The Modern Girl's fashion was often heralded as a sign of progress for women and a sign of health. As one young man reported, "I think the dress of the modern girl is sensible."[52]

Consumption of individual goods, ideas, and images were not simply individual or meaningless acts, as purchasing and using particular goods – from magazines to lipsticks – enmeshed women's everyday acts with much wider cultural changes, from changes in magazine culture and advertising techniques, to changes in the dominant rituals of feminine beauty. None of this was straightforward. As the editors of *The Consumption Reader* argue, "the semantic ambivalence" of the very term "consumption" "entails both an act of *destruction* ... and an act of *creation*."[53] For Modern Girls, this ambivalence was heightened and personal, written on their very bodies. Indeed, commodities did more than transform appearances. As part of the web of feminine modernities, commodities were part of a wider and more complicated system that shifted visual techniques and appearances beyond the corporeal. Advertisements, in particular, revealed the possibility of seeing what was once deemed unseen, private, or beyond the realms of respectable society. In short, advertisements reflected (as opposed to solely produced) new ways of seeing women's bodies, and reflected new visual access and expectations about public bodies. For women, consumer culture offered new ways of appearing, performing, disciplining, and destroying their bodies based on elusive promises of pleasure, change, and success. These acts of discipline and of production were destructive on a number of levels, as women used goods to transform their bodies and lives; nevertheless, there were also small, although not insignificant pleasures in being able to purchase, dress up, make over, attempt to meet standards of beauty, and care intimately for the body, even for a fleeting moment.

Discipline, Commodities, and the Production of the Modern Body

Commodities were deeply implicated with the bodies and identities of women. The Modern Girl was defined by her look, and commodities (especially cosmetics, clothing, and personal care items), shaped and defined her body as modern. Commodities were not simply about purchasing, despite the potential delights of doing so, but were also about use, and the related transformations of the body by goods were incorporated into daily lives and routines. Face powder, for example, was purchased to perfect the skin, which represented something about the woman who wore it, and was thus part of a women's modern subjectivity. As Rita Felski argues, "The emergence of a culture of consumption helped to shape new forms of subjectivity for women, whose needs, desires and perceptions of self, were mediated by public representations of commodities and the gratifications that they promised."[54] The production of the modern body and self were intimately connected to goods that were produced and purchased with specific needs in mind, and the production of the good was intimately tied to the production of the body at the other end of the good's own life cycle.

Goods were also woven into different means of disciplining the body in order to develop a certain status of modern femininity.[55] Modern femininities required the navigation of a complex consumer landscape filled with very particular messages of how to care for, perform, and create a desirable body. Make-up, for example, was a key aspect of the Modern Girl's look, and had to be applied, removed, and prepared for (in the evening and morning) using specialized concoctions at each step. Treatments also required a significant investment of time. Mme. Jeannette's Beauty Treatment for Pompeian Bloom, for example, suggested three "quick and easy" steps: *"First,* a bit of Pompeian Day Cream to make your powder cling and prevent 'shine.' *Next,* apply Pompeian Beauty Powder to all exposed portions of the face, neck and shoulders. *Lastly,* a touch of Pompeian Bloom. Presto! The face is beautified in an instant."[56] The obvious use of cosmetics – once the reserved paint of loose women, prostitutes, actresses and those seen as unable to claim middle-class respectability – had become a middle-class standard for those wishing to appear beautiful.[57] Make-up promised a dramatic, even magical transformation of parts of the body. It was not simply paint that darkened lashes or reddened cheeks and lips, but special preparations, aids, and beauty secrets that transformed the body itself. Powders promised "velvety skin;" rouge, when carefully applied, gave the look of health; Maybelline Eyelash Beautifer did more than darken and elongate lashes, it turned eyes into "expressive shadowy pools of enchanting loveliness."[58] Goods promised a radical transformation of the body.

Though complex terrain, the body itself was essential to consumer culture. As Mike Featherstone argues, in consumer culture the "inner body" (health, disease, deterioration, aging) and the "outer body" (appearance, the "body within social space") are intimately woven together.[59] While the surface was incredibly important, the body's exterior was connected to complex internal processes that still needed monitoring and discipline. Even seemingly ordinary internal functions, like bowel movements and vaginal cleansing, could not be left to nature. Through a "real life" narrative of a working woman named "Betty," an advert for Kellog's All-Bran Cereal suggested that irregular bowel movements could sap women of their beauty, and that the body required internal cleansing. The ad stated: "Betty was the office mystery. Once pretty, her beauty now lay masked behind an unwholesome complexion. Once vivacious, she now seemed eternally tired – a drooping figure of disappointment and dismay. Too bad she didn't realize that it was constipation which was stealing her strength."[60] Given the frequency of comments on "internal cleansing" in working women's letters to the Ontario Industrial Hygiene Board, this message seems to have been taken up. In fact, constipation was described as "the most frequent ailment of business girls."[61] Advertisements for other internal cleansing products and toothpaste blamed "soft" modern diets for causing new medical problems that required increased body maintenance facilitated by the use of commodities. Despite the lauding of modern life as progressive, scientific, and constantly overcoming old problems, the fear of degeneracy was present. For women, degeneracy was sometimes cast as the natural, if not inevitable process of aging, and it was in regard to age that two of the most popular beauty discourses collided.

Two overriding and frequently interconnected concerns for the constant disciplining of the Modern Girl's body were youthfulness and slenderness. An advert for Marmola prescription tablets bluntly stated "Keep Thin to Keep Young. Fight excess fat, whatever else you do for youth, beauty and vitality. Fat is not popular today."[62] For women, rules for looking young and beautiful were absolute, and girlishness conflated thinness and youth. Thin, angular body lines that de-emphasized hips and breasts deliberately mimicked a youthful or even pre-pubescent look, often described at the time as "boyish." This has often been read as a trope of mature masculinity connected to ongoing panics about wider shifting gender relations, perhaps most dramatically marked by some Canadian women's enfranchisement.[63] Yet, boyish implies childhood, and also employs a patronizing tone. Further, many of the visual clues of the Modern Girl remained distinctly feminine, as the focus on make-up, jewellery, and other feminine adornments reveal.

Regardless, the focus was overwhelmingly on a new feminine look tied to youth. Beauty culture in the twenties emphasized remaining young as a solution to everything from marital problems to being passed over for a promotion at work, and told women to hold on to their youthful beauty at any cost.[64] Natural beauty could be spoiled and even a natural process like aging could and should be carefully controlled, if not avoided entirely. Women were told that old age had become optional in the age of modern science, and that "intelligent care of their bodies every day will postpone old age, indefinitely."[65] Women over the age of forty were warned that their bodies did not "show up well in a room full of flappers."[66] As potential consumers, women's bodies were targeted for constant maintenance during their entire life cycle as an effort to ensure the preservation of the idealized adolescent body. Preserving a youthful look was touted as the goal for both younger and more mature women. An advertisement for Woodbury skin preparations asked, "After Thirty – can a woman still gain the charm of 'A Skin you Love to Touch'?"[67] Mothers were advised to train their daughters in the proper regimens of bodily care. Right through to their senior years, women were told to be diligent in preserving a youthful appearance, and were warned to "Keep that Schoolgirl Complexion." Another advertisement went on to warn readers that the time to preserve youth's appearance was in youth. It stated, "It's not only in the thirties and forties that Youth Preservation presents itself as a problem. It starts in the late *teens* and the early twenties, with the admonition of experts that the time to safeguard youth is *in* youth." Although women might have natural beauty or charm, they were warned that these could be spoiled through neglect. Advertisements suggested that a woman should be "A Vision of Loveliness" at all times.[68] Ignoring the inevitable process of aging and the stresses of work, childbearing, childrearing, and illness, beauty culture worked to set the standard of beauty firmly in the realm of youth, thereby neglecting the realities of women's lives.[69] For young women, however, this cultural narrative emphasized their claim to beauty by virtue of their youthfulness. The shop girl then might have been at a distinct disadvantage by her class, but her youth remained an advantage in selling and prescribing style.

The cultural push towards maintaining and celebrating youthfulness was sometimes translated into radical bodily interventions. According to her biography, Elinor Glyn was so dedicated to preserving a youthful look that in 1926 she submitted to undisclosed treatments on her face so extremely painful that she was restrained for over a week.[70] While magazines carried advertisements for surgical and chemical treatments, such as injecting paraffin wax to smooth wrinkles, beauty columnists and physicians remained skeptical and informed readers and colleagues of the dangers associated with these "cures." Tellingly, beauty culture "experts" derided both the doctors and the women who undertook these procedures. Doctors were seen as reckless or dismissed as quacks, while the women were ridiculed as being pathetic. In 1928, a *Saturday Night* article called "The 'Magic' of Plastic Surgery" warned especially of "alleged professional gentry from the United States already discredited in their own country." The article was in reference to an American doctor speaking in Toronto about how plastic surgery could make women more beautiful and "eradicate" the look of "illness, sorrow, disease or accident" in order to return them to "a youthful and attractive appearance." Perhaps the most damning reaction to the surgeries was that, despite the expense and pain of these treatments, they were too obvious and thus only revealed a pathetic grasp at youth rather than the look of youthfulness itself.[71]

An important aspect of the production of Modern Girlhood, regardless of age, was the maintenance of a thin body with a firm, flat bust and narrow hips. Slenderness was promoted by a wide range of companies from clothing retailers to food companies, and advertisements boldly declared that "Fat Is Not in Fashion."[72] Girls and women appear to have received the message. Joan Jacobs Brumberg noted that in the 1920s, young American women increased the amount of time they devoted to body image and weight loss.[73] Yet, while the Modern Girl's image bordered on an unrealistically slim figure, women were warned that one could be too thin. Advertisements for yeast and cod liver oil declared, "Nobody Loves a Skinny Woman," "No Woman Is Beautiful Who Is 'Skinny'" while another stated "You Can't Be Good Looking If Skinny."[74] The women in the advertisements were shown to establish the difference between desirably thin and undesirably skinny.[75] Food refusal and dieting had to be maintained in a certain way so that it was not confused with the ongoing problem of malnutrition in Canada.[76] As such, thinness had to be performed as deliberate and marked out class distinctions. To deny oneself food in the name of appearance spoke to a privilege afforded exclusively to middle and upper-class Canadian women.

Disciplinary tactics to maintain the young and thin body often seem dramatic, painful, and wrought by self-denial. Yet, there was also the potential for pleasure – both social and personal – for women who maintained the appearance of normative femininity. Adverts did not represent women fighting their bodies, but rather women gently, even seductively caring for them. In the busy modern world, a few moments of personal care could be deeply pleasurable and rewarding. Women of the twenties were promised social and cultural power for appearing beautiful. Advertisers tapped into the coexisting discourses of pleasure and fear of social and personal failure using real-life judgments of women and their ability to meet normative standards of femininity.

A Lux soap advertisement used the "horror" story of an anonymous housewife who recounted a discomforting experience during a dinner party for her husband's boss. The evening became a "failure" when she was "pouring coffee, and for the fraction of a second his [the husband's boss's] glance rested on my hands," which were "red and rough" and an embarrassment. She felt that her lack of care reflected poorly on her husband. After the dinner she began to use Lux soap that left them "soft, smooth and white."[77] While this advert tapped into older notions of women being judged by their hands, the solution – a particular commodity – was definitely modern. Fear and pleasure were also caught up in the expected female competition for husbands. An advertisement for Pompeian Day Cream showed two women and a man walking together. The man's eyes were focused on one woman while the other looked over at her as well. It read: "Both were young and one was beautiful. His eyes followed on, lingering on the smooth velvet of her cheek, her warm color, his senses delighting in the elusive fragrance that floated near. The other was forgotten – yet she, too, was young." On the heterosexual scene, where success still equaled marriage, such competition between women in attracting potential mates could mean social and even economic success, given women's paltry wages and the deeply rooted expectation of a male breadwinner.[78]

Such advertisements taught women how to measure themselves against the competition and how to succeed in winning. Romance was indeed a competitive scene and Modern Girls often found themselves discussed (and described themselves) at an advantage in gaining romantic attention. Modern Girls with paint and powder were in demand and young women reported that make-up was essential to heterosexual success.[79] The grooming and production of the Modern Girl's body was caught in a web of discourses framed by both loathing and love. Her body was disciplined through various discourses of beauty that focused on dieting and remaining youthful, but was also "dressed" by discourses and designs of fashion.

Fashion and Clothing

Watching and caring for parts of the body were essential to maintaining the look of the Modern Girl, and so too was fashion. As Monod reports, "the average Canadian adult woman in 1927 spent $80–100 on her own ready-made clothing (not including footwear or furs), almost half of which went to dresses and suits. This latter sum might not sound like much, but a mid-quality dress in the mid-1920s cost $12–15, so our 'typical' woman could afford a modest wardrobe each year."[80] The exception of furs is also significant, given the restructuring of the industry in the twenties to provide cheaper, more accessible furs to more Canadian women, including working women.[81]

Fashions certainly also helped to promote the slender body as the modern body. Along with obliterating breasts and hips, the look revealed much more of the figure. Hemlines, which reached their peak at the knee, rose and fell through the seasons but typically showed a good deal of the calf. Arms were bare, and the back and clavicles exposed. As Mary Louise Roberts observes in her book on interwar France, fashion was a politicized and anxiety-ridden visual language that was symbolic of a host of issues related to the remarkable social and cultural changes brought by the First World War.[82] While the Canadian context is different from that of interwar France, the idea of the political language of fashion is significant, not only in regard to clothing, but a myriad of other commodities including cosmetics and hair tonics. Moreover, France became an almost mystical land of high fashion in many Canadian adverts. Paris had long been the epicentre of fashion, and the designs of Coco Chanel and her contemporary Paul Poiret among others became internationally desired, even if only a tiny fraction of women could afford authentic *haute couture*. Poiret's high fashion style borrowed from Art Deco and widely popular Orientalist motifs. The results were abstract, geometric styles that highlighted a linear shape of the body. Chanel also focused on modern design, opting for sporty, boyish and "poor" looks that were simplified and made from less indulgent materials, notably jersey. The overall style trends coming from Paris's *haute couture* designers de-emphasized traditional feminine curvy styles and focused on straight, flat lines that stressed geometric patterns.[83] Advertisements in Canadian magazines for Canadian stores highlighted French fashion as the high style of the moment, and promised shoppers the latest clothes and accessories from Paris at more reasonable prices. A 1927 advert for the Robert Simpson Company promised that every dress was "a clever copy of some approved Paris original!" If Canadian women could never see Paris, a Chanel show, or an authentic Poiret design, they could experience the prestige of an up-to-date copy. Canadian women were told they could be as chic and moder as women in fashionable international centres. A *Chatelaine* article declared that "a fashion expert was saying the other day that Canada is now no farther behind Paris than the length of an ocean voyage."[84] Modernity, at least superficially in regard to consumption, seemed to smooth over the gaps and differences in social structure. As a result, clothing also connected Canadian women to global markets and trends. London, New York, and especially Paris were emphasized as the cores of global styles.

Companies often tried to appeal to a sense of Canadian pride while still using images of the Modern Girl. Even American-made goods joined in: an advert for Colgate's Talc Powder read, "Dear to the Women of Canada" in an attempt to appeal to a sense of national pride.[85] Women's nationalistic pride could be expressed through purchasing Canadian goods without sacrificing style or fashion. Some advertisements for Canadian-made goods promised that they would meet or exceed the standards set by the global fashion capitals, especially New York City, and depicted a "Canadian" Modern Girl in their ads as evidence. A Penmans Hosiery advertisement stated, "From these famous centres experts send Penmans the latest styles – the newest shades – and Penmans incorporates them into their hosiery so that Canadian women may be 'in the mode' just as soon as fashionable New York." In this way, Penmans suggested that Canadian women, rather than being left behind, could compete with fashionable New Yorkers. Modern Canadian women would not, it seemed, be excused simply by their distance from the fashion epicenters of the modern world.

Being in tune with modern fashion was a difficult task, since one of the aspects of being fashionable was keeping up with rapid, if subtle, changes in style. Seasonal changes were sometimes scant – a shortened hemline or changes in fabric colour – but the quick pace of fashions and their rapid transmission around the globe, at least visually in advertisements and articles, echoed the quickening of life in general. To be modern meant keeping up with the pace of change, and advertisers promised that this was possible. Ashes of Roses by Bourjois revealed their goods were "new from Paris" and that "sophisticated New York and beauty-worshipping Paris have approved the new 'nature tones' created by Bourjois in Ashes of Roses Face Powder."[86]

Mass-produced clothing and accessories at multiple price points also meant that the Modern Girl's fashion was accessible to a wide range of Canadians. Technological developments that improved transportation meant faster and cheaper movement of goods, and leading cultural fashion experts like *Vogue* magazine offered clothing patterns so people could sew their own stylish pieces at home.[87] If modernity seemed to promise democratization, at least of fashion, this was as troubling to some as it was promising to others. The Modern Girl's look partially obscured other bodily visual clues related to class and ethnicity, and the inability to read these cultural categories was disturbing in a society with rigid notions of racial and class hierarchies. In rural Saskatchewan,

McGill sociologist Charles Young observed that "on summer Saturday nights the streets thronged with the beautiful bright-eyed Ukrainian girls who, in dress and deportment, could not be distinguished from our most typical Anglo-Saxon."[88] Ready-to-wear clothing made from cheap synthetic fabrics and produced in a range of prices flattened the look of class, and that mimicked larger cultural concerns about the co-mingling of classes. But class differences did not disappear.

Commodities required disposable income, and even if there was a wider range of accessible goods, very real material barriers remained which dictated the extent to which one could appear as a Modern Girl. Poverty certainly restricted the possibility of Modernity Girlishness for some Canadians, but that did not necessarily diminish her power as a desirable object. As Carolyn Steedman reminds us, women regardless of class were capable of desiring goods even if they were firmly beyond their reach, and more to the point, that the very desire for goods marked women's lives.[89] Women who could afford to keep up with the latest styles sometimes criticised whatever ounce of democracy mass-produced clothing offered in an attempt to reaffirm their class status. In a typical dispatch on fashionable modes from Britain and Europe, *Chatelaine* writer Mary Wyndham noted that "Chanel's necklaces of round diamonds or amethysts or topazes are fading out. Smart women will not wear them because they can be copied too cheaply and the department stores are making festoons of them by the thousands."[90] For other women, cheap goods provided a way of accessing a look and the possibility of transforming their bodies, while stretching (as opposed to devastating) their budgets. As another example, Monarch hosiery promised richness, opulence, beauty and luxury in a pair of their stockings: "Other woman of taste and high standards are doing it. So can you. Just notice how the power of your stocking money is increased when you buy Monarch Hosiery."[91]

In other ways, the new styles were difficult to achieve. For many post-pubescent women achieving a long, slender look required uncomfortable physical restrictions in addition to dieting or long-term interventions. Jane Walters, who came of age in the twenties, recalled,

And the clothes! They were hard to take. Do you know, there was a time at that stage when they wore dresses absolutely straight and flat across here, and some of them used to bind their bosoms to get into these dresses! I had a singer's body and believe me, I had a big bosom, and I had the most awful time getting dresses – all the girls did. We just went through that stage of flat bosoms. It was a bad time. You can't buck nature and not get some bad results from it.[92]

One long-standing means of bucking nature was corseting which did not disappear in the 1920s.[93] A body-shaper advertisement was titled "For the woman who would be slender" and promised that the product's results could be instantly seen. In drawing attention to the model who posed in a corset, the advertisement drew attention to the way the device reshaped the flesh into long lines. It demanded, "See how the line of beauty flows over the curve of the bust into the waistline, indicating but not emphasizing it, how it continues down over the hips, and the thigh line, in perfect, unbroken symmetry. Note the supported, youthful lines, the smoothed, curved contours of the entire figure."[94] In another corset advertisement, the product was presented as being able to give "average or stout figures ... a perfect straight front and a small hip effect."[95] The connection between slenderness, straight lines, and youthfulness implied that the Modern Girl's body, although seemingly adult-like, held on to youthful, if not childlike, qualities.

As the ideal, however, Modern Girls were not girl-children who could be victimized, taken advantage of, or closely and carefully parented. Instead, they were supposed to be a smart, savvy young women who retained the best of child-like beauty and a sense of carefree fun as they matured, got wiser, and maybe even sophisticated and street smart. A troubling complication was that as this cultural shift occurred, the Girl's mother was sometimes dismissed as incredibly old-fashioned and out-of-date. As American historian Laura Davidow Hirschbein argues, the image of the flapper was often juxtaposed with images of older women. Expressing the alleged clash between the generations allowed critics "to explore the implications of new and old in American society and to organize rapidly shifting social, cultural, political, and economic worlds."[96] Advertisers implied that older women were unable to understand or offer advice to their thoroughly modern daughters. The world had changed and she had not. Conveniently, of course, this meant that advertisers, movies, magazine columnists, and other members of popular culture could fill a mother's place in advising Girls, and rise to the exalted position of expert. They did not, however, dispense with mothers even as they ridiculed them. Advertisers in particular recognized mothers' influence as consumers, and by the 1920s, ideas of brand loyalty (where daughters would grow to use the products their mothers did) directed advertising techniques. Moreover, modern motherly advice was distilled through a host of medical and quasi-medical experts who had the latest knowledge, and advertisers and other modern beauty experts also looked to those experts for direction.[97] The gap between mothers and daughters was also emphasized through hairstyles, and one in particular – the bob – dramatically marked out generational differences.

Hair

Bobbed hair was one of the most dramatic and problematic symbols of the Modern Girl. The bob was a fashionable and popular hairstyle in Canada and internationally, and its popularity is often attributed to French fashion designer Coco Chanel who acquired the cut in 1916. Although the bob was a fashionable haircut throughout the twenties, it was also a source of tension and discussion. Jake Foran later recalled that bobbed hair was so significant and surprising that he took pictures of it. He said, "I have pictures of the first girls I ever saw with bobbed hair. That was considered wicked almost, bobbing one's hair. The older people thought the world was going straight to hell because they bobbed their hair and shortened their skirts."[98]

When stenographer Vivian Maw bobbed her hair in December 1922, other employees at the Winnipeg Grain Exchange discussed it for days. Five years later in Calgary, four nurses in training were dismissed for bobbing their hair. Newspapers reported that this was the second time nurses had been fired for donning the popular hairstyle. A student nurse in Halifax was required by her superintendent to retrieve her recently bobbed hair and pin it in a bun onto her head.[99] Nurses in particular were constructed to be sexually pure, and defending the look of purity in their uniforms was especially important. Kathryn McPherson concludes that while the bob eventually won out in nursing in the 1920s, other changes like shortening skirts were more successfully resisted.[100]

The bob was part of a larger visual economy in which cultural anxieties were debated. Prior to the 1920s, a woman's hair was frequently seen as her crowning glory, and long hair was an important symbol of femininity and desirability. In girlhood the hair could be worn down and loose, while pinning the hair up was a sign of maturation into womanhood. In Lucy Maud Montgomery's iconic novel *Anne of Green Gables*, Anne's bosom friend Diana Berry announces, "In four more years we'll be able to put our hair up." She continues, "Alice Bell is only sixteen and she is wearing hers up, but I think that's ridiculous. I shall wait until I'm seventeen."[101] Long hair was powerful because it could seduce or charm, while cutting one's hair could be seen as an act of defacement, a renunciation of (hetero)sexuality, or even a violation. In F. Scott Fitzgerald's classic short story "Bernice Bobs Her Hair," and the 1925 *Maclean's* story "Pokey and Her Flapper-Masher Bob," ugliness and bad behaviour seem to be among the best consequences of bobbed hair.[102] Bernice's bob is a way of getting the attention of men, even though she announces that she thinks the bob immoral, feels like "Marie Antoinette bound for the guillotine" on the way to the barber, and thinks the hair-cut is "ugly as sin" on her. In the *Maclean's* story, Ruth, a married woman with a child, tells her husband that she wants to bob her hair because her friend Betty did and "she looks sixteen." Although her husband disapproves, Ruth still cuts her hair. After an altercation with young men on the street, Ruth is accused of asking "for some dope" and the police bring her to the station where she runs into her husband and his boss as they defend the mashers, unknowingly calling Ruth a "hussy." To rectify the situation, and save her and her husband from embarrassment, Ruth lies and appeals to constructions of the New Woman, saying she bobbed her hair "for the protection of my weaker sisters … I am president of an association for the apprehension of mashers, and in order to help round them up and so protect the thoughtless girls who might be victimized I sacrificed my hair – my beautiful hair … that I might look flapperish and so attract the species of human insect known as the flapper-masher." Ruth's story exemplifies the differences between New Women and Modern Girls, but also the blurred the lines between them. While she desires to look younger and "flapperish," to protect her and her husband's status she appeals to the legacies of self-sacrifice and duty in protecting young, urban women – a popular project for early twentieth-century middle-class women. However, her deception ultimately reveals her shallowness, especially since she uses this story to get twenty dollars from her husband for a permanent wave. Such stories suggest a duplici-tous nature in appearing as a Modern Girl. That disciplining and pro-ducing a modern body could overtake any sense of authenticity (or at least the discourse of authenticity) suggested a far more troubling shift from the internal to the external. The superficial was what mattered. Ultimately, Ruth's story reaffirmed conservative stereotypes of working-class flappers, their sexual availability, and their inability to meet .

middle-class ideals of respectability. That Ruth "wins" by claiming protection of other women, and her reward is money for a perm, both highlight the significant class tensions in the appearance of the Modern Girl.

As Ruth's story also reveals, hair required the investment of time and money. Hair required specific cleansers, the face required a myriad of products from creams to soaps to powders, and the body required specific care in a variety of ways from hair removal to odour prevention (including bad breath) to care of the hands and nails to internal cleansing of the mouth, the vagina and the digestive system. While carving up the body into increasingly specific areas in need of improvement or maintenance, the disciplining of the modern female body also connected the parts. An advert for Marmola Prescription Tablets warned, "You must be slender to have bobbed hair – For the shingle bob or the straight bob you must have a youthful silhouette. One simply can't be stout – or even overweight."[103] All of these products promoted specific techniques of the self that promised the seemingly elusive, fragile, and fleeting look of beauty.

More generally, hair was a troublesome issue for women as there were a myriad of products to improve, perfect, and remove it. A certain amount of expertise was needed to evaluate which hair was good and should be emphasized, and which was bad and needed to be removed or covered. X-Bazin adverts declared, "With daytime frocks of gossamer thinness and revealing evening gowns your skin must be free from hair blemish and your arms from armpit to wrist immaculate." Princess Complexion Purifier promised to cure a range of pesky skin problems including superfluous hair. The opening sentence of one advert offered "an easy remedy for an ugly skin," and made it clear that unwanted hair was equal to rashes, eruptions, and general dermatological problems. While articles and advertisements promoted the use of mascara to increase the intensity of the look of eyelashes, eyebrows were a trickier matter with some of the hairs being a necessity and others a hassle to be tweezed. In a series of lengthy articles syndicated in Canadian newspapers, British actress Gladys Cooper gave advice on "How to Become Beautiful" to Canadian women. She devoted an entire chapter to the eyes in which she gave detailed advice on how to care for eyebrows and eyelashes that involved bathing, brushing, tweezing and moisturizing treatments. Grey hair, however, was always negative as it indicated old age, and companies like Kolor-Bak, Brownatone, and Inecto promised to "banish" grey and restore the look of beauty and youth.[104]

She's Got Legs: Commodities, Pieces of the Modern Body, and the Private in Public

The crafting of modern femininities helped to delineate care of the body into finely tuned compartments with matching specialized goods. At times, it connected women's bodies with products that had no natural association at all. The visual dismemberment of the body also did strange things to the pieces it brought into focus. Advertisements for Legacy Silverware included a strangely shaped woman's head on an oddly thick and elongated neck with disproportionately long hands and fingers appearing below a comparatively large, upright standing fork.[105] A casual flip through a commercial magazine from the 1920s reveals dismemberment of the female body – or to use the language of film, a "close-up": heads, hands, legs, each of which emphasized a particular connection to a commodity such as a hat, dress, powder, cream, diet aid, cigarette, or car. Because of close-cropped hair and cloche hats, heads appeared free-floating and disembodied in many advertisements. Eaton's adverts for cloche hats, for example, frequently included drawn head shots of women with rectangular skulls and necks so disproportionately long that they would have been almost twice the length of the face. Within this multiplicity of pieces, certain body parts garnered more attention than others, and legs garnered far more attention than other parts of the body. Modern fashion remapped the body, and rendering most of the upper body and hips flat and geometric, legs came into full focus.[106]

In 1928, *Saturday Night*'s resident beauty columnist Valerie reminded women of the significance of their legs, and that others – both men and women – were watching. While attending a performance at Toronto's Massey Hall, Valerie observed: "There were scores of women on the platform in the 'stage audience,' and most of them made a display of beige hosiery that made one think of Friday bargains. There was hardly a decent pair of knees to be see in that applauding crowd ... Perhaps some day the Canadian woman will realize that her knees might be improved and will betake herself to a gymnasium and indulge in the exercises which will make the feminine knee more shapely than it now appears. Of course, longer skirts would help."[107] Valerie's statement was loaded with class and gender judgments. Middle-class women were otherwise told to envy the youthfulness and slenderness of the shop girl, and were subtly chastised for a reliance on her cheap goods. Maintenance of more and more of the body (as Valerie suggested exercise and more sophisticated consumer practices) required further investments of time and energy.

1.2   Legacy Silverware Advertisement, *Saturday Night*, 17 November 1928.

The twenties saw women's legs garnering significant attention. In Paris, France in 1926 a legal trial brought attention to the tyranny of thin legs when a cosmetic surgeon was sued for a botched operation to remove "excess fat" from a woman's legs. After the loss of her leg to a gangrene infection, the doctor and the increasingly popular specialization of cosmetic surgery went on trial – one that was closely followed in France and North America.[108] That same year the sensational story of the Australian film hopeful Lotus Thompson broke. On the screen, Thompson's legs had been used in montages with other actress' faces. Frustrated by the spectacle of her disembodiment, Thompson poured acid over her legs.[109] Such a dramatic statement was hardly common, yet it does speak to the intensification with which women experienced modern urban culture, which frequently focused on pieces of their bodies.

In the Victorian period women's lower legs were fetishized by their absence, so that catching a glimpse of an ankle or calf could be erotic; the twenties saw a revelation of the legs, including the upper portions of legs becoming fashionable while maintaining their erotic appeal. Fetishizing parts of women's bodies was not unique to the 1920s, and yet the means of display and their subsequent meanings were an essential ingredient in feminine modernities of the period. These dominant discourses mapped out erotic territory, and a new geography for viewing them. As Abigail Solomon-Godeau argues, "The legs of Betty Grable or Marlene Dietrich, or the prominence of legs in modern advertising, are evidence of the enduring potency of this particular mapping of the erotic ... the salient fact is that until the twentieth century it was only the legs of dancers or entertainers that were publicly on display."[110]

The Modern Girl was a key figure in shifting the revelation of legs from the potentially disreputable performances on stage to more everyday performances by middle and working class women. Legs, more specifically long, thin legs, became a dominant image and revealed more than changes in fashion. Rising skirt lengths, the introduction of rayon (artificial silk) and changes in knitting technology meant an increasing display of more and more of women's legs. An advertisement for Kayser silk hosiery revealed upper portions of the thigh visible through transparent fabric and offered a quick, voyeuristic glance at the upper portion of the (disembodied) legs while the skirt was blown upwards. In a 1928 *Saturday Night* article called "Those Dancing Girls," an author writing under the pseudonym "A Mere Man" reflected on a recent social engagement where there were "girls – a hundred of them to pick from, all prinked out in the pretties of fluffy, feminine frocks and displaying the daintiest of silken calves and ankles! What more could a man want!"[111] Indeed, the focus on bits of women's bodies, especially legs in a private setting, reinforced patriarchal viewing practices and objectification. Such a culture of desire existed particularly around seeing women's legs. In responding to the debates over the display of nude paintings at the 1927 CNE (discussed in chapter 5) one commentator chastised writers complaining about nudity in the sanctity of an art gallery and questioned: "Can any one avoid seeing the extraordinary display of silk stockings and short skirts every day in evidence, not in art galleries but on our public streets?"[112] The author of the letter was not alone in singling out women's legs and stockings for special attention. *The Catholic Register* quoted physicians, criminologists and sociologists who argued that there was a direct link between the revelation of women's bodies and crime. Rolled stockings in particular were problematic, and whether or not women who wore them were "innocent," they caused crimes of passion.[113] This was the double bind of commodities that women faced. The erotic appeal of women's legs had clearly been reaffirmed, and existed as a site of objectification and the production of modern, female subjectivity.

Revealing new parts of the body, particularly legs, was still clearly a point of anxiousness for the public in the 1920s, as it was previously limited to the privacy of bedrooms and dressing rooms. The unveiling of this gloss of privacy simultaneously increased the ads' voyeuristic qualities. There were and are multiple ways to read this aspect of feminine modernities – for women it meant potential scrutiny, if not literal peeping toms, increased intensity regarding the number of body projects, and the public opening of the intimate – a place previously reserved for the culturally suspicious, the disreputable, or the pornographic. There is no doubt that the fetishizing of women's legs was connected to the long-standing, although shifting erotic economy of women's bodies that by the 1920s had found a niche in middle-class women's magazines. They showed images of women in private settings partially dressed in corsets or undergarments. An advert for Harvey Hosiery and Lingerie included what would later be considered a classic pin-up picture of a young woman seated seductively, dressed in scanty undergarments (and, somewhat surprisingly, high heels), fully made up, and staring back at the viewer. Her coquettish pose adds a sense of naivety or innocence, but simultaneously amplifies the appeal to mature sexuality and voyeurism, despite the childish title "Adorable" that appears across the top of the ad. Her right

1.3 Harvey Hosiery Advertisement, *Chatelaine*, May 1928. Used with permission of Stanfield's Limited.

leg escapes the cameo-shaped frame, and together with her posture, suggests her moving towards us – stepping out to meet us. Her pose makes it seem that she is not simply an image, but a moving woman.

The imaging of women partially dressed with exposed legs in motion was a popular theme. Gossard corsets adverts were some of the few who used photographs in their ads, and they did so to startling effect. A full-page ad included a photograph of a woman standing in her corset and stockings. Despite the fact that the setting seems to be a private space in the woman's home, the image belies a public quality in that she is fully accessorized, wearing high-heeled shoes and makeup, and seems to be posed in a moment where she has briefly stopped in the frame of the photograph before continuing her way elsewhere. We've caught her in a moment in-between public and private – seemingly right before she puts on her dress to step out – offered to us by new visual technologies. Modern technologies of image reproduction like photography and film opened up new avenues to the intimate.

Through these practices women were encouraged to simultaneously take on the role of voyeuristic viewer and embodied subject: they could both see the legs and imagine how it would feel to have them covered in silk. Harvey Hosiery and Lingerie's advertisement played upon the double meaning of seeing and being seen. In their advertisement a woman poses in her underwear in front of a large oval. In the picture it is unclear whether we are seeing the woman or seeing her through the other side of her mirror as she stares into her own reflection. The caption reads: "To the eye enchantment! To the wearer, contentment because of her knowledge that the finest materials, perfect fit and beautiful lasting shades are what she buys when she insists upon Harvey Hosiery."[114] A 1928 advert for Harvey Hosiery and Harvey Tailored Lingerie encouraged the idea that physical preparation was pleasurable, rewarding, and that women could take pride and flaunt their well-maintained bodies. The woman in the advert looks into a large handheld mirror striking a confident pose and looking pleased with herself. Promising "perfection," the copy suggested that "Careful dressing is the surest passport for women in business and social life." In this single advert, there were four different images of women's bodies: two images of the entire body and two close-ups of the legs in particular. The four images revealed the woman's body in different positions and different contexts, sending the message that being seen was a constant in the modern woman's life. Even when women were not the main attractions, they were still to expect scrutiny of their bodies. There was no time to relax. Significantly,

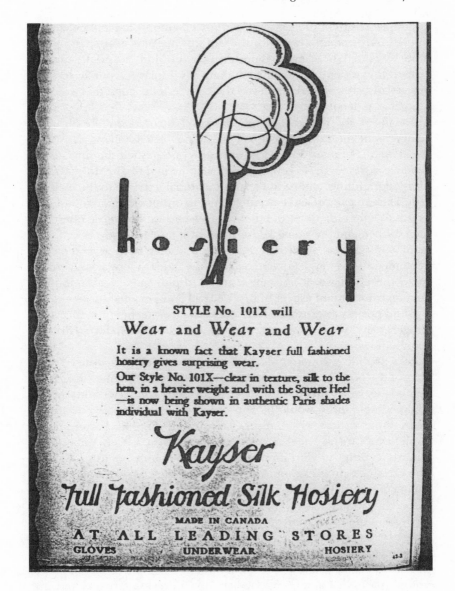

1.4   Kayser Full Fashioned Silk Hosiery Advertisement, *Saturday Night*, 24 September 1927. Used with permission of Kayser-Roth Corporation

the two close-ups of the legs were part of a common concept image that showed only women's legs with the calf or knee at eye-level, and sometimes suggested the sexualized posturing of the Modern Girl. Reminding women that all parts of their body were on display for public scrutiny, hosiery adverts revealed that it was the body, not the good that would be ultimately judged.

An advert for Kayser "All Silk Hosiery" focused on the "brilliant achievement" of two identical pairs of legs depicted walking away from the viewer. Like many hosiery adverts, this one pushed the limits of acceptable skirt lengths to reveal portions of the mid-thigh. Moreover, the flimsy, tight-fitting, almost transparent material left little to the imagination. The two pairs of legs extremely close to one another, surrounded by beams of light radiating from them suggested a uniform style offered by the product, and the potential for a uniform modern body as well. Like many others, these adverts suggested that women's "achievement" was dependent on her appearance. Because the modern look was so indebted to the purchase of consumer goods, it also made consumption a seemingly important aspect of professional and personal success. Thus, legs and hosiery encapsulated the performances, techniques, pleasures, dangers, and ways of seeing that connected the Modern Girl and commodities.

Legs provide a concrete example of the carefully constructed mapping of the body and its associations with modern feminine subjectivity. Being modern meant taking on a particular look connected with specific commodities, and it would be almost impossible to imagine a Modern Girl without a short skirt and silk-like stockings. Yet, the anxiousness of public exposure of knees and stockings points to a deep ambivalence towards feminine modernities. Self-display was simultaneously associated with freedom, progress, and modern subjectivity, as well as sexualized danger, disrepute, and patriarchal objectification. Specified care of parts of the body was intimately connected to the visual fracturing of women's bodies and the concurrent voyeurism of once intimate parts of the body. Images allowed viewers to get close-up looks at particular parts of the body and glimpses up skirts; to hone in on specific pieces of the body like an outstretched leg; and to peer into women's dressing rooms and other private spaces.[115] Cameras opened up once foreclosed spaces and provided the possibility of looking close up while remaining at a safe distance without time limits of personal interaction.

1.5   Kayser Introduces the New Haf [sic] Heel Advertisement, *Saturday Night*, 17 November 1928. Used with permission of Kayser-Roth Corporation.

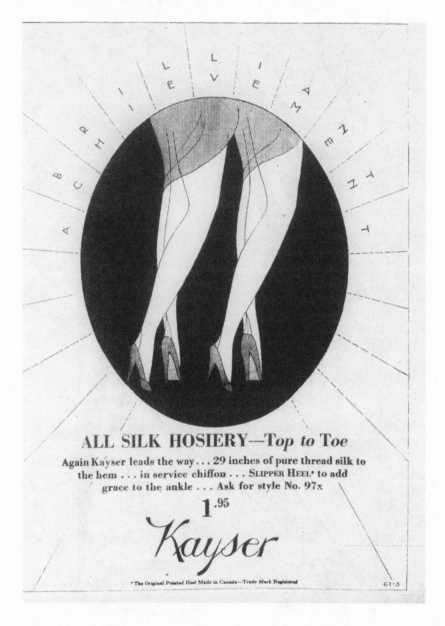

1.6   Kayser Brilliant Achievement "All Silk Hosiery" Advertisement, *Saturday Night*, 24 November 1928. Used with permission of Kayser-Roth Corporation.

Conclusion: The Modern Girl and Things

Consumer culture had within it irresolvable contradictions: mass produced goods promised individuality and personal satisfaction; advertisers created "problems" with the female body that could be pleasurably resolved; one's own body was to be scrutinized as if it were disembodied; and disciplinary tactics for the body could have pleasurable rewards.[116] Further, women's bodies (as discussed in chapter 6) were used to sell seemingly gender-neutral goods. If the body was central to consumer culture, it was predominantly a female body, which sold, spectacularized, made safe, and made appealing a wide variety of goods, ideas, and processes. As such, the female body was never simply about the body itself. It was central to understanding, contesting, and shaping the deeply gendered meanings of the very modernities that were intimately interwoven into consumer and popular culture.

The Modern Girl was a new female type enmeshed with powerful aspects of modern culture, particularly consumer culture (including the powerful projectors of ideal feminine types: advertising and filmmaking), which influenced styles of disciplining the body. As part of the powerful discourse regarding the body disseminated through consumer culture, women's bodies were seen as imperfect at best, and at worst, potentially hazardous to personal, professional, and even national success unless given a lifetime of care, discipline, and maintenance. The repetitive tasks required in the production of a modern, feminine body were complicated and encompassed the entirety of the body, which was broken down into small parts in need of specialized care and attention. That the Modern Girl's body was politicized should not be entirely surprising – it was at the centre of a complicated discourse of beauty that encompassed wider cultural shifts in the care of and appearance of female bodies. Changes in fashion were also changes in fashioning the body. As care for the body became increasingly specific, women found that their bodies as a whole and in pieces were at the centre of public discussions. Moreover, the new geography of the female body required women to simultaneously perform, scrutinize, and defend their bodies. This was complicated and troubled terrain. As the next chapter reveals, women's relationship to the ever-changing consumer landscape was mediated by beauty experts who allegedly helped women perform and appear modern in appropriate ways. Moreover, experts participated in discourses of pleasure and magic that made such time-consuming and difficult work seem pleasurable and rewarding.

2 Dear Valerie, Dear Mab: Beauty, Expert Advice, and Modern Magic

In the 29 September 1928 edition of the Canadian periodical *Saturday Night*, the resident beauty columnist Valerie responded as usual to letters from anxious Canadian women in need of special beauty advice. To "Peggy," Valerie replied, "Thank you for the kind words said about this paper and this column. I have indicated where you may get the cleansing cream – also the nourishing one. The homemade article of this nature is hardly worth while. There are ever so many good soaps nowadays of which you may take your choice but most modern women prefer a cleansing cream."[1] Valerie's response to an unprinted query is indicative of a number of important aspects of feminine modernities in 1920s Canada: women seeking advice on how to negotiate the increasingly complicated consumer scene; the position of the beauty expert as a trusted source of information; and the connection between appearing modern and specific mass-produced products. In dispensing advice, Valerie did more than offer beauty tips, she helped Canadian women navigate the modern scene where new "techniques of appearing – the manner and means of execution of one's visual effects and status" – were intimately interwoven with consumer culture and modern feminine subjectivities.[2] As a "trusted expert" in becoming beautiful, individuals like Valerie provided Canadian women with important details on how to create and maintain modern, female bodies like that of the Modern Girl, as they helped to normalize, and at times contest, her appearance. Closely reading these columns along with advertising and articles in mass-market, commercial Canadian magazines reveals the peculiarly modern mix of women's visibility, mass consumption, and objectification. They also give us a glimpse into Canadian women's personal concerns, as the columnists addressed individual letters from women across the country.

Bodies did not simply transform into being modern, but were carefully produced through a host of techniques intimately connected with the culture of mass consumption. Feminine visibility was a key aspect of modern life. As part of being modern, women experienced this intensification of the visual scene in a number of ways, such as new means of producing a modern body, and having their bodies be increasingly judged. Techniques of appearing became inherently tied to the consistent use of particular commodities, especially cosmetics, which helped to create a modern female subjectivity exemplified by the Modern Girl. *Chatelaine*'s beauty columnist Mab summarized the work required when she wrote, "To- day, beauty demands that a woman be slender, graceful, and exceedingly well groomed. This is the age of revelation. We have no billowy skirts, false hair or veils to hide our defects, and eternal youth is the cry of the hour. For the most part beauty is not obtained or retained without a good deal of personal effort."[3] This particular and popular narrative of the twenties was not the first to structure the critical judgment of women's bodies. It reveals, however, the new intense criticism of women's appearance in the modern scene, and the type of work expected to produce a modern female body.

The Modern Girl was deeply connected to commodity culture. Magazines with beauty culture "experts" played an important role in delineating modern femininities within the new logic of commodity culture, visuality, and display. As Penny Tinkler and Cheryl Krasnick Warsh have recently argued in regard to *Vogue*, magazines encouraged women "to imagine themselves as participants in the modern world and encouraged [them] to remake themselves as modern feminine subjects through their consumption practices."[4] Magazines and other periodicals were diverse in their composition with editorials, articles, advertisements, and sometimes a number of columnists. As a result, they provided a heterogeneous voice and, although I draw from multiple parts of the magazines, this chapter focuses particularly on beauty expert columns and advertisements. Advertisers became modern "experts" on bodily care and techniques of appearing; similarly columns usually reinforced advertisers' messages of body maintenance and consumption, while supporting the message of bodily preparation for women.[5] Not surprisingly, both experts' columns were flanked with advertisements for a range of beauty products directed almost exclusively to women. It would have been hard to miss the message, as the columns and adverts usually reinforced each other.

Both *Saturday Night* and *Chatelaine* contained regular beauty columns, which are an excellent source to explore how messages of consumption were reinforced and modified for Canadian women. *Saturday Night*'s beauty columnist Valerie wrote a column entitled "The Dressing Table" and *Chatelaine*'s columnist Mab was the author of "The Promise of Beauty."[6] Columnists cultivated relationships with readers through monthly or bi-weekly columns that were meant to provide direction and expertise to English-speaking women across the country. These were more intimate, personal, and direct than advertisements or articles. The columnists followed a typical formula of discussing key issues related to beauty, fashion, and dieting, and also responded to individual letters and queries (either directly or indirectly), often providing glimpses into their own "real-life" experiences, beauty practices, and concerns. As a result, the columns created a sort of intimacy that worked especially well given the sort of personal advice readers sought. Readers were further encouraged to write to their beauty columnist if they wanted personalized advice on how to improve their appearance. *Chatelaine* readers were told, "It may be that you are dissatisfied with the condition of your skin, your hair or your figure. Mab will be glad to answer your individual questions if you will write her in care of "The Chatelaine," enclosing a stamped addressed envelope." In the early 1920s, readers of the *Saturday Night* columnist were informed, "Correspondents throughout the breadth of this Dominion, so greatly blessed with cold cream and hair tonics, are warned that in future, all demands for private replies must be accompanied by a stamped and addressed envelope." By 1923, the advice to information-seekers became more particular: readers were told to "write on one side of the paper and limit inquires to two in number."[7] Valerie, like cold creams and hair tonics it seemed, was popular.

By critically examining these columns, this chapter explores how expert advice regarding techniques of appearing encouraged the production of modern, female bodies in Canada in the 1920s, where women's bodies were embroidered with a sort of consumer magic that shored up the idea that goods were a necessary investment. I argue that advice columns provided critical information to Canadian women on how to negotiate a complicated consumer scene focused on being modern and beautiful. While I recognize such discourses of beauty as intensely problematic, I also explore the promises of pleasure that made the production of modern beauty potentially appealing. These columns, however limited, show the similarity and disjuncture of discourses of modern beauty in the Canadian context, a much different concern than that of interwar nationalism that has dominated the historiography. Written by Canadians for Canadians, these columns show how a global (although seemingly American-propelled) discourse was suited to a particular land-scape, and subtly reveal a complicated relationship with the global Modern Girl.

Both *Saturday Night* and *Chatelaine* provide excellent examples of the types of advertising and advice that appeared in commercial mass media magazines in Canada. While *Saturday Night* was intended for mixed gen-der audiences, *Chatelaine* was (and still is) a woman's magazine first pub-lished in March 1928. Despite the fact that it appeared so late in the decade under investigation here, *Chatelaine* made a significant and im-mediate impact on the Canadian cultural landscape, selling 57,000 cop-ies a month by December 1928.[8] While it is difficult to measure who was actually reading and writing to the columnists, discussions frequently as-sumed a white, largely middle-class, female readership looking to negoti-ate the boundaries of feminine modernities. That said, columnists often saw themselves as part of a wider project of public education for working-class, rural, and immigrant women.[9] Given the ubiquitous image of the Modern Girl and her relatively uniform look across race, class, and even national lines, assuming a singularly narrow audience could be problem-atic. Yet, as we shall see, the discourses of modern female subjectivity in Canada were interlaced with discourses of age, class, and race. As chapter 1 discussed, the making of the Modern Girl's body was about new disciplinary tactics, which were often packaged with promises of pleasure. This chapter picks up that thread to explore it more fully, par-ticularly in the context of how experts doled out this potential, ultimate-ly making appearing as a Modern Girl seem possible for Canadian women willing to invest time, energy, and money in their bodies. Experts addressed business women, professional women, housewives, and work-ing girls; certainly, though, these columns tell us about middle-class ide-als and the women striving to achieve them.

The Rise of the Beauty Expert

As chapter 1 revealed, the modern body was marketed as a problem in need of ingenious solutions packaged as various consumer goods. This was a complicated problem, and working and middle-class women nego-tiating the consumer scene had a multitude of choices and a sometimes-scary selection of options. Still haunting consumers in the 1920s were problems identified much earlier: shoddy, if not dangerous goods; ad-vertising campaigns that promised far more than their product could deliver; and social and moral judgment tied to the use of particular goods, especially make-up. Other products still on the market were dangerous or painful, like the widely-advertised chemical depilatories that burned through fabrics and skin. How could women deal with such a complicated scene? Such a technical problem in making and maintaining the modern body required a technical solution, and thus an expert to mediate between processes of production, advertising, and consumption.[10]

Helping women make consumer decisions, particularly in relation to becoming beautiful, were beauty culture experts who participated in solidifying the link between commodities and modern women's bodies as they appropriated part of women's culture in the form of intimate "woman-talk."[11] Valerie and Mab were not distinctive in doling out this type of womanly advice. Other magazines offered women different access to advice depending on their area of interest. As Jennifer Scanlon reveals in *Inarticulate Longings*, intimate advice by way of regular columns were common in *Ladies' Home Journal*. Unlike the columns by Mab and Valerie here, however, the advice in the *Journal's* columns focused on housekeeping issues and scientific motherhood. In other locales like Sydney, Australia, for example, magazines such as *Picture Show* and *Photoplay* offered young, working-class women insight into international movies, while offering tips on consuming and beautifying in the way of Hollywood starlets. As Kirsten McKenzie argues, such "strategies illuminate the question of how provincial audiences were bound into an emergent global culture."[12] In this way, Valerie and Mab helped to tailor dominant consumer messages broadcast globally to the Canadian context.

While advertisers also tried to step into the role of offering advice through named and unnamed experts, beauty columnists offered supposedly neutral expert advice; allegedly, because earlier columns hawked particular goods so not to offend powerful advertisers. By in large, this practice had faded by the twenties, and neither Valerie nor Mab offered explicit endorsements of specific products, with one notable exception. Valerie repeatedly referred readers to Lulu Peters' *Watch Your Weight* for dieting advice. While Mab and Valerie had stopped promoting certain brands of consumer goods, they would provide brand names to readers who wrote in requesting advice.[13] Valerie expressed her fear of advertisers, which she described in 1920 as greater than her fear of catching the flu. Given the worldwide devastation the Spanish influenza had just caused in 1919, this was meant to be a significant and weighty statement.[14] Valerie's advice was probably mediated by other constraints, such as her editor, who would have been keenly aware of the need to maintain positive relationships with financially powerful advertisers.[15] Experts had to negotiate their own complicated relationships between advertisers, editors, and readers.

Columns on women's etiquette and beauty were not new in the 1920s, as *Saturday Night*'s columnist Valerie had been writing her column in the 1910s. The initial process for established expertise was unclear, but Mab and Valerie frequently reminded their readers of their connections to famous folk and their deep knowledge of the ever-changing ground of beauty culture. In such a fast-moving market (and the speed of change was something they regularly reminded their readers of), expertise needed to be constantly reaffirmed in order to establish and maintain a relationship of trust. The columnists seemed to respond to individual Canadian women, which established a sense of intimacy and concern over individual, specific problems. Valerie responded to readers in warm and personal ways writing, "I recall your woes of several years ago," which implied that Valerie remembered writers' concerns in ways that cemented a sense of female friendship. And some readers did follow-up by providing their own beauty updates as "Anna" did in August of 1928 when she reported that brighter, longer, and unbobbed hair were the fashion (the latter perhaps significant to Valerie who thought women over thirty like Anna only looked desperate to be young with bobbed hair).[16] Moreover, while letters to the columnists were unprinted, the responses suggested a confessional tone. Women wrote in with intimate problems, confessing a lack of interest, a neglectful period, or even the misuse of products with devastating effect. These confessions, along with reprimands and pardons offered by the columnist, continually reaffirmed the power of Valerie's and Mab's expertise.

The chastisement of women who mistook the columns for something other than beauty and fashion also worked to delineate their discursive territory. To "Sara," Valerie responded: "Dear me, you have made a mistake – just as Marigold did – and you must think this is a 'heart-to-heart department' where women with false lovers or unfaithful husbands bring their woes. My dear girl, I think the woman who must write to a newspaper or magazine about her affairs of the heart is a very poor creature, indeed. You say that you are afraid this young man does not love you. Then why, you silly goose, should you bother about him? I should not take the trouble to dab on face cream and powder – to say nothing of a touch of rouge – for the sake of a stupid and unappreciative young man."[17] There was no doubt where the borders of her expertise were – or how she felt about women in need of such seemingly outdated romantic advice.[18] But, for many women like Sara and Marigold, writing to Valerie or Mab was a means of engaging with modern femininities in another way: a chance for change, or as Barbara Sato describes it in regard to Japanese Modern Girls, "one way to improve one-self or achieve self-cultivation [which] offer[s] the possibility of social fluidity."[19]

In the dominant scripts offered by both advertisers and movies, improvements in physical appearances could pay large dividends in finding or keeping a husband, professional and personal success, and perhaps even social mobility, and beauty experts worked to shore up this message. In chastising "Sara," Valerie suggested that the process of beauty was only worthy of certain men and that women should direct their energy to those worthy (and appreciative) of the effort. Women were subtly assured that corporeal changes could mean changes in their destiny. Since Valerie once wrote that she largely offered advice to the amorphous category of "business women," which implied a salaried or waged woman, such promises held overtones of class improvement.[20] In this case, women's investments in their bodies were not as frivolous as they may have seemed.

Responses from Valerie to readers, which were published after every column, generally covered a rather narrow range of topics: skin, hair, and figure. Within those categories the fields were more complex, although there were patterns: oily skin, acne and a dull complexion were frequent complaints, as were oily, darkening, or greying hair, and along those lines, some women sought advice about bobbing or growing out their hair. In addition, women requested advice on how to maintain their figures and improve specific pieces of the body, especially the hands. Valerie replied publicly to various letters and frequently promised that more specific advice, with specific products, was on its way to the letter-writer. On more than one occasion, Valerie publicly reprimanded the reader for not providing the requisite self-addressed stamped envelope. However, in giving advice about specific issues, Valerie also passed on comments about beauty and consumerism more generally. While Valerie "refuse[d] to guarantee anything" she did declare: "this is emphatically an age of perfect production in soaps and powder."[21] For various skin afflictions, however, she encouraged women to seek out advice from a physician.

Unlike Valerie, Mab responded to concerns from readers in the body of her column. In September 1929 she noted, "In looking over the many letters that come to this department. I find there are two things that more than anything else bring despair to my correspondents. One is unwanted flesh and the other is unwanted hair." One month later, Mab uncharacteristically printed an excerpt from a correspondent who she identified as a woman over fifty who, like others of the same age range, "beg for suggestions that will help them to reduce their weight and obliterate the lines etched upon their faces."[22]

It was in these moments of advice doled out to particular people or smaller groups of women that the experts' contradictions were most fully realized. While Valerie told one woman to ignore the sensationalist stories of husbands leaving their wives because of women's corporeal neglect, both she and Mab contradicted this in their respective columns.[23] As a result, it is important to remember that beauty experts added to the confusion of consumer goods, bodily messages, and physical performance even though they were meant to assist women with them. Yet, these contradictory, opaque, and confusing messages offer an important glimpse into some Canadian women's struggles, hesitations, and triumphs in chancing to occupy the image of the Modern Girl.

Ultimately, it is very difficult to know who was reading the beauty columns and writing to Valerie and Mab. Barbara Sato's work on Japanese Modern Girls, however, is a good reminder that even reading mass women's magazines should be seen as an available act of consumerism available to "less-privileged women."[24] Valerie's own admission that she wrote for business women should suggest a broader cross-section of readers. There are other hints, however, that allow me to speculate that the readers were sometimes not only the working and middle-class women like Valerie and Mab presumed. While men were usually framed as misunderstanding fools who simply could not be trusted for their thoughts on sensitive issues of consuming and beautifying, Valerie did respond to at least two queries from men looking for beauty advice. Once in 1922 and once in 1928 men wrote asking of baldness and blemishes.[25] Valerie also occasionally commented on the pseudonyms women had chosen for themselves and gave advice based on their ethnicity. "Nora," for example, was told she had a good Irish name and that if she was new to Canada would need no cosmetics "since the old country complexions are usually wonderfully fresh and clear and beyond all 'touching up.'" Such judgments also came with ethnic stereotypes: Valerie hoped that "Nora" was one of the peaceable Irish. While Ireland was in the midst of a civil war when Valerie was writing in 1923, one wonders exactly what "Nora's" concern with blackheads had to do with it. Stereotypes of beautiful "old country" complexions were also a theme when the writers revealed themselves to be from the United Kingdom, which exalted the appearance of "preferred" immigrants. Valerie also received letters from women in their teens on a variety of issues from skincare to the cultivation of "charm." Her advice seems to have been on the mark – or at least that is what she wanted her readers to think. As Valerie reported in 1928, she had never received a disagreeable letter. English-Canadian women's concerns were many and they sought out the advice of experts, but chastisements flowed only in one direction.

Do You Believe in Magic?

In October of 1928, Mab waxed poetic about the potential offered by modern beauty products. She wrote, "Shopping for beauty makes one realize the staggering number of things in pots and bottles and sachets that are full of the promise of beauty ... Women are serious in their desire to improve their appearance and they are succeeding beyond their most sanguine expectations. Is it any wonder that they believe in magic?"[26] Throughout the 1920s, the sale of cosmetics and other beauty aids littered the Canadian cultural landscape, most of which promised physical improvement along with other less tangible benefits like freedom, mobility, and power. Commodity magic did not happen by chance, but if used frequently and correctly (Valerie chastised readers for being reckless, not following instructions, and yet expecting results), it promised significant paybacks: an attractive mate, popularity, and personal and professional success. While goods imbued with magic gave consumers a sense of optimism, suspicion of "snake oil" salesmen and products remained. Columnists negotiated the troubled terrain of commodity magic by providing careful recommendations of safe products, while intertwining modern science and magic. In the world of modern science's "fairy magic," Mab extolled, "the scientist is accomplishing truly magical things."[27] A mythical re-enchantment of goods (magic allegedly made safe by the gloss of science) was a significant aspect of modern advertising, and the fact that one could shop for beauty, as opposed to cultivate it from within one's own character, revealed some of the challenges consumer culture presented to more established standards of beauty. The alleged promise of improvement, however, also introduced the "democratic and anxiety-inducing idea that beauty could be achieved by all women – if only they used the correct products."[28] In advocating for the thoughtful use of make-up, Mab bluntly informed readers, "Anything that a woman can do to improve her appearance is right to do." In displacing homemade beauty treatments and remedies, modern beauty, as one advertisement declared, required "the best" and that was often equated with the mass-produced and store bought.[29] For those living on a budget for whom commodity magic may have been prohibitive, columnists provided sly ways to continue to be modern. They offered recipes to teach women how to make some beauty products, but typically only if the alternative was nothing at all. Valerie challenged the argument that "the business woman has not time or money to attend to her beauty." She suggested that business women who "often have a whole free evening to keep her good looks" purchase an extensive list of ingredients, including lemon, milk, hydrogen peroxide, white wax, almond oil, elder-flower water, boracic acid, rosewater, olive oil, a cucumber, a strawberry (when in season), and olive oil soap.[30] These "ingredients" were meant to mimic the effect of mass-produced cosmetics (some being seemingly simpler versions of those goods anyhow).

Despite the fact that Valerie recognized time was at a premium for business women, she implied that time was a better sacrifice than beauty, and subtly reinforced the notion that, in a quickly moving modern world, commercial preparations were simply easier. In letters written to Sylvia Gray as part of the 1922 prize competition for best letter on personal care held by the Ontario Industrial Division of Hygiene, young women noted the difficulties in balancing time and necessary, modern personal care. Their letters describe intimate details about working women's cosmetic use and hygienic care in sometimes difficult, if not inadequate, living conditions. These so-called confessions revealed the significance of consumer products to girls' identities. Gray concluded that deodorants were "an essential factor in the toilet of the modern girl." The letters also showed that women managed difficult living conditions, sometimes compromising their ideals for bathing and hair washing to try to meet modern standards of hygiene and beauty on slender incomes.[31] One letter entitled "Live and Learn" is particularly revealing and worth quoting at length. The contributor wrote,

> I came to the city when I was only eighteen from an old-fashioned home and everything was different and exciting and all my ideas changed in a minute. Seeing girls wearing what looked like lovely evening dresses at work and the gay silk stockings and all, sort of when to my head – I know that sounds funny but, honest, that's what happened. I got the lowest-necked georgette blouse and the shortest skirt I could find and high heels and silk stockings with roses on them and hennaed my hair and somehow I looked so different I began to act different and dropped all my good old habits.

> I went to parties every night and never got to bed before twelve. Well, Sylvia, I guess I'd better come to the point though it's hard to write for it is that I just hadn't time to wash. I'd be so tired I'd get up at the last moment, throw on my clothes, put on a lot of perfume and powder and rush off. I really did think perfume did instead of soap and water. I just thought it a more luxurious city way of keeping clean like silk stockings were a more luxurious city way of dressing.

At work one morning she overhears a colleague describing her as unwashed and having been put in the "dirty corner." Her shame and embarrassment lead her to a new regime of bodily care. "Live and Learn" continued,

> I decided I'd have to go slower and take time to look after my body. I cut out lots of parties, went to bed earlier, got up earlier, and I guess now my hobby is pretty clothes and washing. I've had a bath every day of my life since that awful morning and I'm careful about my clothes and know that everything about me is just as clean and dainty as possible.

Significantly, she does not state or imply that she is giving up luxury city consumer items, only that she had learned to take better care of her things and her body, and has return to regularly washing.[32]

As Valerie's advice and "Live and Learn's" letter reveal, a belief in modern magic was only part of the formula in being a modern woman, as the "desire to improve their appearance" and become modern was ultimately of import. As much as advertisements turned the body into an object for consumption, they also appealed to notions of subjectivity by connecting commodity displays and modern female subjectivity. The line between consumer objects and women's subjectivity was complicated, and representations were closely tied with techniques of appearing. Part of the complication was that women were encouraged to carefully examine the body from the outside – taking on a critical, often masculine gaze – in order to respond to the body's perceived needs. The idea of the body as visual image, in need of constant attention and improvement, "made the body into a project," and imparted the message that it was no longer enough to experience one's body and respond simply to physical sensations or be judged by one's character.[33] Projects were deemed to be constant and specific and were connected to particular commodities.

After a series of instructions on make-up application (one of her many columns on the subject), Mab told readers to remember one important point: "Be your own most severe critic, and study your face from all angles."[34] Mab's advice reinforced a popular discourse that encouraged self-scrutiny on an intensely detailed level and reinforced the idea that women were to study their bodies through a male lens, thus encouraging the co-opting of an intensely misogynistic scopic regime in order to promote further corporeal discipline.[35] Popular advertisements encouraged self-scrutiny by including large photographs depicting women looking into mirrors. The techniques for modern filmmaking with close-ups and the ability to focus in and slow down were adopted in advertising, revealing the intimacies of surveillance. One advert depicted a woman sitting forward looking intently into a mirror and demanded, "Look at Yourself! Are you satisfied?"[36] An advertisement for Pompeian Night Cream included a large photograph of a seated woman holding a hand mirror and studying her reflection. The caption stated: "Miss Van Q. regards *with critical eye* the exquisite beauty of her skin, which she keeps properly cleansed and cared for with Pompeian Night Cream."[37] On crowded urban streets and seemingly anonymous environments like the department store or movie theatre, women were judged by passers-by, who advertisers intimated scrutinized the body and noticed details like cuticles and underarms, making the "critical eye" a necessary part of the process of appearing. Working women seem to get the message: one *Confessions* writer shared with her cohort, "Make constant use of a hand-mirror while dressing. See yourself both going and coming. Always remember the people back of you have a wonderful chance to search out your defects."[38]

The critical eye, however, inevitably led to a new consumer good – a manicure kit or skin cream – to solve the perceived problem. Not only did such products promise magical solutions, but also confidence that one would not have to worry about ragged cuticles being noticed by strangers. In an advertisement for hair removal cream, a young woman sits reclining in her slip with one arm above her head, exposing her underarm. The underarm is marked with an "x" and the caption reads "From the man's viewpoint." The text warns that "should he glimpse the slightest trace of unsightly hair – the whole impression is spoiled; he classifies you from then on as a woman lacking in fastidiousness."[39] The pain of chemical hair removal was, of course, not mentioned, as women were encouraged to recall how "he" would see it – a small, rather intimate piece of the body. The advert suggested that men noticed a lack of care, thus naturalizing a standard of bodily maintenance that made such work both a necessity and inconspicuous. Subtlety in body-work being done was a theme in Valerie's column, and the subject even extended to personal relationships. On 8 October 1927 she recounted the story of a "suburban housewife" who described the significant amount of time and energy that went into looking fresh and young for her husband. Keeping the work from her husband, she revealed the satisfaction in seeing her youthful reflection in his eyes, recalling, "And the reflection that I see in his eyes makes up for all the trouble I've gone to in order to erase the signs of neglect."[40]

The notion of constant surveillance contested the boundaries between public and private displays. In the 1920s, not all body projects were expected to be done in secret or look natural, despite some suggestions made to the contrary; rather, they were part of modern techniques of appearing in which women revealed aspects of their work. If the Gibson Girl appeared effortlessly and naturally beautiful, the Modern Girl flaunted her physical changes by wearing obvious make-up in shades one beauty columnist pointed out were not "humanly possible."[41] Desiring to produce a Modern Girl's body required a tricky sort of cultural negotiation, and advice on how to both create her body and deal with troublesome issues like "touching up" were provided by magazines and advertisements selling particular commodities. Advertisements for Gouraud's Oriental Cream offered a solution to the ongoing problem of maintenance by promising a "24 hour complexion" and declaring "Stop 'Touching Up.'"

Columnists and other writers debated the appropriateness of the oft-witnessed performances of beauty upkeep on Canadian streets. Valerie reported that the Modern Girl had "thrown all boudoir reticence to the winds and produces her compact on all occasions – in the street-car, in the theatre – and even in the crowded ball-room. So far, the compact has not been seen in church – but then the modern girl is not often seen at church." In 1927 *Maclean's* put the Modern Girl applying make-up in church on its cover, which succinctly encapsulated these practices and their problems. It depicted a Modern Girl sitting in a church pew with her bible held up in front of her face as though she were diligently reading it, but from our angle as a viewer, we see her make-up compact is held inside the bible and she is, in fact, touching up her face.[42] The viewer of the image is "in" on her secrets: the appearance of religious obedience while being engaged in a superficial practice, and the need for her look to be constantly maintained – even in public. Specific technology opened up the possibility of such performances. Small, handheld compacts were a recent development, and as Joan Jacob Brumberg

2.1 X-Bazin Advertisement, *Maclean's*, 1 February 1926

argues, these mirrors were significant "because they allowed women to scrutinize and 'reconstruct' the face almost anywhere, at a moment's notice."[43] Further, Mab argued that the freshness of make-up on the face could not be maintained all day when one was in contact with "the busy world." She advised that it was "absolutely necessary to carry restoratives to repair the damage," although she warned that it was "undesirable" to be seen applying lipstick, powder, or rouge in public. While touching up openly and obviously in public was seen as crass, the standards of constant and consistent maintenance of Modern Girlishness often deemed it necessary. [44] Moreover, in order to appear constantly at their best (even for a 24 hour period), women were almost perpetually engaged in the process of appearing modern, lest they be faced with critical judgment.

Notions of constant public surveillance of one's appearance, the constant and time-consuming process of disciplining the body, and the need to be up-to-date with the latest techniques of appearing had a nefarious side. The twenties were a significant decade for Canadian women, who by the early years of the decade had fought for and won the right to vote at the federal and provincial levels, with the exception of Quebec.[45] Increasing access to higher education for the white middle class, and a growing presence in the public helped to spark a reordering of gender relations. It seemed, however, the idea of female emancipation was quickly reduced to conspicuous consumption. As Cheryl Krasnick Warsh argues, "The fragile figure of the flapper, the emphasis on short-term gratification, and the espousal of the value of fashion – ephemeral and unproductive – dissipated some of the anxieties caused by increasing public roles for women. Power was now defined as purchasing power, the goal of which was the traditional one of pleasing a man."[46] The many body projects including bobbed hair, make-up, and a complicated skin care regime promoted in advertisements and articles encouraged women to spend their available time engaged in improving their appearance, and associated their physical improvement with power. Further, increasing feminine visibility added another layer to the physical mastery women were expected to have before entering into the public. Agnes Macphail was elected as Canada's first woman Member of Parliament in 1921 and endured bitter attacks on her "mannish" behaviour and "plain" style.[47] Despite other successes, women were constantly reminded that their bodies were on display, and power was associated with attracting positive attention through the eyes of others. As professionals, wives, and mothers, women were warned to take on proper techniques to look modern in order to achieve success, keep their husbands, and act as

2.2 *Maclean's* Cover of Modern Girl Secretly Touching Up in Church, *Maclean's*, 15 February 1927. Used with the permission of *Maclean's* Magazine.

"emancipated mothers." These issues were explicitly addressed in the dialogues beauty columnists had with readers, who wrote in asking for help with specific problems.[48] As a result, these discussions made both the threat of professional, social, and personal failure and the solutions, embedded as they were in consumer culture, seem real.

A single advert often tied many of these different themes together. A Bovril ad made connections between the product and modern femininity by appealing to women's "need" to look thin and young. The copy stated "Keep Your Youthful Figure" and "her friends chuckle behind her back when she puts on *excess* weight." The women in the image were clearly engaged in behaviour that suggested a normalization of the cultural policing of women's bodies through surveillance. The dialogue between two women made it clear that the third was "a dear old soul," but quite clearly this did not matter as much as the appearance of her figure. Moreover, not only was the non-modern woman depicted as old and "suffering" from excess weight, she was also clearly out-of-date. She was wearing clothing from at least a decade earlier and was seated alone in a domestic setting.[49] This image of "sad," outdated tradition was juxtaposed with young, thin, modern women, who were clearly out having fun in public. In a somewhat paradoxical appeal given the Modern Girl's figure, the advert also suggested that consuming Bovril gave women the strength to "resist epidemics," and therefore implied some sort of health benefit.

Overall, we are certainly meant to feel sorry for the lonely, old-fashioned, and perhaps unhealthy woman, but the underlying implication was that she chose to be old, and with that came a wide-reaching set of cultural assumptions. In Canadian beauty columns, youth was defined as having alertness, elasticity, vitality, energy, and enthusiasm, while old age was described using words and phrases like "fatty degenerations," misshapen, conceited, lazy, flabby, and having "lost the magic of youth."[50] It is difficult to know the precise age of the woman being mocked in the Bovril advert. Perhaps more important is the fact that she is presented as choosing to be old, out-of-date, and unstylish because, unlike her supposed friends, she has not updated her clothing or disciplined her body to be thin, elongated, and lissom as was expected.

Indeed, there was no shortage of advice on how to retain a youthful appearance. Valerie attempted to explain the complex negotiations of age in which Canadian women were expected to participate. Although she disclosed that she knew a three-year-old concerned about her hair colour, her overall advice was that a "woman of twenty or thirty does well to go in for prevention or take steps to hold on to what she's got. But there is no valid reason why a woman of forty, fifty, seventy or ninety should not conserve also and repair."[51] Almost every month, the beauty column in *Chatelaine* lauded youth as the main characteristic of beauty and provided tips for women to hold on to it. For example, women were told that "a tiny fund of youth ... can be tapped by right thinking and right exercise and lotions and by keeping strict account of calories." Women were also told that old age had become optional, and that "intelligent care of their bodies every day will postpone old age, indefinitely." In passing along some New Year advice, Mab quoted an unnamed beauty expert who declared that growing old "is a thing that can be controlled and even prevented indefinitely. That fat, settled, weak, inadequate look and feeling can be thrown out of the window like an unbecoming hat. The twentieth century has opened the window, it is up to you to toss the hat."[52] Valerie declared, "The woman of today regards her wrinkled cheeks and sagging chin and goes forth to buy a special astringent for which she pays five dollars and a half. Then she applies this tightening preparation, afterwards a vanishing cream, and finally a dash of her favourite powder. Then she throws a kiss to Father Time."[53] Consumption of the right goods would, it seemed, restore the appearance of youth after signs of age began to appear, and this is when the beauty expert's advice was so important. Valerie suggested an alternative for older women who had not kept their bloom: they were literally to clear the floor for beautiful young girls wishing to dance in public. She suggested, "Why not dance in private?"[54] However, women's advice columns also warned of dangerous, desperate, and obvious attempts to remain youthful. Hair dyes, face lifts, and other types of surgical intervention (including one reported case of the injection of paraffin wax to fix wrinkles) by disreputable and unqualified people (often labelled "American") were said to give unfavourable results that only fooled the purchaser.[55] The message was not to consume whatever was available on a landscape littered with items for purchase, but rather to adopt a careful and plotting consumption of the correct goods. To this end, Valerie responded to questions about the safety of cosmetics. Magic, even modern, scientific magic, required ongoing management and careful regulation.

The Promise of Beauty

Cosmetics and the production of a modern body were not only about self-loathing and problematizing a "natural" female body. Part of the lure was also the pleasure one could take in the care of the body and the promise of beauty. As Mab suggested, "Carefully chosen aids to beauty as Christmas gifts will be interesting and satisfying purchases. Such gifts will help to keep youth in the hearts as well as in the bodies of the recipients, because of the promise that they suggest."[56] Even the editors of the confessional letters of working women commented on makeup. They wrote, "there is the question of 'make up,' a question which to many perhaps will seem purely trivial ... On health grounds, however, the subject is not as trivial as it looks and it is, partly, on health grounds that it is used. It is discouraging to see yourself looking tired and unusually plain ..." The passage continued, however, to seriously warn women that makeup could not be used to cover up defects in health or "camouflage uncleanliness."[57] Used properly and appropriately in a wider regime of caring for the body, cosmetics promised satisfaction in consuming and use, as well as confidence and self-assurance.

Pleasure could also be found in the personal time spent caring intimately for the body, and it was this investment of time that were front and centre in debates over consumerism.[58] In *Confessions*, a young worker writing under the pseudonym "Irish" revealed, "What an awful proposition it is trying to keep fit and looking pretty while most of the time is taken up working for a living!" Like many women, "Irish" suggested a very modern cure to the problem: increased efficiency. Many women wrote in with detailed schedules of days and weeks and the pleasures of bathing and care of the self. Mary Griffith "confessed": "I also found it beneficial to have an evening occasionally to simply relax, try one's hair a new way, try on one's gowns and plan alterations, or fix up some little accessory to brighten one's toilet for the next day."[59]

Many North American cultural commentators shared concerns over the appearance of the Modern Girl. A stinging critique of modern youth, especially for women, appeared in the 1919 issue of *Saturday Night* and questioned the dramatic rise in numbers of painted faces. Included in a list of problem behaviours like reading salacious literature, unsupervised dating, and watching questionable films was the use of cosmetics. Famous first-wave feminist Nellie McClung lamented the rise of the young "lip-stick beauty" in an article tellingly entitled "I'll Never Tell My Age Again!"[60] A *Chatelaine* article described the impact of advertisements and the pressure on young women to conform to particular standards. Writing of a "tremendous outside pressure", the author pointed out that "the youngsters of to-day are fortified with nothing but a tyrannical code picked up from each other and crammed down their throats by every type of modern publicity."[61] This was one of many ironic statements made regarding women's relationship to consumption during the decade. While magazines and newspapers played central roles in delivering the messages, they also found ways to critique them.

Appearing modern in public was discussed as both potentially pleasurable and perilous in Canadian magazines. While adverts appealed to notions of pleasure, critics pointed out a more nefarious side. While there was satisfaction in knowing one was being watched, there was also inherent danger. The pleasure in being seen was not limited to the experience of self-surveillance: underlying this notion was that others would find the appearance agreeable and pleasurable. Yet, attracting public attention was still thought to border on the distasteful at best, and dangerous at worst. Women were encouraged to emulate a modern look that was summed up by Mab as "the age of revelation," but they potentially risked their reputations and more in doing so. Modern Girls needed to strike a precarious balance, and columnists, in warning about the right amount of rouge and lipstick, attempted to delineate what that was. As Mab suggested, "experts in make-up put on their paint and powder in successive thin layers, which gives a charming natural effect when properly done. I maintain that any woman can learn to apply make-up properly and expertly, if she cares to give a little time and attention to it."[62]

In response to admonishments from various "authorities in the press and the pulpit," Valerie wrote, "it is true that the women of this continent spend many millions on articles that may properly be described as cosmetics. Yet who shall say that the money is wasted? The world needs all of the prettiness that it can beg, borrow or buy. Too much of the artificial is ugly; but a touch of it is really necessary, unless one is very young." The article continued to warn women whose husbands disagreed with their use of cosmetics, telling them that their husbands' eyes would inevitably turn to the "flapper who has a velvety finish of her favourite powder." Later in the column Valerie dealt with the inevitable pressure advertising placed on Canadian women. In an overtly critical moment, she revealed that she "resented the implications of the advertisements" but nonetheless followed their advice.[63] One year later, in a decidedly more chipper tone, Valerie's column pointed to one of the more neglected aspects of undertaking various performances and techniques of appearing: pleasure. A letter from "Dolores" reinforced a popular narrative of pleasure in the care of the body. She wrote,

> Dolores, who is only eighteen years old, declares that she is an ugly duckling with a "perfectly terrible" complexion. Now, when I awakened this morning, the world seemed cold and drab and I had a complexion to match. So, I

hastened to a pretty sea-green jar and took some nice, smooth cream from it, which I applied to my drab-colored face, "rubbing upward and outward," and finally wiping off with a cloth dipped in cold water. The drabness vanished as if by magic and the world became rose-colored once more. So, Dolores, begin all over again and become a swan.[64]

Magic, after all, implied pleasure, and despite the constant work and anxiety, moments of it were at least promised. The idea was to take pleasure in "curing" a complexion, and by doing so eliminate the dullness and monotony of life (albeit through a regular routine), and return to the promise of beauty. Problems even beyond the complexion, it appeared, could be massaged away with cream from a sea-green jar. This levelling of surfaces and assumption of similarity that Valerie's solution could work for Dolores because they shared the same problem is troubling. The deeper significance of the promise of beauty was an assumption of a singular standard, and in this regard, columnists were in line with other dominant trends of the period. For example, international beauty contests measured "national" beauty against very particular North American standards emerging from the sponsors' desire to find a new Hollywood starlet.

Yet, even the beauty experts who helped women navigate the increasingly cluttered world of commodities did not entirely embrace the complete look of the Modern Girl. Valerie, the more conservative of the two columnists, was particularly hesitant to encourage the bob.[65] While short hair may have had a wide appeal, bobbed hair was also seen as disconcerting to many older Canadians, since it was often affiliated with young women engaged in questionable behaviour like smoking, drinking, and petting. Yet, Dan Azoulay notes that by 1924 complaints about the Modern Girl's use of cosmetics and inappropriate behaviour had shifted dramatically from being undesirable by young men to being attractive. As one male letter-writer to the *Family Herald* from Saskatchewan wrote, "The modern girl appears to be very much more popular than the staid old-fashioned girl who in nine cases out of ten is obliged to play wallflower while her frivolous sister gets all the beaux. The average bachelor, even if he is on the shady side of forty, considers it quite romantic to escort this flashy be-powdered girl about ..."[66] Valerie's concern about the bob, however, was different. She warned readers about the upkeep, how it was not a universally flattering look for all women, and held on to older notions of a woman's hair being her "crowning glory." Valerie's concern was always how women could be their best modern selves in regard to appearance.

While the discourse of the promise of beauty was fairly universal, it did become fractured in regard to climate and race. Climate was a recurring theme in beauty columns, and certain types of goods were laced with national sentiments that modified their use for what was seen as a challenging natural environment. Mab's March 1929 column advocated the use of artificial sunray lamps for Canadian women suffering in the darkness of the northern winter climate.[67] Once considered a sign of the working classes, tanned skin in the 1920s suggested a certain fashionableness. Part of the motif of the Modern Girl was participation in sports like golf and tennis, so tanned skin became tied to athleticism. Pond's cold cream, for example, declared, "It's smart to be sun-tanned!" The advert included Jane Kendall Mason, "society favorite and all-around sportswoman," and stated that sun-kissed skin became popular when an ill "Parisian *élegante*" was told to tan "until she was brown as an Arab." She was returned to health and "achieved an irresistible new beauty which forthwith became the fashion."[68]

According to Mab, not only was tanned skin increasingly fashionable, but "canned sun" also offered the possibility of fortifying the nation's health. Mab reported, "according to one of our Canadian doctors the next generation, by having the right food and the necessary sunlight, will be immune from rickets and other such dwarfing diseases, and will grow up straight and strong. Indeed, he believes that in time, as a result of the wonderful facilities for health that are being constantly discovered, we may have human beings like gods inhabiting the earth!" Yet, Mab argued that since there were no gods inhabiting earth yet, Canadian women needed to rely on commercial enhancements, especially during the month of March. Mab paradoxically pointed out that the "wear and tear of winter" was indiscreetly highlighted by the "merciless" way the sun revealed "defects." The solutions were clear: special cream for the eyes, hot oil hair and face treatments, vanishing cream, powder, lipstick, and blush. These consumer goods were not only necessary for the modern woman, but specifically for the modern Canadian woman fighting a particularly harsh climate.

The northern-ness and ruggedness of the climate was a significant narrative in the constellation of discourses of Canadian nationalism in the 1920s.[69] Intimately connected to issues of race and gender, "the great white north" was seen as an escape from the soft, feminized, racialized landscape of the urban environment. Indeed, the Canadian climate was often used as a justification to exclude people of colour who, it was argued, could not handle the cold, difficult winters. Given Canada's ongoing project of colonization of Indigenous populations and concerns over shifting patterns of immigration, the privileging of whiteness and the naturalization of its association with beauty were coupled with discourses that connected race, progress, and modernity.[70] If white women could briefly "compromise" their whiteness with a touch of sun for the health of the nation, it was a sign of their privilege. Visually, women of colour were largely excluded from dialogues of consumption in Canadian magazines. In fact, the mention of "brown" skin in beauty columns was typically followed by a "cure" to return skin to its "natural" white and was, more often than not, part of a chastisement, especially if one had let a touch of summer sun stay too far into the fall.

For many Canadian women, even those who desired to meet the standards advocated in the columns, many commodities were beyond their reach. Economics, geography, and time hindered access to consumer goods, and promoters were well aware of the limitations. Advertisers and columnists did not, however, allow these limitations to dint the discourse of consumption, and in doing so, reduced structural inequities to personal care issues. For "women in industry" Mab noted the "bondage in the form of blisters, callouses, stains, roughness, broken nails and hangnails." She simply continued to relay advice on hand maintenance that required washing, cream, astringent, and polish.[71] In the world of commodity culture, racism, poverty, distance, and lack of time were no excuse. As such, Canadian women did not become modern as a group, but performed and appeared modern to varying degrees, and this required a constant production and cultural negotiation in a country where modernity was uneven and contested. Yet, the feminine modernities exemplified in columns in commercial, mass-market magazines naturalized being modern and female as a largely white project in the frequency and singularity of its representation.

Part of what was so ingenious about "the promise of beauty" was that it foisted responsibility squarely onto the shoulders of the women seeking it, and heaved a sense of shame on those who wanted to stay beyond it. Further, it was allegedly something that almost all women could achieve if only they followed advice to the letter, put in the time, purchased the correct products, and were unrelenting in the pursuit of the promise of beauty. Such a discourse set women up for failure, and perhaps more nefariously, made them responsible for it. That this idea was so widespread meant that the potential ensuing judgment for not trying or achieving it meant shame – an internalized self-criticism.[72]

Nowhere was this stronger than in the intertwining of fat and aging – both considered signs of neglect and personal failing. As Mab put it, "curbing the appetite improves the moral fibre as well as the figure."[73] Dieting was almost always connected to looking youthful, and thus columns conflated slenderness and youthfulness into a singular disciplinary regime. Mab wrote, "But if the spirit is willing, the flesh though weak and flabby can be made to obey orders, and the result will more than justify the effort. That amazing woman, Edna Wallace Hopper, has proved that it is possible for a woman of sixty-three to look in body and face like a girl in her twenties."[74] Mab and Valerie had plenty of advice on becoming and maintaining slender and young. In November 1928, Mab shared the diet of Mary Garden, who reportedly ate toast in the morning, anything at lunch, and then nothing for the rest of the day. Mab added that, to her mind, the best method was to abstain from food for one day a week.[75] In an attempt to offer women another weapon in the arsenal to fight fat and flabbiness, Mab reported on a chemist's new preparation that, if dissolved into a hot bath three times a week, could dissolve about twelve pounds of fat a month. This was a rare permanent treatment, considering the promising belief that fat dissolved chemically would not return to the body. Mab was careful in recommending this product, however, but ultimately suggested, "This treatment sounds like a perfect godsend to the unfashionably fat. It should not, however, entirely replace care in diet and regular exercise, but should supplement them ... It would be a delicate matter to proffer a box of this diminishing powder to a friend, but one might give it to a hefty member of one's own family as a present from Santa Claus!"[76] Shame, it seemed, could be wrapped in friendship and delivered by way of a gift. In addition to providing much-needed advice on how to consume, then, Valerie and Mab also offered many tips on how *not* to – at least in the case of food. If the promise of beauty could be pleasurable, it could also be premised on painful denial. If women were to develop and maintain a modern body that was both beautiful and young, careful restrictions were in order. In some ways, this advice must have seemed deeply disturbing in a country where malnutrition was still a pressing issue, but the Modern Girl seemed to have a dysfunctional relationship with food ingrained in her being.

Conclusion

Valerie and Mab frequently challenged critics – both male and female – who dismissed their areas of expertise as frivolous.[77] They argued that beauty mattered, and given the far-reaching web that connected individual bodies and techniques of appearing to issues of feminine subjectivity and modernity, it clearly did. While Canadian women faced restrictions in regard to consumption, commodity display advocated techniques of appearing that were expected to be and were employed. For women, being modern meant being a consumer, not only of goods, but also of many of the deeper and perhaps more troubling messages of the culture of consumption that intimately shaped their bodies and lives. Women were encouraged to take on roles of surveillance of their own and others' bodies, acting as unofficial gatekeepers of who appeared modern. If Victorian notions of being judged by character, not looks, had any resonance in the 1920s, the balance had certainly shifted towards an emphasis on appearance. No modern woman could be without particular commodities, and standing outside of the burgeoning commodity culture would mean ridicule and scorn. Age was no excuse as, in 1928, Valerie revealed herself to be sixty-one, a grandmother, and finding it "so easy to keep young – if you know how."[78] Canadian women were not, however, simply dupes of the media and advertisers, and beauty columnists served as experts in helping them steer through a complex consumer landscape. Columnists' answers to mostly unprinted letters reveal that women across the country took many of these issues to heart. Changes in techniques of appearing also connected Canadians to other women influenced by the global Modern Girl. In the manufacturing of surfaces, the Modern Girl's connection to modernity was a complicated mix of power and pleasure, but one that placed increasing emphasis on how women appeared.

3 The Girl in the City:
Urban Modernity, Race, and Nation

The 1 December 1925 cover of *Maclean's* must have startled readers with a depiction of the Modern Girl's alleged sexual aggressiveness. Catching a young man under the mistletoe, she grabs him by the lapels and goes in for a kiss. He looks shocked. The woman's clothing is more revealing than others who graced the cover of the magazine: a good portion of her back and arms are bare, and her dress scoops low underneath the arm-pit. Her skin is dusky, and it is difficult to ascertain her status visually. In some ways this image encapsulated many of the fears of feminine moder-nities: gender imbalance, aggressiveness, and racial and class ambigui-ties most often embodied by the more dramatic and extreme look of the flapper. As Louise Ryan argues, "The flapper, a symbol of modernism, embodied not only those different national characteristics, but also helped to frame the specific debates and concerns of particular national contexts."[1] The conflation of modernity, modernism (as an aesthetic movement), and urban life wove its way into complicated representa-tions of Modern Girls that cut to the quick of the greater anxieties of heterosexuality and race. While the Modern Girl could stir up anxieties about changing gender relations and racial mixing, this chapter explores how she could also shore up ideas about sexual difference and the privi-lege of whiteness in cityscapes increasingly congested with different people, places, and goods. Overall, the Modern Girl and especially the flapper functioned in a matrix of typing, performance, and masking that were part of the dynamic of modern life, the gendered racialization of feminine modernities, and narratives of alleged sexual freedom.

The Modern Girl was intimately related to urban modernity. Central to the Modern Girl's existence was being seen – her performances need-ed to be witnessed and her presence needed an audience. She was born of changes in women's work in the city: their power as consumers and drivers of leisure youth culture. Moreover, changes in the visual economy that placed her at the centre of an increasingly visual and anonymous urban culture reinforced the need for easily identifiable types. Anonymous relations in the city where people needed to identify and sort based on quick, visual analyses led to a hardening of typing, and were often based on gender, race, and class. From the late nineteenth century, advertisers had relied on categorizing particular combinations of hair and skin colour into "types," which were further associated with "exotic" locales and ethnicities. Cleopatra, for example, was a popular type.[2] In this urban environment, the Modern Girl had been most frequently interpreted as disturbing, if not downright disruptive, as she obscured normative gender, class, and racial codes in ways that made typing and reading types increasingly difficult.[3] In some ways she was disruptive of these codes, as she adopted boyish looks and behaviour, participated in working-class and immigrant pastimes, adopted racial masquerades, and suggested sexual freedom. In other ways, however, she was reaffirming, especially in light of concerns over immigration and the racial formation of the nation. This chapter explores the Modern Girl's connections to the modern logic of display in the city and the entire nation, and suggests how her body might have been read and interpreted in conjunction with a soft, feminized, racialized landscape. Moreover, this chapter discusses some of the more subtle (and nefarious) connections of the practices and performances of Modern Girls, and some of the sexualized and racialized contours of feminine modernities. The overwhelming whiteness of the Modern Girl was not a neutral category, and this chapter seeks to situate her within the broader scope of commodity modernism and cultural politics to explore her appeal, as well as the racial contours of her global style in the Canadian context. While in Canada she was often associated with fears over miscegenation, she also worked to shore up the mythology of "the great white north" and the whiteness of modernity. Whiteness was, afterall, an invisible centre for feminine modernities in the period.

In engaging in a cultural analysis of the complicated matrix of modern femininities, race and sexuality, I employ the strong and well-developed literature on histories of girls and women in Canadian cities in the period. Much of this literature has persuasively argued that young women who sought modern lives and appearances faced a significant legal, social, economic, and political backlash in the form of cultural, economic, and judicial penalties that could be both dispiriting and violent.[4] In

3.1   Cover of *Maclean's*, 1 December 1925. Used with the permission of *Maclean's* Magazine.

focusing on cultural narratives of women's alleged erotic choices and their desire to make their bodies sensuous through so-called Orientalized masquerades, I'm adding to this discussion women's cultural power to shape these narratives, and their seductive appeal to women. My analysis, however, reflects two essential points: that patriarchy severely proscribed *living* the cultural narrative of erotic choice, and that racism worked to define whiteness and privilege as the centre of many Modern Girls' claim to modernity and power. Cultural narratives worked to shape women's behaviour and their performances of modernity, and so they should not be seen as separate to Girls' experience. I suggest that women took on these narratives in making themselves up and pursuing modern leisure opportunities in the city, but I do with an eye to the proscriptions and penalties they faced in doing so.

Urban Life and Modern Female Landscapes

Modern Girls embodied modern changes from class and gender relations, to the growth of cities. Strange notes the following about Toronto: "From the Art Deco façade of Eaton's College Street store to the towering headquarters of the Canadian Imperial Back on Commerce, retail and office buildings literally and figuratively overshadowed Toronto's factories as the largest employers of women by the 1920s. As the city began to flaunt the trappings of a metropolis, the women who strode into work in trim suits and high heels took on a new air of sophistication as well."[5] If modern femininities seemed to reorder gender relations in look and appearance, they also suggested changes on the more literal landscape.

Modern Girls were defined by their angular geometric shape, which emphasized long vertical lines and obliterated the curves of breasts and hips. Her thinness was so startling to Dr. H.E. Barnard, president of the Institute of Baking, that he declared in a *Victoria Times* article that he thought the Modern Girl should be forcibly fattened in rat cages.[6] Often drawn unrealistically thin in an elongated almost rectangular shape, she wore short skirts and sleeveless tops that showed off long, thin arms and legs with hands and feet that ended in points.

Roland Marchand argues that the flapper's shape was associated with another symbol of modernity – the skyscraper.[7] Skyscrapers in Canada had begun to make their appearance, and from the beginning of the twentieth century, Canadian buildings competed for the prestige of being the tallest building in the British Empire. However, architectural style remained conservative in Canada until the 1920s when European modernism was incorporated into a Modern Classicism that stylized parts of the urban, Canadian landscape. In the 1890s, American critics commented that "even staid old Canada has of late years erected some tall office buildings ... Canadians are rather slow in adopting novelties." The delay was attributed to a negative reaction to the quick and cheap trends driving American taste.[8] Nevertheless, "staid" Canadian architects opened the pages of the January 1927 edition of the *Journal of the Royal Architectural Institute of Canada* to an advertisement depicting Miss Toronto 1926, learning how to shoot pool in a new Toronto recreation club.[9]

By the 1920s, architectural modernism had made its mark on both cities and bodies. Indeed, Canadian architectural historian Harold Kalman's description of Art Deco buildings could be read to echo the appearance of the Modern Girl. He describes the design as "a popular, non revolutionary modernism, primarily [achieved] through the application of the new decoration. Art Deco office buildings stress verticality, have a multiplicity of planes and angles and decorated flat surfaces, and sometimes appear to have been sculpted from a large slab of plastic material." Moreover, Art Deco did not have strong ties to history or tradition, but was rather a movement caught up in contemporary influences like jazz and the machine aesthetic. Art Deco was also a significant part of the reimaging of the female body as urban and modern, rather than part of an ahistorical natural environment.[10] Following New York's 1916 zoning ordinance, Montreal passed a by-law in 1924 that required skyscrapers to allow light to reach the street in attempt to combat the huge shadows they cast. In advertisements the Modern Girl's body competed with and sometimes trumped the buildings as she towered over them in super human form. Modern Girls thus cast their own challenging shadows, but regulation was far more difficult, if only in part because of the incredible power of commodity culture that was helping to dictate the modern logic of display. Women showed a remarkable degree of sophistication in both the maintenance of their body projects and their activities. As smooth skin, thin bodies, flat chests, and narrow hips were being promoted as the ideal, Girls were expected to negotiate a new and complex urban landscape with ease. Slender, elongated skyscraper-like bodies could easily fit with the new crowded urban landscape where the sky seemed to be the limit. Lithe, streamlined bodies could skim along the crowded sidewalks and slip easily into cars, movie seats, or crowded department stores.

The Modern Girl's towering, decorative, superficial style spoke to a form of modernism that appeared not only in architecture, but also art and fashion. Marchand argues that modernism was familiar to readers of popular magazines because advertisers looked to instill style and prestige into their products did so by incorporating the visual taxonomy of modern art. Technical aspects like diagonal lines, off-centre layout, montage, distortion, and simplicity added excitement and introduced, if only peripherally, audiences to high artistic movements like cubism, futurism, and Art Deco.[11] Advertisements for Eaton's and the Robert Simpson Company included Art Deco-styled women who appeared to blend into architectural details, which suggested their intimate relationship with the urban environment. The woman in a 1927 advert seems to be woven into an architectural detail or modernist sculpture; similarly, a 1928 Eaton's advert shows a young woman in a long tubular winter coat that almost makes her body appear the same as the column behind it. Reflecting a more economic style and design, the advert distilled the woman's body down to its essence, making it almost indistinguishable from the metropolitan landscape. A long, taper-thin pair of legs, an elongated, flat, rectangular torso, a disproportionately long neck, and small head also spoke to the "modernness" of the look.[12]

By 1932, the Museum of Modern Art in New York held an exhibition on modern architecture that coined the term "International Style" in reference to the stark uniformity of modern architecture internationally. The Modern Girls' body fit with this style as there was something both cosmopolitan and common in her look. In this way, her body spoke a language of modernity and modernism that was translated and spoken across different Canadian landscapes as well as globally. That the new fashions came from Paris, London, and New York also emphasized their prestige as these three centres were the fashion capitals of the decade, and offered an international flair to the goods. Fashion advertisements promised the latest looks from these cities, and commodities (both make-up and clothing) could be mail-ordered and shipped across the country. If her appearance was reflective of a modern disorder, it was partially due to the widespread changes that appeared in distilled forms on her body and echoed with wider cultural shifts. And her body – the body of a young, primarily although not exclusively white, middle-class woman – held its own long-standing anxieties intimately connected to issues of racial survival and the development of the nation. In this way, the landscape was both gendered and racialized, and the Modern Girl worked in a number of ways to render and define these aspects of urban modernity.

3.2 Autumn Modes, *Saturday Night*, 22 September 1928. Used with permission of Sears Canada Inc.

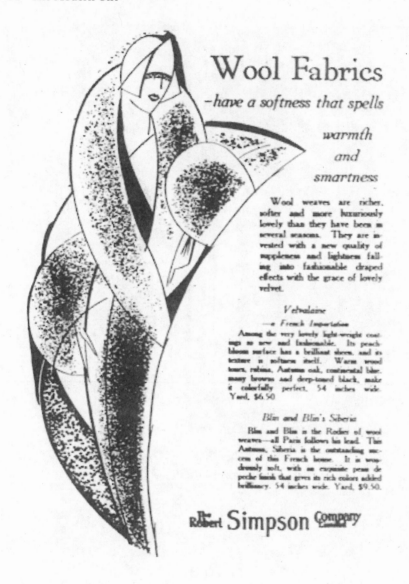

3.3   Robert Simpson's Advertisement, *Saturday Night*, 24 September 1927

The Girl in the City

The period from the 1880s to the 1920s is often framed as a story of remarkable change. The changing nature of work, the rise of the New Woman, the ongoing efforts of the moral and social reform movement, the impact of women's suffrage (often referred in Britain and to a lesser extent in Canada with the rather ironic phrase "the flapper vote") and shifts in the culture of consumerism all created the context into which the Modern Girl emerged, circulated, and was understood.[13] Her look and reception was defined by shifting class relations, changing patterns of immigration, and changing ideas of women, work, the public, sexuality, familial relations, and the rapid rise in consumer culture and mass retail.

By the twenties, women's options for employment in cities had shifted. While women at the end of the nineteenth century were often described as "adrift," by the 1920s Canadian had largely accepted the appearance of women alone in the city.[14] In the first decades of the twentieth century, the nature of women's work changed with the rise of clerical work and the opening of such positions to women, but especially women on the margins of the middle classes. As Donica Belisle argues, working in a department store was seen as preferable for many women because of the perception of respectability.[15] For women of both classes, however, there remained a concern over their work, living conditions, and leisure activities, because of their location within the city and because of the shift to commercial amusements that tended to be cheap (sometimes in both senses of the word) and heterosocial. Social surveys in Toronto (1915) and Montreal (1918) saw young women in search of a good time as a problem. Middle-class reformers in the 1920s continued to link female working adolescents, alleged declines in respectability, lax immigration policies, the breakdown of the family, and urban life.[16]

The rise of the urban business woman did not, of course, temper all anxieties about their lives and leisure. Narratives of sexual danger, improper leisure pursuits, and the value placed on individual women's bodies for the health of the nation continued. The working girls' place in the culture of consumption was intimately wed to other concerns of urban life. A cartoon printed in a 1928 edition of *Saturday Night* provided a synopsis of some of these changes where a young modern woman deliberately draws the attention of two older men.[17] Her behaviour and appearance may have certainly suggested a sexual forwardness, if not a potential act of solicitation. As Comacchio argues, concern over the flapper and the so-called New Morality of the 1920s were caused by a fear of

3.4   Cartoon from *Saturday Night*, 17 November 1928

young women fitting too easily within the new moral order, and their use of sexual capital for their own gain. *Hush*'s "Confessions of a Flapper" series, which described the relationship between a flapper and her much older and married sugar daddy named "Popsy," played on this fear.[18]

For other critics, the look of the Modern Girl took on a negative cast. In 1919, Beatrice M. Shaw, writing for *Saturday Night*, welcomed readers to the "the age of uninnocence."[19] In her article, Shaw touched upon a number of concerns that penetrated the cultural consciousness of the 1920s: the threat of the modern woman with a painted face and fashionable clothing from a department store; the crisis in modern masculinity as a result of a powerful new femininity; the concern over the physical and moral health of the nation; mass consumption; and the never-ending stream of American magazines, literature, and films pouring into Canada, which added to, if not caused, the other problems. Ultimately, Shaw pointed to some of the problems of modernity embodied by the Modern Girl. Others raised warning bells by predicting that men and women would soon be almost indistinguishable in appearance and behaviour. In an article entitled "The Girl of Tomorrow," readers were warned that trends in the masculinisation of modern womanhood would continue to the point that gender divisions would be almost entirely obscured.[20]

Much of this concern was directed at a new modern urban culture that necessitates a discussion of modern cities. Before the 1910s, cities were marked by dirt and decay, while poor sanitation, little regulation, and inadequate services made them physically dangerous. Urban reform efforts, tied in with middle-class efforts for the moral regulation of the urban poor, did affect public health campaigns to chlorinate water, provide vaccinations, and pressure cities to implement proper sewage and water facilities.[21] But while improvements were made, anxieties continued, especially ones marked by racist fears over newcomers. As new Canadians immigrated largely to cities, they came under the watchful eyes of reformers worried about their impact on Canadian society as concentrated in the city. The concern was intensified as patterns in migration shifted from the British Isles to southern and eastern Europe. Strict immigration laws minimized Asian immigration.[22]

The medical, labour, and feminist groups of the twenties were vocal opponents of immigration, and fears over the "Red Scare" and labour radicalism dovetailed with xenophobia. For women of child-bearing years, these arguments became rooted in reproduction, as concerns about "race suicide" were magnified in the wake of the Great War. The world-wide conflict revealed serious problems in child health (by way of recruits' poor health), serious losses of life, and high numbers of disabled soldiers, all of which framed concerns about the health of the Canadian nation. Child-saving campaigns along with "proper" scientific education for mothers were offered as solutions.[23] The family-focus on proper mothering and child rearing were part of a concerted effort to maintain middle-class ideals of domesticity in the face of modern changes. As Cynthia Comacchio argues, "Perhaps the most significant modern trend, in what it seemed to forecast for 'the family,' was the changing role, appearance, and attitude of the 'girl of the new day' ... Armed with the vote, more formal schooling than her mother, new access to jobs, and new ideas about her 'proper sphere,' the flapper appeared a singular threat to middle-class domestic ideals."[24] Concerns over everything from vice to entertainment to poverty were shot through with fears over race and preservation of the white, middle class, and frequently distilled down to focus on young women's bodies, since their health was tied to that of the nation.

Modern femininity did appear to more closely and comfortably fit urban life than masculinity. Young working women, in particular, seemed to acclimatize to the city more easily and were more readily visible because of it. For both middle- and working-class women, however, modern life was deemed to be a potential problem for their physical health. Far removed from an idyllic natural state, urban women were at risk of becoming too civilized for their proper reproductive roles, and physicians in the late nineteenth century repeatedly expressed fears that this was manifesting itself in disease and disorder.[25] Paradoxically, men in white-collar professions were thought to be at risk since modernity seemed to wear away the naturally masculine hardiness of the white, middle class. Escape from the city to the wilderness by way of tourism was deemed essential to their health, and ultimately the health of the nation. By the end of the nineteenth century, the recognition of the need for workers' rest to preserve health and efficiency gave rise to shorter, closer excursions.[26] If modern life was celebrated as progressive, the long list of concerns gave rise to modern cures.

Cities were feminized, racialized spaces of perceived dangers to the social and moral health of Canadians. The city – as a public space – seemed to be feminized by a variety of women's claims on public space. Middle- and working-class women demanded reforms for a host of issues from voting and public health campaigns, to labour rights and better wages. They shopped, walked to work, sought out amusement, and demanded reforms on city streets. More subtly, cultural practices, like those related to smoking, also changed. Once socially proscribed, women smoked publicly, taking up what was once defined as a masculine practice that marked out men's public space. As Sharon Anne Cook has recently argued, working women were essential to the image of the female smoker, as it was working women who lived out fantasies of pleasure and danger by lighting up. Smoking allowed working girls to construct themselves as modern, urbane, and sophisticated, but this still required a careful performance of smoking, given their vulnerable economic position and tenuous claim on respectability.[27] On the front page of a 1928 edition of *Saturday Night* they reported that like smoking, cussing was being feminized. The brief article concluded, "The average man is a simple idiot blissfully unaware that the fair sex is taking one by one and making distinctively their own the delights that were once his by virtue of his manhood. He can thank his stars that he is yet able to make love without being considered effeminate."[28]

While modern life was seen as having an ill effect on almost everyone, those effects were gendered in nature and intensity. Men, in particular white middle-class men, were seen as in danger of losing essential masculine qualities of aggressiveness and decisive behaviour because of the soft, feminized landscape of the city. Such problems were countered by antimodern antidotes that required a literal escape to more "natural," rugged places that offered more "authentic" experiences – and surely this claim to authenticity was partially a reaction to the alleged artifice of the modern city.[29] It was also a restatement of patriarchal privilege and its necessity to the national maturation of the early twentieth century, and propelled further by the First World War. White men's place as the "maturing colonial son" willing to build their own characters of the nation embodied a sort of "white civility" that tied together masculinity and immigration. The latter was never about equality, but about showing maturity through a gentlemanly acceptance of certain immigrants, who by hard work were deemed essential to the nation. Significantly, this particular narrative drew the line at miscegenation and assimilation – a line drawn succinctly in J.S Woodsworth's *Strangers at the Gate*: "Some peoples may not intermarry. The Mongolians, The Hindus, and the negroes will probably remain largely distinct."[30] There was no place for the Modern Girl in the hardy, largely non-urban discourse of manly maturation, except to marry well and have racially-healthy children. A close look at urban life, feminine modernities, and the Modern Girl, however, point to her more "nefarious" associations with racialized men on the "wrong side" of the colour line, and most importantly, how she also worked to maintain racial privilege in her own modern, urban way.

The "Menace," Modern Masculinity, and the Modern Girl

The Modern Girl was a cultural trope intimately connected to discussions of race and nationhood in the 1920s, which were in turn absorbed in the supposed crisis of modern masculinity. Defining the limits of nation were ideas about race, and in the context of the early twentieth century, these ideas were fixed in both biological and cultural discourses that reaffirmed and at times chafed against each other. A particular type of Modern Girl – the flapper – was most often associated with racial crossing and, as it has been often pointed out, this caused consternation across North America. Dancing the Charleston, listening to jazz, and taking on some of the trappings of the Harlem Renaissance, she brushed up against white, middle-class cultural boundaries and flirted with racialized but also immigrant and working-class pastimes.[31] Her ability to temporarily float across some of these cultural divides, however, was a product of her status. Her racial crossings were more often than not dilettantism rather than permanent or political challenges. She could, however, represent the anxiety of racial crossing, especially in the context of pseudo-scientific concerns of the seemingly imminent decline of the white race.

In regard to visual depictions, men and women of colour were far more limited and fixed. There were some set categories in which they appeared, including servile positions (porters, cleaners, servants), nostalgic antimodern primitives (in "authentic" dress often juxtaposed against white modernity), and as an erotic and exotic other (e.g. Rudolph Valentino as *The Sheik*, a popular trope that would take on its own life form in advertising and newspaper stories in the 1920s). But the Modern Girl had a representative mobility unavailable to other types. She crossed barriers and took on a look and the ability to perform it, if only briefly. These crossings were culturally significant because of the racial work they did in connection to discourses of masculinity and nation-building.

One of the striking features of the Modern Girl in the North American context is her *persistent* whiteness. And, in the context of Canada as a white settler society, this is significant as her racial work was different from other locales. As the Modern Girl Around the World Research Group points out, "Whereas anticolonial struggles tended to view the

Modern Girl with suspicion, nationalist projects often mobilized the white Modern Girl as a signifier of 'health' and 'civilized' national femininity."[32] The affirmation of the Modern Girl as a symbol of Canadian civility and progress appeared in a variety of ways. In an article on Turkish women, for example, an anonymous *Victoria Times* author measured "feminine freedom" in terms of dancing the Charleston, bobbed hair, and wearing lipstick.[33] Appearing in evident cosmetics was a sign of progress.

On a more profound level, as part of a global phenomenon, the Modern Girl became part of contemporary discussions that revealed some citizens' ongoing anxiousness about the racial composition of Canada society and concern over "the race" – a synonym for whiteness. As Mariana Valverde argues, "The slippery term 'race' allowed Anglo-Saxons to think of themselves as both a specific race and as the vanguard of the human race as a whole. The ambiguity of the term hence allowed white Anglo-Saxon supremacy to be justified without argument or evidence: it was obvious that as Anglo-Saxons progressed or declined, so would the world." Ideas of racial degeneration were also deeply inflected with ideas of gender, so that William Lyon Mackenzie King in 1919 could claim that legislation was needed to protect white, middle-class working women from potentially harming job strain that could be passed onto their future children.[34] Such concerns were heightened by racist discourses that deemed particular employers – men of colour – as potentially dangerous. Though these fears were rooted in ideas about heterosexual sex and desire, Cynthia Comacchio argues that "eugenic theory intensified anxieties about declining manhood ... [and] sensationalist tales of immigrant sexual depravity fuelled anxieties that were ostensibly about social purity, but also belied worries about the virility of Canadian men."[35]

The New Woman challenged white, middle-class men's social and political power, and this was often seen as a disadvantage. When combined with racial fears about immigrant men, the problem turned into a panic of national proportions. Although Margaret Sanger provided information on "birth control" to families and women across the continent, her methods were attacked as contributing to "race suicide" – defined by the declining rates of births among the white, middle class. Working men and women often thought of the issue differently, as organizations like British Columbia's Canadian Birth Control League (founded in 1924) reveal. Limiting family size meant a chance at a more economically secure life.[36]

An article by George Winter Mitchell published in *The Canadian Magazine* in 1923 reveals some of the ongoing issues of race, Canadian nationhood, and Anglo-Saxon supremacy. Canadians – who Mitchell understood as those descended from "the Nordic race" – belonged in Canada, which he predicted would become the cradle of the Empire. Dismissing other countries, notably the United States, Mitchell argued that Nordic people could reign supreme anywhere, but it seemed that southern climates produced degeneracy and interbreeding, which led to the subsequent demise of the Nordic race. Americans, in particular, had ruined their potential with loose immigration policies. Mitchell wrote, "Canada alone possesses all of the conditions necessary for the preservation of our white civilization, but to attain this high destiny she has need of the severest immigration laws, the wisest use of eugenics, and the renunciation of that life of ease and of premature endeavor [*sic*] to cultivate the arts which has of late years been creeping into the country and which is justifiable only as relaxation from strenuous work accomplished."[37] Canadians – as the Nordic race – were then a far more exclusive category than the actual composition of the country at the time. Mitchell's comments also highlighted the need of work over "play," or the cultivation of arts and culture, and were surely a comment on what many saw as North Americans' slide into the idle degeneracy of popular cultural production. Mitchell's argument also aptly expressed the nationalistic hope for Canada's growing role in the Empire as a point of racial preservation. Thus, his arguments were about much more than immigration policies and cultural production; they were about the preservation of "the race" and the future of humanity.

On the surface, the Modern Girl seemed to imperil the dominant ideas of racial (Anglo-Saxon) preservation and smacked of southern (especially American) degeneracy that seemed to flood northward. Yet, this was only one aspect of her connection to racialized Canadian modernities. There is no doubt she was an important point of concern, as she engaged in previously forbidden behaviours, wore fashionable clothing that would have been an affront to the good taste of her mother's generation, and freely painted her face as prostitutes a generation earlier were apt to do. Significantly, she was also apt to stir up racial anxieties. A 1925 *Saturday Night* article warned Canadian girls to "be careful whom you marry." The article highlighted the allegedly growing number of Canadian (and surely this meant white) women who married a "Chinaman, Hindu, Moslem or African Negro." Along with the fear that these men would depart for their country of origin, the author warned of polygamous marriages, which would have seemed "uncivilized" to many Canadians as it also tapped into fear-inducing stereotypes about racialized men's uncontrollable or even "primitive" sexuality. In calling for the federal government to ban such unions, the article concluded, "In view of the additional fact that such marriages place their white participants and the offspring under various social disadvantages as well as being distinctly undesirable from the point of view of the State, the Federal Government would do well to prohibit them altogether."[38]

Such sentiments echoed social regenerators and members of the moral and social reform movement who frequently expressed concerns over foreign men fraternizing, and perhaps even exploiting vulnerable working Canadian women. Stories appeared in major Canadian periodicals, cautioning that young, single women entering cities looking for work were being seduced and degraded by a "foreign element." Emily Murphy's book *The Black Candle*, in addition to a series of *Maclean's* articles, warned about the potential dangers of miscegenation, and the threats young women faced as a result of men of colour's influence and involvement in the illegal drug trade. The narrative of drug use constructed by Murphy was one of Chinese men luring innocent white, young women into the underworld of addiction.[39] Murphy's sentiments were typical of the ongoing social and moral reform movement. As a judge who took on numerous issues, Murphy sought to address serious social issues around poverty, violence, infant mortality, alcohol consumption, and the dangers of the city. Such issues and problems were addressed by way of moral regulation that constituted and reaffirmed white, middle-class values and privilege.[40]

The Modern Girl's connection to racial politics was more defined by desire than concerns over racial purity. As business women, working girls, and movie goers (which by the 1920s encompassed both working- and middle-class women), Modern Girls expressed desire for foreign men – a trope newspapers and magazines exploited in creating a titillating moral panic. The popularity of Hollywood films in which racialized men like Valentino as *The Sheik* appeared as heartthrobs also fuelled the fear of miscegenation, and certainly provided a context of fear for the sensational stories of Toronto women marrying foreigners. Moreover, the Toronto tabloid *Hush* reported the "Menace of Arabian Sheik Love." While the headline seemed to suggest that the men were the problem, the story warned that there was an epidemic of "neurotic screen-struck women" who "had their heads turned by the sentimental rubbish that is released in certain types of films" and were throwing themselves at

"Arabian Sheiks." The most disquieting aspect of this story was summarized by the subtitle that declared: "New Mania for Colored Men." [41] The mania was reinforced, if not produced, by advertisers and reporters. In an advert for Golden Peacock Bleach Crème, a Modern Girl is being kissed by a man clearly racialized as generically Middle Eastern. The heading announced: "The fascination of a milky white skin – now yours almost overnight!"[42] The advert clearly proposed that white skin was alluring, especially to men of colour. In 1924, a *Globe* headline announced: "Dusky Midway Sheik to Wed Toronto Girl." The bridegroom was part of the "India Show" at the Canadian National Exhibition, and was reportedly a "Mohammedan." In 1927, the *Toronto Daily Star* ran a series of articles on a "Toronto Girl" who was to marry a Persian Prince. Hilda Palmer – the would-be princess – was the epitome of a Modern Girl. Pictures depicted her with fashionably bobbed hair, obvious cosmetic use, and fashionable clothing. The marriage plans allegedly fell apart when Prince Farid refused the unstated conditions stipulated by Palmer's parents and fled, shattering Palmer's "dreams of an Oriental romance." Three days later, the *Star* reported that Farid was a fraud.[43]

While this narrative may have reversed the typical one of racialized men improperly lusting after white women, it still tapped into the contemporary fear of racial miscegenation, potential social dislocation, and the failure of the Anglo-Saxon race. Significantly, concern over "Sheiks" and women's desire also reflected anxieties about the achievements of the New Woman, the Modern Girl, and the seeming embattled hegemonic masculinity of white, working- and middle-class Canadian men. The tabloid *Hush* reported frequently on flappers and their sugar daddies, modern women's power over their husbands, modern women deceiving their husbands, flappers' promiscuity, and flappers flirting with mashers – bold young men who approached unknown women. It also reported on flappers' sexualized, racialized crossings, summarized by the reprinting of the racist headline "Toronto Society Woman in Nigger Dive."[44] Women's power as voters, consumers, and spectators helped to create the "problem" or imbalance in modern sexual relations. As Miriam Hansen notes, "the projection of the ethnic and racially male other as sexually potent, uncontrollable, and predatory no doubt reflected anxieties related to the ongoing crisis of WASP masculinity. The source of these anxieties, however, was more likely the New Woman, with her alleged economic independence, liberalized life-style, and new public presence (as voter and consumer), which seemed to advance the articulation of female desire, of erotic initiative and choice."[45]

3.5 Peacock Bleach Crème, *Toronto Daily Star*, 6 September 1927

While the "Sheik" or the "Arabian Prince" were popular racial tropes which supposedly threatened white women's purity, female consumers in fact helped to create matinee idols like Valentino. This revealed women's – particularly working women's – power as consumers. Female spectators drove popular cultural tastes, especially on film, and as such they had avenues to cultural and economic power.[46] *The Catholic Register* warned of movie-struck girls who were becoming "insufferable prigs" because of the lustful visions they watched on screen. The paper warned that these girls could be noticed on the street, and that "every casual glance a stranger gives them they interpret as expressing adoration, or the animal passion so crudely portrayed in their favourite movie-drama!"[47] In the commercialized world of the Modern Girl, Valentino's popularity as a Latin Lover playing roles of ethnic otherness stemmed from women's desire, and their participation in an urban popular culture allowed for such dreams to flourish. Moreover, concern about what the Modern Girl was becoming was also related to the shifting gender relations between modern men and women, since the latter seemed to be taking up the once-coveted white, middle-class masculine territory.

As changes in work opened up opportunities for modern women of the working and middle classes, by the 1920s many women in Canada were enfranchised, their consumer power flourished, and young women took on masculine cultural habits like smoking and swearing. Meanwhile, white working- and middle-class men seemed to be increasingly at a disadvantage.[48] Such a narrative was largely fictional in regard to everything from social capital to claims on respectability to the possibilities of wage earning, but this does not lessen the narrative's cultural power. That racialized and immigrant men became the focal point for women's "erotic initiative" was just one more level of alleged disadvantage for white, working- and middle-class men's already tarnished masculine identity, especially as Valentino's racialized, erotic identity was perceived by critics as being effeminate.[49] Suzanne Morton cites a poem from *The Worker* in 1927 which is revealing in this regard. Twenty-two-year-old Oscar Ryan wrote:

Hell! – first it's the bloody foreman, then
the boss, and now
you.
All you think of
is to run off to those
movie joints and cry yourself
sick over Valentino

But when it comes to the
Fellows in the shop,
you don't fall for us.
We don't put
axel-grease on our hair,
and we wear oil-soaked work shirts.[50]

Canadian men did engage in the culture of consumption and in body projects that helped produce their bodies as masculine and modern.[51] But in regard to race and nationhood, modern masculinities were firmly situated in the discourse of antimodernism, where white, British Canadian men were foundational to the development of the nation.[52] The combined threat of the New Woman, the Modern Girl, and immigrant men in their various arrangements was a serious challenge.

Patriarchal power severely stunted women's claim to "erotic initiative." And, despite whatever cultural power Modern Girls had to define a heterosexual, popular culture impulse, their lives remained bound by misogynistic restrictions. Women (especially young working-class women) who "got themselves" pregnant found themselves unfairly penalized socially, economically, culturally, and sexually. Cultural narratives of erotic choice and freedom were crushed by severe restrictions on legal birth control, misogynistic views of rape, and sanctioned vulnerability for women who found themselves unexpectedly pregnant and unmarried.[53] Unwed mothers were defined by leading child welfare experts like Charlotte Whitton as "delinquent," "immoral," and "inferior mentally." As Lori Chambers' research reveals, young, pregnant, unmarried women in contact with the Children's Aid Society found themselves "questioned extensively not only about the pregnancy itself but also about their other 'bad habits,' such as rouging themselves, smoking, drinking, and attending dance halls and movies."[54]

Rising rates of illegitimacy as well as the decreasing of the age of marriage for young women in the 1920s, suggests that more women were entering into sexual relationships earlier. Young urban working women in Montreal sometimes found themselves caught up in the juvenile justice system for their sexual activity, or for engaging in commercial pastimes like attending movies or dance halls. Defined as delinquents by parents, probations officers, social workers, and judges, women's transgressions were magnified if they crossed racial or ethnic lines.[55] If the Girls' love of finery had been accepted by *Chatelaine* writer Anne Elizabeth Wilson, racial fears persisted. The advert for chorus girls, Wilson noted, was carried in major Canadian dailies. Women who auditioned for the "presupposing mulatto" were promised training, international travel, and Wilson direly noted "a life of vice against her will."[56] Such warnings, no doubt, rang alarm bells for beauty contest critics, as the advertising and promised rewards were strikingly similar to those offered to pageant hopefuls. In regard to the Modern Girl's expression of heterosexuality, then, it remained one that was used against her as a weapon to shore up the alleged loss of white men's power, and to socially penalize her for heterosexual acts, both wanted and unwanted. Erotic initiative may have driven cultural fantasies, and film and advertising industries were clearly attuned to women's desires, but there remained a deep and wide disjuncture between the cultural narrative of sexual freedom and desire, and the harsh reality of the patriarchal regulation of desire.

Orientalist Fever and the Racial Masquerade

Stories of Canadian women being lured by foreign men or – even worse – lusting over a Sheik stirred gendered racial anxieties and concerns about shifting practices of heterosexuality among young women. Yet, the Modern Girl also worked to soothe racial anxieties by taking on or discarding racialized masquerades that subtlety shored up white privilege. In *The Sheik*, after all, the protagonist was revealed to be a man of European descent masquerading as someone from the Middle East. Perhaps more to the point, the author of *The Sheik* was in masquerade as well. Edith Maud Winstanley took on the pseudonym E.M Hull so as to not bring shame to her family.[57]

The most popular racial masquerade, and one that was employed throughout the decade, was the identification of "Oriental," drawing upon Edward Said's work on Orientalism. Although sometimes specific countries (Egypt, for example) were referenced, the Orientalist fever of the 1920s was a cultural construction only loosely based on geography. In this fashion, notions of desire, exoticism, and racial play fit with the West's simultaneous projection of desire for and fear of the Other. The Orient was represented as dark, mysterious, and feminine, while the West was light, familiar, and masculine.[58] In regard to racial masquerading, masks were superficial signs of racial Otherness provided by cosmetics and other consumer goods.[59] These masks were re-imaginations of both the performance of self by the women who took them on and the discourse of the East, as they appropriated, invented, dislocated, and bastardized aspects of Eastern culture. For the Modern Girl, Orientalism was a gateway to express a new sensuous identity – one that allowed white women to express erotic desirability and initiative in ways otherwise circumscribed by edicts of respectability.

Orientalism in popular and high culture was not new to the 1920s, and represents some shared ground between the New Woman and the Modern Girl.[60] Since at least the mid-nineteenth century in both North America and Europe, racialized performances packed entertainment venues and dovetailed with the rise of primitivism in the art world. If modernity and subsequently modernism felt cold and alienating, primitivism promised the ability to reconnect to something authentic, natural, and sensual. Art and modern dance contained this impulse.

Soon after "Little Egypt" performed at the Chicago World's Fair in 1893, orientalized dancers appeared on the sideshow at the Toronto Industrial Exhibition where so-called Nautch girls and Arabian dancers performed exotic and sexualized dances for predominantly white audiences.[61] Sexually charged and orientalized performances continued on the sideshows throughout the twenties and continued to attract both audiences and critics who often saw the performances as nude shows.[62] Further, films like *Salomé* (1918) starring Theda Bara (who played Cleopatra in a film by the same name in 1917) and another 1923 version of the Oscar Wilde play were part of a longer cultural trend the *New York Times* labelled "Salomania." Plays, operas and ballets employed Middle Eastern themes typically identified as essentially Egyptian in form (even when it was not), and some explicitly drew on the trope of Salomé. Canadian-born modern dancer Maud Allan was famous for her Salomé dancing where she enacted her own version of the Biblical story that concluded with her kissing the lips of John the Baptist's severed head. In her 1908 autobiography, Allan argued that dance had originated in Egypt and was cultivated in Ancient Greece, and Salomé's dancing allowed her to connect to ancient roots through movement.[63] This discourse allowed for artists – and ultimately their audiences – to tap into a more primitive motif, allowing them to move away from the rigidness of Victorianism.[64]

By the 1920s, aspects of Salomania continued as women appeared in Salomé-styled costumes for masquerade balls, dance performances, and on magazine covers. The performance of the racialized spectacle had become more common and popular than its high art predecessors. Following the lead of pioneering modern dancers like the iconic Duncan, Allan, and Ruth St. Denis, white Canadian women adopted the Oriental costume with revealing costumes of beads, gold accents, sheer material,

3.6   Cover of *Kinematograph Weekly*, 25 September 1924.

and covered heads, and performed dances as part of and away from the low culture of burlesque and sideshows. Salomé and orientalized costumes were revealing at best and often used patterns of beads over the breast and vaginal areas to draw attention. While wearing very few clothes, the women were often excessively adorned with jewellery and rich coloured fabrics which hinted at a sort of wealth; this was in opposition with the carefully covered modest look demanded by middle-class fashion sensibilities. Head coverings added an element of mystical, forbidden appeal, while the body was almost fully revealed. Though the Modern Girl toyed with racial masquerades like Salomé, this only shored up the privilege of being white, of being able to temporarily tap into part of the exotic look of the Other, only to cast it off at a moment's notice. The real cause of concern was not the mask, but the fear that it was somehow tied to miscegenation, that playing the exotic would drive the Modern Girl into more dangerous territory and cause her to permanently pollute her body and the nation.

Caught up in discourses of primitiveness as well as the related artistic movement of primitivism, the Modern Girl helped to delineate the racial boundaries of modernity in Canada. A sort of vulgar primitivism was appropriated in advertising and some performances to reveal the body in an exotic state of undress. Being primitive was frequently symbolized by a lack of clothing. In a debate over nude art shown at the 1927 Canadian National Exhibition, one of the many letters to the editor remarked "reasonable covering is a sign of civilization; only uncivilized races and demoralized people go naked."[65] Given white women's symbolic role in notions of progress, the health of the nation, and civilization, taking on an exoticized performance in a state of undress was apt to raise anxiety. And, in the case of the diverse audiences at the CNE who could enter the art gallery for the price of dime, the public display of the nude body did spark debate. Yet, as Alys Eve Weinbaum argues in regard to racial masquerades, "race was treated less as a biological posit than as a performance, posture, gesture, façade, or surface appropriable by she who possessed access to consumer culture."[66] The goods available on the mass market did not necessarily promote the look of nudity, but rather were a means to take on racialized masks that offered women a chance to be modern, seductive, and charming, while on a deeper level, mark out the racialized contours of feminine modernities.

By appropriating an Oriental look, white women could masquerade as the Other in ways that remained safe and even familiar, and in a manner that did not necessarily imperil their own racial power. White, middle-class Canadian women were encouraged to play with stereotypical looks of Asianness as a way of making themselves exotic. Art Deco-styled Modern Girls were often drawn with elongated eyes rimmed in kohl meant to mimic a particular look of so-called Asian eyes, and were carefully draped in ornately patterned silk of saturated colours and golden "imperial" embroidery with stylized Asian prints. Together with special creams that promised to give an air of mysticism, these elements provided a sense of exotic mystery affiliated with Orientalism. This racial masquerade had become deeply entrenched as part of the image of being modern; so much so that one of the symbols of the Modern Girl was her ability to take on Oriental looks as part of her performance. *Saturday Night's* beauty columnist Valerie even told readers that Modern Girls demanded perfumes from the Orient.[67]

Clothing, make-up, and other commodities were marketed as "Oriental" or "Egyptian" to highlight their richness, expense, and exoticism. In March 1920, for example, Eaton's advertised new arrivals from Paris, but the fashion globe-trotting did not stop there. The gown highlighted was described as a "Model from Madeleine and Madeleine in black satin, with Egyptian tunic of antique gold color tulle heavily embroidered in gold and jet beads." The Robert Simpson Company advertised drapery fabric as "illusively Chinese." Popular advertisements for Gouraud's Oriental Cream promised a more complete transformation riddled with stereotypes of the alleged mystique of the East. It promised "An alluring, seductive charm of infatuating mystic depth, bewitching and enamoring [*sic*] all those who behold it. It is just this entrancing touch that renders your skin and complexion an appearance of glowing, fascinating loveliness, bringing you the joy of a new, dominating beauty." Another ad for the same product stated "The seductive touch of the Orient – this alluring fascinating attractive beauty with its subtle mystic appeal can be yours. Possess this bewitching appearance thru Gouraud's Oriental Cream."[68] The cream came in three pale shades: white, flesh, and Rachel, but the ad promised to transform women beyond the ordinariness of whiteness to a mystic, bewitching, and dominating look that gave a power born from exoticized representations of women in the East. Cosmetic adverts – potentially the most troubling since they involved changing the skin – were careful to point out that Oriental masks added exoticism without sacrificing whiteness. Other advertisements for the cream stressed the product as a "secret of beauty" used world-wide that gave a "velvety softness" and "pearly whiteness" to the skin. Pompeian Bloom introduced their Oriental tint as a "beautiful new tone. It seems

And She Used Oriental Tint

HER satin gown and her veil were charmingly arranged — but it was the lovely coloring of her complexion that rewarded her with beauty on her wedding day. Every woman can be just a little lovelier if she uses the right shade of powder and rouge.

Do you know that a touch of bloom in the cheeks makes the eyes sparkle with a new beauty? Do you also know that Pompeian Bloom enjoys the widest use the world over, by all women who need youthful color?

Mme. Jeannette's Beauty Treatment—First, a bit of Pompeian Day Cream to make your powder cling and prevent "shine." *Next*, apply Pompeian Beauty Powder to all exposed portions of the face, neck and shoulders. *Lastly*, a touch of Pompeian Bloom. Presto! The face is beautified in an instant.

Oriental Tint

great pleasure in making special mention of this beautiful new tone. It seems to add a great brilliancy and youthfulness to your complexion. You may want to adopt it for general use—or you may want to use it only when you need to look particularly well and "sparkling."

SHADE } *for selecting your correct*
CHART } *tone of Pompeian Bloom*

Medium Skin: The average woman who has the medium skin can use the Medium shade, the Orange Tint, or the new Oriental Tint.

Olive Skin: Women with the true olive skin are generally dark of eyes and hair—and require the Dark shade of Pompeian Bloom.

Pink Skin: This is the youthful-looking skin that has real pink tones. Medium or Light tone of Pompeian Bloom should be used. Sometimes the Orange Tint is exquisite on such a skin.

White Skin: If you have a decidedly white skin, use Light, Medium, or the Oriental Tint.

Purity and satisfaction guaranteed. At all toilet

3.7 "And She Used Oriental Tint," *Maclean's*, 1 November 1929.

to add a great brilliancy and youthfulness to your complexion. You may want to adopt it for general use – or you may want to use it only when you need to look particularly well and 'sparkling.'" The picture in the advert showed a bride and stated, "And She Used Oriental Tint," implying that even a bride would use the tint on such an important day.[69]

In Canada, women who flirted with racial Otherness made themselves modern and also connected themselves – however obliquely – with contemporary international events. Early in the 1920s, archaeologists discovered the tomb of ancient Egyptian pharaoh Tutankhamen and an Egyptian look was quickly incorporated into fashion. Tutmania introduced repetitive patterns and encouraged a two-dimensional and elongated silhouette.[70] Fashion advertising also incorporated the look of ancient Egypt into the drawings of models who appeared in profile. The Egyptian look complemented existing styles that conflated slenderness, youth, and beauty. The continuation of a more sinister colonial project was also at work in the aftermath of the Great War, where the appropriation of an Eastern look happened at a moment of imperial crisis. In the peace negotiations of 1919, Britain and France worked to carve out their own spheres of influence in the Middle East, and in recognition that the modern world was going to run on oil, fought to protect their current and future interests. Arab and Indian movements for independence, however, were growing in an attempt to throw off the cloak of colonialism, which Egypt did in 1922.[71] Buying into the popular Orientalist look, in particular that of Egyptianness, was another form of commodity racism, and what Anne McClintock describes as "the mass marketing of empire as an organized system of images and attitudes."[72] The exoticization of "the East" thus functioned on a number of levels in female beauty culture: as a means of making white women temporarily exotic, and as a way of defining what was exotic in and of itself. Significantly, playing with racial masquerades was neither to be respectful nor permanent.

In the dabbling of Otherness, the mask was to be temporary and needed to be quickly removed so whiteness was not permanently comprised. Clothing and make-up performed a different function than another popular personal care item: soap. As McClintock argues in *Imperial Leather*, soap advertisements were caught up in discourses of whiteness, civilization, and colonialism by reassuring the supremacy of whiteness and tying cleanliness with the use of soap to notions of progress and the success of the colonial project. Soap and beauty ads in Canadian magazines in the 1920s continued this discourse, using notions of "white cleanliness" to indicate purity, as well as parlaying ideas about racial hierarchy. Advertisements for The Hiscott Institute in Toronto offered "Princess Preparations" for skin that was "Soft and White – Just Right."[73] The racialized discourses associated with commodities and bodily care were further complicated by the appeal of colonial resource extraction for the betterment of the colonizer. In this regard, Palmolive soap advertisements, which were prolific in Canadian magazines, promised a beautiful, youthful complexion because of the unique qualities of "rare" African or Egyptian oils. This was just a part of a wider pattern of adverts tied into colonialist tropes. Exemplifying what T. Jackson Lears calls "imperial primitivism" where "the white man enters the dark interior of a tropical land, extracts remedies, and puts them to the service of Anglo-Saxon civilization," these ads were part of a popular trope used since the late nineteenth century.[74] It served to reinforce the hierarchy between colony and metropole, and suppressed the violence of colonial resource extraction. Adverts for Mi-Rita hair remover depicted a stereotypical image of a young, Middle Eastern woman in a position of servitude. She is seated and looking upwards, offering a bottle of the concoction to someone beyond the frame of the picture. Her head covering, a ceramic container, and the bottle all contain the logo for the company, which contained popular visual allusions of Egyptianness.

Palmolive soap adverts highlighted "A Beauty Secret 3,000 years old" and commodified the legend of Cleopatra's beauty, juxtaposing a scantily-clad Cleopatra-esque woman in a revealing bra top, pouring oil beside a Modern Girl who looks on fully dressed. [75] The Palmolive adverts from the twenties had a particular visual structure, with a beautiful, white, modern woman on the top with a tableau of racialized women (and often men) who appeared as if in Egypt or Africa at the bottom of the page. This structure mimicked many white Canadians' view of an appropriate racial hierarchy. In the Egyptian tableaux, Cleopatra (who was named in the ad copy) is depicted looking at beautiful strings of beads surrounded by a number of men of different rank. Employing Cleopatra allowed the advertisers to tap into notions of timeless beauty and charm that emphasized luxurious and sensuous care of one's own body. This was a sort of corporeal indulgence that ran counter to more Spartan, white, Anglo-Saxon, middle-class notions of developing character and virtue at the expense of the flesh. Thus, women could briefly indulge in such physical care by washing their faces with Palmolive soap. Playing into notions of both the exotic and the erotic (images of Cleopatra showed her with very little clothing), the adverts for clothing, make-up, and other commodities provided enough distance between the desirable and the threatening elements of the Other to create a sort of tense racial ambivalence. The ads were part of the discourse of Orientalism that was intimately connected to the white, female body, an alleged source of fearful desire of the Other, and thus in need of the greatest protection. Yet, here they were taking on the exotic appeal of racialized women without ever permanently damaging their whiteness. There was, after all, plenty of available purifying and whitening soap that could strip off the mask.

This interaction with the Oriental exotic can be seen as another form of racism, and one that in Canada was accompanied by a more explicit racial fear: the so-called Yellow Peril. These notions of racial masquerade came on the heels of the now notorious Quong Wing case wherein the Supreme Court of Canada upheld racist legislation that made it illegal for Asian men to employ white women. The motivation behind the legislation was the assumption that Asian men preyed on white women and lured them into opium dens and the "White Slave Trade." It also operated on the premise that women were especially vulnerable to racial attack, through intermarriage, forced participation in the sex trade, or rape, and that any potential miscegenation had serious consequences for the health of the nation.[76] The Wing case, however, marks out only one dramatic moment in the history of Anti-Asian – especially anti-Chinese – sentiment that had been growing across Canada since the end of the nineteenth century through to the 1920s.[77] An outright panic about the "White Slave Trade" was premised on protecting young, white women from "dangerous" races of men, including the Chinese. It was intimately connected to urbanization, especially the increasing numbers of single, white, young women moving to the city (and away from traditional means of control) in search of work. The urban environment produced a sort of anonymity at odds with established means of judging character and exercising social control. It also produced an atmosphere wherein different groups of people, including new immigrants and the allegedly degenerate urban poor, had the potential to cross paths or comingle. Such a context produced racialized fears like those publicly expressed by Judge Emily Murphy who wrote, "Yes! It is quite certain we do not understand these people from the Orient, nor what ideas are hid behind their dark inscrutable faces."[78]

In this context, the Oriental mask initially seems perplexing, if not contradictory. White, middle-class women with full access to consumer culture, however, were fully in charge of the racial masquerade.[79] They could just as easily slip out of it (by changing clothes and washing their faces to return them to white) as they did into it. In fact, given the peculiarities of its commodification, these acts could not be separated from performing whiteness – and modern, female, whiteness. Masquerading as the Oriental marked out what was not "natural" to Canada or even North America, and such performances continued to show difference and racial hierarchy even as the Oriental was appropriated. In this way, the Modern Girl could experience the alleged cosmopolitanism of global connections (closely tied to imperial projects that "discovered" beauty secrets of exotic women and stripped natural resources from colonies) without challenging the privilege of her whiteness. Moreover, this helped to entrench whiteness as part of being modern in Canada, and upheld white, middle-class women's power and privilege in relation to race and consumption.

As a white settler society, Canada's racialized modernities took on another cast. As Liz Conor's work reveals in the Australian context, Indigenous modernities were discounted by the very absence of their presence as Modern Girls. Racist discourses about Indigenous peoples' "primitiveness" – and therefore the impossibility of being modern – created what Conor describes as "oppressive circumstances [that] dissuaded the social presence of Aboriginal Modern Girls."[80] While white women played with notions of race in adopting certain looks, styles, and cultural acts, the Modern Girl was nevertheless predominantly white, and her ability to take on racial masquerades was premised on that whiteness. Certainly, Canadian government policy and widespread attitudes and beliefs that devastated Indigenous communities also played a role in discounting the Indigenous Modern Girl. The reserve system which severely restricted movement, residential schools, illness, poverty, and cultural dislocation made taking up the performance of a Modern Girl a mighty task, even beyond the powerful cultural prohibitions. It was far more prevalent to depict Indigenous women as antimodern relics or not represent them at all, and in this regard, there were noticeable gender differences in such representations with men being far more prevalent. Government photographers produced images for the nation of Indigenous women that deliberately highlighted their antimodern status, and in the popular media, Indigenous peoples in stereotypical costumes were often juxtaposed with white modernity.[81] The appearance of "authentic" Indigenous peoples at the Canadian National Exhibition in 1927 was enough to warrant the publication of two photographs and a write-up in the *Toronto Daily Star*. In "authentic" dress the men, women, and children were described as a "living link with the old world," which portrayed them as primitive at best and sub-human at worst.[82]

Even when race seems to be secondary it bubbles to the surface in anxious moments: in Fitzgerald's short story "Bernice Bobs Her Hair," for example, Bernice's "Indian blood" is employed as an almost comic device when she is cutting off Marjorie's long hair and says "Scalp the selfish thing." Racial hierarchies and Indigenous women's place in them also played a role in the defining the end of the flapper. Clara Bow – the "It Girl" of the 1920s – marked the end of her career and the flapper in her 1932 film *Call Her Savage*. The ploys and pranks of the flapper existed on the margins of femininity, and Bow's character Nasa was perverse and wild – characteristics distilled down to her alleged savageness and "Indian" blood.[83]

This is not to suggest that Indigenous Modern Girls did not exist in Canada, only that they were not fairly represented in the popular media, advertising, or nation-building projects. Often in film, Indigenous women were even portrayed by white women in racial masquerade that essentialized, stereotyped, and flattened Indigenous cultures in simplistic ways that reaffirmed racial hierarchies. As Daniel Francis argues, representations of "Indians" in early twentieth-century popular culture were based on actual Indigenous practices manifested into often denigrating or romanticized stereotypes.[84] In her book *When the Movies Were Young*, Linda Arvidson (also known as Mrs D.W. Griffith) recalled the process of getting into costume for white women taking on and off the mask of "Indian-ness." She wrote:

> Back at the Inn the Indians would be changing from leather fringes and feathered head dresses to their bathing suits. And when the location party . returned, they'd have reached the green slopes of the Big Basin where, soap in hand, they would be sudsing off the brown bolamenia from legs and arms before the plunge into the cool waters of the Big Basin – a rise and a swim "to onct." The girls who "did" Indians had the privacy of the one bathroom for their cleaning up. So they were usually "pretty" again.[85]

Arvidson's quotation is suggestive of the cleansing of the racial mask and the return to a sort of ordinary attractiveness she describes as "pretty." However, it presents only one side of the issue of racialized performances that continued into the 1920s.

If one popular trope was "playing Indian" in the movies, there were other, far more positive precedents for the representation of Indigenous modernities. As Ruth Phillips argues, "performance offered the most favourable site for Native negotiations of the dominant culture's images of

Indians as pre-modern, degenerate, and vanishing."[86] E. Pauline Johnson as a New Woman and performance artist toyed with colonial racial dichotomies in a career that spanned from the 1880s to her death in 1913.[87] Two early twentieth-century Indigenous performers Esther Deer and Molly Spotted Elk (Molly Nelson) were modern dancers and entertainers who complicated notions of Indianness and primitiveness. Their popularity, which peaked in the twenties and thirties, did so along with the rise of primitivism, an artistic movement that was part of modernism and inflected popular culture.

As others have argued in regard to Art Deco, such "high" or "fine" artistic movements were not cleaved apart from the low forms of popular arts like advertising and graphic art, especially in regard to race. In an advertisement for drape fabric, the Robert Simpson Company highlighted the material's connection to modern art three times using phrases like "geometrically fashioned medallions fit into the modernist scheme of art." Significantly, the fabric was also connected to the appeal of primitivism with statements like "Art modern is gracefully blended with the traditional in exquisite Drapery Fabrics presenting delightful colour harmonies for the very modern as well as the more conventional home."[88]

Man Ray's famous image *Noire et Blanche* which first appeared in *Vogue* magazine in 1926 juxtaposed white (and significantly female) modernity with a "primitive" black mask, and is in some ways emblematic of the intimate connections between primitivism, popular culture, high art, and masking. Masks suggested primitiveness, whereas whiteness was firmly associated with modernity; the very juxtaposition of white faces with racialized, "primitive" masks helped delineate the racial boundaries of modernity. Five years before the publication of Man Ray's photograph, however, Esther Deer, a Mohawk from Kahnawake, juxtaposed her face with an Iroquois False Face mask. Phillips argues that this juxtaposition makes Deer's own face seem "white and flapper-modern," and that Deer "inverts two colonialist tropes of the European and the Other, the trope of colonialism mimicry later expressed by Fanon in *Black Skin, White Masks*, and the Primitivism trope of appropriation that Man Ray would express in his famous 1926 photograph *Noire et Blanche*."[89] This limited evidence suggests that Indigenous women could use tropes of primitivism to make room for Indigenous female modernities.

Significantly, however, these are examples of female modernities created by *temporarily* inverting dominant codes of masking and masquerading. Yet, both Molly Spotted Elk and Esther Deer took on the performance of Orientalness as part of their performances, particularly when they travelled to Paris, France. As Phillips argues, these adaptations of eastern dances grew out of friendship and collaboration with dancers from India, Indonesia, and Malaysia.[90] This is different than the often crass commercialism that promoted a sort of consumer false face mask at the expense of the culture of origin; or indeed, of the simple exoticization of the desire for Middle Eastern or Oriental sensuality that was so prevalent in Canadian popular culture.

Conclusion

Heterosexual choice was one of the hallmarks of the Modern Girl – it framed her social relations and her perception. It also drove cultural narratives that sold movie tickets, goods, and ideas. Practicing "choice" was another matter altogether in the patriarchal society of early twentieth-century Canada. Her erotic initiative, when combined with fears of miscegenation and race suicide, made "problems" more acute. Nonetheless, racial masquerades and the sensuousness that they evoked were an important part of the performance of feminine modernities. The Modern Girl was a dynamic woman who shored up notions of whiteness, racial supremacy, and helped to partially close the doors of modernity to women under Canada's fierce colonial project, all the while making tenuous connections to the empire. The total effect was a deeply sexualized and racialized modernity delineated by the performances and masks one could choose to take on. Here the white Modern Girl had the most privileged fluidity of all: the privileged canvas. Ongoing concerns over the "girl problem" which had shifted by the 1920s from their predecessors, rendered white working women as still vulnerable but increasingly sophisticated in the urban environment. Sophistication, however, was no match for the legal, social and cultural penalties of being young, pleasure-seeking, and sexually active. As such, her racial work and alleged sexual freedom tied her to discourses of nation-building, declines in WASP masculinity, and a seemingly fluctuating racial order. Others who started with racialized canvasses found that performing white modernity was more difficult, and taking on the other masks more challenging. It is significant that the whiteness of the Modern Girl worked to bolster notions of white privilege and discount other racialized modernities, especially Indigenous ones, in the white settler context of Canadian society.

Modernity was a sometimes startling and dislocating experience, but the appearance of the Modern Girl drew together the dialectic of pleasure and anxiety in a culturally meaningful form. Delineating aspects of modernity – and sometimes its contestation – was a significant aspect of the Modern Girl's symbolic work, which was intimately related to facets of urban modernity and the changing cityscape. Discourses enmeshed with the Modern Girl worked to maintain specific racial hierarchies through commodity modernism, specifically racial masquerades. White women could take on the role of the exotic Other in order to reveal more of their own bodies in an often erotic performance. In doing so, they shored up the privilege of men's claim to heterosexuality and whiteness while simultaneously revealing who remained Othered in Canadian society. Because the Modern Girl was so dependent on constant and consistent production and performance of her body, there were gaps and opportunities for opposition and negotiation. Her body came into existence through disciplinary projects and techniques that were based on modern expertise (advertisers and beauty columnists) and commodities that were widely available. This meant that others who did not meet her white, middle-class status could copy her look as with Indigenous Modern Girls. Even if they were beyond the limits of popular representations, this did not mean that they could not take and perform her look and find a place for themselves in the construction of new female subjectivities. That said, they did so without the privilege of being able to easily occupy her image as it was popularly represented.

4 The Beauty Pageant:
Contesting Feminine Modernities

Another type of Modern Girl appeared on the cultural landscape in the 1920s and she was not confined to a particular geographic area, although she purportedly represented a place. She was the beauty contestant, who by the end of the twenties appeared as one form of the global Modern Girl. In Canada, the beauty contestant embodied rapidly transforming cultural values and their concurrent contestations. Ideas of degeneration and anxiety in relation to gender, youth, and public exposure were part of popular discussions and debates over the beauty contest and the potential pleasures and perils it offered young women. One of the more troubling aspects of the Modern Girl was her visibility, and beauty contests became another means for young, thoroughly modern women to appear in modern culture. This chapter explores the beauty contest as a public performance intimately connected with modern visual culture, specifically the gendered visual regimes of appearing and self-surveillance closely associated with consumerism. As Liz Conor argues, "Appearing facilitates rethinking how the visual extent of the modern signifactory scene spectacularized the feminine and produced a new subjectivity in which the performance of the feminine became more concentrated on the visual."[1] Contests also reveal the close associations between beauty contestants and some of the dominant producers of modern popular culture, especially Hollywood filmmakers. As such, the contests provided fertile ground for public debates on contests' appropriateness and wider changes in modern femininities. As a result, this chapter also explores the tensions of class, sexuality, and respectability that were essential aspects to beauty contestants' appearing, and the protests the contests garnered.

My analysis of the class dynamics of contestants is certainly more spec-ulative than absolute, given that I know few biographical details of the women, even their names. Yet, the documentary evidence provides sub-tle clues that these were working women who were pushing the limits of modern femininities and making a claim to untraditional, modern op-portunities for fame and fortune, thus making them integral to moder-nity as a whole. Overall, the beauty contestant was another type of Modern Girl on the Canadian cultural landscape. As such, she relates to the wider projects of imaging ideals of women's bodies, class tensions, and the cultural promotion of specific feminine body projects in con-junction with women's public appearances. Beauty contests by real wom-en (who self-selected to perform on their own volition) reveal how individual women took up the messages of modernity, gender, and the body, and subsequently performed them in public. Young working wom-en from the working and lower middle classes performed as contestants and were used as symbols of deeper cultural change.

In live performances, in print, and on screen, images of beauty contes-tants were prolific, and contests offered young women the opportunity to perform feminine modernities. By doing so they added another feminine archetype to the growing list of screen starlet, flapper, and mannequin. The beauty contestant was part of a wide web of visual culture that con-nected commercial culture, women's bodies, and public performance in ways that promoted self-scrutiny and competition on a common level – to be a Modern Girl meant subjecting your body for public judgment. Moreover, beauty contests demarcated wider cultural, social, and genera-tional shifts as Canadians found themselves confronted with a new type of modern femininity, this one firmly embedded in commercial culture. Gone was the romantic, quiet, respectable Gibson Girl, and in her place stood a movie-loving, urban, attention-seeking, bathing suit–clad and often painted Modern Girl. If nineteenth-century Canadian women had the choice between moral, self-sacrificing and pious, or pleasure-seeking, sexualized, and selfish, the latter had become more culturally dominant by the 1920s.[2] Beauty contests allowed some young, white, able-bodied women to self-represent as beautiful and modern, while forging public identities based on the characteristics of pleasure, self-promotion, het-erosexual desire, and the deliberate solicitation of attention.

Certainly beauty contests remained unpopular among some more conservative or reform-minded Canadians who saw such public appear-ance as a sign of serious cultural laxity and a celebration of degenerative superficiality. For working-class reformers, pageants also revealed how working women could be taken advantage of by businessmen trying to make a dollar off the cheap exposure of the female body. While this was not an illegitimate concern, it should be noted that a few labour organizations also harnessed the cultural power of beauty contests in the 1920s.[3] Widespread anxiety, however, was not the overwhelming reaction in spite of serious criticism. If any one reaction marked the beauty contestant's public appearance in Canadian culture it was ambivalence. While there were outspoken critics who called for bans on contests and more stringent protection of young women from public exposure, there was also a silent majority that supported, participated in, and embraced beauty contests as an aspect of modern life. The cries for bans were loud, but largely ineffective, and in a few short years, beauty contests transformed from contentious public performances to widely accepted ones that reflected allegedly national standards for beauty.[4]

Recently, beauty contests have become more popular in academic studies because of the legitimization of related areas of study like consumerism and beauty. Much of the historiography on pageants focuses on the United States, in particular the Miss America contest, and much of the early literature is largely celebratory in nature.[5] Recent critical inquiries on early incarnations of pageants, though, have discussed them as "brazen" though troubled performances of femininity; as backlashes against first-wave feminists; as continuations of older celebrations; and as sacrificial rituals.[6] Sociologist Maxine Leeds Craig's book on the history of African American beauty contests in the United States provides a fascinating account of black women's participation in beauty contests from 1891 onwards. Craig discusses the separate contests that had to be held due to the written by-laws excluding black women from competing in Miss America, and the protests women held to change those laws.[7] In addition, there are a growing number of studies on how pageants in the 1920s, 1930s, and 1940s have functioned to embody national and cultural ideas of "race" in countries outside of the US.[8]

Work on Canadian contests or Canadian participation in other contests is more limited, with the important exception of Patrizia Gentile's studies.[9] Some of the American studies mention Canadians competing in early Miss America contests, but with the exception of a few works, the history of Canadian pageants is just being recovered.[10] Taken together, the body of work on beauty contests (and its absences) reveal how multifaceted they were, how diverse their purpose was, and how challenging they have been to interpret. Images of beauty contestants, like images of the Modern Girl, were remarkably flexible and could be tailored to meet local and national ideals yielding a rich field for analysis.

The History of Beauty Queens

Women from Saint John, New Brunswick to Victoria, British Columbia competed in beauty pageants for diverse and often paying audiences. These shows were not limited to larger urban areas, as smaller communities such as New Liskegard, Ontario and Moose Jaw, Saskatchewan were also involved in the trend. There were also international pageants in which Canadian women competed, including Miss America and a North America-wide beauty pageant held by Rudolph Valentino in 1923 (discussed in chapter 6).[11] While Canadian contests were held across the country and were met with both support and controversy, no single pageant captured the imagination of Canadians in the same way Miss America did in the United States. Yet, the idea of a beautiful, healthy, young woman chosen to represent the state was a popular theme in Canadian culture, and one that was not only associated with beauty contests. In Diamond Jubilee of Confederation celebrations in 1927, for example, women were drawn and chosen to be the embodied representation of the country.[12] During the twenties, the moniker "Miss Canada" was used almost indiscriminately to refer to a host of beauty contestants in addition to cartoons, drawings, and performances for national celebrations, and thus was quite ambiguous. Aside from other usages, part of the ambiguity stemmed from the varied types of contests that existed in Canada. Most of the pageants tended to be local and, even in the case of Miss Canada, regional as opposed to national in character. Contestants in the 1920s earned titles that were tied to geographical regions, but there were so far only stirrings of nationalistic pride. In part, the controversy associated with bathing beauty contests in the twenties made the association between them and the nation-state somewhat unlikely. Yet, some of the pageants promoted at least the promise that one could judge and find a young woman who would embody the ideals of womanhood. What this woman would look like – and what values she would represent – remained a contentious point.

Although other types of tournaments for May Day Queens and the like would remain, these were different from the emerging type of modern competition.[13] The new brand of Miss Canada and other local competitions were based entirely on physical appearance, were sponsored by commercial investors, and were closely associated with the entertainment and advertising industries. These beauty contests focused on ways of fashioning the ideal body for young women without formally taking into account her relationship to the community, her values, or the qualities that would make her a good citizen. Nonetheless, contests would strive to achieve respectability and a certain gloss of morality, which furthered older female types. North Americans were not alone in having these types of modern pageants, as they appeared internationally in the 1920s as part of a larger international mosaic of the global Modern Girl.[14]

The ritual process of selecting a young woman as a representative of an event dates back to the Middle Ages. American historian Lois Banner argues that the origins of twentieth-century beauty contests can be traced back to May Day celebrations and nineteenth-century reproductions of medieval tournaments. These events were incorporated into fairs that continued the tradition of selecting queens, although physical beauty was not always the most important criteria. The first known contest where women were chosen based only on their attractiveness was held in the same venue as a display of freaks, wonders, and curiosities by American entrepreneur P.T. Barnum in 1854 (indeed, contests often remained closely linked to carnivals).[15] Realizing the powerful draw of women's bodies, Barnum attempted a beauty contest following his successful bird, dog, flower, and baby contests at the New York City American Museum. After the initial call for contestants was met with only a few entries from women of questionable character, Barnum decided not to have the women compete live, but through daguerreotypes. The contest was a success, and photographic beauty contests spread to major American newspapers.[16] These types of contests still did not meet the demands of middle-class respectability, since many of them ran in publications that used sex and violence to attract an audience. Nonetheless, photographic beauty contests conducted for profit from the late nineteenth century to the 1920s became very popular among working-class men and women, and were aligned with other questionable amusements.[17] Dime museums, especially those in New York's Bowery district, offered beauty contests as part of their displays. By the 1890s, beauty contests were part of travelling sideshows, circuses, and fairs that included Hoochie Coochie dances, girl shows, and other performances in which women were displayed for money, and often appeared in bathing suits or revealing costumes.[18] As early as the 1880s, the cultural terrain was tested for a beauty contest removed from carnival culture. The first Miss United States contest was held at Rehoboth Beach, a family resort in Delaware. It was part of a publicity campaign meant to attract tourists to the summer resort. By the turn of the twentieth century, beach beauty contests were popular at some beaches, but part of the reason why Rehoboth ran a contest without controversy was that the beach catered to working-class patrons.[19] Although the 1880 competition introduced a number of important features that would be appropriated by later contest organizers, beauty contests remained under the moral radar as long as they remained part of working-class culture and were infrequent events.

Early beauty contests did not hold much appeal north of the border, in part because of the failure of entertainment venues like dime museums.[20] At the 1884 Toronto Industrial Exhibition, the Ladies Department attempted to run a beauty contest where entrants would be ranked based on portrait photographs. The list of available prizes (including a fifty dollar gold watch and twenty-five dollars worth of jewellery) was impressive, but there were no interested contestants. Keith Walden argues that "the idea of the beauty contest ran counter to the conventions of modesty, but its complete failure suggests that people, especially women, were reluctant to court public view deliberately, even at a remove."[21] A beauty contest on the fairgrounds was not attempted again until the mid-thirties. Despite the hesitancy to engage in beauty contests on the CNE grounds, by the mid-twenties they had taken root in Canadian culture at beaches and theatres. As modern, commercial culture developed, beauty contests became part of the cultural landscape. In some ways, this represents a deeper class shift in commercial amusements with more working-class leisure opportunities (like movies) becoming part of a wider, cross-class popular culture, driven in particular by young women.[22] Some of them, it seemed, were no longer as hesitant to deliberately attract the public's gaze, and the contests themselves were no longer confined to working-class spaces.

Miss America and Canadian Pageants in the 1920s

The initiation of the Miss America contest was a pivotal moment in the history of modern pageants. In 1920, the hoteliers of Atlantic City met to discuss ways to keep tourists at the beach resort past Labour Day. They decided on a weeklong festival entitled "A National Beauty Pageant/ Fall Frolic," where eight women sponsored by their local newspapers would compete in "Atlantic City's Inter-City beauty contest."[23] Supported by Atlantic City newspaper reporter Harry Finley, the beauty contest was designed with the hope that it would boost circulation. Like earlier contests, contenders from around the country competed in their own local papers.[24] Unlike the earlier contests, however, which attempted to maintain women's respectability by having them compete anonymously or through photographs, preliminary winners of this contest travelled to Atlantic City to compete in a series of live performances. In 1921, eight women, including the eventual winner Margaret Gorman, competed in the Inter-City Beauty Contest.[25] The Miss America pageant was a hit and became the largest and most popular beauty contest in North America in the twenties. Samuel Gompers, President of the American Federation of Labor, declared that the 5'1", 108-pound Margaret Gorman was "the type of woman that America needs, strong, redblooded, able to shoulder the responsibilities of homemaking and motherhood." He continued, "It is in her type that the hope of the country rests."[26] Despite Gompers glowing words that promoted a safe, traditional, and respectable future in marriage and motherhood, the contest still attracted significant public scrutiny.

By 1927, controversies regarding married women's involvement, the participation of professional showgirls, and protests by women's and religious groups brought the pageant to an end. Beauty contests both in the United States and Canada, however, did not disappear, and Miss America's cancellation was only a short hiatus.[27] In its early years, however, the contest set the precedent for the organization of other pageants, and Canadian contests quickly cropped up as numbers for Miss America swelled. In 1922, the number of contestants competing in Miss America reached fifty-seven and included Miss Toronto and Miss Montreal. Notably, Miss America instituted one of the central (and most controversial) features of modern beauty competitions: the swimsuit competition.[28]

Some of the Canadian feeder pageants for Miss America like Miss Toronto 1926 were local contests. By the mid-twenties, the operators of Sunnyside Amusement Park were looking for a means to attract more tourists. The Attractions Manager, having visited Atlantic City and being familiar with the Miss America pageant, suggested a Miss Toronto pageant to be held at the bathing pavilion.[29] During the week of 9 August 1926, Sunnyside held their first Miss Toronto pageant that, according to advertisements, was "authorized by the Atlantic City Pageant Committee." The winner of the Miss Toronto pageant would compete at the Miss America pageant. One advertisement lured that "Fay Lanphier, 'Miss Los Angeles,' made $50,000 as the result of being chosen by her city." Over four hundred women signed up to compete for the title. The explicit rules were that interested contestants had to be female, between the ages of 16 and 25, and a "bona fide resident" of Toronto as of 31 December 1925.[30] After at least two rounds of eliminations, Jean Ford Tolmie won Miss Toronto. In the few weeks before the Miss America pageant, Tolmie made public appearances at Sunnyside. Furnished with a new wardrobe (a significant reward itself given women's paltry wages), and after meeting with Miss Niagara Peach, Tolmie went to the Miss America pageant and, according the Toronto newspapers, won "the cup for beauty of face and grace of carriage."[31] In the fall of 1926, Tolmie left Toronto to tour with Captain Plunkett's 1926 Revue, and on 18 September 1927, the *Toronto Daily Star* happily reported that she married H. Leslie Appleby, the business manager of the Revue in Fort William, Ontario.[32]

Preliminary Canadian contests for the Miss America pageant did not always follow the typical formulation. One Miss Vancouver contest held in 1927 did not include bathing suit competitions or have pictures of contestants in bathing attire appear in local newspapers. Since the eventual winner would have to compete in a bathing suit as part of the Miss America pageant, it is significant that the organizers did not use or promote this aspect of the contest in their preliminary competition. Yet, the men involved in organizing and promoting it emphasized that this was a different style of pageant. The contest was organized under the auspices of the local branch of the Canadian Legion and was decided by a popular vote in which patrons would purchase ballots and the funds thereby raised would go to support First World War veterans. On the opening night of 3 May 1927, General Macdonald stressed the fact that the contest was being held in order to raise money for ex-service men and stated,

> Words cannot express how much we need the support of every citizen of this country and I trust that all will keep before them throughout the contest the fact that in asking votes for themselves in the campaign they are obtaining help for others. If I thought different, I would not be here, nor would I have given this contest my support, but I know that yourselves and every citizen are going to make the campaign a success on account of the wonderful cause.[33]

Macdonald's statement emphasized women's supportive role, and was a continuation of their expected self-sacrifice that harkened back to wartime discourses. Although the contest did have significant prizes, including a new car and an all-expenses paid trip to Atlantic City with public appearances along the way, the real goal for women, as Sergeant Major

4.1   Finalists for the Miss Toronto Pageant, City of Toronto Archives Fonds 1244, Item 1028J. Used with permission of the City of Toronto Archives.

Jimmy Robinson reminded them, was that they would do good for the men of the city and the Dominion.[34]

Despite the variety in geographical contexts and local sponsors involved, beauty contests in the 1920s shared some important features. For one, women competed in them exclusively. While it is unclear why individual women entered contests, anecdotal evidence suggests there were a variety of reasons. Donica Belisle notes that department store employees were encouraged to enter local pageants so the store could highlight their saleswomen's beauty and attractiveness.[35] Beauty contests advertisements echoed wider claims in popular culture that promised women glamour, excitement and consumer fulfilment in the form of lucrative prizes for entering. As well as being tempting, these promises matched the cultural narratives of working women finding "success" in the form of stardom or upwards mobility in marriage through modern performances. Successful marriage was a promised reward in advertising, and some contestants made headlines for their subsequent marriages. However, Belisle notes it is important to remember that retailers, theatres, and major consumer industries benefitted financially from holding the contests. Few women achieved fame and fortune through beauty contests, but this did not diminish the power of the promises or the potential significance of the smaller, less lucrative prizes of small sums of money or goods like clothing, jewellery, and candy. That four hundred women competed in the inaugural Miss Toronto contest at Sunnyside certainly speaks to the appeal.

Newspapers carried advertisements for the contests, which made appeals to both contestants and audience members. Newspapers were, in fact, central places for the dissemination of information about the contests, and generate the bulk of evidence on early beauty contests. Once contestants signed up to participate, they appeared in public for a full week or more. Ticket prices varied widely from ten cents to two dollars depending on the venue and the contest. During the performances, contestants were evaluated by either a panel of judges or paying audience members. The identities of judges were usually kept a secret, although men described as artists were a popular choice. Artists were chosen because of their alleged ability to judge beauty and their (sometimes oblique) associations with high culture.[36] When the public voted, each admission provided the audience member with the opportunity to cast a ballot. The more "democratic" style of voting, typically used by movie theatres, also encouraged multiple votes and thus admissions, which bolstered revenue for the theatre.

Physical beauty was, however, the overarching feature of the modern beauty contest. Part of the new modern sensibility, the focus on beauty ran counter to Victorian notions that women were to cultivate their personalities and character, not focus entirely on their faces and figures. For some, the dramatic shift in women's visibility caused a level of discomfort. A *Globe* editorial commenting on the Miss Toronto 1926 contest stated that "If the only charm that the entrants in the present contest at Sunnyside can boast of is that of face and figure, they had much better for their own future happiness and peace of mind stay at home and pray the prayer of the old pagan philosopher. 'Teach me to grow beautiful within.'"[37] Despite ongoing, international protests, the quest to find the most beautiful woman in a town, city, country or the globe was popular, and played an important role in delineating and disseminating the idea of modern beauty. While the women who competed were not "cookie-cutter cut outs" without any variation, they did embody a particular standard or idea of female beauty most closely associated with the Modern

Girl. For most potential entrants, there were residential and marital status requirements, but overall the implicit prerequisites to becoming a beauty contest winner in the 1920s were that one was white, young, and able-bodied. However, the contests attempted to render these categories as invisible, normative standards while fashioning a particular "type" or female trope on the cultural landscape.[38]

The Bathing Beauty, the Bathing Suit, and the Modern Body

When Australian swim champion and future film star Annette Kellerman appeared on a Boston beach in 1908 wearing a revealing one-piece bathing suit, she was arrested for indecent exposure and started a trend. [39] By the 1920s, the new one-piece bathing suit was practically the uniform for beauty contestants. The new and more revealing suits were so central to the modern pageants that they were often referred to as "bathing beauty contests." If they competed in anything else – formal dress, for example – bathing suits were still the choice outfit for photographers and newspapers, including the often-critical *Globe*.[40] Neither the contests nor the bathing suit, however, were universally embraced. An anonymous editorial in the *Catholic Register*, later reprinted in the *Globe*, took aim at both. It stated,

> The annual parade of female flesh, the annual blot on American civilization, the annual insult to woman's honour and dignity, the annual exploitation of woman's undraped charms before the gaze of salacious vulgarians gathered from the clubs and dens of the continent, has been proclaimed as about to take place. Our Toronto papers carry advertisements announcing this outrage to American womanhood and asking for girls to present themselves for the dishonor of being 'Miss Toronto' at the Atlantic City's carnival of shamelessness ... The girl who walks our streets in semi-nudity is a law unto herself. She is above the conventions of decency that bound her old-fashioned mother and has become a puzzle to the judicious and the sane.

The editorial predicted the outcome of such dishonour. Beauty contestants would "return home and be forgotten, dissatisfied with their former lives, filled with envy and jealousy of the winner and the prey of unhealthy emotions and unholy ambitions."[41] A war on immodesty was declared as part of a "denunciation" of beauty contests. The fact that large numbers of women paraded in revealing bathing costumes, deliberately courted the view of the public, and competed for prizes of cash,

movie contracts, or cars, exposed the burgeoning culture of visuality
and women's centrality within it. For critics, it also suggested a more
nefarious side of popular culture and potentially smacked of prostitution.[42] The warning in the *Catholic Register* and the *Globe* suggested
that young women were lured into commercial culture, and potentially
(perhaps unwittingly) sacrificed their proper roles as wives and mothers for the promise of cheap thrills and consumer goods. The editorial
fervently expressed more widespread concerns over women's visibility,
young women's dress, public performances, and leisure activities, which
crystallized around debates over swimwear. They also represented only
one side of the issue, which was met with far more ambivalence than
the sharp-tongued editorial suggests. The beauty contestant clad in a
commercially manufactured one-piece remained a popular type of the
Modern Girl, who appeared in advertisements, newspaper articles, photographs, and on film. Beauty contests were a popular craze, and while
certainly contentious, they also reinforced important elements of feminine modernities: spectacularization, production, and care of the body
through the use of mass-produced goods, as well as the normalization
of the male gaze.

Looking more closely at aspects of beauty contests in relation to beauty
culture and the body reveals how they functioned to encourage a particularly critical self-scrutiny as seemingly mandatory for modern women. The
"proximate gaze" helped to define modern beauty culture by encouraging women to live up to a singular ideal – an ideal selected in part through
beauty contests.[43] Contestants were, after all, "real" women selected or
elected (depending on the judging process) as embodying ideals of modern beauty. The most beautiful Girl defined a standard for beauty, encouraged and normalized competition among women in regard to appearance,
made commercial goods (like swimsuits) seem indispensable, and generally flattened the surface of modern femininities. Contests also offered
ordinary women the chance to participate in the elusive yet popular culture of celebrity. Film-goers and fans would know that famous actresses
like Clara Bow had risen to celebrity status because she had been discovered in a beauty contest. Advertisements, like those for Miss Toronto 1926,
also hinged on the culture of celebrity by highlighting the success of other contestants, notably Fay Lanphier. While excluding married women
from competition worked to help define pageants' respectability, there
was another benefit. The competitions selected young, single women and
were thereby broadcasting changes on the heterosexual marriage scene.
Women could compete for the heterosexual gaze and announce their

beauty and desirability in a dating culture that increasingly embraced the Modern Girl and all that she stood for.

In the critical words of W.I. Thomas, young women as a whole in the twenties were "demoralized," "unadjusted," and using their sexuality as "capital" and "a condition of the realization of other wishes." [44] Although he was not, Thomas could well have been describing modern beauty contestants. At the time, femininities meant increased pressure regarding the consumption of goods, self-surveillance, and watching and being watched. It also meant changing standards for appearing in public and changing techniques for appearing. Beauty contests, however, allowed participants a chance to reveal how well they matched up to modern beauty standards. This was a very literal performance in occupying images. We can examine how all of these fused together in beauty competitions by looking more closely at a key aspect of the contests: the bathing suit.

Dress is a symbol of deeper cultural and social changes, and the bathing suit of the interwar years certainly highlighted those changes, especially in terms of public performance. Indicative of the new consumer culture style-setters – youth, European fashion houses, movies, and advertisements – fashion demarcated generational shifts. Donning a bathing suit at a public beach was in many ways performative. And, as Angela J. Latham argues, "public bathing was, after all, an experience largely associated with looking at others and being looked at by them."[45] This experience was heightened for beauty contestants whose purpose was overt, public performances for mixed gender audiences at spaces that threw together classes and ages. Beauty contestants were, after all, a very select (and self-selected) group of women who fit within a particular type and embodied the Modern Girl. As such, they complicate the idea that the Modern Girl did not exist, as contestants negotiated between producing a modern female subjectivity, performing it in a very public way, and offering themselves as objects to be judged.

The bathing suit, worn as a costume by beauty contestants, indicated shifts in morality, respectability, and public performance for the post-war generation. Women's fashions of the twenties were sometimes cause for consternation among some more conservative Canadians who found the flesh-revealing garments to be shocking or even dangerous; meanwhile, shortened skirts and armless tops seemed to pale in comparison to the new style of swimsuits.[46] Without doubt, bathing suits in the 1920s were much more revealing than the bulky dress-like attire worn at the turn of the twentieth century. New and tightly-fitting swimsuits hugged the body and revealed shoulders, arms, legs, back, and portions of the chest, and showed a clear silhouette of the body. In the contests, suits were frequently worn with stockings that wearers rolled down to expose their knees and thighs. But, what swimsuits *didn't* reveal was almost more important. The suits accentuated the breasts, waist, and hips, and according to one pageant historian, had "the disconcerting property of riveting attention right to the crotch."[47] As with other "dress reforms" Canadians were divided on whether or not new swimming styles represented progress or degeneration. In advertisements and articles that appeared alongside announcements for beauty contests in Canadian newspapers, the new styles were touted as representing "freedom" and revealing a more modern, healthy, and athletic view of the female body.[48] Twice in the decade *Maclean's* published covers of Modern Girls in bathing suits, which suggests not only a visual appeal, but also a good measure of acceptance.[49] As the editorial admonition in the *Catholic Register* shows, this view was far from universal.

Competitions on bathing beaches like Miss Toronto 1926 held at Sunnyside Amusement Park attempted to naturalize the fact that women competed in bathing suits. Although the contest took place at the bathing pavilion, and there was an obvious association between frequenting a beach and wearing a swimsuit, Miss Toronto contestants never entered the water. Further, swimming skills were not part of the decision-making and women paraded on stage in their suits and high heels, footwear obviously not conducive to swimming.[50] These contradictions in the performance did not go unnoticed. One year after the Miss Toronto competition, the President of the Canadian National Exhibition J.J. Dixon responded to a complaint about women in bathing suits demonstrating how a shower operated. As part of an exhibit for the shower, women in "ordinary woollen bathing suits" showered to show how the technology functioned. Dixon argued, "I do not object to bathing costumes if are going under the water. But I do not think it is a proper use of them to parade girls in beauty shows, clad in little or nothing, and merely showing their bodies."[51] Apparently to Dixon, performative aspects of wearing a bathing suit were mediated by practicality – a sentiment which weakly defended the voyeuristic, patriarchal, and peeping Tom-like display of watching women shower at the CNE. Dixon even found the highly contentious nude paintings hung in the CNE art gallery in 1927 to be less distasteful than beauty contests where women competed in their bathing suits in front of crowds of men and women.[52]

The new bathing suits were not, of course, strictly made for beauty contestants. While the bathing suit allowed women to engage in swimming as an athletic endeavour, the utilitarian side of the new bathing suits could not completely overcome the shock some people experienced when women wore them. Even for legitimate competitors in sporting events, there was sometimes concern over the impropriety of their outfits.[53] In the early decades of the twentieth century, participation in sports like swimming became increasingly acceptable for Canadian women. Their participation in organized sports was seen as a positive alternative to idle time, so long as the physical activity was limited in the degree of competitiveness and aggressiveness. Medical authorities remained concerned that physical activity for young women could damage their reproductive organs, but in general swimming and other moderate sporting activities were encouraged.[54] Previous concerns that sporting would cause women to lose their femininity or become "mannish" were tempered in part because of the new feminine athletic style.[55]

By 1927, it seemed that some of the concerns surrounding sporting competitions were waning. That year, the Canadian National Exhibition held a marathon swim in Lake Ontario. Female swimmers had their pictures taken on the beach in their swimming attire to no voices of dissent. According to newspaper reports, there were rumours that once in the water, women competing for the substantial prize money planned to quickly strip off their suits and proceed to swim in the nude. Upon hearing this, the Toronto *Evening Telegram* dispatched a reporter to canvas the female swimmers. The results were mixed, with some women favouring simply grease, others a mix of a silk suit and grease, and still others a regular woollen suit with the option to "drop" the suit if it got too heavy. While CNE official Elwood A. Hughes made it clear that his preference was to have all swimmers "have something on at the start," he announced that if bathing suits were discarded in the water a boat would pick them up.[56] Despite the fact that swimmers' bodies would have been obscured by the water, and that swimming in the buff might be safer than in a heavy, water-logged suit, it is unusual given the general state of concern over women's fashions, particularly the bathing suit, that such an act would be met with ambivalence.

These co-ed swimming competitions also reveal important differences in body performance and style. Photographs of the swimmers reveal muscular bodies that were more athletic and less adorned than those of beauty contestants. They wore no make-up, did not pose in attention-seeking ways, and did not take on any of the Modern Girl's usual tech-

Canadian swimmers choose Aberleys!

They double the thrill of water sports

JOHNNY WALKER, Swimming Coach, Granite Club, Toronto, wearing a Men's Life-Guard Aberley, No. 900, priced at $4.00.

"MISS TORONTO" wearing the stylish Aberley in which she won the cup at the 1926 Beauty Contest at Sunnyside. The "Miss Toronto" style is priced at $4.50.

IT'S SWIMMING weather! Get into the swim in an Aberley!

With nothing to sag or bind, an Aberley fits like your own skin! Allows perfect muscle-freedom for every stroke!

Aberleys are made for men and women, boys, girls and children — all 100% pure wool, knit from the famous Aberley yarn with the special Aberley stitch.

MASTER PETER PURDY, a real swimmer at less than three years, wearing a Kiddie's Life-Guard Aberley, priced at $1.50.

Smart, graceful styles with a dash and snap to their design. Bright colors that stay bright.

Swim in an Aberley this summer.

You'll never know how well you'll look in a swimming suit until you get into an Aberley.

"How to Swim the Crawl"

Johnny Walker, Swimming Instructor at the Granite Club, Toronto, and former trainer of George Young, has written a book on swimming that is yours for the asking. Gives clear and concise instructions for mastering this popular stroke, illustrated with diagram. It's free—write for it to

Illustrating a Ladies' Life-Guard Aberley, priced at $5.00.

Aberley Knitting Mills, Limited
Toronto   •   Canada

Aberley
100% PURE WOOL
form-fitting Swimming Suits

4.2   Aberley's Advertisement Featuring Miss Toronto 1926, *Maclean's*, 1 July 1927.

niques of appearing. Women competing in the Great Swim showcased the athleticism of their bodies. Clearly the question of nudity, or "semi-nudity" as the *Catholic Register*'s editorial stated, had much more to do with the beauty contestants' performance of the body on a public beach or in a movie house for a paying audience than the actual act of disrobing. The performance of modern beauty in the hopes of money or valuable consumer goods was clearly more distressing than the promises of money and fame for long-distance swimming. One was demeaned as superficial, and the other exalted as hard-earned skill.

The problem of performance was magnified for competitors in the 1927 Miss Canada contest and its feeder pageants that took place in the western provinces. The contestants competed in movie houses in bathing suits and high heels. During these contests, each woman took her place on a pedestal under a spotlight, and when the curtains opened, the contestant would pose for the audience in hopes to get votes. This type of display, minus the democratic element of voting, may have been familiar to some audience members as the same means of display used in midway girl shows.[57] As pageant historian Frank Deford argues, "The basic, and base, pageant appeal is, and always has been, girl watching – and the fewer the clothes the better."[58] "Girl watching" was as profitable on a number of fronts as movie houses, amusement parks, and other venues that employed beauty contests to generate revenues. Advertisers also found women's bodies to be a powerful draw, using advertisements to signal new techniques of bodily preparation required for modern beauty contestants and other women who sought to appear beautiful on the public scene.

In trying to sell bathing suits, advertisers highlighted their peformative potential. An advertisement for Eaton's focused directly on marketing their product to beauty contestants. One "smart new" suit offered potential candidates "carefully designed simplicity and a perfection of form that would mould to the supple, graceful lines of your figure, leaving no superfluous folds."[59] A 1927 advertisement for Aberley swimsuits suggested that Canadian swimmers chose their suits to "double the thrill of water sports." It stated that not only were Aberley's great to swim in since "an Aberley fits like your own skin," but also that the suits had "smart, graceful styles with a dash and snap to their design." The copy promised, "You'll never know how well you'll look in a swimming suit until you get into an Aberley."[60] The advert also included a photograph of Tolmie, Miss Toronto 1926, boasting that she wore the "stylish Aberley" suit at the competition.

In actual beauty contests, visual appeal beat out functionality as most competitors' suits revealed their ornamental purpose. In the Miss Victoria pageant in 1927, for example, Madeleine Woodman appeared in a white silken bathing suit, while contestant Kathryn McLaren had a suit specially made out of beaded black lace.[61] Other advertisements for bathing suits revealed the fact that being watched was inherent in appearing in a bathing suit. An advertisement for Monarch Bathing Suits stated, "Whether you choose a bathing suit for beach wear or for swimming – Monarch gives you the best choice." The picture that accompanied the advertisement showed a young woman walking along a beach in a swimsuit with two men and one woman in the background watching her.[62] Showing women under public, (both male and female) scrutiny, was a popular trope used in advertising in the 1920s, and advertisements warned that women's bodies were under constant surveillance and public scrutiny in the "beauty contest of life."[63]

While the new suits were touted as freeing women from the constraints of older styles (and made drowning less of a possibility), they in fact introduced new standards of bodily control. In the twenties, bathing suits were produced by three main companies: Cole, Catalina, and Jantzen. The companies used new technology in sewing and mass production to offer cheaper bathing suits. For beauty contestants, finding, wearing, and performing in a bathing suit was a precursor to winning. Long, lean, and increasingly slender standards for physical beauty required dieting and weight management for most adult women in pursuit of the young, thin ideal body of the beauty contestant.

In one of fashion's many catch-22s, wearing a new style of bathing suit required a particular figure, and health and beauty experts argued this could be achieved through swimming. Australian swimming champion and international film star Annette Kellerman wrote a beauty manual that endorsed swimming as a means of becoming physically beautiful. According to Kellerman, swimming built beautiful bodies without developing "the hard knotty muscles of the masculine athlete." Swimming also toned bodies, tapered the form, and "remove[d] the ugly rolls of superfluous fat and put in its place smooth firm tissue."[64] As Kellerman's manual made clear, a muscular, masculine look was to be avoided, and women should strive to achieve a more pre-pubescent look with only modest curves in very particular places. Kellerman also warned that maintaining one's figure over everything else was necessary "for the competition with the passing show of general femininity."[65]

4.3   Monarch Bathing Suits Advertisement, *Saturday Night*, 8 June 1926.

The implication here was clear: any sort of beauty contest (official or part of life) required significant self-modification. Exercise, cosmetics, hair styling, and body hair removal were also part of the recommended regime required for appearing in public. Bathing suits helped to represent the shift in the artificial modification of the body from corseting to dieting. Despite promises from manufacturers, there was little room to "hide" in a suit. Notions of changing the body to appear more beautiful and attractive were not new or unique to beauty contests, but what changed was the style and the means by which it was promoted in adverts. The deep connections to commercial culture drove aspects of body modification, and suggested that women could purchase their way to a new body by attaining particular goods.

Burgeoning scientific standards of the day meant that beauty was more than an artistic idea. Scientific "experts" on beauty were interviewed for newspaper articles related to beauty contests, and they revealed the science of beauty through measurement. In the Miss Canada contest of 1927, women's measurements were published in *The Victoria Times* and compared to two showgirls, Beatrice Roberts and Olive Brady, who were epitomized as exceptionally beautiful. In their photographs, the measurements of various body parts (height, neck, bust, waist, hips, thigh, calf, and ankle) were included. Brady, for example, had a 32 inch bust, 33.5 inch hips, a 7.5 inch ankle, and was 5'5" tall.[66] The newspaper queried whether or not potential Miss Victorias measured up, and highlighted some of the local participants whose measurements closely fit the ideals.[67] Encouraging this proximate gaze attempted to naturalize the competitive nature of beauty contests, and encouraged often unrealistic comparisons to ideals. Like advertisements that focused in on parts of the body, beauty pageants symbolically carved up the body and attempted to attach specific sizes and characteristics to each piece. Still, pageants allowed "real" women to show how they literally measured up to those ideals. As such, they also helped to send the message that the ideals were not simply cultural scripts on paper, but ones that could be met by ordinary women, thereby blurring real and representation.

Beauty contestants were sometimes compared to showgirls because they shared an alleged desire for careers in show business. However, contestants were also likened to classical ideals, including the bastion of beauty, the Venus de Milo, whose measurements were also provided in *The Victoria Times.*[68] This comparison suggested that representative beauties needed to meet certain rigorous and timeless standards of physical beauty, and that they shared some sort of quality with high artistic tradition. According to the measurements of Venus given in the newspaper, the statue seemed to measure up with dimensions very close to the chorus girls' and beauty contestants' measurements, but a significant discrepancy existed in regard to height. Undoubtedly, these ideal dimensions were unrealistic for most Canadian women. While the average Canadian woman born between 1898 and 1917 was between 5'1.5" and 5'2," the ideal for a beauty contestant was 2 to 4 inches taller.[69] Linearity was a key aspect of the cultural push towards the ideal of female slenderness.

Despite widespread claims that women's fashions in the 1920s tended to be "boyish," fashion historian Valerie Steele argues that the feminine ideal is more aptly described as youthful.[70] Beauty contestants were synonymous with youth, as age restrictions typically limited participation to women between the ages of 16 and 25. The explicit rules for the Miss Toronto 1926 contest, for example, stated that interested parties had to be female, between the ages of 16 and 25, single, and a "bona fide resident" of Toronto as of 31 December 1925.[71] The 1927 Miss Victoria pageant had a similar rule requiring contestants to be between 17 and 25 years and unmarried.[72] Such restrictions operated on two levels: they helped to solidify the wider cultural idea that youth was an essential element of beauty, and they tried to ensure contestants were unmarried, thus ensuring that organizers could attempt to defend themselves against claims that they were drawing women away from their duties as wives and mothers.[73] In the wider cultural milieu, being young was seen as vital to being beautiful, and contests highlighted this. Unmistakably, the competitions were about finding and rewarding beauty, and in this sense they worked to affirm and establish cultural demarcations as to what constituted attractiveness and youth. None of this was obvious, natural, or consistent. The need to perfect the body was premised on the careful surveillance of one's own body and of those of others. For women in the audience, beauty contests were simply another opportunity to critically examine the feminine form to see if they measured up. They were also, however, unique in bringing live, local women whose bodies could meet modern standards of beauty to the public.

In advertisements and popular discussions, new styles were often seen as a means to gain attention from the opposite sex. Contact and physical arousal between young men and women was a concern, as some bathing spots in Canada were only recently opened to both sexes. This also increased the general anxiety surrounding youth and the future of the county.[74] Exposure on bathing beaches was particularly disconcerting, and critics argued that women's beach styles bordered on the nude.[75]

Sex appeal – the notoriously defined "It" by Elinor Glyn – was part of the troubling visual symbol of performing in a bathing suit. "It" was a popular interpretation of Sigmund Freud's id and indicated "an undefinable voltage of openly sexual energy."[76] Glyn had coined "It" in regard to beauty contest winner and screen star Clara Bow. Alongside advertisements, articles, and photographs about Miss Vancouver, the *Vancouver Sun* included an article about a beauty queen, a car, and "It." Under the title "Paige Has 'It,' Says Beauty Queen," the article compared the "IT of motordom" to "the IT in human nature made famous by Elinor." The beauty queen was quoted as saying, "To me Paige has that almost indefinable spark of personality which fascinates and enslaves … What is 'it' – well, I am not sure that I can say, but 'it' is there nevertheless."[77] The fact that the beauty contest winner could identify "it" and used it to sell a car suggested a disconcerting sophistication, and a knowledge of sexual desirability that still could only be referred to in couched, if deliberately coy terms.

"It" could also be a problem. Women in suggestive clothing, critics claimed, at best distracted men and boys, and at worst tempted them by "forcing too much of their physical form upon his gaze."[78] In the pamphlets produced by the Canadian National Council for Combating Venereal Diseases, for example, young women were warned that they needed to maintain self-control "in order to avoid arousing the sexual desire of men by words or acts or suggestive clothing."[79] The *Catholic Register* (in separate and related articles to those on beauty contests) quoted physicians, criminologists, and sociologists who argued that there was a direct link between the revelation of women's bodies and crime. Rolled stockings in particular were to blame, and whether or not women who wore them were "innocent," they caused crimes of passion. In the misogynistic legal system of 1920s Canada, women who were sexually assaulted often found their behaviour and dress under scrutiny during the trial.[80] Women were encouraged to emulate a modern look but they potentially risked their reputations and more in doing so.

Despite the burgeoning culture of visuality, women still paid an incredibly high and unfair price for meeting standards encouraged by beauty contests, and young, working-class women bore the brunt of social and moral reform efforts to "clean up" popular amusements by becoming the focus of criticism and reform. Yet, explicit discussion of the threat of violence was absent from discussions on beauty contests:[81] far more ink was spilled on the contestent's swimsuit and the performance. The undertones of the hightly critical commentators correctly identified the fact that women were unable to match the critical, aggressive masculine gaze. They failed to understand, however, that women were encouraged (if not required) to subject their bodies to it in performing feminine modernities. Moreover, the debates underlined that the solution to this imbalance of power was the protection of women and the careful monitoring of women's entry into the public sphere. The patriarchal imbalance was twofold: one, in continuing to render women the object of the masculine gaze, and two, in offering the solution of traditional, masculine protection. The myth that women needed to carefully monitor their own dress and behaviour to stay safe remained and undermined real efforts to assure women's access to the public. Despite political and social gains, women who deliberately courted the public's attention were still viewed as potential threats to themselves or others. Caught up in the new world of commercial culture were concerns that "ordinary Girls" were exchanging sexual favours for commercial goods, and thus willing to debase themselves for cheap (and not-so-cheap given women's wages) goods. As such, the young women were not deemed to be culturally sympathetic victims, but rather women asserting choices, challenging a traditional order of gender roles and behaviours, and being bold and irreverent about it. Beauty contests as part of modern commercial culture may have offered women limited opportunities for fun and perhaps fame and fortune, but it did not fundamentally shift patriarchal relations, which still rendered women (especially young working-class women), as vulnerable. It was these types of concerns over class, sexuality, and respectability that laid the groundwork for the controversy over the Miss Toronto 1926 pageant held at Sunnyside amusement park.

For Roués and Satyrs: Controversies over Beauty Contests and Contestants

In the ancient Greek myth of the judgment of Paris, women competed for Paris to decide who was the most beautiful. The myth had a wide cultural currency throughout Western history, particularly art history, but modern Canadians found themselves once again employing the tale as a cautionary one. In condemning the international trend of beauty contests, the *Catholic Register* warned of "this modern judgement of Paris," clearly working off an interpretation of the myth that drew upon themes of lust, bloodshed, and war.[82] John Berger describes how the myth inserted judgment as a factor in beauty and added a competitive element to the quest for beauty that is mimicked in beauty contests. He argues, "Those who are not judged beautiful are *not beautiful.* Those who are, are given the prize. The prize is to be owned by a judge – that is available to him."[83] While not all contestants or organizers may have seen the element of judgment in connection to ownership, beauty contests do suggest an ongoing "traffic in women" to use feminist theorists Gayle Rubin's terminology. Rubin's argument focused on the creation of a sex/gender system that produced widespread differentials in rights. Such a system allowed for a political economy based on transactions in or exhanges of women through marriage, tribute, or buying and selling. As Karen Newman has more recently suggested, however, Rubin's designation of traffic *in* women does not acknowledge the potential power, pleasure, and reward for women in taking up the status as patriarchal object.[84] These points are significant to the history of Canadian beauty contestants in the 1920s. While middle-class religious, reform, and women's organizations highlighted the cheap aspect of beauty contests and questioned women's sense of decency in entering them (based, it must be noted, on middle-class ideals of decency and respectability), working-class critics saw the contests as capitalist exploitation of working girls. Both matters speak to the patriarchal traffic in women, yet a significant number of working women certainly found participation in contests to be appealing and rewarding. What these debates ultimately reveal are tensions between class-based ideals of respectability and display, and the changing tides of morality.

Perhaps the most outspoken of the critics, the *Catholic Register* fully denounced beauty contests. Its editorial stated that young women were subjecting themselves to be "scrutinized and examined, pawed and handled, measured and weighed" just so that they could claim the "dishonour" of being Miss Toronto, and then were paraded before "the vulgar and impure."[85] Young women, it warned, were exposing themselves to "the gaze of salacious vulgarians."[86] As well, the editor of the *Globe* argued that the contest was morally repugnant and senseless. In starkly racist terms he wrote, "For a woman to 'parade' her beauty is about as sensible as a Negro taking pride in his blackness." Almost every aspect of the Miss Toronto pageant was publicly criticized, and it was not unique in this regard. The Council for Social Service of the Church of England, local and national chapters of the Council of Women, and Social Hygiene Councils all passed resolutions calling for the prohibition of beauty contests.[87] In the spring of 1927 the *Toronto Daily Star* reported that local protests over beauty contests were not unusual, and a nation-wide protest was underway. Presidents of the Mothers in Council in Philadelphia released a copy of their protest for endorsement. Quoted at length in the article, it stated, "The Atlantic City and other such beauty pageants are but another expression of the same spirit abroad in our land, flooding the markets with salacious literature, and the sensuous nauseating moving picture."[88]

Despite the success of the Miss Toronto 1926 pageant, Sunnyside halted its contest after only one year. Months after the initial Miss Toronto pageant, executives announced that they were "making no plans for beauty contests."[89] Although American scholars have argued that there were not explicitly feminist protests against beauty contests, Canadian women's groups did oppose them.[90] The Toronto Local Council of Women passed a resolution condemning the Miss Toronto pageant. In 1927, the National Council of Women asked the Ontario Attorney General to consider legislation to prevent beauty contests.[91] As Patrizia Gentile notes, working-class women also entered into the discussion, but on the basis of different concerns. In *The Woman Worker*, a publication of the Canadian Federation of Women's Labor Leagues, an article from September 1926 noted their disapproval was not the same as "ministers of the church and artists," who "object to the display of feminine beauty in such a vulgar fashion." Their objection was to the exploitation of women's bodies for capitalist gain, in particular that the contest was little more than a cheaply designed advertising campaign to benefit Sunnyside, vendors, and the City of Toronto.[92] In this way, middle- and working-class concern dovetailed around the issue of young women's participation (or exploitation) in modern, commercial amusements. What connected middle-class reformers and working-class labour activists were notions of the protection of young women, who were seen as especially vulnerable in their pleasure-seeking sexualized self-promotion.

While the Miss Toronto contest was officially halted, beauty contestants still made a sort of appearance at Sunnyside Beach in 1927 by way of photographs being displayed of that year's Miss America contestants. The *Globe* described their popularity: "Every evening finds a large crowd gathered about the panels, so keen is the interest in them. Some are in bathing suits, some in dress costumes, and several show head and shoulders."[93] At the same time, the *Globe* reported that Toronto was not the only city concerned with the moral tone and effect of beauty contests. The article included several long quotations from the American group

Mothers in Council who, like their Canadian counterparts, were part of a campaign to save young women from exploitation, and the country from the demoralizing effect of these types of contests. Indeed, 1926 and 1927 were pivotal years in North America for the strength of the protest, at least in the eastern half of the continent. By 1927 the protesting voices surrounding the Miss America pageant, mostly from women's, religious, and social and moral reform groups, was strong. Frank Deford, in his study of Miss America, argues that although the pageant had always faced controversy, by the late twenties the hotelmen who had once championed the spectacle decided that it was "a cheap exploitation of physical beauty."[94]

When various groups and editorials pronounced the pageants offensive, they questioned why parents, but especially mothers, would allow their daughters to participate in such events. In the *New York Times* editorial that described the merits of Rudolph Valentino's beauty contest winner Norma Niblock's cosmetic-free face, this concern was raised:

> what sort of mother and fathers – especially mothers – have they [the competitors] that they failed to get the once more than common home training which would have made them shrink aghast from the very thought of participating in such a competition ... It would not do, because it would not be true, to say that no decent girl would exhibit herself in this way, but certainly none would do it whose instincts were even a little nice or fine, who had been carefully lessoned in modesty and self-respect – who had been familiar in childhood with a mother who exemplified those qualities.[95]

The *Catholic Register* made a plea to parents and "wished that no Catholic father or mother will permit a daughter of theirs to degrade her womanhood before the public gaze."[96] In response to these allegations, some newspaper articles attempted to assure readers that mothers were involved in chaperoning their daughters. For example, when Miss Canada, Madeleine Woodman, made an appearance at the luncheon of the Gyro Club at the Chamber of Commerce, the *Victoria Times* made a point of stating that her mother was with her.[97]

The multi-pronged criticism of the contests was then overwhelmingly focused on the women who participated in them, either directly or by way of an attack on their improper parenting. Although working women's insufficient wages had been a source of concern since the end of the nineteenth century and had sparked legislative reform, there were still tensions regarding the fears of prostitution (the exchange of the body for goods and money), and the desire for women to keep their bodies respectable and pure for marriage and motherhood – the widely understood goals for all women.[98] Beauty contests revealed the tensions regarding new morality, which was heavily influenced by popular culture. Being part of a public spectacle was part of modern femininities, and references to the "beauty contest of life" and the "passing show of femininity" reveal that the gap between contests and everyday practices were not as wide as some of the criticisms might suggest. As Joan Jacob Brumberg argues, "modern femininity required some degree of exhibitionism or, at least, a willingness to display oneself as a decorative object."[99]

While newspaper editors took aim at the women and their alleged indecency for even participating in the contests, limited evidence suggests working women did not see a contradiction between being a contestant and being respectable. The rules of the 1927 Miss Victoria contest stated that "The contestants must be of good character."[100] When Miss Cincinnati and her mother visited Toronto as part of their tour of America sponsored by the *Cincinnati Post*, her mother spoke out about her support for her daughter. Mrs. Riga explained that it was not harmful to have a beautiful woman be proud of the gift God had given her. She stated, "If a girl's heart is in the right place, she will take the admiration for what it is worth, and will not get her head filled with silly thoughts." Being a beauty queen was explained as a temporary break from the regular routine, and when Miss Cincinnati returned home she would go back to her job as a cashier at the movies.[101] Other women, newspapers themselves reported, found happiness post-contest in marriage. In 1922, Miss Toronto made headlines in the *New York Times* for spurning a millionaire suitor to marry her mechanic boyfriend after competing in Atlantic City in the Miss America contest. The *Times* lauded her decision as proof that young women could compete and remain unaffected by the attention. The article stated,

> Behind this [wedding] announcement is a story of a pretty girl who refused to let her head be turned by admiration and attention at Atlantic City. Her friends say her most persistent suitor was a young millionaire of 'the States.' She did not forget her Canadian sweetheart, however, nor did she wish to desert her Canadian home for New York or Hollywood, and today's simple wedding is the result.[102]

It was newsworthy that a working girl did well and fought against the tides of raised expectations that critics warned only led to exploitation and disaster. Despite the condescending tone of the *New York Times*, the story is suggestive of working women's ability to claim respectability as a beauty contestant. Few beauty contestants left records about their thoughts on the contests, but the numbers of women participating in them during the decade, combined with what we must acknowledge as the possibility of young women's agency, should suggest that women saw benefits and rewards in line with modern ideas of morality and respectability. Women's slender incomes, the very real demands to look and perform modern, and influence of consumer culture meant that there could be material draws to becoming a contestant. In addition to the fun and the potential non-monetary rewards of fame, pageants could offer women material comforts in cash, clothing, and other consumer goods.

The strength of the opposition against beauty pageants in Central and Eastern Canada is in contrast to the West, where in 1927 three successful Miss Canada pageants were met with little protest. In the years prior to the Great Depression (which eventually halted the competitions), women from Winnipeg to Victoria were welcomed to compete in representing Canada at an international beauty contest. The only groups to take issue with the event were the Girl Guides and the Local Councils for Women who passed resolutions against beauty contests in general and bathing beauty contests in particular.[103]

In May of 1927, as two Miss Vancouver pageants were run, nation-wide plans to celebrate the Diamond Jubilee of Confederation were also underway. While women were used to represent Canada in floats across Canada under the title of Miss Canada, bathing beauties were not selected. Typically for the Diamond Jubilee festivities, women who held prominent positions in the community were chosen to represent the provinces and Canada on floats. The general committee for the city of Vancouver even eliminated the unsanctioned bathing beauty contest from the aquatic sports committee's schedule. One of the women on the general committee led the protest, arguing that such parades exploited womanhood. For the July celebrations in Vancouver, Jean Cameron was selected as Miss Canada because she was British Columbia's Oratorical champion.[104]

A different controversy over a Vancouver beauty contest held by the Canadian Legion of the British Empire erupted in May of 1927, when a dispute between two finalists continued to the courts. Part of the prize package included a brand new car – the new Auburn – a substantial prize that would have been beyond the means of the average working family. The declared winner, Velma Rogers, had her victory clouded in controversy when Kitty Salmon sued the Canadian Legion, the contest itself, and Rogers.[105] Salmon sued on the grounds of breach of the rules, fraud, and negligence. Her mother (Kitty was not old enough to file the suit) alleged that some of the Miss Vancouver pageant contestants were either married or over the age of twenty-one, both infractions of the rules. In addition, Salmon argued that people had bribed the organizers and were allowed to cast ballots after the voting had officially closed.[106] Such scandals marred some of the gloss of acceptability that the contests had gained. Competition over being the most beautiful was seen by some as distinctly distasteful, but the allegation of married women's participation as well as the fight over material goods seemed crass. Beauty contestants like Salmon may have been enticed by opportunity and consumer goods, but to critics their desires reflected fears of the cultural influence of the working classes and their unwillingness to accept class subordination.

Conclusion

Appearing required multiple areas of examination of the face and body, and in that way beauty was restricted to a particular yet often ill-defined age range within the amorphous category of youth. Contests encouraged very particular standards of the body, especially thinness, and in relation to other image-makers, disseminated those images along with carefully couched suggestions that regular women could and should live up to the ideal. For the modern woman, appearing required sufficient self-surveillance and regulation. Beauty competitions were not isolated events or performances, but rather a part of the wider webs of visuality connected to advertising and movies, and through all of these, the beauty contestant appeared as a new type of Modern Girl. Certainly, there were objectors, and with good reason. Beauty contests were deeply problematic in their promotion of attractiveness as the most significant feminine quality, and in shoring up connections between whiteness, thinness, and beauty. Women who entered them found themselves in public debates in addition to being under scrutiny for their appearance. Notably though, women were not simply taken advantage of or to blame for their participation. As problematic as they may have been, beauty contests did offer working women an opportunity for pleasure, self-display, and reward both personally and financially. That those qualities were so culturally valued is the real problem, not the women who pursued their goals through them. There were ambivalent responses to beauty contests in the 1920s which suggest a measure of appeal and success. As modern as contests were, there were also conservative elements inherent in them:

men judging women's looks, the open gaze of working women's bodies, and the affirmation of hierarchies of race, class and gender. The tensions over age, beauty, exposure of the body, and the Modern Girl were not unique to beauty contests. And, as discussed in the next chapter, these tensions erupted at the 1927 Canadian National Exhibition over the display of nude paintings.

5 Modern Art and the Girl:
Nude Art and the Feminine Threat

When the Modern Girl appeared on canvas embroidered with the look of mature, female sexuality at the Canadian National Exhibition in 1927, a controversy erupted that lasted from the opening day to weeks and months after the closing of the gates. The three nudes in question were John Wentworth Russell's *A Modern Fantasy*, George C. Drinkwater's *Paolo and Francesca*, and Rosalie Emslie's *Comfort*.[1] They were not the only nudes hanging on the walls of the fine art gallery, but they were the ones that sparked a contentious debate carried out in newspaper columns and over one hundred letters to the editor. These were not simply images of the Modern Girl – they were nude paintings in the figurative realist style that incorporated and eschewed aspects of her cultural profile and techniques of appearing, especially in regard to age. Reading the paintings and the debates through the lens of the Modern Girl reveals not only the limits of her acceptance, but also how her representation could reveal more profound cultural changes and contestations in gender, class, and sexuality. In particular, it reveals the resiliency of patriarchy in framing and understanding the Modern Girl. This chapter picks up on the theme of the feminine threat to explore how what initially appear to be rather banal images of women raised concerns about changes in women's appearance, as well as changes in culture that challenged normative gender, class, and age codes. The feminine threat appeared to destabilize the ordering of spaces and people, and made it seem as if popular culture was eroding a foundational high culture. This claim was certainly linked to other well-documented cultural debates on the depravity of American popular culture and its influence in Canada. The particular case of the nudes at the CNE, however, provides fertile ground for exploring the Modern Girl's threat in relation to class, sexuality, and patriarchy. As challenging as she was to cultural norms, fears of the Modern Girl helped to bolster masculine authority and privilege in the 1920s. Delineating her as a problem reinvested authority in traditional, masculine forms.

Nude art held (and still holds) a simultaneously contentious and prestigious place within the canon of artistic production.[2] It should come as no surprise that Canadians debated its place in a public exhibition, but the nature of the discussion over these particular nudes is significant. On the surface it may seem obvious that a controversy over nude art would erupt in "Toronto the Good." Yet, the complexities of Toronto's urban environment in the 1920s mean that the debates require a more intricate analysis than the simple dichotomy of moral Toronto versus nude art allows. Toronto certainly had a reputation for blue laws, an eager Morality Department, and an active Social Purity movement, but the notion of "Toronto the Good" obscures the self-constructed discourses of goodness, morality, and purity, as well as the diversity of experiences available in the burgeoning urban area. Moreover, the controversy was not just a prudish reaction by a Canadian (particularly Toronto-based) public unable to appreciate the artistic qualities of nude art.[3] During the twenties nudes were shown in the CNE's art gallery that received little attention from the press or the public. Other CNE catalogues from the decade contain a number of nude paintings which sparked little discussion.[4] Referring to the 1927 display, Canadian artist Lawren Harris noted that "there were other nudes on the gallery walls, notably one by the Englishman, Proctor, that was clear, beautiful and unnoticed."[5] A spokesperson for the Local Council of Women stated, "It isn't that we object to nude pictures. There are very beautiful nude pictures which anyone should admire. 'Eve Triumphant' at the Exhibition last year was a beautiful picture. It was a nude, yet no one could object to it. It is the sensuous nature of the pictures shown this year that makes us want to rule them out." The "sensuous nature" of the three particular paintings provides a starting point to explore why the controversy erupted, and the underlying cultural tensions that emerged from it. Still, not only did the content of the paintings matter, but so too did the space in which they were hung. The Council, for example, also objected to having them hanging in "such a public place at the Exhibition, where not only art lovers, but all classes and all ages of people, come to see them."[6]

The Modern Girl proper may have seemed strange on canvas, since she was more a product of cheap newsprint and celluloid – pop culture products for all classes but especially the working class. A nod to her in high art – and in the apogee of the female nude at that – may have seemed troubling in and of itself. The three paintings all tapped into notions of the private lives of women, which challenged neat (although troubled) dichotomies of private versus public. Viewers often took what they saw in the paintings and made assumptions about real women's bodies in public spaces, and from there, to the private behaviours that seemed to be reflected in the public. Popular sensibilities did not often discriminate between reading the body and reading actions of it.

This chapter studies the three paintings in the wider context of the emergence and representation of the Modern Girl to reveal how her appearance (if somewhat subverted in actual representation) opened debates on the anxieties of feminine modernities. It also explores how the Modern Girl became a lynchpin for the seeming collision of high and mass culture, and ultimately the alleged breakdown of dichotomies that separated spectators, places of viewing, and types of images based on class, gender, and age. Here, the Modern Girl stands not only as a representation of feminine modernities, but also a deeper and more troubling feminine threat to masculine, bourgeois ideals about high culture and access to it.

Nudes at the CNE, 1927

Emerging in Paris in the 1860s, the narrative of artistic modernism typically begins with Edouard Manet's *Olympia*, a painting that sparked its own scandal when first exhibited. As T.J. Clark argues, *Olympia* tapped into the ongoing anxiety over class, as well as prostitution and venereal disease so prevalent in mid nineteenth-century Paris. In regard to composition, Russell's painting may well have seemed derivative of *Olympia* at best. By far the most contentious painting, Russell's *A Modern Fantasy* depicted a reclining nude who was almost perfectly prone with an exposed vaginal area. [7] Rather than being offered flowers by a servant, the woman is completely taken by the table of goods next to her bed, which includes china figures of a jazz band, dancers, and vases – one is clearly not needed as it is empty. Her head is resting on a number of pillows and behind them is some ornate fabric. The woman is bound by excess and, as her hand slowly creeps towards one of her many goods, she seems entirely unconcerned with being seen. She is so taken by trinkets that her nudity seems to disappear – at least to herself. In this regard, she is much different than Manet's *Olympia* who looks out challenging viewers, while covering her pubic area in a noticeable, if defensive way. With

5.1   John Wentworth Russell's oil on canvas *A Modern Fantasy*. Used with permission of the Estate of Anna Russell.

Olympia the viewer was put on the spot and expected to pay to gain access, while Russell's nude was so distracted by goods that she lay open and revealed.

Russell's take on "fantasy" seems to be twofold: first as the fully exposed nude, and second as the desire for consumer goods. How had the woman amassed such a collection? Was she "crazy for bargains" – an out-of-control middle-class female shopper irresponsibly spending her husband's hard-earned dollars and thus in need of strong male authority? Was she engaged in the casual modern world of "treating," or the more nefarious work of prostitution, or was she part of the middle-class "orgy of shopping?"[8] Like the masquerade of the Middle Eastern dancer, Russell's model was also surrounded by racialized excess – the peacock-feathered

5.2 Rosalie Emslie's oil on canvas *Comfort*. Reproduced from the 1927
Catalogue of Fine, Graphic and Allied Arts and Salon of Photography. Licence granted
by the Copyright Board.

print fabric and the jazz band figurines. In juxtaposing the nude body with a whole host of consumer goods, Russell suggested excess, desire, and the erotics of consumer goods. As such, his painting revealed that consumerism was far too real and practical to maintain a disengaged, repressed viewing of a classical nude. There seemed to be very little distance between high art, pop culture, and consumerism.

George Drinkwater's painting *Paolo and Francesca* revealed the same sort of concern over sex and consumer goods, in this case seductive texts. In the original story, Paolo and Francesca were brother and sister-in-law as Francesca had married Paolo's older brother. One day, Paolo and Francesca were sitting together reading aloud the story of Lancelot and Guinevere. They were overwhelmed by the section where Lancelot kisses the queen, and began their own affair. Francesca describes how, "Several times our reading caused our eyes to meet and our faces to pale; but it was one point alone that overcame us."[9] The lovers were caught; they were shot by her husband, and ushered into hell. The painting depicted Paolo and Francesca naked and pinned together by a sword with which Francesca's husband had stabbed them.[10] One viewer described Francesca as "a flapper, bobbed-hair and blonde of 'the complexion that gentlemen prefer'" who seemed "entirely undisturbed by the assassin's dagger."[11] The modernization of Francesca suggested a connection between the painting and contemporary concerns over cheap fiction, theatre, and films.[12] That Francesca's modernity was symbolized by bobbed hair was something all three paintings shared, yet neither Russell's nor Emslie's nudes could veritably be described as Modern Girls. *Comfort,* for example, depicts a woman with short, dark hair, sitting naked in a club chair with a piece of crumpled fabric underneath her. Her body is not that of an idealized classical nude, or even a perfect rendition of the idealized body of a Modern Girl. Her neck and shoulders are muscular and defined. Her legs look powerful. The angular lines used by Emslie around her head and shoulders imply a hardness or roughness. Her breasts and stomach, however, reveal a softness of the female body not typical of the angular, sparse physique of the Modern Girl. Despite her bobbed hair, the body is not youthful and taut, and her position implies a sort of settled stillness that is, in some ways, the antithesis of the Modern Girl's almost constant sense of movement. In addition, her face looks mature.

In a way, both paintings imply a sort of crassness of maturation imitating youth, but they do so maintaining the confidence of a mature, if not bold, sexuality. The bodies were ones that consumed too much – too

many things, too much pleasure, too much idleness, too much of themselves. But, as we shall see, commentators conjured up images of Modern
Girls when they saw the paintings. The symbols of modernity were so
caught up with the Modern Girl that they were almost indistinguishable,
even when artists sought to trouble or subvert them. These paintings,
however, take on an even more complex meaning when situated in the
wider artistic movement in Canada in the 1920s.

Art in Canada in the 1920s and Competing Visions of Modernity

As Art Deco–inspired images and goods appeared in magazines, advertisements, fashion, and other venues of popular culture, the wider artistic movement of modernism was not entirely distant from Canadians. As
chapter 3 suggests, the Modern Girl was embroidered with some styles of
modern art, making limited connections between high, graphic, and
popular art. Moreover, Canadian artists were not removed from international artistic developments. For decades, Canadian artists had travelled
to Paris to learn, practise, and experience the cultural landscape. By the
1920s, the art gallery at the CNE had at least a gloss of cosmopolitanism,
despite the fact it was in generally poor shape, was in need of better organization, and according to some members of the Fine Art Committee,
needed to show a better quality of art.[13] The CNE's gallery showed work
from Canadian, British, and European artists, and individual pieces of
art reflecting an international artistic community were also hung as part
of the annual show.

The CNE's connection to fine art fits with the dominant narrative of
Canadian modern art in the twenties, which is tied to various interpretations of the Group of Seven and their far-reaching artistic presence.
Building upon the desire to create a uniquely Canadian culture in the
wake of the First World War, the Group was one of the foundations
for Canadian cultural nationalism in the interwar period. By 1927, the
Group's reputation had been well established, but they existed as part of
a flourishing and diverse group of Canadian artists who founded a number of important groups or associations including Beaver Hill Hall and
the Sculptors' Society of Canada. They also played a role in the significant artistic production by Indigenous peoples across the country, who
were largely discounted as artists in the maintenance of false, racialized,
and gendered categories of art versus craft versus ethnological display.[14]
Although the Group of Seven declared that they had founded a new
school of painting and sought to distance themselves from European

traditions, many painters who composed the Group had studied in Paris, and art historians have argued that the Group owed a debt to impressionism as well as Scandinavian artists of the period.[15] Nonetheless, the Group received praise for developing a "Canadian" artistic style and was generally heralded by critics.

The Group's vision of the landscape as a rugged, harsh, wild, untamed area appealed to the nostalgic antimodern impulse of the 1920s, and was distinctly masculine in its representation. Like other Canadian painters before them, the members of the Group of Seven were influenced by the land. From their first exhibition in May 1920, the motif of the rugged "Northern" wilderness that would epitomize the Canadian spirit proved popular, even if their vision was more stunted than the appeal to nationwide sentiment suggested.[16] The Group's landscapes became "icons of moral and sexual purity" as a representation of an idealized, antimodern therapeutic space separated from the feminizing and racialized influences of urban life. As Paul Hjaratarson persuasively argues, the Group's landscapes effectively played upon the trope of "virgin land" to simultaneously render Indigenous peoples as prehistoric and equate women with "the land," effectively countering movements by both the claim of public space and full citizenship.[17] It was a conservative countering to women's increasing public presence as political actors and modern consumers. The Group's work was not simply a retreat into an idealized, antimodern past; it was an attack on the present – a present defined by shifts in industrialization, urbanization, and consumer culture embodied by the Modern Girl.

The Group's profound influence on cultural nationalism was based on their abilities to appeal to middle-class English-Canadian nationalist sentiments on canvas, and somewhat ironically, their harnessing of modern publicity. Their landscapes melded many different contemporary concerns over labour disputes, immigration, modern women's increased cultural and political presence, and Indigenous rights by way of their erasure from the "virgin land."[18] *Maclean's* tellingly described the Group's now iconic paintings of Northern Ontario as able to "be labelled Canada, for in their stark intensity they typify the spirit of a race."[19] The Canadian public generally embraced the work of the Group, and their exhibitions drew crowds and earned the support of the national artistic community.[20] The artists also managed to create controversy around their work, and adding to their popularity were the sometimes deliberately constructed myths about themselves and their movement. For one exhibition in Ottawa, they reprinted Hector Charlesworth's harsh review of their painting in the catalogue. Members of the Group continued to use the negative comments about their work to cultivate an image that they were the young, new order fighting against the old establishment.

Despite the overwhelming support of the National Gallery of Canada, Prime Minister William Lyon Mackenzie King was not a fan. In his journal, he recorded his reactions to the 1927 art display at the CNE. He wrote,

> I was immensely interested in the other buildings as well, went thro' the Art Exhibit. While I liked some of the paintings I have a positive dislike for the work of the New School which is seeking to call itself 'Canadian.' Russell had a figure of a nude woman which may be good painting but seemed to me an immoral exhibit and not the kind of thing we should seek to accustom our people to, there was an even worse allegorical painting of two figures which I think should be burned instead of exhibited.[21]

What King's comments on the exhibition as a whole reveal are that the nudes in question were juxtaposed directly with the Group, who offered a much more romantic, antimodern image of Canada that may have seemed preferable (although not to King), or at least less offensive to many gallery-goers. King's statement reveals the significant presence of the Group of Seven at the CNE in both the gallery and on the Fine Art Committee, who in 1927, made the decision to hang the three nudes. Therefore, within the space of the CNE's art gallery are competing visions of Canadian modernity. One is anchored by antimodernism revelling in the "unique," "Canadian" landscape represented and interpreted in masculine terms: harsh, rugged, empty, bodiless, and an example of sexual, moral, and racial purity. The other calls upon the tropes of feminine modernities and represents aspects of it, including the modern body, consumerism, and female sexuality. The nude paintings were not exactly binary opposites, as they still engaged with a masculinist gaze of the female body, but that too was part of feminine modernities.

Yet, the connection between the Group as Canadian modern artists and the Modern Girl hints at the deep disjuncture in Canadian modernity: the Group's vision of modern art seems to be at odds with the very existence of the Modern Girl. The representation of a remote, wild, harsh, and masculine landscape were attacks on the urban, industrial, commercial, feminized, and racialized cities that were so intimately connected with the Modern Girl. The locales met, however, around the harnessing of modern publicity. But popular reactions provide another point: the

Group had a great deal of popular support in their conservative, masculine, antimodern view of Canada and Canadian-ness in the 1920s. It was a view antithetical to the Modern Girl, with her working-class associations, her appreciation of popular culture, and her femininity. That the Group had been so well received at the CNE provides significant context for the contentious reception of the three paintings in question, especially given that the debates on them focused on gender, class, and sexuality.

"Cheap Sensation," Publicity, and the Art Gallery

The artists who made up the Fine Art Committee would have realized the potential for controversy. The Committee was composed of prominent artists and businessmen, including Fred S. Haines, George Agnew Reid, A.H. Robson, and Frederick Herbert Deacon. The Committee represented a powerful selection of elite men with strong connections to other artistic institutions like the Art Gallery of Toronto and the Ontario College of Art, as well as the graphic art firm Grip where members of the Group of Seven got their start as commercial artists. The question remains, however, whether or not the paintings were deliberately selected to generate publicity and increase attendance for the gallery. In 1927, the art gallery more than tripled its expected attendance and profits with approximately 158,000 people passing through its doors spending almost sixteen thousand dollars.[22] An increase in attendance may have been expected in 1927 given the special events planned for the celebration of the Diamond Jubilee of Confederation, and because the CNE's attendance had been growing over the course of the decade.[23] Neither of these factors alone, however, explains the threefold increase in gallery attendance. The Ontario Society of Artists described the attendance as "phenomenal partly owing to the newspaper publicity given to paintings to which exception was taken by some of our citizens."[24] The notion of cheap publicity (usually coupled with accusations of editors playing up sexual aspects) and of debate being developed day after day in newspapers spoke to the modernness of the scandal itself. Fine art could be many things, but cheap wasn't supposed to be one of them; cheap was reserved for Hollywood films, mass-produced goods, and the women who consumed them.[25] The controversy, however, became caught up in liminal cultural spaces – an art gallery on the fairgrounds, a painting reproduced on newsprint, and a discussion of high art unfolding in cheap newspapers.

The newspaper coverage of the paintings began on the first day of the exhibition, which was not in itself entirely unusual. The CNE was still an important annual event covered in great detail in Toronto newspapers. On the opening day in 1927, newspapers discussed the gallery's offerings and one even printed a photograph of Russell's painting.[26] What was different was that the first strains of the controversy were reported on the opening day, and some newspapers warned that gallery-goers would find the three nudes offensive.[27] The *Evening Telegram* printed a curiously placed letter in the main section of the paper rather than the typical editorial page. In the letter signed "Father," the author expressed outrage at the exhibition arguing, "it is obvious that our 'art leaders' have nothing to tell our youth that will help them along the road of happy, healthy, helpful, wholesome citizenship." In the late edition of the *Star*, the editors ran a lengthy article with the headline "'Nudes' Hung at Exhibition Likely Cause Controversy: but Art Gallery Committee Is Standing Pat on What It Has Shown – John Russell's 'Modern Fantasy' Excites Comment."[28] Perhaps not surprisingly, some sceptical readers, artists, and critics accused the editors of stirring up "cheap sensationalism" for the art gallery.[29] From the beginning then, much of the debate occurred in letters to the editors, giving it a cacophonous quality, and extending the debate well beyond the fairgrounds.

On September 3, CNE officials responded to the accusation that the box office rush was only due to the nudes. One official was quoted as saying, "We are getting a good class of people in the gallery, not just the seekers after a cheap sensation or a thrill. Our sales of the art catalogue are much greater than ever before. Casual callers who are looking for nudes do not as a rule buy catalogues. The art lovers do." Within three days of the denial, a conflicting report appeared in a different Toronto newspaper wherein one official allegedly thanked the paper for printing a reproduction of one of the nudes. He was quoted as saying, "I figure that the publicity given the picture by *The Telegram* was worth at least 30,000 admissions."[30] Both seem like plausible responses given the internal tensions of the Fine Art Committee. Sybille Pantazzi has suggested that there were conflicting interests with artists desiring to cultivate public appreciation for art, and businessmen wanting sensational works to increase profits.[31] More than a few commentators wondered if artists, who they believed were entirely responsible in selecting the paintings, were too distanced from contemporary Canadian culture to be in charge of selecting what would be exhibited in such a public space to a very heterogeneous audience.

Given the track record of the CNE, it may be likely that the paintings were chosen because they would cause debate and spark people's desire to see them. Certainly this occurred in 1927: a number of people admitted in their letters to the editor that they were stirred to see the paintings for themselves after hearing of or reading about the controversy. One letter was particularly revealing, if only for its ironic depiction of the event. The author wrote,

> Having seen in the press news about there being in the art gallery at the Exhibition certain pictures of the nude that ought not to be there, I decided to go and see those pictures so that I could decide for myself about them. But imagine my disgust when, on reaching the place, I could not get in owing to the long line of people ahead of me. Those people were going to see those pictures drawn by vulgar curiosity. I went out again the next night about dark but again found the same disgraceful crowding and was unable to get in ... It is evident from the way the crowd acted that we have a large element in the city that is attracted by the coarse and prurient so that a clean minded man can't get near the place.[32]

In another letter, one woman admitted that after hearing about the exhibit she marched down to see it for herself, but would not let her children go. In trying to attract this sort of publicity, however, the Fine Art Committee risked offending patrons, especially those who frequented the gallery. According to one writer, the gallery was crammed with people from "whom one would never expect either a knowledge or appreciation of art in any form." These people simply wanted to be directed to the nudes and were willing to spend their dime on them.[33] Their patronage was temporary and, it was assumed, did not necessarily turn into long-term gallery support.

There were other reasons to get people into the art gallery, which in the 1920s had seen a decline in the quality of art and the interest expressed in it. The Art Committee wanted a new gallery to replace their current space, and increased attendance and profits would give a wash of credibility to their demands. Fred S. Haines, a member of the Fine Art Committee and Director of the Art Gallery of Toronto, actively pushed for a new building for the CNE's art gallery.[34] The decision in support of one was made by the Committee a month after the closing of the 1926 CNE. The Committee also wished to increase sales of art, expressing concern that they would not be able to attract artists in the future given the slim chance of selling pieces at the CNE.[35] In the Annual Report for 1927, the attendance at the CNE was heralded as proof of "the ever increasing appreciation that Art is receiving at the Canadian National

Exhibition, and stresses the need for a new gallery."[36] One letter writer, however, objected to the use of the nudes to garner interest, and ultimately financial support for a new gallery, saying, "One thing is certain. The Exhibition directors will not get the taxpayers to vote money for a new Art Gallery so long as the crowded condition is due to the display of 'nudes' that so many people are ashamed to be seen looking at except perhaps furtively and at a distance."[37] The 1928 Annual Report of the CNE noted how the interest expressed in 1927 was sustained in the following year. But in 1928, the gallery was significantly less crowded and revenue fell by almost five thousand dollars.[38] The gallery clearly wanted to increase attendance, newspapers needed to be sold, and there did seem to be a disjuncture between "visions" on the Art Committee, all of which may have helped to create the controversy. That alone, however, could not sustain it. Simply hanging potentially scandalous paintings and advertising their existence would not cause such a raucous debate. There had to be a connection between the paintings and the larger cultural atmosphere.[39] The increased attendance suggests that people wanted to see the paintings; moreover, people wanted to debate what they saw in them and expressed opinions in letters to the editor. The concerns over the paintings, however, extended beyond the actual images to deeper cultural concerns over the Modern Girl. Using the suggestion of the collision of high and low culture, the next section explores the politics of space.

The Sites and Sights of the Canadian National Exhibition

Despite the impossibility of the dichotomy between high and low culture, there was a real investment in maintaining it. The three nudes hung in 1927, however, revealed the increasing pressure on, if not the collapse of, the dichotomy structured around differences in space, images, and privilege based on class, gender, and age, and this was apparent in the discussions over space. Never neutral, spaces shaped and were shaped by experiences and ideas, and it played a key role in fashioning the debates of the paintings on a number of levels. First, the fairgrounds of the Canadian National Exhibition were a unique space in terms of education, order, goals, regulation, and the mixed assemblage of people and places. The CNE was touted as appealing "to all classes and creeds and colors of people" who would all "find something to wonder at, to admire, to appreciate, to enjoy." But even this openness was tempered by existing ideas of identity and privilege.[40] Second, as part of the CNE, the art gallery was shaped and differentiated by its place on the grounds and its relationships to other venues of education and entertainment. Its status as an art gallery, however, was mediated by its increased accessibility as part of the fair. As one person described, "the Exhibition art gallery is not an ordinary art gallery visited only by lovers of the beautiful. It is one of the buildings 'to be done.'"[41] This helps to explain why when the paintings were moved to the Toronto art gallery in 1928, a staff writer for *Saturday Night* reported that quite possibly the most shocking aspect of this collection was that it no longer shocked the Canadian public.[42] Despite the arguments for the gallery's accessibility, interactions in the space were mediated by class and gender as well as expectations about behaviour. Third, both the CNE and the art gallery were related to other spaces of amusement and concerns over them, particularly as they related to issues of class, gender, and age. Namely, the association was most often with the midway.

American historian Robert Rydell argues that fairs performed a hegemonic function because they replicated the ideals and values of the county's leaders, and offered their ideas as "the proper interpretation of social and political reality."[43] The social and political reality that was being publicly promoted at the Canadian National Exhibition was that of moral reform, education, and progress. Organizers of the "Ex" billed the 1927 CNE as:

a panorama of Canadian progress since the early days. It affords opportunity for gathering the latest information regarding progress in all fields of Canadian endeavour and it is the assembling place for the latest achievements in Science, Art, Industry and hosts of other activities that stamp themselves upon the face of Canadian history, a tremendous effort to place before the Canadian people the last and best word in the realm of progress in all that is of interest and concern to every citizen.

The CNE was also likened to an "industrial university."[44] Organizers of the exhibition saw their purpose extend beyond highlighting progress and achievement, to education and the encouragement of moral standards. This conception of the Ex was part of the late-nineteenth-century drive to reform the fair from a space of pleasure and disorder to an educational one. This pedagogic impulse sparked moments of tension on the fairgrounds well into the 1920s. The contention between established ideas of moral education and new standards espoused by popular culture seemed in flux, and the paintings afforded an opportunity to debate these changes. Some patrons questioned what type of educational impact the paintings would have on viewers, with one person describing Russell's painting as "of such a subtle, daring, grossly indelicate and sensual character, that it cannot fail to do incalculable harm. What a picture for our young people from all parts of Canada to visualize and carry home with them!"[45] The debate also included the type of education and moral standard the CNE was attempting to impart, and whether or not, given the accessibility of the Gallery, this was even possible.

The Art Committee of the CNE, in particular, was supposed to play an important part in applying ideas on moral reform and education, as well as shoring up cultural hierarchies. The separation of art from the rest of the fair began in the decades leading up to the controversy. At the turn of the twentieth century, the establishment of an art gallery was part of the middle-class drive to create a moral space that would provide inspiration for morality, decency, idealism, and beauty. Art had been part of the exhibition since the incorporation of the Toronto Industrial Exhibition in 1879. In 1902, the gallery was separated from commercial exhibitions and, because of the ambition of the Ontario Society of Artists, had its own building erected. In 1905, a more permanent, fireproof structure was built. Both galleries were constructed with inspiration from classical Greek styles, an architectural representation of "high culture." In the first twenty-five years of the twentieth century, the CNE's gallery was one of the few places where visitors could see foreign art. The close connections between the CNE, the Ontario Society of Artists, and the Art Museum of Toronto suggest that the CNE's art gallery was an important place for exhibiting art. [46]

One of the central thrusts in the move to separate art from practical objects was the increasingly popular idea that art could serve a social role as a civilizing force that underscored elite leadership and taste. Further, art was supposed to serve as a moral force lifting viewers from a preoccupation with their appetites to instead focus on developing their spiritual character. It is not a coincidence then that as the gallery was being constructed the midway was being moved from a central location to the periphery of the fairgrounds with its own separate entrance.[47] Yet, as Tony Bennett argues, the sensational and raucous carnival haunted gallery spaces, as the two were historically related.[48] Indeed, this did affect the minds of CNE patrons in 1927. As much as organizers desired the art gallery to be a space of self-improvement based on middle-class standards, it could never entirely live up to this claim. Rife with contradictions, the CNE grounds were far less a space of social control and far more one of ongoing negotiation and ambiguity. The frequent comparisons between the midway and the art gallery allow for an exploration of its inherent expectations and contradictions.

The debate over space revealed the tension between areas on the fairground and the educational goals of the CNE. While the distinction between the two spaces was frequently troubled in practice, the divide remained sharp in some fairgoers' minds as they expected differences between them. When the lines seemed blurred by the nudes, they spoke out. One writer cheekily suggested that midway operators be in charge of choosing the next year's paintings since the Fine Art Committee had selected "circus pictures."[49] Another person questioned if, given the lack of censorship in the art gallery and the ostensibly perpetual surveillance of the midway, there was a different artistic law for the rich and for the poor.[50] Under the headline of "An Exhibition Mistake," the editor of the *Globe* commented: "If these works of art had been exhibited in a Midway booth at ten cents a view, as they were in the Art Gallery under the auspices of the Exhibition management, the place would have been closed within five minutes."[51] D. McTavish, writing on the opening day of the CNE, expressed shock that the "blot on the CNE" was to be found in the art gallery and not, as usual, on the midway.[52] The notion that there was a different standard for the midway and the art gallery was true. In spite of all the rhetoric surrounding education and morality, the fair was also a place of amusement. Different spaces sought to achieve these goals in diverse ways, were orientated to altered expectations, and had their own standards for behaviour.

Visitors who had once claimed the art gallery as their place of reprieve from the chaos of the exhibition grounds now argued the gallery was crowded and, perhaps more to the point, distressing. The *Evening Telegram* reported that people expecting their "quiet half hour" in the art gallery this year would be disappointed since "long after the hour when the doors of the gallery are usually closed, a line-up four deep" remained. It was not, they warned, the "usual crowd of art lovers."[53] Walden argues that urban space was delineated by class, as the middle classes sought "to quarantine problematic social groups, isolate unpleasant activities, and insulate their own territories from competing sources of power."[54] The exhibition was advertised as open to everyone, and rigorous definitions of class and space were crossed by people who ventured into all corners of the fair. However, there were also limits, and specific definitions and accompanying codes of decorum existed for the different areas.

Visitors were welcome to the gallery if their viewing practices and behaviour matched the established middle-class standard, but with the popularity of the nudes, this standard was often challenged. A *Globe* editorial succinctly described the shift when it noted the "long queues of cigarette-smoking youths and giggling girls who stood in line daily to see paintings which to most of them must have been merely pictures."[55] Concerns about young members of the working-classes viewing the paintings simply as a quick pleasure were repeated in a number of letters to the editor. The Toronto Local Council of Women protested against the hanging of two of the nude pieces in the art gallery on the grounds that they were hung in a public place where "mixed classes" could view them.[56] While they did not wish to debate the artistic merits of the paintings, they argued that the paintings were too accessible for "children and adolescent youth and scoffing and sneering people with no artistic sense [who] could pass in for a dime."[57] Similarly, an anonymous writer to the editor of the *Globe* who appreciated the art still did not want any more nudes to be hung in order to protect the art from the "sacrilege" of the "vulgar gaze of people who do not understand even the rudiments of art."[58] Another letter writer suggested that the gallery should attract a certain class of "people of the finer type in which the intellectual and the moral and spiritual faculties predominate and the grosser physical qualities are not so much in evidence."[59]

One means of regulating the space was the price of admission, and although art was supposed to uplift the masses, it was not one of the free exhibits. The admission of ten cents to the gallery was the same as or less than displays on the midway, and half the price of unlimited midway rides. While the price of admission was not unduly prohibitive, it did suggest a shift in space and played an important though largely symbolic role. Only those with the necessary money and the willingness to spend it had the ability to look at the art work. The charge forced fair-goers to decide where to spend their sometimes limited resources, as the art gallery competed with other spectacles, vendors, and spaces. Visitors to the fair were well aware that the art gallery at the CNE was different from other galleries in the city exactly because of the eclectic composition of the people who gathered there. In 1927, there was concern that the exhibit was attractive only because of the nudes.

The issue of class was closely tied to gender as well. One "Indignant Mother" wrote, "One glance at those pictures was sufficient, I hung my head in shame and made a hasty retreat. There were young boys there about sixteen, and scores of men jeering and laughing and making rude remarks. Were they lovers of art, think you?"[60] Another woman reported that she decided to leave the gallery when she realized that there were few if any other women there.[61] People being provoked by the paintings led to potential danger for women, and as the Local Council of Women argued, led to aggression against women. In an appeal to the president of the CNE, one woman said that "after a somewhat similar picture had been shown in Toronto some years ago there were a number of offences against women."[62] These concerns reveal two issues related to the construction of space. First, the art gallery was a space defined by class and gender. Second, it was an area that shared a social and cultural logic around looking that could be compromised by images that attracted different viewers with different viewing practices. These two issues beg further exploration in relation to the gallery and its counterpoint on the fairgrounds – the midway.

Women were concerned that cultural institutions like the art gallery relied in part on women's alleged moral influence in constructing the space as a pedagogic one. Women – in particular white, middle-class women – were expected to bring a level of decorum and a civilizing force to the gallery, [63] and it was hoped that their influence would allow others to learn from and emulate "proper" behaviour. This idea was premised on the fact that women would find the space tenable to their sensibilities as "respectable" women.[64] But in 1927, the hanging of the three nudes chafed against this construction. They were not the wholesome, uplifting image of white, middle-class womanhood; in fact, the paintings could be read as a critique of that group of women, who seemed consumed by goods, narcissistic, and driven by sexual desire. When women reported disruptive behaviour from males around them, or fled the gallery when they realized it was crowded with men, it signalled a shift in the construction of the space and its purpose. Laughing and jeering at nude images was far more suited to rough, male, working-class culture than the accepted social logic of the art gallery.[65] The desire to create an educational space where the civilizing force of the middle class could be imparted on other people was potentially placed in jeopardy if the nudes, more often than not, attracted people who broke those conventions.

Underlying the claim to space was the multiple ways of looking in the gallery. Ostensibly art was the main attraction, but bodies, intentionally or unintentionally on display, were also intriguing. Some women expressed concern about potentially becoming the object of other people's – especially men's – attention in the same space where sensuous nudes were hung. The crowded nature of the fair, which mimicked that of the growing Canadian urban landscape and its diversity of people, meant that looking at other people was a necessity that could be pleasurable or dangerous. The expectation that middle-class women's behaviour would be watched and mimicked assumed that they would be studied respectfully as opposed to leered at. After all, ogling semi-nude and scantily-clad women's bodies was most acceptable on the midway where lines of race, class, and gender established different hierarchies of who could look, and who was the object of that look.[66] These subtle shifts in looking reflect that seeing, like space, was not neutral.

Appetites of all kinds were encouraged and satiated on the midway. Despite continuing efforts to clean it up, it remained a space where "low" culture was experienced, and social and cultural norms were tested.[67] As a low form of entertainment that was physically and psychically separated from middle-class attractions and ideals of progress, it stood in stark contrast to the well-ordered exhibitions of farm machinery, new and useful household products, or the history of Canada spectacle in the grandstand.[68] Despite the challenges of the midway, it remained a necessity as people expected such amusement, and it provided substantial amounts of money for the CNE.[69]

The midway, with entertainment features like the "two-headed cow positively alive" and a semi-nude, grossly obese woman, was the place where people went to gawk at "unusual" bodies on display, to look at the exotic, and to experience the raucous and sometimes aggressive carnival. Part of the carnival culture was the acceptability of staring at bodies. Freak shows, commercial displays, and public performances were areas where bodies were deliberately used for entertainment or advertising. On the midway, different bodies or the bodies of racial "Others" were the most frequently viewed. In particular, women were shown in the semi- or fully-nude as part of exotic and erotic spectacles. These sexualized and racialized performances sought to reaffirm dominant constructions about gender, race, and ethnicity. Available for visual consumption, for example, were scantily clad women in girl shows, or diving beauties who performed acrobatic tricks in bathing suits for money. Earlier shows highlighted things like "hootchie coochie" performances.[70]

Nude art had also appeared as a sideshow amusement. Astley Cooper's painting *Trilby* was on display in 1900 and excited comment from one female visitor who expressed concern about the men leering at the painting.[71] Earlier in the twenties, the midway included a nude painting entitled *Stella*, which could be seen as a pay-per-view exhibit. *Stella* was a life-sized painting of a nude, blonde-haired, blue-eyed woman reclining on her side.[72] These types of displays sometimes caused public protest, and Walden argues that such controversies cropped up when traditional constructions of middle-class identity were challenged. The controversies revealed the beginnings of a subtle and contested social shift from character and restraint as the defining qualities of the middle class to "pleasure, expression, and consumption."[73]

In some ways, the 1927 controversy continued this trend, and the idea of "pleasure, expression, and consumption" could well describe how people felt about popular culture in the 1920s. As with all changes in social logic, however, this shift happened unevenly and, in relation to the nude art, continued to spark public debate in the cultural milieu of the twenties when working-class culture was increasingly enjoyed by the middle classes. In 1927, however, there was one important difference that made this controversy unlike those earlier ones. The controversy erupted not in regards to a sideshow exhibition, but rather to art hung in the gallery. To some, the cheap thrills of the midway had made their way into the art gallery.

The threads of debate related to space, education, class, and gender were revealed in a lengthy letter to the editor on September 13. "Stenographer" wrote to the *Globe* and brought into sharp relief some of the concerns in reaction to Russell's painting. The writer identified herself as a young, educated woman, and her chosen pseudonym indicated she was one of many white-collar female workers. She made a conscious effort to define herself as one with good moral standing, stating that she was "pure-minded" and did not typically patronize the midway. Earlier in the decade, however, the writer and a friend had seen the pay-per-view nude painting *Stella* on the midway (though it was with hesitation that they did so). Upon gazing at *Stella*, she was

Spellbound ... The golden ringlets, the dancing life in the blue eyes, the dimples, the lips that looked as though they were just about to speak to us, the pretty, pretty hands and shapely feet – and the absolute innocence and naturalness of her, just held us breathless – never had I looked upon such loveliness, such beauty of body, but even far more striking, the beauty of the young girl's soul and spirit that shone at us. A lump in my throat and my thoughts were something like this: "Oh, what glorious beauty! Could any woman be so altogether lovely? Surely only God could make such beauty, and if God made her then He is indeed to be worshipped, humbly and adoringly." I was filled with delight and reverence and cried out: "That – that – is art!"

It seems that the two young women had an almost religious experience being "spellbound" by *Stella*'s beauty. The nudity allowed Stella's soul and spirit to shine through, making Stenographer realize the splendour of God's creation. The painting was more than inspiring, as it actually inspired positive moral and religious thoughts. Upon hearing about the pictures being hung in the gallery, Stenographer went to see them in hopes of having a similar experience. She was disappointed, and described *A Modern Fantasy* as

> Simply the naked body of a young woman, shapely and most beautifully tinted and shaded, it is true but where was the soul and the inspiration? Utterly lacking – in fact, the first sight of that picture sent such a bolt of horror through my being that my heart actually tightened, and I just longed to rush forward with a knife and rip it to shreds – I even wondered if the nail-file in my purse would do the job – but, like the others, I merely turned quietly away, for was I not, after all, in the Art Gallery?

Whereas *Stella* was ennobling and uplifting, *A Modern Fantasy* was "so lewd that even the cushions and the silk coverlet seemed to shriek licentiousness."[74] In her estimation of the two paintings, purity and grace were on the midway and the dirty picture was in the art gallery. Similarly, others described the art as muck, unclean, low, or "art in a mud hole." "Father," another writer to the editor, described the woman in the painting as "indolent, luxurious, naked and unashamed ... lounging, lolling, frenzied, dead, freak postured."[75]

The dichotomy between "high art" and what was essentially a girl show image was inverted. The psychic inversion of space revealed the related social hierarchies as well as the difficulties in regulating spaces and the need for constant policing. The midway could be pedagogic and spiritually uplifting, and the art gallery could appeal to low and basic impulses. The things on display continued to shape the space and its purpose. Yet the constructions of space did not completely collapse, as Stenographer reveals through her own suppression of the violent impulse to destroy *A Modern Fantasy* – with a tool from her nail kit.

Despite the outrage, not all viewers were concerned about the apparently collapsing relationship between the gallery and the midway. In defence of the pictures a writer chastised a *Globe* editorial for conflating the two spaces, which the writer maintained were very different.[76] One man argued that people should turn their attention away from the art gallery and focus it on the midway, which in his opinion had none of the redeeming qualities of education, artistic merit, or social value. To him, the midway was a place where "the hideous deformities of both man and beast are open for public inspection; half nude dancing girls, without art as an alibi, performing at the bidding of the public, and so on."[77] Others upheld the gallery/midway dichotomy by extolling the virtues of the gallery and discrediting the troublesome displays of the midway. One letter to the editor by "Artist's Daughter" juxtaposed the beauty of the woman's body in *A Modern Fantasy* to the "disgusting" freak show bodies. She wrote that the paintings belonged in the gallery because they displayed beauty unlike the four hundred pound sideshow performer who had "masses of superfluous flesh."[78]

The passionate arguments on both sides revealed the disparate feelings surrounding the spaces and bodies, but more than likely many patrons of the CNE visited both the midway and the art gallery. Since the end of the nineteenth century, the middle classes were increasingly comfortable with such commercial entertainment, but there remained limits (always shifting and uneven) still carefully patrolled by consumers like Stenographer. Her position as a viewer of nude paintings suggested even deeper changes in female spectatorship and a link to popular culture, especially films.

The Modern Girl, Spectatorship, and Cultural Change

Judging from the reaction to the paintings printed in letters to the editor, one must wonder what viewers actually saw, for there seemed to be little consensus about what was exactly was hanging on the walls of the 1927 Ex. This is in itself a reminder that what people saw was contextual and informed by social and cultural concerns which were linked to shifting practices of spectatorship. Amid accusations of poor technique, nakedness, muck, genius, indecency, and beauty, letter writers clearly saw intimate connections with the Modern Girl. Interwoven into the debates on the paintings were the appearance and activities of the Modern Girl, including movies, beauty contests, modern fashion, marathon dancing, and motoring. It is, then, unsurprising that she was so present in the art gallery. In *The Birth of the Museum*, Tony Bennett argues that the museum is a heterotopia or a space where other cultural institutions "are simultaneously represented, contested and inverted."[79] The gallery as contested site was certainly true in this case, and the contest clearly had connections to the Modern Girl.

The changes occurring in popular and feminized culture were implied and made explicit in the letters to the editor. Writers underscored changes in the way people saw and reacted to the paintings, highlighting the influence of and appearance of the young working classes in the gallery. In short, they identified changes in the "ways of seeing" in relation to the people and things around them in the gallery, and more broadly, in popular culture.[80] Writers who defended the paintings noted how curious it was that in an era of allegedly loosened sexual mores and a sexualized popular culture such paintings caused controversy at all. A columnist for the *Toronto Daily Star* questioned whether "a generation accustomed to the modern dance, public or private, to beauty contests, or even the accepted bathing attire, finds much in any genuinely artistic picture to shock or even startle it." [81] The very fact that a generation of Canadians might be used to this type of display and not be shocked by it was in itself a problem. John Wentworth Russell responded to a reporter who asked him about the effect his painting might have on the morality of youths by asking, "Did you ever see anything more sophisticated than the young people of to-day?"[82]

"Sophistication" relates to the pressing question of what made these images so potentially dangerous in the eyes of some viewers; after all, the paintings were simply "the exposure of an inanimate figure on a two-dimensional picture."[83] The answer lies in the gallery space as it reflected broader issues related to modern society. Modern popular culture had seeped into the art gallery, and some people argued that the art needed to be protected from the "sophisticated" minds of youth. John C. Reade, writing to defend the exhibition of the paintings, made it quite clear that the problem was not the art but those who looked at it. He pointed out that to "the vast army of tolerant and serenely minded people," the paintings were "a natural subject produced with skill and honesty." Furthermore, it was in the distorted minds and "erotic and sensuous imaginations of callow youths" that these pictures became an affront to womanhood.[84]

A key concern was that popular culture from Europe and especially the United States was warping the minds of Canadian youth. How could a generation raised on salacious popular culture appreciate the finely skilled artistic qualities of the apogee of painting? Main Street had come to Canadian culture in the form of dime novels, jazz, movies, dancing, and beauty contests, and was trapping youth in a debauched world.[85] Concerned citizens complained that homes and schools were no longer moral training ground. Now movies, amusement parks, and dance halls educated young Canadians in ways that seemed to run counter to traditional Canadian values. Further, reliable venues for moral education like the art gallery now seemed to be taking a dangerous turn. Implicit (and occasionally explicit) in these judgments were that some overly-permissive parents, but especially mothers, were no longer doing their duty in raising the next generation of citizens.[86] Such arguments made feminine modernities seem foreign rather than part of a modern, Canadian landscape. Neither wayward daughters nor American goods were new to Canada in the 1920s, but what had changed – the real source of the concern – was the influence of working-class cultures in the middle classes. These concerns were heightened especially in regard to sexuality, gender, and age.

Letters to the editor expressed concerns about the relationship between physical exposure and behaviour, with one author going so far as to suggest that the sexual behaviour of Paolo and Francesca was repeated "daily on any popular bathing beach."[87] Certainly this is an exaggeration, but apprehension over generational changes in style and the spaces of heterosocial amusement remains important. If *Fantasy* was "womanhood … so disgustingly portrayed," as one angry letter described it, many found the painting far less offensive than what they saw marriageable daughters – and some of their mothers – wearing and doing on the street.[88] One writer argued that

Many women are indignant because they consider themselves exposed. Have women not been unnecessarily exposing themselves for some years now? What do we see in our offices, on our street cars, on our streets, at bathing beaches and summer resorts, to say nothing of fashion parades and beauty shows – mothers and daughters alike all flapping their sex before the eyes of man and flaming youth.[89]

J.W. Jones wrote,

It seems to me rather funny that people can get shocked over this when the general decree of fashion these days is to border as close to the nude as possible. Can any one avoid seeing the extraordinary display of silk stockings and short skirts every day in evidence, not in art galleries but on our public streets? After all to exhibit the nude is not half as sinful as to exhibit that which creates an evil suggestiveness in the mind … If they think these things should be censored, then let short skirts, lipsticks, petting parties, and cigaret [*sic*] parties and open spooning come in also for a little of their attention.[90]

The suggestion of sensuousness and sexual activity were disconcerting, and nudity in art seemed to be a lesser concern in an age where Modern Girls allegedly ran wild, engaged in seedy behaviour, and dressed in ways that were offensive at best and imperilled the future of the nation at worst.

Changes in art seemed to be less of a concern than changes in femininity. In May 1927, the Royal Canadian Legion celebrated Velma Rogers winning the Miss Vancouver contest and published her picture in the *Vancouver Sun*, revealing her bobbed hair and masculine dress (shirt, tie, and jacket). At the same time, an article on American soprano Alma Gluck announced that flappers were now mature women with ages from thirty to fifty. The article began by explaining that Gluck saw these mature flappers as the real point of the degeneracy of the home, since "teen-age boys and girls come home to find their mothers are away playing bridge, attending matinees, smoking cigarettes and drinking liquor." She continued, "It is they, not the young people, who are to blame."[91] The concern over flighty, easily impressionable women drawn into popular culture at the expense of their roles as wives and mothers was widely expressed, but that anxiety was heightened by age. Beauty culturists and other critics regularly warned Canadian readers of the danger of older women trying desperately to take on the appearance of the Girl. While holding on to one's youthful appearance was almost incessantly promoted, there was also a line into desperation that women crossed if they tried too hard or were "too old" to hold on anymore. Furthermore, the behaviour of these mature flappers seemed to most firmly challenge the long idealized roles of wife and mother. If some Modern Girls could be excused and accepted on some level, part of that was a privilege of their youth. While still a dangerous time that needed to be protected, a certain level of immaturity and pleasure-seeking could be understood, if not wholly accepted. The presence of maturing aping flappers was more serious.

A deeper shift was suggested by the debates over the paintings and the look and behaviour of women in public. In the nineteenth century, "public women" (those who "flapped their sex" in public and created an "evil suggestiveness in the mind") were likened to prostitutes. However, by the 1920s the idea of women in public changed,[92] and middle-class white women made new claims to the public. Resulting economic, social, and cultural shifts in work, amusement, and leisure pursuits gave female entertainers an increased claim to respectability. Nonetheless, the older concerns about the "public woman" were never completely lost, and the well-known connection between studio models for nude paintings and prostitution likely made this link stronger. Yet, the paintings in 1927 challenged the older conception of "public woman" with a new one.

Russell's work in particular reflects not a prostitute but a mature woman of leisure; indeed, one casually lying about in the nude surveying her collection of mass-produced, commercial goods. Russell's painting could be read as a critical commentary on the middle-class flappers of Gluck's imagination, only laid out naked in public. If "indignant" women were the key ones complaining about the painting, it was surely connected to disturbing trends in pop culture that seemed to pull their daughters further and further away from their own familiar life course. But, the outcry from middle-class women could be seen as a reaction to Russell's criticism of their own cultural place and practices. Here was the middle-class department store shopper run wild.

In addition, women who had fought for a more public role in terms of suffrage, prohibition, and education faced criticisms for publicly going against their "natural" roles and psychically (and sometimes physically) aping men. Young women in the 1920s seemed to appropriate and exploit these criticisms with fashions that emphasized boyish bodies, shorn hair, and behaviour like public smoking and drinking.[93] The impact of youth culture seemed to be an increasingly part of the dominant popular culture. Despite being modern, women in public still carried reminders of the difficulties in understanding the changes in traditional categories. How would people tell the differences between working girls, "working girls," public women, and "public women"? The multiplicity of meaning framed the dialectic of cultural hierarchies, which by the end of the 1920s seemed to suffer at the hands of "progress" in modern Canada.

Nonetheless, there were defenders of the paintings and gallery-goers who celebrated the changes and signalled an acceptance of the new day. The fact that the paintings remained on the walls, despite calls for censorship and an investigation by Toronto police, reflects an acceptance of modern feminine images. The Morality Department of the Toronto Police briefly became involved, but quickly quashed the rumour that they had asked the CNE directors to remove the paintings using section 207 of the criminal code, which referred to obscene pictures tending to corrupt morals. Inspector McKinney argued that there was nothing objectionable about the pictures, although "it would be different if the pictures were shown elsewhere than in an art gallery."[94]

Changes in femininity that shaped how people viewed and reacted to the paintings were important, but another anxiety percolated to the surface: the relationship between images and actions. One of the somewhat oxymoronic ideals of nude paintings – and here the genre is most certainly historically dominated by female nudes – is that viewers were to be removed from bodily impulses and sexual desires. Part of the underlying tension of the debates in 1927 was a result of the "sensuousness" of the paintings – to use the word of the Local Council of Women. Most certainly, the imaging of sexuality and the potential responses to it were imbued with concerns over the sexuality and new morality embodied by the Modern Girl. Yet, the response by viewers cut across other lines of the debate on popular culture, art appreciation, and space. Women's reactions to the paintings were varied, but there was a distinct theme that emerged across numerous letters to editors: a theme of concern of how they would be seen beyond the space of the gallery. That the imaginary line between oil-painted image and flesh and blood woman would be erased or crossed was not an illegitimate fear. A letter in the *Evening Telegram* on 19 September summed up the problem: "A Husband and Father" wrote, "I had the pleasure of viewing that very beautiful painting by John Russell at the CNE Art Gallery ... I sat down and fed my heart on its loveliness. It certainly was a great relief to some of us poor hen-pecked husbands who have nothing much to look at home."[95]

There was a pervading sense of distress in a number of the letters over what John Berger has described as a sort of psychic split of women's identity, as they took on simultaneous positions of surveyors and the surveyed. He writes,

A woman must continually watch herself. She is almost continually accompanied by her own image of herself. Whilst she is walking across a room or whilst she is weeping at the death of her father, she can scarcely avoid envisaging herself walking or weeping. From earliest childhood she has been taught and persuaded to survey herself continually. And so she comes to consider the *surveyor* and the *surveyed* within her as the two constituent yet always distinct elements of her identity as a woman.[96]

This fractured identity was represented in numerous individual letters, as women revealed how looking at the paintings in the gallery made them aware of their own bodies, especially in regard to issues of personal shame and safety. How were women to appear modern and mature while maintaining a sense of security in a culture rapidly shifting between misogynistic discourses? One woman decided to leave the gallery when she realized that the viewers were mainly men.[97] "A Daughter" wrote to the *Evening Telegram* objecting to the paintings on the grounds that, "As a woman, I do not approve of certain pictures of my sex being hung in art galleries, especially where every Tom, Dick, and Harry can gaze on them out of plain curiosity."[98] The look, even at the fair when it was deliberately encouraged, could be provoking and dangerous; for women it could mean a loss of respectability and perhaps even the fear of sexual violence. The paintings collapsed the difference between an image of a woman and images of one (female) self. Women, unable to return the critical and aggressive gaze (and possibly fearful of aggression itself), avoided or removed themselves from the situation.

If feminine modernities challenged masculine ones, they did so without fundamentally shifting the nature of patriarchy. The feminine threat – the threat of a popular culture undoing high art and its middle-class values – never challenged the threat of being female. Modern women were told they were always under surveillance and that they should watch and perform their bodies with that in mind. The threat of perpetual surveillance was rarely addressed in magazines and adverts that instead appealed to the pleasurable aspects of being watched. Women in the art gallery who were fearful for their own safety and respectability reveal the problem with that discourse, and the persistence of the patriarchal need for male authority to discipline women.

The appearance of the Modern Girl in the art gallery – on canvas, in person, and as an analytical device with which to understand the paintings – led to the faltering of the bourgeois ideal of the gallery as contemplative, uplifting, and quasi-spiritual space. For some, her alleged birth in movie houses and subsequent appearance in an art gallery was too wide a gap to cross – a gap of class. As such, the nudes were interpreted within the context of a particularly disturbing popular culture (especially through movies) that revealed and revelled in exposing the female body. Film was a culture for the masses that had little claim to art: its use of sex, violence, and nudity were not allegorical but literal. That popular culture was threatening the wholesomeness of Canadian culture and its youth was a serious concern, but if it was attacking bourgeois standards – the last bastion of white, middle-class good taste in a world consumed by cheap things – that was another entirely. In a lengthy letter, one viewer of the paintings decried Drinkwater's canvas as "the unstudied Kodak-like composition and commercial color scheme."[99] If artists were guilty of crass commercialism, a far deeper issue arose from the connection to movie culture. Movie houses were implicated as spaces where viewers were incorrectly educated in the ways of looking. In terms of film and its predecessor photography, Lynda Nead argues, "here was a medium which had introduced a new way of showing and looking at the female body."[100] As the controversy over nude art raged in newspapers, many commentators compared the offensive paintings in the CNE's art gallery to what they saw as the lowest form of modern entertainment – the movie. One person wrote a letter questioning whether the nude paintings could be worse than popular movies which lacked beauty and idealism. They inquired, "Can a few weeks at the Exhibition make much difference to children trained so early in crass vulgarity?"[101]

The cinema was not the place for disembodied viewing, and this was perhaps the most disturbing of all of the problems. Moving pictures did not expect an intellectualized disassociation of seeing from the body that was expected in art galleries and dictated in formal art education. Movies required that viewers associated with and understood physical suggestions on the screen. Cinematic vision, Nead argues, requires that we know "what it is to touch things in the world."[102] This was key to both the trouble with movies and their power outside of the theatre, for they spread not only in terms of the fads they offered but also their cultivation of this new perception. Considering such changes in viewing practices with the introduction of new technologies like film, this also framed how the diverse gallery-goers saw the nude paintings at the CNE and watched others looking at them. Film, in particular, introduced what art historian Lynda Nead has described as "a particularly intense form of embodied, haptic spectatorship." She argues that with mechanical technology came a

> new perception of viewing that was in direct opposition to the traditional ideal of the detached contemplation of beauty. If art promoted the intellectual and contemplative consumption of the image in which the body had been trained not to look, then film and the optical machines of the mid- and late nineteenth century reintroduced the viewer's body as an integral part of its attraction.[103]

Moving pictures certainly startled some early viewers, who, when introduced in 1896, were engrossed in the illusion of movement to the point of experiencing it themselves. A newspaper reported that "On one occasion, an old lady in the audience, quite unable to suppress a scream, started up in her seat and tried to scramble out, and in doing so knocked over the person behind her in her endeavour to get away from the horses; many more cases of the same sort have been known."[104] To be removed from one's body in the act of watching was a middle-class ideal that movies challenged. In the conservative world of the CNE Art

Gallery, this threat was embodied by the Modern Girl, both in the trappings of her on canvas, and in her standing in lines to laugh at high art.

On year later, a telling letter was penned that suggested a shift in power was at the heart of the controversy. It was written to Ontario Provincial Treasurer J.D. Monteith and connected the art controversy at the 1927 Canadian National Exhibition and the Canadian film industry. It stated,

> In the first place if the Government is going in for moving pictures they must be of a distinctly Canadian atmosphere – this alone will not make a picture a success, you must give the people what they want.
>
> Last year at the Toronto Exhibition [Canadian National Exhibition] the Art Gallery had a couple of paintings of nude women on view. Now there was nothing vulgar, or immoral, or unhealthy, or indecent about this, it was art, and as I understand it the hall in which these pictures was [sic] exhibited was thronged with people eager to see them. Of course we had some kill-joys, blasphemous hypocritical sanctimonious psalm singers, and religious hocuspocus [sic] artists, shouting their lungs out against these pictures being shown, but the holipolli [sic] flocked to see them, they were what they wanted so they went.
>
> Now what I want to bring out is this: if you are going to make pictures that are going to be [a] success you must have a 'kick' in them, along with the 'kick' you can get in a lot of educational work, but there is no use producing pictures that the people are not going to pay their money to go and see, and talk about them after they have seen them; get this into that part of their anatomy, of your censors, where most people originate their ideas. Give the people what they want, then you can successfully compete with American, European, or any other film producers."[105]

That movies might learn "kick" from an art gallery seemed to invert the dominant cultural codes, but clearly they were already challenged on a number of fronts. Movies in general, and popular culture in particular, seemed to have already reshaped the eyes and ideals of modern generations. That the Modern Girl was a dominant representation around which these ideas and changes were debated is unsurprising, especially given her particularly complex representation in the three nudes that sparked the controversy. More to the point, the masses had the purchasing power necessary to shape modern cultural values. The feminine threat was just that – their collective power to consume. The fact that it revealed itself in the context of a controversy over nude paintings in an art gallery, however, is reflective of the maintenance of patriarchy.

The feminine threat was not a subversive, feminist attack on the underlying patriarchal values that made it acceptable to look at nude, female bodies in high culture. It was changing the terms of seeing – making it embodied, introducing raucous laughter, and destroying the pretence of looking at a distance from oneself. That women found themselves the subject of the painting, the subject of criticism, and the embodiment of the problem suggests that despite age and class differences, there was no way to win.

Conclusion

In December 1927, William Lyon Mackenzie King was questioned regarding a rumour that the National Gallery of Canada was planning to purchase *A Modern Fantasy*. King responded, "I have not heard anything about buying Russell's painting for the National Gallery. It may be so, however. An Art Committee deals with these matters. I saw the painting at the Exhibition and thought it a marvellous work."[106] King's comment contradicted his earlier and private sentiments about the "immoral exhibit" which contained a painting worthy of burning. The contradictory statements could be explained by a hesitancy to express his private views to the public, or perhaps time had softened King's view. It may also be that his reaction to the painting was only fleeting. In this respect, fleeting may well describe the controversy as a whole. For weeks the nudes were hotly debated in newspapers as people promoted their own understanding of the issue, but then faded away, only to resurface a few times in the 1930s when nude art once again caused a stir. In a way, the conflicting nature of King's comments reveals the very character of the debates, if not the Modern Girl: ephemeral, contradictory, and enigmatic.

In this chapter, I have suggested that the controversy in the summer of 1927 arose out of the particular context in which the paintings were hung, and were marked by ambivalences and ambiguities in defining and understanding the Modern Girl. The art gallery absorbed and refracted issues related to its own construction as well as the wider culture in which it was situated. How the moral standards and pedagogic impulse of the CNE and the gallery could be maintained with sensuous nudes was a point of discussion that incorporated dialogues regarding the midway, the collision of high and low cultures, and shifts in gender, class, and age. As a microcosm of society, the CNE allowed people to literally see and discuss wider cultural changes through readily accessible lenses. What they revealed was an essence of being modern, defined by a female body. Exploring this small moment for its internal workings and contradictions exposes the contested changes in being modern – in a feminine way - experienced in the 1920s. The nudes provided an opening for discussion, which made cultural changes palpable and more readily discernible. It was a brief moment made from a constellation of forces – the content of the paintings, the publicity, the space, and the current cultural concerns. They all converged in 1927 to reveal anxieties over the unsettled dynamics of feminine modernities, how they were simultaneously powerful and threatening, and how they were subsumed under a misogynistic and patriarchal discourse of shame and fear. The modern publicity machine relied on images of modern women, but feminine modernities remained at once uncomfortable and appealing. Moreover, the presence of such sensual images in the art gallery revealed the ruse of the bourgeois illusion of uplifting art. If only subtly, the controversy exposed the cracks in masculine, antimodern visions of Canada, the significant pressure of feminine modernities, and ultimately, the resiliency of patriarchy.

6 Modern Girls and Machines: Cars, Projectors, and Publicity

In F. Scott Fitzgerald's classic novel *The Great Gatsby*, protagonist Nick Caraway meets a Modern Girl and makes the following observation:

> I enjoyed looking at her. She was a slender, small-breasted girl, with an erect carriage, which she accentuated by throwing her body backward at the shoulders like a young cadet. Her grey sun-strained eyes looked back at me with polite reciprocal curiosity out of a wan, charming, discontented face. It occurred to me now that I had seen her before, or a picture of her, somewhere before.[1]

Given the popularity of the Modern Girl, Nick Caraway would have certainly "seen her before, or a picture of her, somewhere before." The woman he is entranced by is Jordan Baker, a quintessential Modern Girl: cool by disposition, somewhat masculine in appearance, athletic, and mobile. Even her name, chosen by Fitzgerald from two automobiles, speaks to her modernity and mobility.[2] The passage above, like many in the book where Caraway watches Baker, speaks to the pleasure ingrained in looking at her body, the omnipresence of her image, and to her expected role as a figure *to be seen*. The connection between Jordan Baker and consumer culture is also suggested by her connection to the car. As such, this quotation speaks to the popular cultural projection of the Modern Girl and her deeper connection to consumer goods like cars and films – all of which projected specific ideas of being modern as they interlaced gender and modernity.

This chapter looks specifically at the connection between three things: women's bodies, film, and the car, to reveal how commodities, the body, and entertainment wove together a complex landscape that marked out both goods and bodies as modern and gendered. It focuses specifically on how these three things reinforced each other in the gendering of modernities. In returning to beauty contests, this time commercial ones sponsored by film companies, this chapter shows how modern publicity machines promised opportunities that were as superficial and artificial as the performances required to get them, but in doing so, made suggestive connections between reality and fantasy. Thus, the Modern Girl as starlet and beauty contestant seemed not to be merely a fictionalized representation of feminine modernities, but a real flesh and blood possibility. As with cars and films, the line between fact and fantasy was blurred. Ultimately, I am interested in these three particular commodities not as spaces for consumer culture, but in their cultural value as representations of feminine modernities. In this regard, I build from Victoria de Grazia's wider definition of consumerism that includes not only the literal buying of goods, but also the desire for things and images.[3] This is not to suggest that the actual commodities were not significant; on the contrary, both automobiles and films were important parts of the wider consumer landscape, both literally and figuratively.

Prior to the First World War, automobiles were restricted to the more privileged classes in Canadian society. By the 1930s, however, the patterns of consumption had changed, and automobiles ranked third – behind food, clothing, and shoes – as a percentage of every dollar Canadians spent on consumer goods.[4] Movie houses were readily available and well patronized in the 1920s, especially in urban areas, but also in smaller communities. By 1928, there were approximately one thousand theatres in the country. In addition to urban movie houses, other spaces like halls, churches, rural schools, and colleges transformed themselves into theatres on Saturday nights. In 1928, Valance Patriarche, a member of the Manitoba Censor Board, told readers in the *Dalhousie Review* that despite a scattered population and many rural communities, three million Canadians attended the movies each week. By 1929, weekly ticket sales for Canadian theatres reached two million a week. Even in the heart of the Depression four years later, one study in Edmonton and Calgary estimated that urban youth still attended at least one movie per week.[5]

Cars, the Modern Girl's body, and moving pictures also shared some remarkable similarities in the 1920s: standardization, objectification for mass consumption, a focus on speed, and a preoccupation with fun. Significantly, they were all also "vehicles" for the transformation of patterns of consumption, cultural habits and the performance of the body.

Newer technological innovations had two significant effects on modern life: the apparent speeding up of time, and the related collapse of space. Cars, the Modern Girl's body, and moving pictures formed the matrix of the image of change and helped to delineate the cultural propulsion towards perpetual speed. Deeper cultural transformation was premised on a change in perception.[6] The "new" way of seeing was based on multiple, and often competing, understandings of modernity that were deeply gendered, and reaffirmed the feminine's contradictory symbolic status as marker of modernity and also representative of a nostalgic "tradition."

The Modern Girl was closely tied to cars, films, and machine-age aesthetics in that her body appeared in line with ideas of the aesthetically-pleasing smooth, cool surfaces of modern and rationalized production that appeared to run at an ever-increasing pace. As Cynthia Comacchio argues, in the late nineteenth and early twentieth centuries, the understanding of the human body from scientific, medical, industrial, and health perspectives became imbued with machine metaphors. Alongside industrial management techniques, the overall goal was to make bodies more productive, efficient, and modern. While the new human machines were often conceived of in masculine terms, women's bodies fit with the machine metaphor in regard to "their responsibility for reproducing productive bodies and socializing them into 'citizenship'"[7] The Modern Girl was more often than not depicted at play rather than at work (paid or unpaid), and the anxieties regarding her existence often related to her rejection of traditional female roles. The care of her body fit a sort of industrial routine where the whole product was produced in pieces, and the time and effort spent on the body was fractured into individual tasks. The total effect, however, was a smooth, shiny surface.

Feminine modernities extended beyond the body proper to seemingly gender-neutral commodities. In this way, cars, film, and women's bodies formed a nexus through which commodity modernism was shaped and defined. Technological advances in the film and automobile industries were not disconnected from technologies of the modern body. In regard to cars, corsets, and cigarettes, Penny Tinkler and Cheryl Krasnick Warsh argue that "the slippage between descriptions of women and cars created the impression that women's bodies were commodities, an impression reinforced by the body display of women's bodies and references to the modern body's production."[8] The perpetual production and consumption of bodies was a significant aspect of feminine modernities that helped define them and also shaped a sense of increasing speed of cultural change. Women's bodies, like those in beauty contests, were produced in specific ways that were deeply connected to commodities, and in turn, sometimes turned into commodities themselves. Women's bodies also sold goods in ways that gendered items, and even practices of selling that formed part of the modern publicity machine.

Commodity Fetishism and Canadian Culture: Cars/Bodies

A 1928 advertisement for Fisher car parts reveals some of the connecting axis of commodity culture, gender, and the body. Drawn by American illustrator McClelland Barclay, this "Fisher Body Girl," like others in the series, does not include an image of the modern car, but instead seems to be selling "style." While the logo for "Body by Fisher" appears in the centre-right of the advert, the dominant image is a drawing of a young, modern couple. Both are well dressed in modern clothing and exude confidence with their body language. They are certainly stylish and, as the text reminds us, "today style is all-important." What is particularly intriguing about this image is the disconcerting connection between the company's logo of a Napoleonic coach and the back of the women's dress. Almost in line with each other, situated at the very middle of the advert, the back of her dress seems to mimic the shape of the "body" logo used by Fisher. The shading of her dress over the buttocks almost disproportionally emphasizes the round shape, as does the rather strange way her skirt unnaturally gathers up between her legs. While the dress seems to be moving because of a gust of wind, neither his overcoat nor pants are affected. In the end, we are left unsure about which "object" of style the word "body" refers to: the motor car or the woman's body. A more nefarious association could possibly be drawn between the fact that Fisher sold car *parts* and it is a specific, fetishized part of the woman's body most directly connected with the machine in the advert. Regardless, the advert suggests that style, the car, and the women's body are somehow connected and available for consumption. The ad elided the differences between consumer goods and women's bodies; both spoke to style, beauty, luxury, and manufactured surfaces. Both the car and the body alluded to a desirability of an object for consumption, and this suggestion ran through Fisher's extensive advertising campaign of the 1920s. Further, as a company selling cars and car parts, it was not alone in using an elision between a modern machine and a modern women's body as an advertising strategy.

Jean Baudrillard argues that bodies, and more specifically women's bodies, became "the finest consumer object." He writes, "In the consumer

MacLean's Magazine, November 1, 1928   33

STYLE

WHEN it comes to style in motor cars—and today style is all-important—all the world looks to Body by Fisher. For Fisher is the authority, the leader, tried and proven; the chief source and center of beauty in motor car design.

GENERAL MOTORS OF CANADA, LIMITED

Cadillac · LaSalle · McLaughlin-Buick · Oakland · Oldsmobile · Pontiac · Chevrolet

6.1 "Body by Fischer" Advertisement, *Maclean's*, 1 November 1928. Used with permission of General Motors.

package, there is one object finer, more precious and more dazzling than any other – and even more laden with connotations than the automobile, in spite of the fact that that encapsulates them all. That object is the BODY."[9] As Baudrillard suggests, automobiles and bodies shared a certain cultural status of "desirable object" imbued with codes of meaning, but those codes worked in tangent to provide meaning for both the female body and the car. Part of what so intimately connected women's bodies, film, and cars was the sexualization of things and the subsequent process of commodifying women's bodies. If objects were deemed desirable – often by way of their forced relationship with women's bodies – those bodies were in turn discursively constructed as commodities. This is what late-nineteenth-century sociologist Thorstein Veblen posited was a key part of the practices of conspicuous consumption of middle-class women. They were both consumers and commodities.[10] Further, Abigail Solomon-Godeau argues, "One of the most conspicuous features of commodity culture is its sexualisation of the commodity, its eroticization of objects, which in turn inflects, if not determines, the psychic structures of consumer desire … In becoming not only the commodity's emblem but its lure, the feminine image operates as a conduit and mirror of desire, reciprocally intensifying and reflecting the commodity's allure."[11]

This particular car advert, however, was neither an unusual trope used by Fisher nor an atypical image for the 1920s. Barclay's "Fisher Body Girl," for example, would have been recognizable to North American magazine readers as both an advertising persona and occasional magazine cover girl.[12] Her modern body stood in for the automobile's body and was described as "always first," "the originator of the finer body styles," and offering "the complete satisfaction."[13] The Fisher Body Girl was also accompanied by a young, attractive, modern man, and this imbued both her body and the commodity it was meant as a stand-in for with a heterosexual tension. *Sexy body* and *sexy car* became synonymous and feminized. In particular, what the adverts were ostensibly offering were custom-made bodies – something that modern women were expected to do for their own flesh. The Modern Girl's own carefully constructed and manufactured figure stood in for the fine craftsmanship of the automobile's body. Women in the adverts plainly revealed that they had followed the dictates of modern body projects and achieved success. Their physique was meticulously fine-tuned, with everything from hair and hands to dress and comportment having been perfected. The care of the body promoted by advertisers went beyond selling specific goods to a wider project of care of the modern body. As Conor argues, "the logic of display was itself feminized, not only because women were seen to be more susceptible to spectacle but because they were seen to identify with it."[14] The Fisher Body Girl is a prime example of this type of connection, though many car adverts frequently imbricated the good with a particular discourse of gender.

While the Fisher body implicated the body of the Fisher Body Girl, the connections between goods and women's bodies were sometimes more explicitly drawn. An advertisement for the Ethyl Gasoline Corporation used the drawing of a young woman on the move as the embodiment of their product. Under her image in handwriting was, "I started something! Ethyl." What she (allegedly) started was the movement towards high compression engines "with consequent increase in efficiency."[15] The Modern Girl personified a product that made faster and more efficient motor cars seem real to potential consumers. A New York *Evening Post* article, reprinted in the Canadian magazine *Saturday Night*, announced that Ford's new Model A was "a girl." In lamenting the passing of the "masculine" Model T, the writer critiqued the easy, beautiful, and responsive Model A:

> The old Ford, the old, black, rusty, cantankerous, obstinate, sputtering Ford brought wisdom to many fools and made many wise men go raving, tearing mad. This new lily of the valley isn't going to teach us anything. It looks as if it would run indefinitely without complaint, which is all wrong. It is made for serenity and comfort, which is also all wrong ... Back to the pioneer days when we threw sand under the fan belt and tightened the horn with a dime – the days when the Ford was a boy![16]

Gentleness, ease, and beauty made the car female, while an independent, free-willed vehicle like the Model T was male. Historian David Nye argues in the American context that men envisioned and watched the development of technological progress, but women made it safe, and embodied it. While Nye implies that this role was marginal, this was not always the case.[17] The female body was used to sell goods to emphasize their modernity, beauty, and sensuality along with their ease and convenience. New motor cars were emphasized as being advantageous to women drivers, and the technology was made to seem safe, familiar, and domestic. In this way, women's bodies provided an important trope for making the machine sensuous and desirable as well as fast, smooth, and efficient. The Modern Girl sexualized things as they made her modern.

ETHYL PAVED THE WAY TO HIGH COMPRESSION

SINCE the advent of Ethyl Gasoline, the compression of automobile engines has been steadily raised, with consequent increase in efficiency.

In 1927 approximately 14 per cent of the leading car models were of so-called high compression (a "5 to 1" ratio or higher). In 1928 roughly 56 per cent were high compression. And this year about 77 per cent are in this category.

It was Ethyl that made the high-compression engine commercially possible.

© E. G. C., 1929

This is the reason: Engines of this type cannot run properly on ordinary gasoline. Even the best of it "knocks" and loses power when it is compressed beyond a certain point. "What can we *add* to gasoline which will control the combustion rate as compression is raised?" asked automotive science. After years of research

it was found that Ethyl flui containing tetraethyl lea was the answer. Leading o companies add it to their gasoline form Ethyl Gasoline, which improv the performance of any car. Sta riding with Ethyl today and see f yourself the big difference it makes.

Ethyl Gasoline Corporation, 2 Broadway, New York City; 56 Chur Street, Toronto, Can.; 36 Queen Anne Gate, London, England.

ETHYL
GASOLINE

6.2   Ethyl Gasoline Advertisement, *Maclean's*, 15 July 1929. Copyright Ethyl Gasoline Corporation, 1929, used with permission of owner.

A joke printed in a 1926 issue of *Maclean's* revealed a popular connection between flappers and cars. It went:

Mary: "Why do you call your car 'Flapper'?"
Elmer: "Streamline body, swell paint job, quick pick-up, all kinds of speed, keeps me broke, warms up quick, and is always ready to go."[18]

The association between flappers and cars, the shape of their body, and paint (as a process of female beautification) was not unique to this joke. Advertisements, like those for the De Soto Six, made parallel suggestions.[19] Speaking at the Art Gallery of Toronto (later the Art Gallery of Ontario) in 1929, Toronto architect John M. Lyle quoted Willys-Overland president John North Willys as saying: "To find a wide market, a car must be mechanically sound, but that is not enough. It must be beautiful."[20] How the car functioned was secondary to its style. In a similar fashion, modern movie patrons demanded "gloss and finish" but also "swift-moving drama, mechanical perfection, youth and beauty."[21] Through a variety of popular cultural media, women's bodies and machines were linked with each other and with modernity.

In regards to cars and movies, women were singled out as primary consumers and also as targets for making the technology seem safe and exciting. In film serials directed towards women, the stories helped to prepare viewers for changes and suggested that women "should be prepared to accept and learn about technological change."[22] In a similar way cars promised women ease and safety by accentuating features like "smooth as velvet" brakes, a "big and powerful engine," and easy steering.[23] Advertisements sometimes featured pictures of dashboards with descriptions of how the different instruments worked along with detailed explanations. For example, "You easily depress the small lever (A) at the left – and the velvety-powered Haynes engine with its dependable force and strength in reserve is in motion softly humming in readiness to propel your new series Haynes."[24] The description emphasizes what the driver will see, hear, and feel as a way to ready them for the physical and sensory experience of driving. Moreover, copywriters often made the experience of being in – rather than owning – a car paramount. In marketing automobiles to women, advertisers quoted other female drivers as stating, "The joy I get out of motoring is in having a peppy, responsive engine, " and "Long, low, racy ... just the kind of car I was sure would do the most thrilling things, quite easily."[25] The car also came equipped with "Lovejoy Shock Absorbers." Cars, like their theatrical counterpart, became a space for adventure, excitement, and quite possibly a private space for sex. The elision of differences between representations of machines and modern women's bodies was a significant aspect of feminine modernity. Women's bodies were represented in cityscapes as modern machines. If women had long been associated with and even embedded in landscapes, the impulse of feminine modernities was a far more urban representation.[26] Interlocking discourses of speed, progress, efficiency, youth, and beauty further brought together modern women's bodies, cars, and movies with the theme of desire and want for both bodies and goods.

Time, technology, and the bodily experience of speed and pleasure connect cars, moving pictures, and the modern visual economy. Historian Kristin Ross writing on post-World War II France argues that film and cars "reinforced each other. Their shared qualities – movement, image, mechanization, and standardization – made movies and cars key commodity-vehicles of a complete transformation in European consumption patterns and cultural habits. Much of that transformation involved a change in perception – a change in the way things were *seen*."[27] Women's bodies were also central to this project. They connected inanimate goods to embodied needs and desires in consumers, and films, in particular, broadcast the look of femininities. With movies and cars, the relationship between women's bodies and modernity articulated a concern over the increasing speed of life and modern change. As one car advertisement told readers, "The busy world of today pays homage to the motor car."[28] The 1928 Annual Report of the Ontario Board of Censors declared that film "was the greatest advertising power in the world."[29] Movies and cars broadcast styles of bodies and fashions to be emulated, showed changes in behaviour, and kept up with the quick-paced cycles of change and consumption. Movies were especially significant in exposing a wide audience to popular fads and fashions. Popular film critics even credited the power of films with how women behaved in public and participated in beauty contests. A particular concern of film was that borders between fiction and reality seemed to be repeatedly crossed with the encouragement of fantasy and desire. The magazine *Hush* made an effort to dispel Hollywood love scenes by reporting on how actors made scenes so real when in fact "film love is just cold-blooded acting."[30] In Canada in the 1920s, continuous motion was very much a part of the problem with movies and film culture, and efforts were made to slow the speed of change. It is of little wonder then that the Modern Girl – herself an embodiment of perpetual motion – came to be a central figure. She appeared frequently in car advertisements along with friends who were motoring for fun and adventure, and cars were frequently described in similar terms to Modern Girls and their apparel. Advertisers promised cars that had "the streamline effect of the body," "conspicuous good looks," "long, graceful lines," and "slender profile."[31]

Film, Car, Body: Practicalities

In the 1920s, magazines and newspapers were inundated with advertisements for automobiles. For those who could afford them, cars freed people from spatial limits and provided the potential for new and exciting experiences. Road trips to more remote locales became a possibility, motoring became a high-speed pastime, and cars became a private space for sexual experimentation among youth. In short, cars represented freedom, desire, and escape for those who purchased them.[32] Driving a car promised excitement and adventure, and these possibilities were often directed towards women, especially young, middle-class women. Yet, despite the decreasing prices for automobiles and the increasing numbers of them – by the end of the twenties there were over one million automobiles registered in Canada – they remained beyond the means of many Canadian families.[33]

What cars provided for the select, movies gave to a much wider audience. Films provided a literal and imaginative escape from home, work, school, and the street for a small charge. They gave ticket-holders the possibility to see foreign places, travel back or ahead in time, and imagine themselves in a variety of exciting dramatic or comedic situations.[34] Like cars, theatres provided a dark, quasi-private space for dating rituals.

One young man recalled that in the twenties, young men "needed a car to make it with girls."[35] One of the more troubling aspects of the modern age was the change in courting practices that moved away from adult chaperoned places to automobiles, movies, and other commercial recreation spaces. Like movies, much of what cars and their advertisements sold was fantasy. While traditions were changing, familial and community control, the expectation of marriage, and strictures against teen pregnancy worked to ensure that the new morality was tempered with traditional values.[36] Cars might have promise freedom, but as Lori Chambers' research reveals, they were also sites of rape and terror.[37] The unease surrounding cars and movies had people crying out for regulation.

Critics of films remained concerned about the appropriateness of movies and the erotic initiative of patrons, especially women. V.S. Patriarche commented,

In discussing the Cinema one need not confine one's self to the films; and there are other things at fault besides those pictures which are banal, vulgar or objectionable. There are the patrons, the theatres, and the reviewers. The embracing lovers, the morons unable to appreciate anything but the crudest thrills, hypocritical older men and – more often – women who patronize pornography and profess not to have understood the meaning of it, and parents who see a sex play on Friday and imagine some divine dispensation makes it suitable for their children on Saturday because they can get in for a dime![38]

An anonymous *Hush* columnist of modest means reported how university co-eds were corrupting him. In his column "Petting among the Highbrows," he told readers about the inner world of young, upper-class women in higher education. Week after week, "Junior" reported about the escapades that young women took him on. On one occasion a young woman named Ellen took him to a movie theatre and told him "You've got to learn about making love in the movie-houses if you are ever going to get anywhere." Of the experience, he reported to readers that "It was a surprise to me to find out how much petting you could do in a couple of theatre seats and how much was always going on. Ellen pointed out a few couples to me. Some of it was raw enough to make me blush but it didn't seem to bother her."[39] If movies lured young men and boys to violent action, people worried that for young women and girls, the moral cost of films was sexual activity and potentially the spread of venereal disease.

Indeed, venereal disease was an important concern for Canadians in the 1920s. Although concern over the sexual health of the nation originated in the nineteenth century, the occurrence of World War I brought the issue to the forefront.[40] By 1917, the National Council of Women pressed the federal government for a nation-wide campaign to study and control sexually-transmitted diseases.[41] By the end of the war, the social hygiene movement was emerging with force and began to encourage education as a means to combat the spread of venereal disease. On 11 April 1919, the federal government established the Department of Health with one of its ten divisions focused on venereal disease. Sex education was introduced in schools in the 1920s, and government-produced pamphlets were printed and distributed to the public.[42]

A lengthy pamphlet published in Canada by the Canadian Social Hygiene Council warned young women to avoid accepting dates from "chance acquaintances," to ride in cars or go to movies. These types of dates were offered with "the intention of leading them [young women] into sex relations."[43] According to prominent social hygiene lecturer

Arthur Beall, part of what made the environment so conducive to the spread of sexually transmitted diseases was the morally impairing influence of suggestive movies.[44] In addition to the cry to clean up the movies and regulate the images that were available to youth, the government screened educational movies about venereal disease. In the 1910s, the Ontario Board of Censors rejected movies about venereal diseases like the unsubtly-titled *Damaged Goods*.[45] But by the 1920s, such movies were exhibited as long as they met certain restrictions. Similar movies like *End of the Road* and *Open Your Eyes* were shown under the supervision of the Canadian National Council for Combating Venereal Diseases, restricted to audiences sixteen years and up, and with separate screenings for men and women.[46]

Other very real dangers existed, and newspapers were also filled with stories of automobile crashes that killed people and destroyed property. The Ontario Department of Highways advertised the possibilities for tourism and recreation that cars provided, but gave warnings about the necessity of good driving. One advertisement stated, "when you go out into the country to refresh body and mind by feasting your eyes on autumn tints, remember you owe it to yourself and to others on the road to show common sense and courtesy in driving."[47] In response to various road traffic problems, the government installed traffic signals, regulated parking, altered street patterns, had police apprehend speeders, and called for the "re-education" of pedestrians in order to stop "reckless walking."[48]

In a similar manner, individuals and groups decried the popularity of moving pictures, and pointed to a variety of related social, cultural, and physical dangers. Motion pictures tended to glorify heterosexual relationships, romance, leisure, and conspicuous consumption. Critics alleged that Canadians, especially young women, were trying to reproduce the magic of the screen in their lives. This took many forms, from mimicking a starlet's particular look or behaviour to desiring her entire life. Newspapers reported on girls running away from home in search of the love, adventure, and lifestyle that was depicted on the silver screen. In 1920, two Chatham, Ontario girls fled their homes and crossed into the United States, allegedly following one girl's actress sister in an attempt to appear in movies.[49] This was no anomaly. Beginning as early as 1914 and becoming an extensive "problem" in the 1920s was the number of "movie struck girls" who had left their homes for Hollywood studios. More generally, in 1928, *Hush* reported that two thousand women fled to New York City every year. The article suggested the reason was a dangerous mix of unemployment, bad homes, and a deep desire to have one's picture in the newspaper. Critics were concerned that for the most susceptible, young, working-class women, this might lead to a flawed character and higher expectations.[50] Articles in *Chatelaine* and *The Woman Worker* warned of lonely working girls in the city who attended movies and became prey of men cashing in on the discrepancy between the realities of their lives and what they watched on the screen. The author of the *Chatelaine* article also warned that movie tickets were used to lure young women into prostitution.[51] Certainly, many films encouraged a fantasy life that broke away from traditional models of home, work, and family. The burgeoning star system of the 1920s created myths of actresses' lives that mimicked screen roles, adding to the believability of the fantasy. Further, advertising and cosmetic companies sold "star secrets" in products that promised to provide consumers with a little bit of that star's glamour.[52] Movies provided an escape both literally and imaginatively from everyday existence, and they created a fantasy that had the potential to lure people into dressing, acting, and consuming differently.

Popular film genres appealed to women's fantasies and, in the moral panics of the 1920s, this allure had dangerous associations. The discourse of women running away, lured by popular culture, and duped by media, suggested that they were dangerously susceptible to the image and could not differentiate between real life and fantasy. Member of Parliament P.F. Casgrain noted the potential for disruption in 1920. Addressing the House of Commons he stated,

> Another point I want to make against these moving picture institutions is that they are responsible, in Montreal, Quebec and other large cities for a great deal of evil that is being committed. In many cases a moving picture show is a common rendezvous for a certain class of people who want to hide themselves ... The pictures that are exhibited are suggestive, and in some cases they lead to very bad results. They are an invitation to the people of the poorer classes to revolt, and they bring disorder into the country.[53]

In fighting against Hollywood, provincial governments tried to use film to both spread a counter-message and censor Hollywood films. At a meeting of provincial censors in 1921, representatives from six provinces declared that these types of themes did not conform to Canadian standards of family life.[54] In fact, government initiatives in Canadian filmmaking in the 1920s have frequently been seen as attempts at cultural nationalism. They were also a way to intervene and undercut female spectator's power and erotic choice, as government filmmakers used them to spread wholesome, if condescending and paternalistic messages about women's bodies and their value to the state.[55] If women were understood to be highly susceptible to the power of the image and the lures of consumer culture, working-class women were seen to be even more at risk. In part, this would seem to lie in the belief that they had more to escape from and a deeper desire to do so.

The link between cars and film goes beyond similarities in the use of space, entertainment, the calls for regulation, and the negotiation of class tensions. Both technologies appeared in the mid-1890s, became markers of modern life, and changed how people perceived social and cultural landscapes and bodies themselves. Movies and automobiles were often singled out as special symbols of modern life, particularly the negative aspects: quick-paced, thrill-seeking, and reckless. Moving pictures represented "life as a wild succession of hair-breadth escapes, thrilling feats, erratic adventures, and give the youth of the present day a weariness and distaste for the monotonous routine of well-ordered existence." In regard to cars, the *Catholic Register* warned that "the craze for speed, which has its vent in the driving of high-powered motor-cars at a reckless pace" symbolized youth's "unhealthy" and "abnormal" preoccupation with perpetual fun.[56] Coming into a continual stream of new movies and objects for consumption, youth were singled out as the modern generation, as consumers, and as leaders of mass cultural movements. Movies were directed towards an increasingly culturally powerful generation of youth, and cars tapped into the widespread discourse on the desire to be young. One advertisement described their product as "a creation that embodies the vibrant spirit of youth, a car that fairly breathes life and vigor and confident class."[57] The car being advertised was the Haynes Special Speedster and the woman behind the wheel was a Modern Girl. Like women's bodies, cars and movies changed drastically in a matter of a few decades. One contemporary noted, "Films, once crude, halting, episodic, have become finished, smooth-flowing and closely knit."[58] Surfaces of all kinds were smoothed over.

Producing New Starlets for Consumption

The movie and advertising industries both perpetuated and capitalized on the discourses of a fast-moving, commodity-fetishizing society interlaced with the Modern Girl's body. The 1927 Miss Vancouver contest organized by the Canadian Legion employed an interesting advertising strategy. Full page adverts were taken out that publicized the contest, the contestants, and the sponsors. They managed this by associating individual sponsors' goods with a particular contestant. The result was an ambiguity between bodies and products. Take, for example, the advert for Stevenson's Bread. Like all of the adverts, one of the contestant's portrait photographs appears at the top; underneath is the slogan "When Health and Beauty Reign Supreme." The sophistication of this advertising strategy was that the slogan could be equally applied to the contestant and the bread, eliding the differences between a body (a fine example of health and beauty) and a particular good (promising health and beauty). An advert for Auburn Cars declared: "The last word in style and smooth-running facility."[59]

In general, the divide between reality and fiction and bodies and goods was certainly fuzzy, as film companies offered opportunities that wove together fantasy, consumerism, and reality in the search for new starlets. Such a search was rendered a necessity by an increasing volume of interest in idealized women's bodies. Not only did some women desire being in the movies, but movies in turn needed fresh faces for audiences hungry for new films and goods. Industry leaders used both sides of this appeal to provide tangible opportunities for "ordinary" women to turn into starlets, and worked to make the fantasy of being "discovered" seem like a real possibility. As discussed in chapter 3, beauty contests reveal important messages about bodily standards for beauty and regimes of corporeal care. Beauty contests also connected women's bodies, movies, and cars, and this section reveals the intimacies and intricacies of this connection. Stories of "discovered" starlets made it seem possible that almost any woman could be discovered if the right opportunity presented itself; or, perhaps more accurately, a woman presented herself to be judged. This created a perfect storm for using beauty contests as a means of finding new talent. If Hollywood beamed images of the Modern Girl across the globe in the beginning of what would soon become American cultural dominance in film, Hollywood executives were also keen to use other national markets in an attempt to find the next star or "It" girl, and firm up the complex web of commodity culture.

One such case occurred in 1923 when international film star Rudolph Valentino hosted North American-wide beauty contests sponsored by Mineralva beauty clay. In the early 1920s, Valentino's career was temporarily hindered because of a quarrel with the studio that owned his rights. In 1922 he left Famous Players, and the studio sued him for breach of contract and obtained an injunction stopping him from making films or

6.3   Detail of advertisement for Miss Vancouver 1927 contest, *Vancouver Sun*, 23 May 1927.

appearing on stage.[60] The difficulties Valentino was experiencing in his career were further complicated by the problems in his personal life. In March 1922 Valentino divorced Jean Acker and in May married Natacha Rambova. Unfortunately, the decree for his divorce stated that the separation from Acker would not become final for one year, and Valentino was subsequently arrested for bigamy.[61] Under severe financial constraints and fearing being forgotten by the public, Valentino entertained other options. In an effort to gain funds and spend time with Rambova, Valentino agreed to host beauty competitions with the beauty company Mineralava. In return for seven thousand dollars a week, the couple would give free dance performances, and Valentino would give a short talk discussing how Mineralava beauty clay gave Rambova a lovely complexion.[62]

For seventeen weeks Valentino and Rambova toured eighty-eight cities in North America dancing the tango and judging local beauty contests. The tour was wildly successful. In part, this was because of Valentino's success as a film star and, as an additional enticement, advertisements stated that the winner of the contest would star opposite Valentino in his next film.[63] In Toronto, the Arena theatre hosted the dancing couple and beauty contest on 16 April 1923. The day of the contest, Toronto newspapers carried large advertisements stating that both Valentino and his wife used Mineralava: "In this day and age no man is ashamed to borrow a suggestion from a woman..Mr. Valentino noticed his wife's purity of complexion and learned she made a daily habit of using MINERALAVA BEAUTY CLAY." The advertisement quoted Valentino as saying he would "insist that they [Valentino and Rambova] keep their skin perfection by the constant use of MINERALAVA."[64] Such an endorsement also speaks to Valentino's rather unique position as an embodiment of modern masculinity. In some ways, taking consumer-related beauty advice from his wife fit the dominant mode of modern woman as consumer and beauty care expert. However, the production of Valentino's body, with the sense of sexual ambiguity, certainly complicates this picture.

After touring around North America and choosing preliminary winners, the contestants gathered for the final competition at Madison Square Garden. Even with tickets priced from one to five dollars per seat the show sold out.[65] The winner was Norma Niblock of Toronto. Returning to Toronto after her win, Niblock made a number of appearances at the Murray-Kay store, and was billed as "Toronto's Own Beauty" in a special attraction at the King Edward Hotel.[66] In December, Niblock was selected by the Shriners in order to participate in the Oriental pageant for their fundraising circus.[67] In the end, however, Niblock never starred in a movie with Rudolph Valentino, although as part of the top sixteen women in the New York contest, she was offered theatrical engagements with the B.F. Keith Vaudeville Exchange.[68]

Valentino's decision to choose Niblock garnered more press attention than Niblock herself. After announcing the winner, Valentino told the press he picked her because she did not wear make-up. A *New York Times* editorial pointed out how winning beauty contestants tread the line between "old-fashioned notions" and the new trend of women showing their "feminine delicacies" in public competitions. The saving grace of the pageant was that Niblock, who won the contest, was unpainted. When the *Globe* proudly reported the Canadian's win on the front page of the newspaper, the article stated that Niblock used no beauty preparations or make-up.[69] According to the *New York Times*, the "old-fashioned person" could find satisfaction in the fact that "the winner of the first prize was a girl who confronted her judges with her charms unassisted by any touch of paint or powder!"[70] Niblock was not the only winner of a beauty contest to be selected on this accord, and Canadian newspapers often thought it was newsworthy when any unpainted winner was chosen.[71] The problem, of course, was that this contest was sponsored by Mineralava beauty products, so Valentino's choice and reasoning of a winner were troublesome for company intent on selling beauty aids. Indeed, part of Niblock's responsibilities as the winner was to appear in advertising campaigns for the product, but the problem was lessened by a touch of advertising genius: Mineralava enhanced natural beauty, but did not give the look of a painted face. In advertisements that appeared immediately after Niblock's win, the copy stated that the beauty aid improved natural beauty so that cosmetics did not have to be used. The advertisement under the banner "How I won the Mineralava Valentino Beauty Contest" stated,

> We asked Miss Norma Niblock to what she ascribed her recent success –
> Here is her reply: 'Last winter after I was chosen winner at the Arena I
> started using Mineralava and I found that after a few applications it kept
> my skin so clear and full of natural color that I did not have to use cosmetics and they say that was largely why I won. I use Mineralava regularly now
> of course for I find it keeps the pores wonderfully healthy and clean and
> makes my skin softer and more radiant than it has even been before.'[72]

Perhaps the most significant aspect of Valentino's contest was that it was filmed and released as a short movie.[73] The filming of the contest extended its life beyond a single moment, but more importantly, it broadcast ordinary women in an extraordinary situation. It also allowed more men and women to participate in consuming the images of beauty contests and become their own judges of beauty. The film also deliberately raised anxieties. In an obviously rigged scene, one contestant is caught flirting with an organizer, thus revealing the tensions of the Modern Girl and modern heterosexuality. In car adverts, for example, heterosexuality was carefully controlled: cool, clean, and contained. In the film, however, the scene played into concerns over the seduction of a star-struck young woman in search of a modern fantasy. If beauty contestants were physically compared to showgirls in the 1927 Miss Canada contest in Vancouver, pageants themselves shared other more dangerous associations with theatres and women working on stage.[74]

The lure of Hollywood was also formalized through commercial beauty contests. The Miss Canada competition held in Vancouver in 1927 was sponsored by Famous Players Lasky, and was, in reality, a talent search for potential starlets. For the contest, western cities including Winnipeg, Brandon, Regina, Saskatoon, Moose Jaw, Calgary, Edmonton, Nanaimo, Nelson, and Victoria held preliminary competitions. In late April and early May preliminary winners competed at a local Vancouver theatre for the title of Miss Canada, as well as prizes including a screen test in Los Angeles and a chance to compete at the International Pulchritude Contest in Galveston, Texas.[75] In eastern Canada, though mostly Ontario-based, pageants were also held in June with the final competition for Miss Ontario happening in early July 1927. In Ontario, the contest was not called a beauty contest, but rather a "screen opportunity contest" with the winners being promised a trip to Hollywood and a screen test, as well as a car (for both the winner and the first runner-up), money, clothing, a silver cup, and toiletries. The second place winner was promised an Overland Whippet Four Special Sport Roadster, and cash prizes for third to sixth places varied from fifty to two hundred dollars, certainly significant amounts of money. Women who placed highly in the results were rewarded with prizes intimately associated with living the idealized life of the Modern Girl, and with their winnings, the possibility of embodying her image could be more fully realized.[76]

The preliminary contests in Ontario were held in conjunction with MGM's film *Tillie the Toiler* starring Marion Davies. Based on the popular comic strip, Tillie was a Modern Girl who, like many young women by the twenties, experienced a period of paid work between school and marriage. Tillie, however, spent far less time working than trying to land a wealthy, if somewhat lecherous, husband. Fashionably dressed with an innocence that took "years to acquire," Tillie was exactly the young, modern station-climber that middle-class reformers feared. A *New York Times* review described the plot: "Tillie's toil consists of putting one piece of paper into a typewriter, after which she concentrates her efforts on capturing the attention of a millionaire named Pennington Fish, familiarly known as 'Penny' Fish."[77] *Tillie*, it should be noted, was not an entirely unique story line. Many films from the time depicted working women in ways that helped create a specific persona subsequently appealed to in film-industry sponsored beauty contests. While many young women worked and turned over pay packets or portions of them to their parents, working girls on film were generally free of such constraints. Working girls were beautiful heroines rewarded with rich husbands and comfortable lifestyles. Although Tillie did not compete in a beauty contest, she did embody the onscreen desires of young working women who were targeted by Famous Players Lasky as potential starlets, and the beauty contest was an ideal way to simultaneously garner publicity, boost audience numbers, and possibly find a new star.

Tillie the Toiler was part of one popular femininized narrative trope filmmakers drew upon in the 1920s. Focusing on young, modern working women, films had wild storylines rooted in just enough familiarity to allow women to connect to them and daydream about the possibility of casting off factory work and a shabby room for the promise of a more comfortable middle-class lifestyle facilitated by marriage. "The movie Moderns" were promoted in conjunction with a powerful system of starlets whose appearances beyond the silver screen (often in advertisements) blurred the lines between reality and fiction. Fan magazines and publicity released by film companies often highlighted stars' huge salaries, beauty, and seeming sexual freedom in being able to marry – sometimes multiple times – while still working in their glamorous careers.[78]

Tillie's comic strip cohort, Winnie Winkle, a stenographer in pursuit of a more glamorous lifestyle, did enter and win a beauty contest for the title of "Miss Movie Queen" in a series of strips published in 1927. After winning, Winnie Winkle's father points out the discrepancy between her public persona, which is depicted as both modern and traditional, and Winnie's actual Modern Girl lifestyle. Her father laughs at pictures highlighting Winnie's domestic skills like cooking and sewing as well as her resting on the couch reading a dictionary. He declares, "I should'a give you a pair of my socks to sew for that picture!! But that photo of you layin' on th' couch eatin' candy would be netcherl, if y'didn't have the book in yer hand!!"[79] The cartoon eschewed the typical beauty contest

discourse of the Modern Girl, who was still attracted to "traditional" domestic women's roles, and suggested it was farcical. Winnie clearly knew
what game she was supposed to be playing to appeal to the public. As
such, the cartoon undercut the discourse of the duped young star-struck
woman being taken advantage of, and challenged it with a conniving
one. Examining the western Miss Canada competition in 1927 allows us
to gauge how women may have balanced these competing discourses.
Moreover, the limited but exceptional evidence left by one contestant
situated in the wider context of the pageants allows an obscured look at
how a young, Canadian woman negotiated her body, the sexing of things,
movie and advertising industries, and her own desires.

In the spring of 1927, while the Miss Ottawa and similar pageants were
being held, cities in the western provinces were holding their own preliminary beauty contests for the Miss Canada title. After the city winners
were chosen, a train called the Miss Canada Special made the journey
from Winnipeg to Vancouver and picked up the local contestants along
the way. The organizers ensured that the Miss Canada pageant was an
unprecedented publicity event. Edith Grant, Miss Regina, recalls that
when she departed from Regina on the Miss Canada Special in May
1927, over two thousand people came to see her off. According to Grant,
the popularity of the contest in Regina was matched in other cities. She
recalled, "and every city was the same. There was just a mob to meet us
and they had to fight us you know through the crowd, you know, to the
hotel."[80] Even at one thirty in the morning, over one thousand citizens of
Moose Jaw showed up to send off their local contestant.

The organizers made efforts to avoid negative publicity on the cross-
country trip by ensuring the women were chaperoned by one of the
band members of the Winnipeg Capitolians, Earle Hill, and his wife.
Local contests ensured that chaperones watched carefully over their
charges and this fact was well publicized. Official rules of the local contests included that "Contestants will be in direct charge of their official
chaperone and must abide by her decision at all times. This rule will be
strictly enforced."[81] Like the Hills, chaperones often included women
who had some professional connection to the entertainment industry,
which was a problem. Miss Victoria 1927's chaperone, Eileen Allwod,
was a "stage star," while Miss Canada 1927's chaperone was Leila Auger
Thomas, Principal of the Famous Players School of Music and Allied
Arts. Photographs of each of these women appeared in local newspapers revealing their more mature look, but some audience members
must have been suspicious about the respectability of such chaperones.

Despite the rules, Edith Grant recalled that the contestants were not always happy about their strict schedules and sometimes tried to give their chaperones the slip. At one stop on the way from Winnipeg to Vancouver, a few of the contestants decided to enjoy the local nightlife. They were caught leaving the hotel, and after that the Western Manager of Famous Players-Lasky and others took turns sitting outside the elevator to ensure that none of the women could sneak out during the night.[82]

At every stop, the increasing throng of potential Miss Canadas would make three appearances a day at the local theatre. Once they arrived in Vancouver the contestants would make nightly appearances in the local Capitol theatre so that the voting audiences could get a good look at them before deciding who should be Miss Canada. Since the winner was decided by popular vote there were concerns that Miss Vancouver had an unfair advantage. In an attempt assuage this fear, the Miss Vancouver contest was held simultaneously from preliminary district winners. Both Miss Canada and Miss Vancouver would compete in the International Pageant of Pulchritude. In the end, Miss Victoria Madeleine Woodman won Miss Canada and was accompanied by Miss Fraser, Eliza A. Dixon, who won the Miss Vancouver contest. The winning contestants were taken to Hollywood for screen tests. As part of their stay they also had lunch with two famous actresses: Fay Wray and Clara Bow.[83] Famous Players-Lasky thus got at least two benefits from the contest: at least a week of packed movie houses and possibly a new starlet. After their short stay in Hollywood the Canadian representatives made their way to Galveston, Texas for a much different pageant. The International Pageant of Pulchritude was held on the boardwalk and contestants were shown off on decorated floats. After her float of green and gold maple leaves passed in front of the judges, Miss Canada placed an impressive fifth out of more than fifty contestants. She won one hundred dollars. [84]

The women who placed in the Miss Canada competition were given a seven-week contract to appear nightly at various movie theatres in Western Canada. In addition, film was taken of the potential Miss Canadas from the time they arrived in Vancouver until the last days in Galveston. This film was then shown in local theatres in order to encourage patrons to pay again to see the bathing beauties. One newspaper reported that

> The girls who go to Galverston will become world famous as scores of camera men will be there to 'cover' the big spectacle from every angle and thousands of feet of film will be taken of every entrant ... These pictures

6.4 Group Photograph of Miss Canada Contestants in Victoria, BC. Detail from Gail (Edith) Grant's scrapbook from the 1927 Miss Regina and Miss Canada contests, Gail Grant Ryan Fonds, Dance Collection Danse. Credit: Courtesy of Dance Collection Danse.

will be seen by millions of people all over the world, besides undergoing the critical inspection of scores of movie magnates and directors who are always on the lookout to find a new type to exploit on the silver screen.[85]

The screen tests usually proved to be futile efforts and few beauty contests were signed to lasting contracts. As the *Victoria Times* wrote, "Beauty winners come and go, appear and disappear; they win places in the films, but try to remember one who held it for more than a few moments."[86]

In reacting to the anxiety over the contests, organizers attempted to tread the thin line of modern expectations, and in doing so, the beauty contestant became a hybrid of sorts who was frequently praised for maintaining traditional values. In this context, marriage and motherhood were sacrosanct. Potential beauty contestants had to be single in order to avoid any potential scandals in drawing married women away from their homes and children. As Carolyn Kitch argues in regards to the flapper, beauty contestants challenged the traditional roles of women for a brief period in her youth, but did not represent an overthrowing of the main goals for women as marriage and motherhood.[87] Amidst the media whirl around the Miss Victoria and Miss Canada contests in 1927, the *Victoria Daily Times* printed an article by American illustrator Haskell Coffin. Coffin, like a number of other American illustrators including Norman Rockwell and James Montgomery Flagg, had been a beauty contest judge. In the article Coffin discussed his standard of female beauty, arguing that beauty should be "natural," so he favoured long hair and a "youthful bloom" untainted by artificial aids and make-up. Moreover, what made a "real beauty" of the eventual winner of the unidentified contest he judged was that her ambition, unlike the other contestants who wanted to become movie stars, was "to get married and have five children." According to Coffin, this statement was accompanied by a "facial expression [that] reflected genuine feminine sweetness that most men, even modern ones, value. It gave a quality of real beauty to her."[88]

Although many of the young women entered in order to gain exposure and hopefully make their way into the sometimes-lucrative business of feature films or other entertainment-based careers, not all contestants were pleased at having been entered into the pageant. Beauty contests in the 1920s had an unusual structure in that women could be entered into them without their approval or even knowledge. Margaret Gorman, for example, who went on to win the first Miss America pageant, had no idea that her photograph had even been entered into the local contest until she was informed, while shooting marbles, that she had won.[89] At least one of the contestants from the 1927 Miss Canada pageant had a similar experience. Although Edith Grant had competed in the local pageant she did so with some reservations. Upon being notified that she had won, her response was "I don't want it. Give it to the next one."[90] The Capitol theatre owners Jack Hunter and Peter Egan had to go to her house and promise her that she could take ballet lessons while in Vancouver in order to convince her.[91] And, despite her hesitation to participate in the Miss Canada contest, Grant made and saved a scrapbook that included cut-out newspaper photographs of each contestant and their signatures. The other contestants wrote words of luck or encouragement, such as those from Winnifred Moffat, Miss Moose Jaw, who penned, "Hoping you will not forget your old friends when you become 'Miss Canada.'" Some even provided advice like that of Peggy Gold, Miss Nanaimo: "Love many –trust few *and* always paddle your own canoe."[92]

Ultimately, only the winners of the contests had the chance to become film stars, and none from Canada managed to make herself into a famous starlet. Nonetheless, the title of beauty queen did translate into

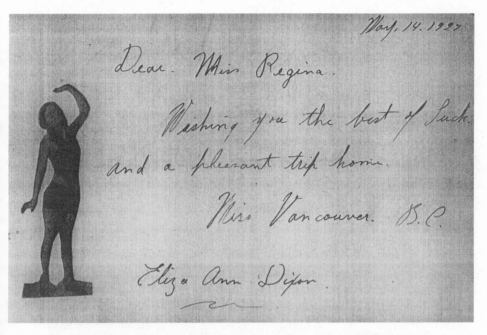

6.5   Eliza Ann Dixon, Miss Vancouver's note to Edith Grant, Miss Regina.
Detail from Gail (Edith) Grant's scrapbook from the 1927 Miss Regina and Miss
Canada contests, Gail Grant Ryan Fonds, Dance Collection Danse. Courtesy of
Dance Collection Danse.

work, even on a limited basis, for some women. The winner and the
runners-up often had theatre contracts until their names and bodies no
longer drew in crowds. Others who wanted to make their way into other
entertainment careers found their titles to be useful. Edith Grant found
that her title as Miss Regina did translate into increased opportunities
for her as a dancer. The Grant family struggled with the devastation of
droughts and recessions, and although jobs were difficult to come by,
Grant's success in the beauty contest allowed her to make daily, and more
importantly paid, appearances dancing in local movie theatres for fif-
teen dollars a week. Despite the grinding poverty surrounding her,
Grant survived throughout the 1930s by dancing, first in Winnipeg and
then in New York.[93] For as much as modern femininities were a reordering of patriarchal gender relations that put women in difficult to negotiate places, women's experiences like Grant's reveal that they did carefully
negotiate this complicated terrain – and sometimes to their advantage.

Conclusion: Projections and the Modern Girl

When Nick Caraway commented that he had seen quintessential Modern Girl Jordan Baker, he could have been referring specifically to Baker or to her look – one that was transmitted widely. The Modern Girl was a central feature in modern, urban culture because she existed in a complicated nexus of modern publicity machines that broadcast her body for a multitude of reasons. She made things modern as she gendered them, she attracted audiences, she consumed and was consumed. Commercial beauty contests, run by businesses and film distributing companies, recognized the powerful draw of the Modern Girl as they searched for new starlets – a perpetual pursuit given the hunger of audiences for someone new and the need to keep up with the ever increasing speed of modern life. Cars zooming down roads could be a metaphor for the quick pace of city life and cultural change. A letter from R.S. Peck, the Director of the Canadian Government Motion Picture Bureau, argued that motion pictures were more powerful than the press in delivering messages and moulding public tastes and opinions. Peck quoted a writer in *Kinematograph Weekly* who wrote, "It (the movie) leaps to the imagination instantly."[94] Moving pictures – and their own technological mirror image the car – did represent an important change in the modern world: the speed of modernity. Visually and metaphorically, moving pictures and cars symbolized the potential of the rapid succession of change not only technologically but also culturally and socially and at the centre was a particularly fashioned modern female body. Together, they helped provided spaces for fantasy, desire, and escape that were framed by discourses of gender and class, and because of the fantastical promises of freedom the Girl was seen as especially susceptible. Commercial beauty contests exploited these discourses as they compelled Modern Girls to participate in the spectacle. For Grant, the experience was marked with ambivalence. What wove together modern machines (cars, movies, publicity) was the promised a new way to experience the body – at top speed – and not about to slow down. Jean Graham's column "At Five O'Clock" announced on 25 August 1928: "The motor car is mediocre; the aeroplane is becoming commonplace; but the Goddard rocket hurling us through space of a week-end with the Martians is a real adventure. Of course, the rocket goes at a fairly fast rate; in fact, it may attain the velocity of seven miles per second, which ought to satisfy the most extravagant modern taste for speed."[95]

Conclusion:
Losing the Modern Girl

On 5 May 1927, *The Halifax Herald* announced: "Champions of the Modern Girl Lose." The previous night men in Antigonish had debated whether or not "the modern girl is preferable to the old-fashioned girl." None of the content of the debate was reported, although it was noted that "it is doubtful if the discussion of any subject in any similar previous contest provided so much genuine pleasure and entertainment as did the debate last evening." Half the article was devoted to describing the "girls on stage" – all seven of them attired as either Modern Girls or old-fashioned ones (and one has to wonder what exactly the latter looked like to the men of Antigonish in 1927). Apparently, they "presented a lovely picture."[1] In debating their preferences for the Modern Girl, men of Antigonish added their voices to wider cultural discussions and debates on her appearance. And how fitting that the Modern Girl be on display while men assessed and discussed her; how very modern indeed. In another circumstance, this could very well have been a less competitive cousin to the modern beauty contest.

From publicly sporting and applying make-up, to working girls' thoughtful "confessions" on the care and maintenance of their bodies, to beauty contestants, discussions of the Modern Girl were popular in English-Canada in the 1920s, as people tried to absorb the changes of feminine modernities. The body of the Modern Girl provided rich territory in which to try to understand both the literal changes in women's bodies and what they meant in the wider cultural context of urban, modern life. For Girls, however, the projects were as intimate as they were public. Creating, reproducing, and caring for the female body required time, energy, and money. The rewards could be remarkably simple: time spent taking care of oneself, the pleasure in knowing you looked beautiful, the ability to compete on the heterosexual scene where success meant marriage, and quite possibly a more secure future away from the poorly paid, demanding work of female labour and pink ghettos. Perhaps there was also some joy in knowing that as a shop girl you defined style, had youth to flaunt, and could feel change happening around you – change that seemed to revolve around your very being. Penalties were frequent and well broadcast, and Girls were not strangers to assault, attack, and violence, yet many continued to be Girls. For women they were certainly historical agents involved in self-selecting to make themselves modern and feminine, and in flaunting it by way of beauty contests or even just walking down the street. Certainly the latter was common, as commentators on the nude art scandal of 1927 liked to point out.

It is important to not only consider the debates, but also to read the evidence for why the image of the Modern Girl would have been one so enticing for women to occupy. In doing so, one must take the desires and motivations of the Modern Girl and how they were integral to feminine modernities seriously. This includes the lure of being modern, as well as the figurative place of the Modern Girl in debates and discussions of modernity. Another important element is taking the consumer force of working girls as a force. The shop girl and the beauty contestant were not merely flighty women taking on whims of whatever advertisers dealt them – not that such cultural pressures were insignificant. The Modern Girl was created from a far more complex constellation: changes in women's work, urban life, and mass consumerism, the formation of an influential youth culture, and of course women's own desires and initiative. Most certainly their lives were shaped by patriarchy in countless ways: from the jobs and wages available to them, to their experiences in criminal courts and social workers' offices, to the reception of their public performances of beauty, to the cultural script that encouraged them to change every part of their body and constantly survey themselves because others were watching. That women found opportunities – limited ones but opportunities nonetheless – to express their opinions, dress up, take care of themselves, take up public space, seize financial rewards by being modern, and demand pleasure and fun speaks to their resilience as well as their place in defining modern female subjectivity and modern femininities more broadly.

Although superficial, artificial, and made up (literally in some ways) of temporary performances, the Modern Girl represented significant changes in women's lives, the Canadian nation, and culture. Many forces challenged an older order: the force of consumerism; the influence of popular culture; the global incarnation of the Modern Girl that seemed at odds with antimodern, cultural nationalism of the period; and the influence of female, working girls culture (like movies and their erotic initiative). This was not simply a flight of fancy terminated by the end of the twenties. Even in the depths of the Depression in the 1930s, consumerism and women's production of a modern body did not dissolve.[2] Styles certainly changed and economic exigencies made clothing, mascara, or silk stockings very difficult goods to consume, but the production of feminine modernities remained, as did the expectations. On 6 April 1934 a starving, out-of-work young woman, Elizabeth McCrae, wrote to Prime Minister R.B. Bennett in a plea for assistance. Hungry and unwilling to compromise her respectability, she reported being turned down for jobs because of her shabby clothing: "many prospective employers just glanced at my attire and shook their heads and more times than I care to mention I was turned away without a trial."[3] Girls writing "confessions" to Sylvia Gray had noted the importance of appearance to securing work in the 1920s. Given the imperativeness of appearance in the culture of personality, this is not entirely surprising. Perhaps, then, investment in the body was neither artificial nor superfluous, but even if it was not connected to employment the fact that the message was there and that women took it up is enough to give it historical significance.

It would be difficult – if not impossible – to imagine the production of the modern body at any point in or after the 1920s without techniques of appearing facilitated by consumer goods. And that was complicated terrain. New disciplinary techniques, practices of consumption, and techniques of appearing produced a modern female body – or variations of it. These techniques and practices also represented more profound cultural change in how women were represented and what that meant for a culture caught in the tides of change. A sign of pleasure, a generation quickly going awry, a feminine threat to the established order, changes in practices of viewing, changes in the understanding of goods, changes in gender relations – all of these discourses helped in her production and the understanding of feminine modernities.

I'm left puzzling at the end of this story over a photograph of my maternal grandmother in Toronto in about 1926 dressed as a Modern Girl. It is the only photograph I have of her in her youth. She stands straight, looking away from the camera, wearing a shortened skirt, high heels, and fashionably bobbed hair. There are hints of make-up. The

7.1   Florence (Nan) Beeston and friend, Toronto, c. 1926.

photograph belies the fact that Florence Beeston did not live a life of gin, jazz, and motoring. Like many women of the decade, her biography reveals a complex web of relationships between family, work, and community. Yet, this photograph suggests that she could have been easily mistaken for "flaming youth." I return to the photograph frequently in the face of the often-repeated conclusion that the Modern Girl was simply a media representation and seemingly did not have a real existence, or that her existence does not require historical attention or deliberations on women's agency in shaping modernity in Canada. Where are the boundaries of existence in a modern world saturated with images? The Modern Girl came into being through the expressions of pleasure and anxiety, through women copying aspects of her look, through people believing she existed. As such, the boundaries of existence seem blurred and confused, rather than neatly divided between lived experience and prescription. Modern women's subjectivity was intimately connected to a culture that constantly used images of women's bodies to circulate ideas of modernities, racial and class hierarchies, discourses of age, ideas of surveillance, and discipline. Taken together with ideas of a feminine threat in pop and high culture, this was a dominant discourse of beauty that was fraught and politicized in many ways. To live as a modern woman was to live in connection with these images, almost regardless of whether or not they accurately reflected one's own lifestyle. Moreover, images of modern femininities were used to circulate, sell, and gender goods in ways that made them modern, safe, and desirable, so her body was embroidered throughout the fabric of modernities.

Women – thinking, savvy, sophisticated women – took on these images and they became essential parts of their identities as modern women. My grandmother was one of them. When I was a child she suffered a brain aneurism and catastrophic stroke. After weeks in the hospital she returned home, and eventually she and my grandfather moved from Toronto to Thunder Bay to be closer to my mother, who could help with her care. Right after the aneurism and stroke almost her entire functioning was compromised: walking, speech, and personal care. What came back did so slowly, and much of it not at all. She did not lose, however, her desire to put on make-up, and while she didn't remember what went where (she had blush on her eyes, lipstick on her cheeks, and eye shadow on her mouth) the compulsion to "put on her face" remained. I remember people expressing embarrassment over this – at how she put on her make-up and at why she would even try. They were embarrassed because "the real Nan" would never have wanted to appear in public like that – she was always so fastidious in her personal appearance. Maybe it was because I never really knew "the real Nan" or my memories of her were obscured by the child's eyes I had witnessed her through, but I've always been struck by this memory as it seemed, to me, to encapsulate her – a gentle tenacity, a beautiful grace, a compelling performance of twentieth-century beauty, a pleasure in consuming. Perhaps people were embarrassed because she tried, because putting makeup on such a compromised body seemed ridiculous. But such a perspective is deeply troubling. Her actions spoke to how deeply ingrained the performances of femininity were – and the phrase "putting on her face" reveals that. Additionally, it speaks to a more hurtful narrative that such performances do not belong to certain bodies. That Nan continued to put on make-up when she didn't know her own name reminds me of the significance of these performances of modern femininities: that they did, in fact, produce a body, that they were so naturalized by everyday practices as to appear banal and normal until suddenly they weren't, that they were delicate and ephemeral, and that they mattered to the women who performed them as well as those who witnessed them. My Nan knew Sylvia Horn – the Girl whose photograph opened this book. The night Sylvia died I went to her room to say my last goodbye. On her nightstand in the hospital was an expensive jar of face cream and as I kissed her cheek I smelled the distinct fragrance of Chanel.

Notes

Introduction

1 I've deliberately chosen the term popular culture over mass culture as the latter seems to imply a uniformity and has condescending overtones. The term popular culture is, to my mind, more respectful, despite the fact that it sometimes takes elements of democratization and agency too far. As Richard Ohmann notes, "neither term is adequate." See his *Selling Culture: Magazines, Markets, and Class at the Turn of the Century* (London and New York: Verso, 1998), 14.

2 Penny Tinkler and Cheryl Krasnick Warsh, "Feminine Modernity in Interwar Britain and North America: Corsets, Cars, and Cigarettes," *Journal of Women's History* 20, no. 3 (2008): 114.

3 The Modern Girl Around the World Research Group uses the Modern Girl as a heuristic device as well. They define it as: "'serving to find out or discover.' A heuristic device cannot be taken as a given a priori; rather, it emerges in and through the research process and possesses a future orientation." See The Modern Girl Around the World Research Group, "The Modern Girl as Heuristic Device: Collaboration, Connective Comparison, Multidirectional Citation," in *The Modern Girl Around the World: Consumption, Modernity, Globalization,* The Modern Girl Around the World Research Group (Alys Eve Weinbaum, Lynn M. Thomas, Priti Ramamurthy, Uta G. Poiger, Madeleine Y. Dong, and Tani E. Barlow), eds., (Durham and London: Duke University Press, 2008), 2.

4 For work on these important areas, see Cynthia Comacchio, *Nations Are Built of Babies: Saving Ontario's Mothers and Children, 1900–1940* (Montreal and Kingston: McGill-Queen's University Press, 1993); Katherine Arnup, *Education for Motherhood: Advice for Mothers in Twentieth-Century Canada*

(Toronto: University of Toronto Press, 1994); and Sarah A. Leavitt, *From Catharine Beecher to Martha Stewart: A Cultural History of Domestic Advice* (Chapel Hill and London: The University of North Carolina Press, 2002).

5 Sumiko Higashi, *Virgins, Vamps and Flappers: The American Silent Movie Heroine* (Montreal: Eden Press Women's Publications, Inc, 1978).

6 For the latter, see Ann Douglas, *Terrible Honesty: Mongrel Manhattan in the 1920s* (New York: Farrar, Straus, and Giroux, 1995).

7 Bryan Palmer, *Working Class Experience: The Rise and Reconstitution of Canadian Labour, 1800–1980* (Toronto: Butterworth, 1983); Suzanne Morton, *Ideal Surroundings: Domestic Life in a Working-Class Suburb in the 1920s* (Toronto: University of Toronto Press, 1995). For a response to Palmer, see Cynthia Wright, "'Feminine Trifles of Vast Importance': Writing Gender Into the History of Consumption," in *Gender Conflicts: New Essays in Women's History*, eds. Franca Iacovetta and Mariana Valverde (Toronto: University of Toronto Press, 1992), 237–8.

8 Jon Stratton, *The Desirable Body: Cultural Fetishism and the Erotics of Consumption* (Manchester: Manchester University Press, 1996), 25–58; and Liz Conor, *The Spectacular Modern Woman: Feminine Visibility in the 1920s* (Indianapolis: Indiana University Press, 2004), chapter 1.

9 "Imagined community" is, of course, from Benedict Anderson's well-used work that argues print culture forged a sense of community from largely disparate groups spread over a large geographical area and was central to the forging of modern nationalism. Benedict Anderson, *Imagined Communities: Reflections on the Origin and Spread of Nationalism* (London: Verso, 1983), 5–7.

10 Roland Marchand, *Advertising the American Dream: Making Way for Modernity, 1920–1940* (Berkeley: University of California Press, 1985). On the Canadian context, see Russell Johnston, *Selling Themselves: The Emergence of Canadian Advertising* (Toronto: University of Toronto Press, 2001).

11 The literature in these areas is significant. For key studies on workers, social reformers and mothers, see Joan Sangster, *Dreams of Equality: Women on the Canadian Left, 1920–1950* (Toronto: McClelland and Stewart, 1989) and her *Earning Respect: The Lives of Working Women in Small-Town Ontario, 1920–1960* (Toronto: University of Toronto Press, 1995); Linda Kealy, *Enlisting Women for the Cause: Women, Labour, and the Left in Canada, 1890–1920* (Toronto: University of Toronto Press, 1998); Morton, *Ideal Surroundings*; Mercedes Steedman, *Angles of the Workplace: Women and the Construction of Gender Relations in the Canadian Clothing Industry, 1890–1940* (Toronto: McClelland and Stewart, 1997); Comacchio, *Nations Are Built of Babies*; and Arnup, *Education for Motherhood*. On medicalization, see Wendy Mitchinson, *The*

Nature of Their Bodies: Women and Their Doctors in Victorian Canada (Toronto: University of Toronto Press, 1991); and James Opp, *The Lord for the Body: Religion, Medicine, and Protestant Faith Healing in Canada, 1880–1930* (Montreal and Kingston: McGill-Queen's University Press, 2007). On discourses of gender, class and sexuality, see Carolyn Strange, *Toronto's Girl Problem: The Perils and Pleasures of the City, 1880–1930* (Toronto: University of Toronto Press, 1995); Joy Parr, *The Gender of Breadwinners: Women, Men, and Change in Two Industrial Towns, 1880–1950* (Toronto: University of Toronto Press, 1990); and Mariana Valverde, *The Age of Light, Soap and Water: Moral Reform in English Canada, 1885–1925* (Toronto: University of Toronto Press, 1991).

12 See Wright "Feminine Trifles of Vast Importance;" Cynthia Comacchio, *The Dominion of Youth: Adolescence and the Making of Modern Canada, 1920 to 1950* (Waterloo, ON: Wilfrid Laurier University Press, 2006); and Donica Belisle, *Retail Nation: Department Stores and the Making of Modern Canada* (Vancouver: University of British Columbia Press, 2011).

13 I borrow this perspective from Adele Perry, *On the Edge of Empire: Gender, Race and the Making of British Columbia, 1849–1871* (Toronto: University of Toronto Press, 2001). Perry notes in particular the *Left History* debates of the 1990s.

14 Veronica Strong-Boag, *The New Day Recalled: Lives of Girls and Women in English-Canada, 1919–1939* (Toronto: Copp Clark Pitman, 1988).

15 Billie Melman, *Women and the Popular Imagination in the Twenties: Flappers and Nymphs* (London: Macmillan Press, 1988); Nancy Cott, *The Grounding of Modern Feminism* (New Have: Yale, 1997), especially chapter 5; Weinbaum, et al., *The Modern Girl Around the World.*

16 For an excellent overview see Kathleen Canning, *Gender History in Practice: Historical Perspectives on Bodies, Class, and Citizenship* (Ithaca: Cornell University Press, 2006), chapter 1.

17 Franca Iacovetta and Mariana Valverde, "Introduction" in *Gender Conflicts: New Essays in Women's History* (Toronto: University of Toronto Press, 1992), xii. This perspective was reflective of the fracturing of the category of "woman" that sparked heated debates in feminism in the 1980s and 1990s. At the centre, for historians, was often Joan Wallach Scott, *Gender and the Politics of History* (New York: Columbia University Press, 1988).

18 Strange, *Toronto's Girl Problem*, 3. For a comparable study on women in Vancouver see, Lindsey McMaster, *Working Girls in the West: Representations of Wage-Earning Women* (Vancouver: University of British Columbia Press, 2008).

19 Three influential works are Joan Jacobs Brumberg, *The Body Project: An Intimate History of American Girls* (New York: Random House, 1997); Valerie

Steele, *Fashion and Eroticism: Ideals of Feminine Beauty from the Victorian Era to the Jazz Age* (New York, Oxford University Press, 1985); and Kathy Peiss, *Hope in a Jar: The Making of America's Beauty Culture* (New York: Metropolitan Books, 1998).

20 For a more detailed overview of the field, see Jane Nicholas and Patrizia Gentile, "Contesting Bodies and Nation in Canadian History," in *Contesting Bodies and Nation in Canadian History* (Toronto: University of Toronto Press, 2013).

21 Canning, *Gender History in Practice*, 189.

22 Elizabeth Grosz, *Volatile Bodies: Toward a Corporeal Feminism* (Indianapolis: Indiana University Press, 1994), x; and Kathleen Canning, *Gender History in Practice: Historical Perspectives on Bodies, Class, and Citizenship* (Ithaca: Cornell University Press, 2006), 26.

23 Scott, *Gender and the Politics of History*.

24 Two classic examples from different generations are Betty Friedan, *The Feminine Mystique* (New York: W.W. Norton and Company, 2001 [1963]) and Naomi Wolf, *The Beauty Myth: How Images of Beauty are Used Against Women* (New York: Vintage, 1991).

25 Tinkler and Warsh, "Feminine Modernity in Interwar Britain and North America."

26 Conor, *The Spectacular Modern Woman*, 8.

27 Keith Walden, *Becoming Modern in Toronto: The Industrial Exhibition and the Shaping of a Late Victorian Culture* (Toronto: University of Toronto Press, 1997).

28 Karen Newman, "Directing Traffic: Subjects, Objects, and the Politics of Exchange," *Differences* 2, no. 2 (1990): 41–54.

29 On the politics of women's looks and the making of feminine modernities in a Western European context, see Mary Louise Roberts, *Civilization Without Sexes: Reconstructing Gender in Postwar France, 1917–1927* (New York: Columbia University Press, 1994); and Mila Ganeva, *Women in Weimar Fashion: Discourses and Displays in German Culture, 1918–1933* (Rochester: Camden House, 2008).

30 The Modern Girl Around the World Research Group, "The Modern Girl as Heuristic Device," 9–10.

31 See Roberts, *Civilization Without Sexes* and Priti Ramamurthy, "All-Consuming Nationalism: The Indian Modern Girl in the 1920s and 1930s," in *The Modern Girl around the World*, 147–173.

32 See The Modern Girl Around the World Research Group, "The Modern Girl as Heuristic Device," in *The Modern Girl Around the World*, 8–9.

33 A detailed discussion on this development can be found in Belisle, *Retail Nation*, chapter 1.

34 Walden, *Becoming Modern*, 333–4.
35 On Benjamin, see Susan Buck-Morss, *Dialectics of Seeing: Walter Benjamin and the Arcades Project* (Cambridge, MA: MIT Press, 1989).
36 Griselda Pollock, *Vision and Difference: Femininity, Feminism and the History of Art* (New York and London: Routledge, 1988), 67. In the Canadian context, see Cynthia Wright, "Rewriting the Modern: Reflections of Race, Nation, and the Death of a Department Store," *Histoire sociale/Social History* 33 no. 65 (2000): 153–67. For an introduction to the theoretical considerations, see Rita Felski, *The Gender of Modernity* (Cambridge, MA: Harvard University Press, 1995). For a reassessment of the debates, see Vanessa R. Schwartz, "Walter Benjamin for Historians" *American Historical Review* 106 no. 5 (December 2001): 1732–3.
37 See Cecilia Morgan, *"A Happy Holiday": English Canadians and Transatlantic Tourism, 1870–1930* (Toronto: University of Toronto Press, 2008), 19.
38 Walden's *Becoming Modern in Toronto*; Patricia Jasen's *Wild Things: Nature, Culture, and Tourism in Ontario, 1790–1914* (Toronto: University of Toronto Press, 1995); Cheryl Krasnick Warsh's "Smoke and Mirrors: Gender Representations in North American Tobacco and Alcohol Advertisements Before 1950," *Histoire sociale/Social History* 31, no. 62 (1999): 183–222; and Belisle's *Retail Nation* stand as exceptions. If popular Canadian textbooks are any measure, however, the narrative remains persistent.
39 The mythology around the Group of Seven and their work illustrates this point. See Peter Mellen, *The Group of Seven* (Toronto: McClelland and Stewart, 1970), 6–22; and John Herd Thompson with Allen Seager, *Canada 1922–1939: Decades of Discord* (Toronto: McClelland and Stewart, 1985), 163–5. See also Carl Berger, "The True North Strong and Free," in *Nationalism in Canada*, ed. Peter Russell (Toronto: McGraw-Hill Ryerson Ltd., 1966), 3–26; and Brian Osborne, "The Iconography of Nationhood in Canadian Art," in *The Iconography of Landscape: Essays on the Symbolic Representation, Design and Use of Past Environments*, ed. David Cosgrove and Stephen Daniels (Cambridge: Cambridge University Press, 1988), 162–78. For critical perspectives on the mythology and its place in historiography, see Lynda Jessup, "Bushwackers in the Gallery: Antimodernism and the Group of Seven," in *Antimodernism and the Artistic Experience*, ed. Lynda Jessup (Toronto: University of Toronto Press, 2001), 130–52; and Leslie Dawn, *National Visions, National Blindness: Canadian Art and Identities in the 1920s* (Vancouver: University of British Columbia Press, 2006).
40 See Paul Rutherford, "Made in America: The Problem of Mass Culture in Canada," in *The Beaver Bites Back: American Popular Culture in Canada*, eds. David H. Flaherty and Frank E. Manning (Montreal and Kingston:

McGill-Queen's University Press, 1993), 260–280; Maria Tippet, *Making Culture: English-Canadian Institutions and the Arts Before the Massey Commission* (Toronto: University of Toronto Press, 1990), 7–8; and Mary Vipond, "Canadian Nationalism and the Plight of Canadian Magazines in the 1920s," *Canadian Historical Review* 58, no. 1 (March 1977): 43–63.

41 Andreas Huyssen, *After the Great Divide: Modernism, Mass Culture, Postmodernism* (Bloomington and Indianapolis: Indiana University Press, 1986), chapter 3. Antimodernism, while at times appropriating aspects of female folk culture and promoted by women, remained comfortably masculine as an alleged return to authentic culture and a shift away from the superficiality and artificiality of modern, consumer culture. Antimodernism provided a haven in reassuring a proper gender order, in establishing the tamed yet wild landscape of retreat from an urban environment, and in providing the comforts of an imagined past facilitated by modern conveniences. See T.J. Jackson Lears, *No Place of Grace: Antimodernism and the Transformation of American Culture, 1880–1920* (Chicago: University of Chicago Press, 1981); and Ian McKay, *The Quest of the Folk: Antimodernism and Cultural Selection in Twentieth-Century Nova Scotia* (Montreal and Kingston: McGill-Queen's University Press, 1994).

42 Daniel Coleman, *White Civility: The Literary Project of English Canada* (Toronto: University of Toronto Press, 2008).

43 On the homefront reaction to human costs of modern warfare, see Ian Hugh Maclean Miller, *Our Glory and Our Grief: Torontonians and the Great War* (Toronto: University of Toronto Press, 2002), 38–49.

 In his seminal work on the Great War, myth, and modernity, Paul Fussell points out "the way the dynamics and iconography of the Great War have proved crucial political, rhetorical, and artistic determinants on subsequent life. At the same time the war was relying on inherited myth, it was generating new myth, and that myth is part of the fibre of our own lives." Paul Fussell, *The Great War and Modern Memory* (London: Oxford University Press, 1975), ix. Canadian intellectuals such as Frank Underhill participated in the mythmaking, but Vance argues that in the end it was ordinary Canadians who were responsible for the myth. Jonathan Vance, *Death So Noble: Memory, Meaning, and the First World War* (Vancouver: University of British Columbia Press, 1997), 7, 228–9. On Underhill, see Carl Berger, *The Writing of Canadian History: Aspects of English-Canadian Historical Writing since 1900*, 2nd ed. (Toronto: University of Toronto Press, 1986), chapter 3 especially 58–9.

44 Gail Cuthbert Brandt et al, *Canadian Women: A History*, (Toronto: Nelson, 2011), 164–9.

45 An In-Between [pseudo.]., "Ready-Made Youngsters: A Plea for the Younger Generation," *Chatelaine*, April 1928, 1. Comacchio, *The Dominion of Youth*, 39, 64.

46 Roberts, *Civilization without Sexes*; Melman, *Women and the Popular Imagination*; Mary Lynn Stewart, *Dressing the Modern Frenchwomen: Marketing Haute Couture, 1919–1939* (Baltimore: Johns Hopkins University Press, 2008); Cott, *The Grounding of Modern Feminism*; Miriam Silverberg, "The Modern Girl as Militant," in *Recreating Japanese Women, 1600–1945*, ed. Gail Bernstein, (Berkeley: University of California Press, 1991), 239–66; Conor, *The Spectacular Modern Woman*; Brigitte Søland, *Becoming Modern: Young Women and the Reconstruction of Womanhood in the 1920s* (Princeton and Oxford: Princeton University Press, 2000); and Weinbaum et al., *The Modern Girl Around the World*.

47 See Søland, *Becoming Modern*, 169–70. Important exceptions to note here in the English-Canadian literature are the works of Cheryl Krasnick Warsh and Donica Belisle. For an early example of a dismissal, see Mary Vipond, "The Image of Women in Mass Circulation Magazines in the 1920s," in *The Neglected Majority: Essays in Canadian Women's History*, Susan Mann Trofimenkoff and Alison Prentice, eds., (Toronto: McClelland and Stewart, 1977), 116–24. More recently, in regard to the lack of serious consideration, the newest edition of *Canadian Women: A History* provides these examples: "The 1920s has often been portrayed as a period during which young people asserted their independence and challenged the moral and social dictates of their parents. In reality, however, the lives of working-class daughters throughout Canada largely replicated those of their mothers." And: "Services provided by such organizations were regarded as essential in the 1920s in a society alarmed by the media image of the flapper – the girl who indulged in so-called immoral pursuits, such as drinking, smoking, wild dancing and party-going." The reduction of the flapper to a media-image, and the discussion of her existence only in regard to immorality and the problems of pleasure-seeking, casts this particular formulation of the Modern Girl as a spectre.

48 The frivolity and consumerism of the Modern Girl is often seen as at odds with feminism. Some of the concern stems from the second-wave feminist movement, which explicitly took on fashion and beauty as feminist problems. For an overview of the extensive literature, see Joanne Hollows, *Feminism, Femininity and Popular Culture* (Manchester: Manchester University Press, 2000), especially chapter 7.

49 David Monod, *Store Wars: Shopkeepers and the Culture of Mass Marketing, 1890–1939* (Toronto: University of Toronto Press, 1996), 115.

50 On this point of strength I'm indebted to Wendy Mitichinson's work on women's agency. See, for example, *The Nature of Their Bodies.*
51 Peter Baskerville, *A Silent Revolution? Gender and Wealth in English Canada, 1860–1930* (Montreal and Kingston: McGill-Queen's University Press, 2008).
52 Marchand, *Advertising the American Dream,* 13.
53 Conor, *The Spectacular Modern Woman,* 112.
54 I should note here that while I did use databases to aid in my research, the material gathered here is largely from reading the texts in full and not simply searching databases by keywords. On methodological issues with databases, see Ian Milligan, "Embracing the 'Big History' Shift: Social Historians and Digital History (or 'how I learned to stop worrying and love the n-gram')," unpublished paper.
55 See Johnston, *Selling Themselves*; Fraser Sutherland, *The Monthly Epic: A History of Canadian Magazines 1789–1989* (Markham, ON: Fitzhenry and Whiteside, 1989); Marjory Lang, *Women Who Made the News: Female Journalists in Canada, 1880–1945* (Montreal and Kingston: McGill-Queen's University Press, 1999); Valerie Korinek, *Roughing It In the Suburbs: Reading Chatelaine Magazine in the Fifties and Sixties* (Toronto: University of Toronto Press, 2000); Dean Irvine, *Editing Modernity: Women and Little-Magazine Cultures in Canada 1916–1956* (Toronto: University of Toronto Press, 2008); and Janice Fiamengo, *The Woman's Page: Journalism and Rhetoric in Early Canada* (Toronto: University of Toronto Press, 2008).
56 In the Canadian literature, see Korinek, *Roughing It in the Suburbs.* For American examples, see Jennifer Scanlon, *Inarticulate Longings: The Ladies' Home Journal, Gender and the Promise of Consumer Culture* (New York and London: Routledge, 1995); Richard Ohmann, *Selling Culture: Magazines, Markets, and the Class at the Turn of the Century* (London: Verso, 1998); Helen Damon-Moore, *Magazines for the Millions: Gender and Commerce in the Ladies' Home Journal and Saturday Evening Post, 1880–1910* (New York: State University of New York Press, 1994); and Tom Pendergast, *Creating the Modern Man: American Magazines and Consumer Culture, 1900–1950* (Columbia and London: University of Missouri Press, 2000).
57 Conor, *The Spectacular Modern Woman,* xiv–xv.
58 Carolyn Kay Steedman, *Landscape for a Good Woman,* (New Brunswick, NJ: Rutgers University Press, 1987), 22.
59 Valerie, "My Lady's Dressing Table," *Saturday Night* (20 March 1920).

1 Making a Modern Girl's Body

1 Gertrude S. Pringle, "Is the Flapper a Menace?" *Maclean's* (15 June 1922), 19.

2 There were women working in advertising, although their numbers remained far more limited. They often found themselves speaking to the alleged "woman's viewpoint." Systemic discrimination against women was apparent in the industry as women made less money than male counterparts and were often excluded from professional organizations. See Marchand, *Advertising the American Dream*, 33–5.

3 Donica Belisle, "Toward A Canadian Consumer History," *Labour/Le Travail* 52 (2003): 187. The classic text on the deception of consumer culture, which Belisle notes is also misogynistic, is Theodor W. Adorno and Max Horkheimer, "The Culture Industry: Enlightenment as Mass Deception," in *Dialectics of Enlightenment* (New York and London: Verso [1944], 1972), 120–67. For a critical perspective that challenges the negative view of consumption, see Huyssen, *After the Great Divide*.

4 Kathy Peiss, "Girls Lean Back Everywhere," in *The Modern Girl Around the World*, 347–53.

5 For an overview of the development of the field, see Canning, *Gender History in Practice*, 28–32. See also Maggie Andrews and Mary M. Talbot, "Introduction: Women in Consumer Culture," in *All the World and Her Husband: Women in Twentieth-Century Consumer Culture*, Maggie Andrews and Mary M. Talbot, eds., (London and New York: Cassell, 2000), 1–9.

6 Angela McRobbie, *Feminism and Youth Culture: From Jackie to Just Seventeen* (London: Macmillan, 1987) and Susan Bordo, *Unbearable Weight: Feminism, Western Culture, and the Body* (Berkeley: University of California Press, 1993).

7 Wright, "Feminine Trifles of Vast Importance".

8 Victoria de Grazia, "Introduction," in *The Sex of Things: Gender and Consumption in Historical Perspective*, Victoria de Grazia with Ellen Furlough, eds., (Berkeley: University of California Press, 1996), 4.

9 "Swift Cyclone of Elation Sweeps Down Town Region," *Globe*, November 8, 1918.

10 Mariana Valverde, "The Love of Finery: Fashion and the Fallen Woman in Nineteenth Century Social Discourse," *Victorian Studies* 32, no. 2 (Winter 1989): 185.

11 On regional variations, see Margaret Conrad and Alvin Finkel, *History of the Canadian Peoples: 1867 to the Present*, volume 2, 3rd edition (Toronto: Addison, Wesley, Longman, 2002): 91.

12 The statistics on Montreal are in reference to the city of Montreal and not the "Greater City" statistics of 1931. The later topped one million. John Herd Thompson with Allen Seager, *Canada, 1922–1939: Decades of Discord* (Toronto: McClelland and Stewart, 1986), 1–5.

13 Walden, *Becoming Modern in Toronto*, 224–5.

14 Conrad and Finkel, *History of the Canadian Peoples*, 132–137; Walden,
    Becoming Modern in Toronto, 225–6; and Morton, *Ideal Surroundings*.
15 Thompson with Seager, *Canada 1922–1939*, 6; Angus McLaren, *Our Own
    Master Race: Eugenics in Canada, 1885–1945* (Toronto: McClelland and
    Stewart, 1990); and Peter Ward, *White Canada Forever: Popular Attitudes and
    Public Policy Towards Orientals in British Columbia* (Montreal and Kingston:
    McGill-Queen's University Press, 1978).
16 Walden, *Becoming Modern in Toronto*, 84. For the shift from character to per-
    sonality see the classic essay by Warren I. Susman. "'Personality' and the
    Making of Twentieth-Century Culture," in *New Directions in American
    Intellectual History*, John Higham and Paul K. Conkin, eds., (Baltimore:
    Johns Hopkins University Press, 1979), 212–26.
17 Mariana Valverde, *The Age of Light, Soap and Water: Moral Reform in English-
    Canada, 1885–1925* (Toronto: McClelland and Stewart, 1991), chapter 6;
    and Margaret Little, *No Car, No Radio, No Liquor Permit The Moral Regulation
    of Single Mothers in Ontario, 1920–1997* (Don Mills: Oxford University Press,
    1998).
18 Tamara Myers, *Caught: Montreal's Modern Girls and the Law, 1869–1945*
    (Toronto: University of Toronto Press, 2006). See also, Strange, *Toronto's
    Girl Problem*; Joan Sangster, *Regulating Girls and Women: Sexuality, Family, and
    the Law in Ontario, 1920–1960* (Don Mills, ON: Oxford University Press,
    2001); and Comacchio, *The Dominion of Youth*.
19 Strange, *Toronto's Girl Problem*; Myers, *Caught*; McMaster, *Working Girls in the
    West*.
20 Lenore Davidoff and Catherine Hall, *Family Fortunes: Men and Women of the
    English Middle Class, 1780–1850* (London: Hutchinson, 1987); Andrews
    Talbot, "Introduction," in *All the World and Her Husband*, 3; and Rachel
    Bowlby, *Just Looking: Consumer Culture in Dreiser, Gissing, and Zola* (London:
    Methuen, 1985).
21 Wright, "'Feminine Trifles of Vast Importance,' 240; Belisle, *Retail Nation*,
    29–30. Home-made clothing in the nineteenth century also had connec-
    tions to mass production and consumption through the distribution of pat-
    terns and the changes in sewing machine technology of the 1850s. On the
    mass marketing of dress patterns to women in magazines in the mid-nine-
    teenth century, see Margaret Walsh, "The Democratization of Fashion: The
    Emergence of the Women's Dress Pattern Industry," *Journal of American
    History* 66, no. 2 (September 1979): 299–313.
22 Monod, *Store Wars*, 109; Belisle, *Retail Nation*, 29–30.
23 Comacchio, *The Dominion of Youth*.

24 Mike Featherstone, "The Body in Consumer Culture," in *The Body: Social Process and Cultural Theory*, Mike Featherstone, et al, (London: Sage, 1991): 170–96.

25 Marchand, *Advertising the American Dream*, 166.

26 For the gender imbalance in post-World War One England in regard to the Modern Girl, see Melman, *Women and the Popular Imagination in the Twenties*.

27 Thompson with Seager, *Canada, 1922–1939*, chapter 1.

28 Strong-Boag, *A New Day Recalled*, 62. Married women still worked in waged labour. Their participation was largely defined by economic need, yet they faced serious social and political proscriptions. Legislation, the still-dominant domestic ideology that made marriage and work incompatible, and the need for women to care of small children often meant women took in piece work in the home.

29 Strong-Boag, *The New Day Recalled*, 42–3.

30 Morton, *Ideal Surroundings*, 146.

31 Cuthbert Brandt et al, *Canadian Women*, 290–1.

32 Strong-Boag, *The New Day Recalled*, 44–45; and Conrad and Finkel, *History of the Canadian Peoples*, 97.

33 Joan Sangster, "The 1907 Bell Telephone Strike: Organizing Women Workers," *Labour/Le Travail* 3 (1978).

34 Belisle, *Retail Nation*, 140–56. As Joy Parr's work on automatic laundry machines in the post-WWII period reveals, Canadian women balanced a number of factors in making purchasing decisions. Joy Parr, *Domestic Goods: The Material, The Moral, and the Economic in the Postwar Years* (Toronto: University of Toronto Press, 1999), chapter 10.

35 Strange, *Toronto's Girl Problem*, 116–17; Mary Kinnear, *A Female Economy: Women's Work in a Prairie Province, 1870–1970* (Montreal and Kingston: McGill-Queen's University Press, 1998), 123–4. Kinnear provides no explanation for how women made up the shortfall or even if they did, although she does note some women's budgeting for amusements like movies.

36 W.I. Thomas, *The Unadjusted Girl with cases and standpoint for behaviour analysis* (Boston: Little Brown and Co, 1923), 109; Sangster, *Regulating Girls and Women*, 89; and Strange, *Toronto's Girl Problem*, chapter 5.

37 Wright, "Feminine Trifles of Vast Importance"; Belisle, *Retail Nation*, 36–44; Strong-Boag, *The New Day Recalled*, 114; and Monod, *Store Wars*, 113.

38 Sharon Anne Cook, *Sex, Lies, and Cigarettes: Canadian Women, Smoking, and Visual Culture, 1880–2000* (Montreal and Kingston: McGill-Queen's University Press, 2012).

39 On working women in particular, see Sharon Anne Cook, "'Liberation Sticks' or 'Coffin Nails'? Representations of the Working Woman and Cigarette Smoking in Canada, 1919–1939," *Canadian Bulletin of Medical History* 24, no. 2 (2007): 367–401; and on youth culture as driving cultural force in Canada in the period, see Comacchio, *The Dominion of Youth.*

40 On these types of changes, from a business history perspective, see Johnston, *Selling Themselves.*

41 Monod, *Store Wars,* 113–15.

42 Ohmann, *Selling Culture,* 76.

43 Matthew Schneirov, *The Dream of a New Social Order: Popular Magazines in America, 1893–1914* (New York: Columbia University Press, 1994), chapter 3.

44 Cott, *The Grounding of Modern Feminism,* 171.

45 T.J. Jackson Lears, "From Salvation to Self-Realization," in Richard Wightman Fox and T.J. Jackson Lears, eds., *The Culture of Consumption* (New York: Pantheon Books, 1983), 18; and Marchand, *Advertising the American Dream,* 10.

46 On men's beauty culture, see Jane Nicholas, "Representing the Modern Man: Beauty Culture and Masculinity in Early Twentieth Century Canada" in *Canadian Men and Masculinities: Historical and Contemporary Perspectives,* Wayne Martino and Christopher Greig, eds. (Canadian Scholars' Press/ Women's Press, 2012); and Cott, *The Grounding of Modern Feminism,* 174.

47 Peiss, *Hope in a Jar,* chapter 4.

48 Carol Lee Bacchi, *Liberation Deferred? The Ideas of the English Canadian Suffragists, 1877–1918* (Toronto: University of Toronto Press, 1982); Ernest Forbes, "The Ideas of Carol Bacchi and the Suffragists of Halifax," in *Atlantis* 10, no. 2 (Spring 1985): 199–226; and Janice Fiamengo, "Rediscovering Our Foremothers Again: Racial Ideas of Canada's Early Feminists, 1885–1945," *Essays on Canadian Writing* 75 (2002): 85–112.

49 Cuthbert Brandt, et al, *Canadian Women,* 230–40.

50 Warsh, "Smoke and Mirrors": 183–222.

51 Cott, *The Grounding of Modern Feminism,* 172–4.

52 Barbara E. Kelcey, "Dress Reform in Nineteenth Century Canada," in *Fashion: A Canadian Perspective,* Alexandra Palmer, ed., (Toronto: University of Toronto Press, 2004), 229–48; and Dan Azoulay, *Hearts and Minds: Canadian Romance at the Dawn of the Modern Era, 1900–1930* (Calgary: University of Calgary Press, 2011), 215.

53 David B. Clarke, Marcus A. Doel, and Kate M.L. Housiaux, "General Introduction," in *The Consumption Reader,* David B. Clarke, Marcus A. Doel, and Kate M.L. Housiaux, eds. (New York and London: Routledge, 2003), 1.

54 Rita Felski, *The Gender of Modernity* (Cambridge: Harvard University Press, 1995), 62.

55 On such "technologies of the self" and disciplinary strategies, see Michel Foucault, "Technologies of the Self," in *Technologies of the Self: A Seminar with Michel Foucault*, eds. Luther H. Martin, Huck Gutman, and Patrick A. Hutton, (Amherst: University of Massachusetts Press, 1988); and Michel Foucault, *Discipline and Punish: The Birth of the Prison* (New York: Vintage, 1995). Feminist critics have rightfully pointed out the issues regarding gender and the body in Foucault's work, where he either saw the body as gender-neutral or in strictly male terms, but have still fruitfully engaged with his ideas. In interpreting Foucault's work on discipline, feminist philosopher Sandra Lee Bartky argues "that the imposition of normative femininity upon the female body requires training, that the modes of training are cultural phenomena properly describes as 'disciplinary practices,' and that the discipline they represent is disempowering to the woman so disciplined ... Disciplines of the body in general fragment and partition the body's times, its spaces, and its movements; in this case they drill the recruit to the disciplinary regime of femininity in the proper techniques necessary to maintain the current norms of feminine embodiment." See Sandra Lee Bartky, "Suffering to Be Beautiful," in *Gender Struggles: Practical Approaches to Contemporary Feminism*, Constance L. Mui and Julien S. Murphy, eds., (Lanham, MD: Rowman and Littlefield Publishers Inc., 2002), 244–5.

56 See, for example, *Maclean's* 1 November 1925. Emphasis in the original.

57 Peiss, *Hope in a Jar*.

58 *Saturday Night*, May 7, 1927, 32.

59 Mike Featherstone, "The Body in Consumer Culture," *Theory, Culture and Society* 1 no. 2 (September 1982), 18.

60 *Maclean's*, December 15, 1925, 64.

61 Business Women, *Health Confessions of Business Women*, Division of Industrial Hygiene, Provincial Board of Health of Ontario (Toronto, 1923), passim, quote from 119.

62 See, for example, *Maclean's*, 1 May 1927, 100.

63 There were significant exceptions made on the basis of race, which continued the disenfranchisement of Asian-Canadian women as well as Aboriginal women. Women in Quebec were not granted the provincial ballot until 1940. On the suffrage movement in Canada, see Catherine Cleverdon, *The Woman Suffrage Movement in Canada* (Toronto: University of Toronto Press, 1970); Veronica Strong-Boag, *The Parliament of Women: The National Council*

of Women of Canada, 1893–1929 (Ottawa: National Museum, 1976); and Bacchi, *Liberation Deferred?*

64 See, for example, *Chatelaine,* July 1928, 32; January 1929, 28; and February 1929, 30.

65 *Chatelaine,* February 1929, 30.

66 Quoted in Strong-Boag, *The New Day Recalled,* 85.

67 See, for example, the advertisements in *Saturday Night,* 4 February 1928, 28; and *Maclean's,* 1 February 1925, 32.

68 See *Maclean's,* 1 February 1925, 32, and the advertisement for Luvisca lingerie in *Saturday Night,* 25 February 1928, 36.

69 Peiss, *Hope in a Jar,* 184–5.

70 Anthony Glyn, *Elinor Glyn: A Biography* (New York: Doubleday & Company, Inc., 1955), 303.

71 "The 'Magic' of Plastic Surgery," *Saturday Night,* 10 March 1928, 28; Valerie, "The Dressing Table," *Saturday Night,* 3 September 1927, 24; and 15 October 1927, 32

72 *Manitoba Free Press,* 28 April 1927, 3.

73 Brumberg, *The Body Project,* 97–107. In the American context, see also Margaret Lowe, *Looking Good: College Women and Body Image, 1875–1930* (Baltimore, MD: Johns Hopkins University Press, 2003), chapters 5 and 6.

74 *Victoria Times,* 12 May 1927, 6.

75 See, for example, the advertisements in *Globe,* 2 September 1927, 6, and 20.

76 Aleck Ostry, *Nutrition Policy in Canada, 1870–1939* (Vancouver: University of British Columbia Press, 2006). Concern over malnutrition in the period was particularly acute for infants.

77 *Saturday Night,* 29 September 1928, 16.

78 The literature on breadwinning, work, and gender is dense. For particularly thorough examples from different theoretical and methodological perspectives, see Parr, *The Gender of Breadwinners;* Strange, *Toronto's Girl Problem;* and Sangster, *Earning Respect.*

79 Azoulay, *Hearts and Minds,* 213–16.

80 Monod, *Store Wars,* 111.

81 George Colpitts, "The Domesticated Body and the Industrialized Woman's Fur Coat in Canada in the Interwar Period," in *Contesting Bodies and Nation in Canadian History,* Patrizia Gentile and Jane Nicholas, eds., (Toronto: University of Toronto Press, 2013).

82 Roberts, *Civilization Without Sexes,* 65–6. On high fashion and the Modern Girl, see also Stewart, *Dressing the Modern Frenchwomen,* chapter 10.

83 Roberts, *Civilization without Sexes,* 67–9.

84 "Fashion Commentaries on the Canadian Mode," *Chatelaine*, April 1928, 20; and Mary Wyndham, "Paris Favors A Feminine Mode," *Chatelaine*, March 1928, 22–3, 65.

85 See, for example, the advertisements in *Saturday Night*, 8 July 1922; 30 July 1927; and 22 September 1928.

86 See, for example, *Saturday Night*, 24 November 1928.

87 Tinkler and Warsh, "Feminine Modernity in Interwar Britain and North America," 114.

88 C.H. Young, *The Ukrainian Canadians: A Study in Assimilation* (Toronto: Nelson, 1931), 71 quoted in Comacchio, *The Dominion of Youth*, 163.

89 Steedman, *Landscape for a Good Woman*, 8–9, 28–9.

90 Mary Wyndham, "Paris Favors a Feminine Mode," *Chatelaine*, March 1928, 66.

91 *Saturday Night*, 23 February 1929, 3.

92 Jane Walters, interview in *The Great War and Canadian Society: An Oral History*, D. Read and R. Hann, eds., (Toronto: Hogtown Press, 1978), 214.

93 On the continuation of corseting designed to produce a modern female body, see Tinkler and Warsh, "Feminine Modernity in Interwar Britain and North America."

94 *Chatelaine*, March 1928, 33.

95 *Canadian Magazine Advertiser*, 58 (November, 1921), 20.

96 Laura Davidow Hirschbein, "The Flapper and the Fogey: Representations of Gender and Age in the 1920s," *Journal of Family History* 26, no. 1 (January 2001): 113–4. See also Levine, *The Devil in Babylon*, 299.

97 On modern motherhood, see Comacchio, *Nations Are Built of Babies*; and Arnup, *Education for Motherhood*.

98 Jake Foran interview in Read and Hann, eds., *The Great War and Canadian Society*, 213.

99 Allen Levine, *The Devil in Babylon: Fear of Progress and the Birth of Modern Life* (Toronto: McClelland and Stewart, 2005), 298–9; *Manitoba Free Press*, May 1927, 1; and *Vancouver Sun* 4 May 1927, 2.

100 Kathryn McPherson, "'The Case of the Kissing Nurse': Femininity, Sexuality, and Canadian Nursing, 1900–1970," in *Gendered Pasts: Historical Essays in Femininity and Masculinity in Canada* edited by Kathryn McPherson, Cecilia Morgan, and Nancy M. Forestell (Don Mills: Oxford University Press, 1999), 186.

101 Lucy Maud Montgomery, *Anne of Green Gables* (Toronto: Seal Books Edition, 1996), 207.

102 F. Scott Fitzgerald, *Bernice Bobs Her Hair and Other Stories* (New York: Signet Classics, 1996); and "Pokey and Her Flapper Masher Bob," *Maclean's*, 1 February 1925, 14, 47, 49–50.

103 *Maclean's*, 1 February 1925.
104 See, for example, the adverts that appear in *Chatelaine* April 1928. For Cooper's column, see Gladys Cooper, "How to Become Beautiful," *Winnipeg Free Press*, 16 April 1927, 14.
105 See *Saturday Night*, 17 November 1928, 27.
106 Carolyn Comiskey, "Cosmetic Surgery in Paris in 1926: The Case of the Amputated Leg," *Journal of Women's History* 16, no. 3 (Fall 2004): 33.
107 Valerie, "My Lady's Dressing Table," *Saturday Night*, 21 January 1928, 28.
108 Carolyn Ward Comiskey, "'I Will Kill Myself … If I Have to Keep My Fat Calves!': Legs and Cosmetic Surgery in Paris in 1926," in *Body Parts: Critical Explorations in Corporeality*, Christopher E. Forth and Ivan Crozier, eds., (Lanham, MD: Lexington Books, 2005), 247–63. See also her "Cosmetic Surgery in Paris in 1926," 30–54.
109 The tale is recounted in Conor, *The Spectacular Modern Woman*, 1–3.
110 Abigail Solomon-Godeau, "The Legs of the Countess," *October* 39 (Winter 1986): 88. On the influence of new visual technologies in this regard see also Conor, *The Spectacular Modern Woman*, 25–6.
111 A Mere Man [pseudo.], "Those Dancing Girls," *Saturday Night*, 10 March 1928, 29.
112 J.W. Jones, letter to the editor, *Globe*, 22 September 1927, 4.
113 *The Catholic Register*, 11 March 1926, 4.
114 *Chatelaine*, May, 1928.
115 See, for example, the adverts that appear in *Maclean's*, 15 December 1923; *Saturday Night*, 24 September 1927, and 17 November 1928.
116 On this point, see Belisle, "Toward a Canadian Consumer History."

2 Dear Valerie, Dear Mab

1 Valerie, "The Dressing Table," *Saturday Night*, 29 September 1928. Valerie's column changed from "My Lady's Dressing Table" to "The Dressing Table" on 10 March 1928.
2 Conor, *The Spectacular Modern Woman*, 2.
3 Mab, "The Promise of Beauty," *Chatelaine*, October 1928.
4 Tinkler and Warsh, "Feminine Modernity in Interwar Britain and North America," 113. For an overview of the Canadian historiography on consumption, see Belisle, "Toward a Canadian Consumer History," 181–206.
5 Lang, *Women Who Made the News*, 164.
6 There were differences between the two columns that are important to note, if only briefly. Valerie dealt with a greater range of things, including

women's behaviour than did Mab, who was more singularly focused on consumer goods and appearances. Valerie's columns also had the tendency to be slightly more critical of recent changes, although this did not temper the overall message of the column during the period under study here.

7 Mab, "The Promise of Beauty," *Chatelaine*, September 1929; and Valerie, "My Lady's Dressing Table," *Saturday Night*, 31 July 1920; and *Saturday Night*, 27 January 1923.

8 Korinek, *Roughing It In the Suburbs*, 33–5.

9 Lang, *Women Who Made the News*, 2.

10 Don Slater, *Consumer Culture and Modernity* (Cambridge: Polity, 1999), 85–7.

11 Margaret Beetham, *A Magazine of Her Own? Domesticity and Desire in the Woman's Magazine, 1800–1914* (New York: Routledge, 1996), 209.

12 Kirsten McKenzie, "Being Modern on a Slender Income: 'Picture Show' and 'Photoplayer' in early 1920s Sydney," *Journal of Women's History* 22, No. 4 (Winter 2010): 115.

13 On the changes in beauty columns, see Lang, *Women Who Made the News*, 177. See, for example, Valerie, "My Lady's Dressing Table," *Saturday Night*, 28 January 1928.

14 Valerie, "My Lady's Dressing Table," *Saturday Night*, 20 March 1920. For a wider discussion of women's newspaper columns and the role of the expert in Canada, see Lang, *Women Who Made the News*, chapter 6.

15 Lang, *Women Who Made the News*, 172–3.

16 Valerie, "My Lady's Dressing Table," *Saturday Night*, 8 July 1922 and 11 August 1928.

17 Valerie, "My Lady's Dressing Column," *Saturday Night*, 29 October, 1927.

18 On the shifts in romantic advice regarding the Modern Girl in the period, see Azoulay, *Hearts and Minds*, 210–22.

19 Barbara Sato, *The New Japanese Woman: Modernity, Media and Women in Interwar Japan* (Durham and London: Duke University Press, 2003), 10.

20 Valerie, "My Lady's Dressing Table," *Saturday Night*, 28 January 1928.

21 Valerie, "My Lady's Dressing Table," 19 November 1927 and 15 September 1928.

22 Mab, "The Promise of Beauty," *Chatelaine*, September 1929 and October 1929.

23 See, for example, Valerie, "My Lady's Dressing Table," 19 November 1927; and Mab, "The Promise of Beauty," *Chatelaine*, February 1929.

24 Barbara Sato, "Contesting Consumerisms in Mass Women's Magazines," in *The Modern Girl Around the World*, 274.

25 Valerie, "My Lady's Dressing Table," *Saturday Night*, 1 July 1922 and 4 February 1928.

26 Mab, "The Promise of Beauty," *Chatelaine*, October 1928.
27 Valerie, "My Lady's Dressing Table," *Saturday Night*, 15 September, 1928; and Mab, "The Promise of Beauty," *Chatelaine*, October, 1928. On myth, enchantment, and advertising, see Buck-Morss, *The Dialectics of Seeing*, chapter 8. On "safe," "modern" cosmetics see Valerie, "My Lady's Dressing Table," *Saturday Night*, 9 July, 1927.
28 Kathy Peiss, "Making Up, Making Over: Cosmetics, Consumer Culture, and Women's Identity," in *The Sex of Things*, 311.
29 Mab, "The Promise of Beauty," *Chatelaine*, April 1928; and see the Monarch Hosiery advert in *Saturday Night*, 25 February 1928.
30 Valerie, "My Lady's Dressing Table," *Saturday Night*, 28 January 1928.
31 Barbara Brookes, "'The Glands of Destiny': Hygiene, Hormones and English Women Doctors in the First Half of the 20th Century," *Canadian Bulletin of Medical History* 21, no. 1 (2006): 57.
32 *Health Confessions of Business Women*, 157.
33 Brumberg, *The Body Project*, 101; Strong-Boag, *The New Day Recalled*, 85–6.
34 Mab, "The Promise of Beauty," *Chatelaine*, March 1929.
35 The term "scopic regime" was coined in relation to film studies by Christian Metz in the 1970s. I'm using it in the broader sense in which it is now employed in the literature. See Martin Jay, "Scopic Regimes of Modernity," in *Vision and Visuality*, ed. Hal Foster (Seattle: Bay Press, 1988), 3–23.
36 *Saturday Night*, 24 September, 1927.
37 *Maclean's*, 15 February 1926, 33 (my emphasis).
38 *Health Confessions of Business Women*, 168.
39 *Maclean's*, 1 February 1926, 54.
40 Valerie, "My Lady's Dressing Table," *Saturday Night*, 8 October 1927.
41 Mab, "The Promise of Beauty," *Chatelaine*, April 1928.
42 *Maclean's*, February 15, 1927, front cover.
43 Brumberg, *The Body Project*, 70.
44 See, for example, Valerie, "The Dressing Table," *Saturday Night*, 10 March 1928; and Mab, "The Promise of Beauty," *Chatelaine*, April 1928. See the advertisement printed in *Saturday Night*, 9 July 1927.
45 For an overview of these events, see Prentice et al., *Canadian Women*, chapter 8.
46 Warsh, "Smoke and Mirrors," 200.
47 Doris Pennington, *Agnes Macphail: Reformer: Canada's First Female MP* (Toronto: Simon and Pierre, 1989), 41–3; and Terry Crowley, *Agnes Macphail and the Politics of Equality* (Toronto: James Lorimer, 1990), 57–60.
48 See, for example, Valerie, "My Lady's Dressing Table," *Saturday Night*, 8 October 1927, 15 October 1927, and 18 August 1928.

49 For an example of this advert, see *Chatelaine*, September 1929.
     Unfortunately, I was unable to attain permission to reprint this advert.
50 See, for example, Mab, "The Promise of Beauty," *Chatelaine*, July 1928,
     January 1929, and February 1929.
51 Valerie, "My Lady's Dressing Table," *Saturday Night*, 19 November 1927.
52 Mab, "The Promise of Beauty," *Chatelaine*, September 1929, February 1929,
     and January 1929.
53 Valerie, "My Lady's Dressing Table," *Saturday Night*, 24 December 1927.
54 Valerie, "The Dressing Table," *Saturday Night*, 11 August 1928.
55 See, for example, Valerie, "My Lady's Dressing Table," *Saturday Night*,
     3 September 1927 and 15 October 1927. A 1928 article in *Saturday Night*
     warned especially of "alleged professional gentry from the United States
     already discredited in their own country." See "The 'Magic' of Plastic
     Surgery," *Saturday Night*, 10 March 1928, 2.
56 Mab, "The Promise of Beauty," *Chatelaine*, December 1928.
57 *Health Confessions of Business Women*, 70 and 15–16.
58 On the significance of time consuming, see Slater, *Consumer Culture and
     Modernity*, 15.
59 *Health Confessions of Business Women*, 215, 70.
60 Beatrice M. Shaw, "The Age of Uninnocence," *Saturday Night*, 24 May 1919,
     31; and Nellie L. McClung, "I'll Never Tell My Age Again!" *Maclean's*,
     15 March 1926, 15.
61 An In-Between [pseud.], "Ready-Made Youngsters: A Plea for the Younger
     Generation," *Chatelaine*, April 1928, 1, 4.
62 See, for example, Mab, "The Promise of Beauty," *Chatelaine*, April, 1928,
     March 1929; and Valerie, "My Lady's Dressing Table," *Saturday Night*,
     28 February 1920 and 22 October 1927.
63 Valerie, "The Dressing Table," *Saturday Night*, 19 November 1927 and
     24 September 1927. On men condemning the use of cosmetics, but also be-
     ing attracted to women who used them see, Valerie, "The Dressing Table,"
     Saturday Night, 10 March 1928.
64 Unusually, Valerie responded to Dolores's letter as part of her regular col-
     umn rather than in the letters section. Valerie, "The Dressing Table,"
     Saturday Night, 14 January 1928.
65 Valerie, "My Lady's Dressing Table," *Saturday Night*, 27 January 1923, 23;
     July 1927, 30 July 1927; and 6 August 1927.
66 Azoulay, *Hearts and Minds*, 215.
67 On the connection between cosmetics and the rising popularity of sun tan-
     ning in the interwar period, see Devon Hansen Atchison, "Shades of
     Change," in *Consuming Modernity: Changing Gendered Behaviours and*

Consumerism, 1919–1940, Cheryl Krasnick Warsh and Dan Malleck, eds., (Vancouver: University of British Columbia Press, 2013). Atchison correctly notes that moderation in tanning was advised.

68 See, for example, the advert that appears in *Maclean's*, 15 July 1929.

69 The classic text is Carl Berger, "The True North Strong and Free," in *Nationalism in Canada*, edited by Peter Russell, (Toronto: McGraw-Hill Ryerson Ltd., 1966), 3–26.

70 For overviews see, for example, J.R. Miller, *Shingwauk's Vision: A History of Native Residential Schools* (Toronto: University of Toronto Press, 1996) and Donald Avery, *Reluctant Host: Canada's Response to Immigrant Workers, 1896–1994* (Toronto: McClelland and Stewart, 1995).

71 Mab, "The Promise of Beauty," November 1929.

72 On women's internalization of shame see, Sandra Lee Bartky, "Shame and Gender," in *Femininity and Domination: Studies in the Phenomenology of Gender* (New York: Routledge, 1990), 83–98.

73 Mab, "The Promise of Beauty," November 1928. Peter N. Stearns, *Fat History: Bodies and Beauty in the Modern West* (New York: New York University Press, 2002), 122.

74 Mab, "The Promise of Beauty," *Chatelaine*, October, 1929.

75 Mab, "The Promise of Beauty," *Chatelaine*, November 1928.

76 Mab, "The Promise of Beauty," *Chatelaine*, December 1928.

77 See, for example, Valerie, "My Lady's Dressing Table," 20 *Saturday Night*, March 1920; and 19 November 1927, and Mab, "The Promise of Beauty," *Chatelaine*, August 1928; and March 1929.

78 Valerie, "The Dressing Table," *Saturday Night*, 18 August 1928.

3 The Girl in the City

1 Louise Ryan, "Locating the Flapper in Rural Irish Society: The Irish Provincial Press and the Modern Woman in the 1920s," in *New Women Hybridities: Femininity, Feminism, and International Consumer Culture, 1880–1930*, Ann Heilman and Margaret Beetham, eds. (New York: Routledge, 2004), 91.

2 Peiss, *Hope in a Jar*, 146–50.

3 Morton, *Ideal Surroundings*, 145–7 and Comacchio, *The Dominion of Youth*, 64–5.

4 Strange, *Toronto's Girl Problem;* Myers, *Caught;* Lori Chambers, *Misconceptions: Unmarried Motherhood and the Ontario Children of Unmarried Parents Act, 1921–1969* (Toronto: University of Toronto Press, 2007); Joan Sangster, *Regulating Girls and Women: Sexuality, Family, and the Law in Ontario, 1920–1960* (Don Mills: Toronto, 2001).

5 Strange, *Toronto's Girl Problem*, 175.

6 Roy J. Gibbons, "Eat! – For Your Country's Sake – EAT!" *Victoria Times*, 16 April 1927.

7 Marchand, *Advertising the American Dream*, 155, 181–4.

8 Quoted in Angela Carr, *Toronto Architect Edmund Burke: Redefining Canadian Architecture* (Montreal and Kingston: McGill-Queen's University Press, 1995), 110.

9 See advertisement for The Brunswick-Balke-Collender Company in *The Journal of the Royal Architectural Institute of Canada*, January 1927, xxviii.

10 Harold Kalman, *A History of Canadian Architecture*, vol. 2 (Toronto: Oxford University Press, 1994), 762; Lucy Fischer, *Designing Women: Cinema, Art Deco and the Female Form* (New York: Columbia University Press, 2003), 26–32. For another reading on Art Deco, Modern Girls, and gender politics, see Ageeth Sluis, "BATACLANISMO! Or, How Female Deco Bodies Transformed Postrevolutionary Mexico City," *The Americas* 68, no. 4 (April 2010): 469–99.

11 Marchand, *Advertising the American Dream*, 140–7.

12 See, for example, the advert appearing in *Saturday Night*, 24 September 1927 and 22 September, 1928.

13 Melman, *Women and the Popular Imagination*, 2. Valerie makes reference to the "flapper vote" in her column "My Lady's Dressing Table," 17 December 1927.

14 See Strange, *Toronto's Girl Problem*, chapter 6. For literary representations on women in the west that follows Strange's argument, see McMaster, *Working Girls in the West*.

15 Belisle, *Retail Nation*, 167.

16 Strange, *Toronto's Girl Problem;* Myers, *Caught*, chapter 3; Comacchio, *The Dominion of Youth*. For women's own take on the inadequacy of their living conditions, see *Health Confessions of Business Women*.

17 *Saturday Night*, 17 November 1928.

18 See, for example, the columns that appear in *Hush*, 16 August 1928; 31 January 1929; 7 February 1929; and 14 February 1929.

19 Beatrice M. Shaw, "The Age of Uninnocence," *Saturday Night*, 24 May 1919, 31.

20 "What a Sight She'll Be – The Girl of To-Morrow!" *Victoria Times*, 2 April 1927, 6.

21 Thompson with Seager, *Canada 1922–1939*, 3–4; Richard Harris, *Creeping Conformity: How Canada Became Suburban, 1900–1960* (Toronto: University of Toronto Press, 2004), 50.

22 For excellent discussions of how these laws worked to both isolate and build communities post-migration, see Enakshi Dua, "Racializing Imperial Canada: Indian Women and the Making of Ethnic Communities"; Midge

Ayukawa, "Japanese Pioneer Women: Fighting Racism and Rearing the Next Generation"; and Isabel Kaprielian-Churchill, "*Odars* and 'Others': Intermarriage and the Retention of Armeian Ethnic Identity," in *Sisters or Strangers?: Immigrant, Ethnic, and Racialized Women in Canadian History* (Toronto: University of Toronto Press, 2004).

23 Comacchio, *Nations Are Built of Babies,* chapter 3.

24 Cynthia Comacchio, *The Infinite Bonds of Family: Domesticity in Canada, 1850–1940* (Toronto: University of Toronto Press, 1999), 73.

25 Mitchinson, *The Nature of Their Bodies,* 74–6.

26 Jasen, *Wild Things,* chapter 5.

27 Warsh, "Smoke and Mirrors," 183–222; Jarrett Rudy, *The Freedom to Smoke: Tobacco Consumption and Identity* (Montreal and Kingston: McGill-Queen's University Press, 2006); and Cook, "'Liberation Sticks' or 'Coffin Nails'?" 367–401.

28 "When Girls Begin to Swear," *Saturday Night,* 7 January 1928.

29 Jasen, *Wild Things*; and Tina Loo, "Making a Modern Wilderness: Conserving Wildlife in Twentieth-Century Canada," *Canadian Historical Review* 82, no. 1 (March 2001): 100.

30 Coleman, *White Civility,* chapter 5. The quote is from page 202.

31 Ann Douglas, *Terrible Honesty: Mongrel Manhattan in the 1920s* (New York: Farrar, Straus, and Giroux, 1995).

32 The Modern Girl Around the World Research Group, "The Modern Girl as Heuristic Device: Collaboration, Connective Comparison, and Multidirectional Citation," in *The Modern Girl Around the World,* 17.

33 *Victoria Times,* 14 May 1927, 6.

34 Valverde, *The Age of Light, Soap, and Water,* 109–10.

35 Cynthia Comacchio, "'A Postscript for Father': Defining A New Fatherhood in Interwar Canada," *Canadian Historical Review* 78, no. 3 (September 1997), 390.

36 Comacchio, *The Infinite Bonds of Family,* 101.

37 George Winter Mitchell, "Canada – Saviour of the Nordic Race," *The Canadian Magazine* 61, no. 2 (June 1923): 138–40.

38 *Saturday Night,* 15 August 1925.

39 Valverde, *The Age of Light, Soap, and Water,* 111–12; and Strange, *Toronto's Girl Problem,* 152–7. Emily Murphy, *The Black Candle,* (Toronto: Thomas Allen, 1922; reprinted Coles Canadiana Collection, 1973). On Murphy in the wider context of drug addiction in Canada in the period, see Catherine Carstairs, *Jailed for Possession: Illegal Drug Use, Regulation, and Power in Canada, 1920–1961* (Toronto: University of Toronto Press, 2006), chapter 1.

40   On the social and moral reform movement and moral regulation, see
     Valverde, *The Age of Light, Soap and Water*, and Little, *No Car, No Radio, No
     Liquor Permit.*
41   *Hush,* 18 October 1928, 9.
42   For a sample of the advert, see *Toronto Daily Star,* 6 September 1927.
43   "Dusky Midway Sheik to Wed Toronto Girl," *Globe,* 4 September 1924, 12;
     "Report Hilda Palmer Toronto Stage Star to Wed Persian Price," *Toronto
     Daily Star,* 14 September 1927, 19; "Toronto Dancer to Wed Picturesque
     Persian," *Toronto Daily Star,* 15 September 1927, 23; "The Moving Finger
     Writes, and Having Writ, Moves On," *Toronto Daily Star,* 19 September 1927, 1;
     "Persian Attaché Declares Farid Is Not A Prince," *Toronto Daily Star,* 20 Sep-
     tember 1927, 21.
44   *Hush,* 29 December 1927, 2 August 1928, 16 August 1928, 6 September
     1928, 1 November 1928, and the quote is from 18 July 1929. On tabloids in
     the interwar period, see Susan E. Houston, "A little steam, a little sizzle, and
     a little sleaze': English-Language Tabloids in the Interwar Period," *Papers of
     the Bibliographical Society of Canada* 40, no. 1 (Spring 2002): 37–59.
45   Miriam Hansen, *Babel and Babylon: Spectatorship in American Silent Film*
     (Cambridge, MA: Harvard University Press, 1994), 255.
46   Karen Chow, "Popular Sexual Knowledges and Women's Agency in 1920s
     England: Marie Stopes's "Married Love," and E.M. Hull's "The Sheik,"
     Feminist Review 63 (Autumn 1999): 76–7.
47   *Catholic Register,* 6 February 1922, 4.
48   Christopher Forth, *Masculinity in the Modern West: Gender, Civilization and the
     Body.* (New York: Palgrave Macmillan, 2008).
49   Gaylyn Studlar, "'The Perfect Lover'? Valentino and Ethnic Masculinity in
     the 1920s." in *The Silent Film Reader,* eds., Lee Grieveson and Peter Krämer
     (New York: Routledge, 2004), 290–304.
50   Cited in Morton, *Ideal Surroundings,* 151–2.
51   Nicholas, "Representing the Modern Man."
52   Coleman, *White Civility.*
53   McLaren and McLaren, *The Bedroom and the State*; Karen Dubinsky, *Improper
     Advances: Rape and Heterosexual Conflict in Ontario, 1880–1929* (Chicago:
     University of Chicago Press, 1993); Sangster, *Regulating Girls and Women.*
54   Chambers, *Misconceptions,* chapter 3. Whitton is quoted on page 58.
55   Myers, *Caught,* 160–1.
56   Anne Elizabeth Wilson, "The Problem of the Missing Girl," *Chatelaine,*
     March 1929.
57   Melman, *Women and the Popular Imagination,* 90.
58   Edward Said, *Orientalism* (New York: Vintage Books, 1978).

59 Alys Eve Weinbaum, "Racial Masquerade, Consumption and Contestation of American Modernity," in *The Modern Girl Around the World*, 124–6.

60 On the New Woman, see Hilary Fawcett, "Romance, Glamour and the Exotic: Femininity and Fashion in Britain in the 1900s," in *New Woman Hybridities*, especially 150–3.

61 Walden, *Becoming Modern in Toronto*, 157–8.

62 Archives of Ontario, RG 23-26-20 File #1.50 Box I Circuses and Travelling Shows, 1920–1921.

63 For a full account of Allen's interpretation in which she interprets Salomé acting on the demands of her mother, see her autobiography: Maud Allan, *My Life and Dancing* (London: Everett and Co., 1908), 123–7. On the ancient roots of modern dance, see 12–13.

64 Rachel Shteir, *Striptease: The Untold History of the Girlie Show* (New York: Oxford University Press, 2004), 47–8.

65 Decency, *Globe*, 17 September 1927, 4.

66 Weinbaum, "Racial Masquerade, Consumption and Contestation of American Modernity," 131.

67 *Saturday Night*, 10 April 1920; and 16 July 1927. For an example of the elongated, kohl-rimmed eye, see the advertisement for Canadian Elgin-Watch Co., Ltd in *Saturday Night*, 17 November 1928.

68 See, for example, the adverts that appeared in *Saturday Night*, 20 March 1920; 7 May 1927; 15 October 1927; and 29 September 1928.

69 Gouraud's adverts were prolific. For some examples of different campaigns see, *Saturday Night*, 8 October, 1927; 15 October 1927; and 25 August 1928. For the Pompeian advert, see *Maclean's*, 1 November 1925.

70 Ronny H. Cohen, "Tut and the 20s: The Egyptian Look," *Art in America* (March/April 1979), 97.

71 Margaret Macmillan, *Paris 1919: Six Months that Changed the World* (Toronto: Random House, 2001), chapter 27.

72 Anne McClintock, *Imperial Leather: Race, Gender, and Sexuality in the Colonial Contest* (New York: Routledge, 1995), 209.

73 See *Saturday Night*, 31 January 1920.

74 T. Jackson Lears, *Fables of Abundance: A Cultural History of Advertising in America* (New York: Basic Books, 1994), 146.

75 See *Saturday Night*, 12 August 1922. For other examples of the Cleopatra trope, see *Saturday Night*, 4 August 1923; and *Maclean's*, 1 March 1924.

76 James W. St. G. Walker, *"Race," Rights and the Law in the Supreme Court of Canada* (Waterloo: Wilfrid Laurier University Press, 1997) chapter 2; and Constance Backhouse, *Colour-Coded: A Legal History of Racism in Canada, 1900–1950* (Toronto: University of Toronto Press, 1999), chapter 5.

77 See, for example, Peter Ward, *White Canada Forever: Popular Attitudes and Public Policy Toward Orientals in British Columbia,* 3rd edition, (Montreal and Kingston: McGill-Queen's University Press, 1995, 2002); Kay Anderson, *Vancouver's Chinatown: Racial Discourse in Canada, 1875–1980* (Montreal and Kingston: McGill-Queen's University Press, 1995); Lisa Rose Mar, "The Tale of Lin Tee: Madness, Family Violence, and Lindsay's Anti-Chinese Riot of 1919," in Marlene Epp, Franca Iacovetta, and Frances Swyripa, eds., *Sisters or Strangers? Immigrant, Ethnic, and Racialized Women in Canadian History* (Toronto: University of Toronto Press, 2004), 108–29; and Lisa Rose Mar, "Beyond Being Others: Chinese Canadians as National History," *BC Studies* 156 (Winter 2007–2008): 13–34.

78 Murphy, *The Black Candle,* 96.

79 Weinbaum, "Racial Masquerade, Consumption and Contestation of American Modernity," 120–46.

80 Liz Conor, "'Blackfella Missus Too Much Proud': Techniques of Appearing, Femininity, and Race in Australian Modernity," in *The Modern Girl Around the World,* 223–4.

81 On photographic projects in the 1920s serving to frame particular discourses of Indigenous peoples' relationship to modernity, see Peter Geller, *Northern Exposures: Photographing and Filming the Canadian North, 1920–45* (Vancouver: University of British Columbia Press, 2004).

82 "Indians Special Attraction at the C.N.E.," *Toronto Daily Star,* 29 August 1927, 4. On this point see also Keith Regular, "On Public Display," in *Alberta History* 34, no. 1 (Winter, 1986): 1–10; Daniel Francis, *The Imaginary Indian: The Image of the Indian in Canadian Culture* (Vancouver: Arsenal Pulp Press, 1992); Jasen, *Wild Things;* H.V. Nelles, *The Art of Nation-Building: Pageantry and Spectacle at Quebec's Tercentenary* (Toronto: University of Toronto Press, 1999); Ian Radforth, *Royal Spectacle: The 1860 Visit of the Prince of Wales to Canada and the United States* (Toronto: University of Toronto Press, 2004), chapter 6; Ian Radforth, "Performance, Politics, and Representation: Aboriginal People and the 1860 Royal Tour of Canada," *Canadian Historical Review* 84 no. 1 (March 2003): 1–32; and Wade A. Henry, "Imagining the Great White Mother and the Great King: Aboriginal Tradition and Royal Representation at the 'Great Pow-wow' of 1901," *Journal of the Canadian Historical Association* n.s. 11, 2000: 87–108.

83 Mary P. Ryan, "The Projection of a New Womanhood: The Movie Moderns in the 1920s," in *The Projection of a New Womanhood: The Movie Moderns in the 1920s,* William G. Shade and Jean E. Friedman, eds., (Boston: Allyn and Bacon, 1976), 381.

84 Francis, *The Imaginary Indian*, chapter 5.
85 Linda Arvidson, *When the Movies Were Young* (New York: Benjamin Blom [1925] 1968), 123. Bolamenia was a red-brown make-up used in the movie industry to "transform" actors and actresses into "natives."
86 Ruth B. Phillips, "Performing the Native Woman: Primitivism and Mimicry in Early Twentieth-Century Visual Culture," in *Antimodernism and the Artistic Experience: Policing the Boundaries of Modernity*, ed., Lynda Jessup (Toronto: University of Toronto Press, 2001), 27.
87 Veronica Strong-Boag and Carole Gerson, *Paddling Her Own Canoe: The Times and Texts of E. Pauline Johnson Tekahionwake* (Toronto: University of Toronto Press, 2000).
88 *Saturday Night*, 29 September 1928, 19.
89 Phillips, "Performing the Native Woman," 38–9.
90 Phillips, "Performing the Native Woman," 41.

4 The Beauty Pageant

1 Conor, *The Spectacular Modern Woman*, 6.
2 Loo and Strange, *Making Good*; and Cook, *Sex, Lies and Cigarettes*, 148.
3 See, for example, Morton, *Ideal Surroundings*, 123.
4 For a longer history of beauty contests in Canada, see Patrizia Gentile, "Queen of the Maple Leaf: A History of Beauty Contests in Twentieth Century Canada," PhD dissertation, Queen's University, 2006.
5 See Henry Pang, "Miss America: An American Ideal, 1921–1969," *Journal of Popular Culture* 2, no. 4 (1969): 687–96; Frank Deford, *There She Is: The Life and Times of Miss America* (New York: Viking Press, 1971), chapter 7; and A.R. Riverol, *Live From Atlantic City: The History of the Miss America Pageant Before, After and in Spite of Television* (Bowling Green, OH: Bowling Green University Popular Press, 1992), chapter 2.
6 See Lois Banner, *American Beauty* (New York: Alfred A. Knopf, 1983), chapter 12; Deborah Sue Wolfe, "Beauty as Vocation: Women and Beauty Contests in America," PhD dissertation, Columbia University, 1994, chapter 2; Jennifer Jones, "The Beauty Queen As Sacrificial Victim," *Theatre History Studies* 18 (June 1998): 99–106; Sarah Banet-Weiser, *The Most Beautiful Girl in the World: Beauty Pageants and National Identity* (Berkeley: University of California Press, 1999) chapter 1; Angela J. Latham, *Posing a Threat: Flappers, Chorus Girls, and Other Brazen Performers of the American 1920s* (Hanover, NH: University of New England Press, 2000); Kimberly A. Hamlin, "Bathing Suits and Backlash: The First Miss American Pageants,

1921–1927," in *There She Is, Miss America: The Politics of Sex, Beauty, and Race in America's Most Famous Pageant*, ed. Elwood Watson and Darcy Martin (New York: Palgrave Macmillan, 2004), 27–51; and Elwood Watson and Darcy Martin, "The Miss America Pageant," and Watson and Martin, "Introduction," in *There She Is, Miss America*, 1–23. On second wave feminists protests over beauty contests, see Marlene LeGates, *Making Waves: A History of Feminism in Western Society* (Toronto: Copp Clark, 1996), 311; and Margarita Jimenez and Laura Mulvey, "The Spectacle is Vulnerable: Miss World, 1970," in *Visual and Other Pleasures*, Laura Mulvey (London: MacMillan Press Ltd, 1989), 3–5.

7 Maxine Leeds Craig, *Ain't I a Beauty Queen? Black Women, Beauty and the Politics of Race* (New York: Oxford University Press, 2002).

8 See Colleen Ballerino Cohen, Richard Wilk, and Beverly Stoeltje, *Beauty Queens on the Global Stage: Gender, Contests, and Power* (New York and London: Routledge, 1995); Rick A. López, "The India Bonita Contest of 1921 and the Ethnicization of Mexican National Culture," *Hispanic American Historical Review* 82, no. 2 (2002): 291–328; Jennifer Robertson, "Japan's First Cyborg: Miss Nippon, Eugenics and Wartime Technologies of Beauty, Body and Blood," *Body and Society* 7, no. 1 (2001): 1–34; Kate Darian-Smith and Sara Willis, "From Queen of Agriculture to Miss Showgirl: Embodying Rurality in Twentieth-Century Australia," *Journal of Australian Studies* 71, (2001): 17–32; and Judith Smart, "Feminists, flappers, and Miss Australia: contesting the meanings of citizenship, femininity and the nation in the 1920s," *Journal of Australian Studies*, no. 71 (2001) 1–16.

9 Patrizia Gentile, "Searching for 'Miss Civil Service' and 'Mr. Civil Service': Gender Anxiety, Beauty Contests and Fruit Machines in the Canadian Civil Service, 1950–1973," (master's thesis, Carleton University, 1996); and Gentile, "Queen of the Maple Leaf."

10 Mary Ann Shantz, "Citizenship Embodied and the Body as Spectacle: Nudist Pageants in Postwar Canada"; and Tarah Brookfield, "Modelling the UN's Mission in Semi-Formal Wear: Edmonton's 'Miss United Nations' Pageants of the 1960s," in *Contesting Bodies and Nation in Canadian History*, edited by Patrizia Gentile and Jane Nicholas (Toronto: University of Toronto Press, 2013); Donica Belisle, *Retail Nation: Department Stores and the Making of Modern Canada* (Vancouver: University of British Columbia Press, 2011), 121–5; Katie Pickles, "The Old and New on Parade: Mimesis, Queen Victoria, and Carnival Queens on Victoria Day in Interwar Victoria," in *Contact Zones: Aboriginal and Settler Women in Canada's Colonial Past* (Vancouver: University of British Columbia Press, 2005); David Goss, "The

Fairest Girl," *Beaver* 83, no. 1 (February/March 2003): 29–32; Karen Rennie, *Moon Magic: Gail Grant and the 1920s Dance in Regina* (Toronto: Dance Collection Danse, 1992), 18. For American studies that include discussions on Canadian participation in Miss America, see Deford, *There She Is*, passim; Watson and Martin, "The Miss America Pageant"; and Wolfe, "Beauty As Vocation," chapter 2.

11 See, for example, *New York Times*, 15 October 1922, 30; *New York Times*, 28 November 1928, 14; *New York Times*, 30 November 1923, 14; "Paintless Girl Wins," *New York Times*, 29 November 1923, 30; "Toronto's Beauty Best in America," *Globe*, 29 November 1923, 1; and "A Bystander at the Office Window," *Globe*, 4 December 1923, 4. For an example of the advertisements that appeared in Toronto, see *Globe*, 16 April 1923. On Valentino's participation, see Irving Shulman, *Valentino*, (London: Leslie Frewin, 1967 and 1968), 223- 6 and 228–30; and Norman A. Mackenzie, *The Magic of Rudolph Valentino*, (London: The Research Publishing Co., 1974), chapter 6.

12 Jane Nicholas, "Gendering the Jubilee Gender and Modernity in the Diamond Jubilee of Confederation Celebrations, 1927," *Canadian Historical Review* 90, no. 2 (June 2009): 247–4.

13 For an example of this type of continuing pageant in Canada, see Goss, "The Fairest Girl," 29–32.

14 Conor, *The Spectacular Modern Woman*; A. Holly Shissler, "Beauty Is Nothing to Be Ashamed Of: Beauty Contests As Tools of Women's Liberation in Early Republican Turkey," *Comparative Studies of South Asia, Africa and the Middle East* 24, no. 1 (2004): 107–22; Bat-Sheva Margalit Stern, "Who's the Fairest of Them All? Women, Womanhood, and Ethnicity in Zionist Eretz Israel," *Nashim: A Journal of Jewish Women's Studies and Gender Issues* 11 no. 1 (Spring 2006): 142–63. For more contemporary studies on pageants globally, see Ballerino Cohen, Wilk, and Stoeltje, *Beauty Queens on the Global Stage*.

15 Banner, *American Beauty*, 257.

16 Banner, *American Beauty*, 250–7; Banet-Weiser, *The Most Beautiful Girl in the World*, 34; and Ballerino Cohen, Wilk, and Stoeltje, *Beauty Queens on the Global Stage*, 4–5. The use of beauty contests to promote newspapers happened in Mexico as well. See López, "The India Bonita Contest of 1921 and the Ethnicization of Mexican National Culture," 297.

17 Banet-Weiser, *The Most Beautiful Girl in the World*, 34.

18 A.W. Stencell, *Girl Show: Into the Canvas World of Bump and Grind*, (Toronto: ECW Press, 1999).

19 Banner, *American Beauty*, 266.

20 On early working-class amusements see Gerald Lenton-Young, "Variety Theatre," in *Early Stages: Theatre in Ontario, 1800–1914*, Ann Saddlemyer, ed., (Toronto: University of Toronto Press, 1990), 166–213.

21 Walden, *Becoming Modern in Toronto*, 155.

22 Comacchio, *The Dominion of Youth*, chapter 6.

23 The Miss America contest was initially called "Atlantic City's Inter-City beauty contest." Watson and Martin, "Introduction," in *There She Is, Miss America*, 2–3.

24 On the development of the Miss American pageant, see Deford, *There She Is*, chapter 7; Riverol, *Live From Atlantic City*, chapter 2; Watson and Martin, "The Miss America Pageant," 106–8; Banet-Weiser, *The Most Beautiful Girl in the World*, 33–7, Watson and Martin, "Introduction," *There She Is, Miss America*, 2–4.

25 Hamlin, "Bathing Suits and Backlash," 30.

26 Quoted in Ann Marie Bivans, *Miss America: In Pursuit of the Crown* (New York: Mastermedia, 1991), 10.

27 The Miss America pageant was discontinued in 1928, revived for one year in 1933, and then permanently revived in 1935.

28 Although beach beauty contests had existed since the turn of the century, they were casual affairs and did not typically involve swimsuit competitions. John Kasson, *Amusing the Millions: Coney Island at the Turn of the Century* (New York: Hill & Wang, 1978).

29 Sunnyside was completed in 1919 after having its construction delayed as a result of the First World War. Located on the waterfront, Sunnyside was an accessible place for visitors to enjoy midway-like rides and games, dancing, swimming, and general leisure activities. Mike Filey, *I Remember Sunnyside: The Rise and Fall of a Magical Era* (Toronto: Brownstone Press, 1981), 96; and Randall White, *Too Good To Be True: Toronto in the 1920s* (Toronto: Dundurn, 1993), 52.

30 *Globe*, 31 July 1926, 2. Fifty thousand dollars was an incredible amount of money as, in 1929, the Department of Labour estimated that a Canadian family needed $1,430 to survive. In 1931, the average female wage was $559 a year. While the amount of money was certainly exaggerated, the statement obscured the fact that Lanphier's success came not from being Miss Los Angeles but from being Miss America 1925. Lanphier had been awarded a movie contract as part of her prize package and starred in the motion picture *The American Venus* in 1926 with Louise Brooks.

31 *Globe*, 19 August 1926, 2; *Globe*, 27 August 1926, 10; *Globe*, 2 September 1926, 13; and *Toronto Daily Star*, 19 September 1927, 22.

32 *Toronto Daily Star*, 19 September 1927, 22; and 20 September 1927, 3.
33 "Big Contest Inaugurated," *Vancouver Sun*, 3 May 1927, 16.
34 "Big Contest Inaugurated," *Vancouver Sun*, 3 May 1927, 16; and "Legion Girls Working Hard for Victory," *Vancouver Sun*, 19 May 1927, 4.
35 Belisle, *Retail Nation*, 120.
36 Judges for Miss America included Norman Rockwell and James Montgomery Flagg. Wolfe, "Beauty As Vocation," 85–6; and Norman Rockwell, *My Adventures as an Illustrator* (New York: Doubleday and Company, Inc, 1960), 204.
37 "The Beauty Parade," *Globe*, 10 August 1926, 4.
38 Conor, *The Spectacular Modern Woman*, 136. On types and typing see Martha Banta, *Imaging American Women: Ideas and Ideals in Cultural History* (New York: Columbia University Press, 1987).
39 Latham, *Posing a Threat*, 69–70. Part of the concern over the Kellerman suit by the 1920s was related to Kellerman's status as a vaudeville and film star and the content of some of her movies. In 1917, for example, in the very successful *Neptune's Daughter*, Kellerman appeared to be skinny-dipping and appeared almost nude as a mermaid with only her hair as a cover. Most of Kellerman's films required her to appear in revealing swim attire. Erdman argues, "perhaps more than with any other single female performer, the imperatives of consumer capitalism and the fetishizing gaze of the heterosexual theatre patron found their surest inscription on the body of Annette Kellerman." On Kellerman's theatrical career, see Andrew L. Erdman, *Blue Vaudeville: Sex, Morals, and the Mass Marketing of Amusement, 1895–1915* (Jefferson, NC: McFarland & Company, Inc., 2004), 93–9.
40 Newspapers covered beauty contests from across North America, but most frequently the coverage consisted of reprinting the picture of the winner in her swimsuit with a small caption explaining which contest she had won. See, for example, *The Hamilton Spectator*, 23 May 1927, 16; 23 August 1927, 8; 26 August 1927, 19; 29 August 1927, 8; and 10 September 1927, 23.
41 *The Catholic Register*, 5 August 1926, 4.
42 At many events the prizes were promised but not delivered. See Goss, "The Fairest Girl," 32.
43 Conor, *The Spectacular Modern Woman*, 131–2.
44 Azoulay, *Hearts and Minds*, chapter 5; and Comacchio, *The Dominion of Youth*, chapter 3. Thomas is quoted in Comacchio on page 84.
45 Latham, *Posing a Threat*, 65.
46 Helen Lenskyj, *Out of Bounds: Women, Sport and Sexuality* (Toronto: Women's Press, 1986), 68.
47 Deford, *There She Is*, 69.

48 See, for example, *Saturday Night*, 12 December 1925, 19; An In-Between [pseud.], "Ready-Made Youngsters: A Plea for the Younger Generation," *Chatelaine*, April 1928, 1; *Victoria Times*, 25 April 1927, 10, and 14 May 1927, 6.

49 *Maclean's*, July 15, 1928 and 1929.

50 Photograph of five finalists of the 1926 Sunnyside Miss Toronto contest. City of Toronto Archives (CTA), *Globe and Mail Photographic Files*, Fonds 1244, Item 1028J.

51 *Toronto Daily Star*, 10 September 1927, 4.

52 "Women State Protest Over; 'Nudes' At Fair," *Toronto Daily Star*, 9 September 1927, 22.

53 Lenskyj, *Out of Bounds*, 68.

54 Prentice *et al*, *Canadian Women*, 287–8; and Lenskyj, *Out of Bounds*, 34–44.

55 Lenskyj, *Out of Bounds*, 67. Bruce Kidd, *The Struggle for Canadian Sport* (Toronto: University of Toronto Press, 1996).

56 "Majority of Women Swimmers Favor Retaining Bathing Suits," *Evening Telegram*, 30 August 1927, 21.

57 Stencell, *Girl Show*, 86.

58 Deford, *There She Is*, 11.

59 See, for example, the advertisement in see *Manitoba Free Press*, 19 April 1927, 8.

60 *Maclean's Magazine*, 1 July 1927, 77.

61 "Ski-ing Beauty Leads Contest for 'Miss Victoria,'" *Victoria Daily Times*, 26 April 1927, 9.

62 See for example the advertisement in *Saturday Night*, 8 June 1926, 3.

63 Marchand, *Advertising the American Dream*, 178; and Strong-Boag, *The New Day Recalled*, 12.

64 Annette Kellerman, *Physical Beauty – How to Keep It: Annette Kellerman Illustrated* (New York: George H. Doras, 1918), 86–7.

65 Kellerman, *Physical Beauty*, 23.

66 *Victoria Times*, 19 April 1927, 2.

67 *Victoria Times*, 19 April 1927, 2; 23 April 1927, 12; and 30 April 1927, 9. See also *New York Times*, 17 July 1923, 31; and *Toronto Daily Star*, 24 September 1927, 8.

68 During the 1927 Miss Canada contest, for example, the *Victoria Daily Times* published the measurements of the *Venus de Milo*. Readers were told that the statue had the following measurements: height – 5'4," neck –14 inches, bust – 34 ¾ inches, waist – 28 ½ inches, hips – 36 inches, thighs – 19 ½ inches, calf – 13 ½ inches, ankle – 8 ½ inches. The *Venus de Milo* was an often-cited example of beauty in the early twentieth-century. See Banner, *American Beauty*, 203; and Wolfe, "Beauty as Vocation," 82.

69 L.B. Pett, "The Canadian weight-height survey," *Human Biology* 28 (1956):
177–188; John Cranfield and Kris Inwood, "The Great Transformation: A
Long-Run Perspective On Physical Well-Being in Canada," in *Economics and
Human Biology* 5 (2007): 215. In 1928, Paul Nystrom estimated that only
seventeen percent of American women were over 5 feet 3 inches in height
and "slender." Paul H. Nystrom, *Economics of Fashion* (New York, Ronald
Press, 1928), 466.
70 Steele, *Fashion and Eroticism*, 239.
71 The Miss Toronto contest of 1926 required, like the Miss America pageant,
that women had to be between sixteen and twenty-five. Other contests, like
Miss Winnipeg, only had a minimum age of eighteen, but the unmarried
requirement limited the age range. *Globe*, 31 July 1926, 2. See *Winnipeg Free
Press*, 16 April 1927, 3.
72 "Final Prize List and Rules," *Victoria Times*, 19 April 1927.
73 Of course, this strategy did not work, but scandal ensured almost every time
a married contestant was publicly exposed. There was one notable exception reported in the *Victoria Times* when a married mother of twins competed for Miss Cambridge and won. She was described as an "old-fashioned
girl" who kept her figure by performing housework and boxing with her
husband. See "If You'd Be Beautiful – Try Twins, Washtub, Boxing and
Plenty of Sleep; It's a Winning Recipe," *Victoria Times*, 7 May 1927, 6.
74 These concerns, of course, rested on the assumption of heterosexuality.
On swimming in Canada, see Ken Cruikshank and Nancy B. Bouchier,
"Dirty Spaces: Environment, the State, and Recreational Swimming in
Hamilton Harbour, 1870–1946," *Sport History Review* 29 no. 1 (1998): 1–20;
Robert S. Kossuth, "Dangerous Waters: Victorian Decorum, Swimmer
Safety, and the Establishment of Public Bathing Facilities in London
(Canada)" *International Journal of the History of Sport* 22 no. 5 (September
2005): 796–815. On the beaches in the 1920s, see Strange, *Toronto's Girl
Problem*, chapter 6.
75 *Globe*, 22 September 1927, 4; and *Toronto Daily Star*, 13 September 1927, 6.
76 Douglas, *Terrible Honesty*, 47.
77 *The Catholic Register*, 11 March 1926, 4; and *Vancouver Sun*, 21 May 1927, 5.
78 *Catholic Register*, 23 May 1929: 4.
79 Suzann Buckley and Janice Dickin McGinnis, "Venereal Disease and Public
Health Reform in Canada," *Canadian Historical Review* 63, no. 3 (1982): 348.
80 *The Catholic Register*, 11 March 1926, 4; Dubinsky, *Improper Advances*;
Chambers, *Misconceptions*, 72–5; and Constance Backhouse, *Carnal Crimes:
Sexual Assault Law in Canada, 1900–1975* (Toronto: The Osgoode Society,
2008).

81 On these efforts, see Strange, *Toronto's Girl Problem.*
82 "Ireland Frowns on Beauty Shows," *Catholic Register,* 4 April 1929, 4.
83 John Berger, *Ways of Seeing* (Toronto: Macmillan, 1972), 52.
84 Gayle Rubin, "The Traffic in Women: Notes on the 'Political Economy' of Sex," in *Feminist Theory: A Reader,* Wendy Kolmar and Frances Bartkowski, eds., (Moutnain Views, CA: Mayfield Publishing Company, 2000), 228–44; and Newman, "Directing Traffic": 41–54.
85 *The Catholic Register,* 5 August 1926, 4. The concern over judges touching and measuring the contestants stems from the Miss America pageant where in different years judges measured the contestants. See Wolfe, "Beauty As Vocation," 85–6; and Rockwell, *My Adventures as an Illustrator,* 204. Rockwell was a judge for the Miss America pageant in the 1920s. In his memoirs he recalls that "The judge who thought it up had a wonderful time measuring all the girls – bust, waist, hips, etc."
86 *The Catholic Register,* 5 August 1926, 4.
87 Archives of Ontario, Attorney General Files, RG 4-32 File 538 [1927].
88 *Toronto Daily Star,* 3 March 1927, 8.
89 *Toronto Daily Star,* 9 March 1927, 1.
90 Hamlin, "Bathing Suits and Backlash."
91 Archives of Ontario, RG 4-32 Attorney General Central Registry Criminal and Civil, A.L. Smythe, National Council of Women, Toronto: Query how legislation might prevent Beauty Contests, 1927.
92 Gentile, "Queen of the Maple Leaf." See also Margaret Hobbs and Joan Sangster, *The Woman Worker, 1926–1929* (St. John's: Canadian Committee on Labour History, 1999), 103, 111.
93 *The Globe,* 1 September 1927, 16.
94 Quoted in Deford, *There She Is,* 129.
95 *New York Times,* 30 November 1923, 14.
96 *Catholic Register,* 5 August 1926, 4
97 "'Miss Canada' Tells Gyros of Plans to Become a Movie Queen," *Victoria Times,* 13 June 1927.
98 On the concern over working women's wages, prostitution, and respectability, see Strange, *Toronto's Girl Problem,* and Belisle, *Retail Nation,* 220–227. On legislative changes, see Kinnear, *A Female Economy,* chapter 7.
99 Brumberg, *The Body Project,* 107
100 The rules for Miss Victoria are reprinted in the *Victoria Times,* April 19, 1927, 7. For other examples, see *Toronto Star,* 22 December 1923, 17; *Victoria Times,* 14 April 1927, 8; *Victoria Times,* 16 April 1927; *Victoria Times,* 22 April 1927, 2; *Winnipeg Free Press,* 16 April 1927, 3; and *Vancouver Sun,* 7 May 1927, 1.

101 *Toronto Daily Star,* 29 September 1927, 4.
102 *New York Times,* 15 October 1922, 30.
103 See for example, "Protest Against Beauty Contests," *Victoria Times,* 3 May 1927, 15.
104 "Bathing Girls Barred From City Parade," *Vancouver Sun,* 26 May 1927, 9 and *Vancouver Sun,* 28 June 1927, 1.
105 Salmon's mother, Letitia Salmon, actually initiated the suit as Kitty was not old enough to file suit under her own name. See "Beauty Contest Case Deferred," *Vancouver Sun,* 20 June 1927, 18.
106 *Vancouver Sun,* 3 May 1927, 16; and 4 June 1927, 1.

5 Modern Art and the Girl

1 On the paintings, particularly Russell's, see Brian Foss, "Living Landscape," in *Edwin Holgate,* ed. Rosalind Pepall and Brian Foss (Montreal: Museum of Fine Arts, 2005), 46–7; J. Russell Harper, *Painting in Canada: A History,* 2nd ed. (Toronto: University of Toronto Press, 1977), 230–3; and Paul Duval, *Canadian Impressionism* (Toronto: McClelland and Stewart, 1990), 70. The whereabouts of Drinkwater's painting remains unknown. Unlike the other two, it was not reproduced in Toronto papers or in the CNE catalogue.
2 Jerrold Morris, *The Nude in Canadian Painting* (Toronto: New Press, 1972), 3–4. Also informative in regards to the nude is Alison Smith, *The Victorian Nude: Sexuality, Morality and Art* (Manchester: Manchester University Press, 1996).
3 On the fiction of "Toronto the Good" as well as a discussion of morality and pleasure in Toronto, see Strange, *Toronto's Girl Problem,* 13–4 and *passim.* The phrase "Toronto the Good" comes from C.S. Clark, *Of Toronto the Good: The Queen City of Canada as it is* (Montreal: the Toronto Publishing Company, 1898; Coles Canadiana Collection, 1970).The idea of an unappreciative crowd was suggested in a few of the responses where writers argued that Canadians were unaccustomed to European artistic sensibilities. Some implied that this was a good thing since European culture had become "coarse." See The Observer [pseud.] "Modern Art and the Old Puritanism," *Toronto Daily Star,* 22 September 1927, 6; and Lawren Harris, "The Nudes at the CNE," *Canadian Forum* 8 no. 85 (October 1927), 392. In his classic work on Canadian painting, Russell Harper argued that "puritanical Toronto shuddered" in reaction to the paintings. See Harper, *Painting in Canada,* 232.

4 The only other incident of public protest over paintings in the art gallery in the period was in 1919 when notable artists and art critics such as P.G. Konody, J.W. Beatty, Arthur Lismer, and J.W. Bengough debated the "cubist monstrosities" that depicted the gas attacks of the First World War. See the debates in the *Globe*, 26 August 1919, 5; 29 August 1919, 2, 7; 5 September 1919, 5; 8 September 1919, 6; 10 September 1919, 6; and 12 September 1919, 6.

5 Harris, "The Nudes at the CNE," 391.

6 "Women State Protest Over 'Nudes' at Fair," *Toronto Daily Star*, 9 September 1927, 22.

7 *A Modern Fantasy* had already been exhibited in Paris and was accorded the highest honour at the Spring Salon de Société des Artistes earlier in 1927. Although Canadian by birth, Russell had a tenuous association with the Canadian art world. Russell left in 1905 to live and study in Paris and was, by most accounts, a maverick on the Canadian art scene known for his "naturally artistic temperament" and his refusal to join Canadian art societies. In 1932, the *Evening Telegram* described him as "John Russell, a member of nothing, honoured (by request) by nobody." Russell was also decidedly outspoken. The exhibition of his work at the CNE marked a homecoming. See Muriel Miller, *Famous Canadian Artists* (Peterborough, Woodland Publishing, 1983), 73; Newton MacTavish, *The Fine Arts in Canada* (Toronto: Macmillan Co., 1925), 118; Duval, *Canadian Impressionism*, 70; and Harper, *Painting in Canada*, 232. On the reclining nude, see Berger, *Ways of Seeing*, 63; T.J. Clark, *The Painting of Modern Life: Paris in the Art of Manet and His Followers* (New York: Knopf, 1985); Gerald Needham, "Manet, 'Olympia' and Pornographic Photography," in *Woman as Sex Object: Studies in Erotic Art, 1730–1970*, ed. Thomas B. Hess and Linda Nochlin (London: Allen Lane, 1972), 80–9; Thomas Crow, "Modernism and Mass Culture in the Visual Arts," in *Modernism and Modernity: The Vancouver Conference Papers*, ed. Benjamin H.D. Buchloh, Serge Guilbaut, and David Solkin (Halifax: Press of the Nova Scotia College of Art and Design, 1983), 215–64; Lynda Nead, *The Female Nude: Art, Obscenity and Sexuality* (New York: Routledge, 1992); and Judy Chicago and Edward Lucie-Smith, *Women and Art: Contested Territory* (New York: Watson-Guptill Publications, 1999), chapter 6.

8 Donica Belisle, "Crazy for Bargains: Inventing the Irrational Female Shopper in Modernizing English Canada," *Canadian Historical Review* 92, no. 4 (December 2011). "Orgy of shopping" is quoted on page 590.

9 Quoted in Renato Poggioli, "Paolo and Francesca," in *Dante: A Collection of Critical Essays*, ed. John Freccero (Englewood Cliffs, NJ: Prentice Hall, 1965), 62.

10 From the reaction to the painting, people were clearly aware of the tale of Paolo and Francesca, but even if they had not been, the Toronto *Daily Star* summarized it for readers on the opening day of the CNE. See "'Nudes' Hung at Exhibition Likely Cause Controversy," *Toronto Daily Star*, 27 August 1927, 22. For the original text, see Dante Alighieri, *Inferno* (New York: Bantam Classics, 1982), Canto 5.

11 The phrasing was originally from an article in the *Evening Telegram* but was repeated in a letter in the *Globe*. See "Letter Presents Artist's Reply to Toronto's 'Viragoes of Virtue,'" *Evening Telegram*, 17 September 1927, 18; and Alice Humler, letter to the editor, *Globe*, 22 September 1927, 4.

12 See Cynthia Comacchio, "Dancing to Perdition Adolescence and Leisure in Interwar English-Canada," in *Journal of Canadian Studies* 32, no. 3 (Fall 1997), 11–17; and Strange, *Toronto's Girl Problem*, 122–7.

13 In the 1920s, the committees involved in art selection made a conscious effort to improve the quality of both the foreign and the domestic art shown in their Gallery, and to make the art show of interest to the general public. Canadian National Exhibition Archives [hereafter CNEA], Minutes of the Canadian National Exhibition Graphic and Applied Arts Committee Minutes, 28 October, 1926.

14 Dawn, *National Visions, National Blindness*.

15 See Harper, *Painting in Canada*; and Roald Nasgaard, *The Mystic North: Symbolist Landscape Painting in Northern Europe and North America, 1890–1940*. For an excellent reinterpretation of the myths of the Group of Seven, see Jessup, "Bushwackers in the Gallery," 130–52.

16 On the Group of Seven, see Peter Mellen, *The Group of Seven* (Toronto: McClelland and Stewart, 1970); J. Russell Harper, *Painting in Canada*; and Muriel Miller, *Famous Canadian Artists*, (Peterborough, ON: Woodland Publishing, 1983).

17 Paul Hjartarson, "'Virgin Land,' the Settler-Invader Subject, and Cultural Nationalism: Gendered Landscape in the Cultural Construction of Canadian National Identity," in *Gender and Landscape: Renegotiating Morality and Space* eds., Lorraine Dowler, Josephine Carubia, and Bonj Szczygiel (New York and London: Routledge, 2005), 203–20.

18 Hjaratarson, "'Virgin Land,' the Settler-Invader Subject, and Cultural Nationalism."

19 Quoted in Thompson with Seager, *Canada, 1922–1939*, 162.

20 Dawn, *National Visions, National Blindness*, chapter 1.

21 William Lyon Mackenzie King, *The Mackenzie King Diaries, 1893–1931.*
    Transcript (Toronto, 1973), 26 August 1927.

22 M.O. Hammond, "Strong Encouragement is given by Exhibition to·All
    Creative Arts," *Globe*, 27 August 1927, 16. The revenues of the art gallery illus-
    trate this point as well. In 1926, the revenues from admission to the art gal-
    lery were $6134.50 and jumped to $15,840.20 in 1927. In 1928, revenues fell
    to $10,866.90. CNEA, The Annual Meeting of the Canadian National
    Exhibition, 22 February 1928.

23 "All Records Smashed," *Globe*, 12 September 1927, 1.

24 Archives of Ontario, Ontario Society of Artists fonds F1140, Ontario Society
    of Artists, President's Annual Report, 1927–8.

25 Kathy Peiss, *Cheap Amusements: Working Women and Leisure in Turn-of-the-
    Century New York* (Philadelphia: Temple University Press, 1986), 140–6.

26 Hammond, "Strong Encouragement is Given by Exhibition to All Creative
    Arts," *Globe*, 27 August 1927, 16; and "CNE Pictures This Year Galaxy of
    High Average," *Toronto Daily Star*, 27 August 1927, 3.

27 The *Toronto Daily Star* described Drinkwater's painting as one that "censori-
    ous people will ask to have turned to the wall." "CNE Pictures This Year
    Galaxy of High Average," 3.

28 A Father [pseud.], "Those Pictures of the Nude At the Exhibition Art
    Gallery," *Evening Telegram*, 27 August 1927, 21 and "'Nudes' Hung at
    Exhibition Likely Cause Controversy: but Art Gallery Committee Is
    Standing Pat on What It Has Shown – John Russell's 'Modern Fantasy'
    Excites Comment," *Toronto Daily Star*, 27 August 1927, 22.

29 "The Nude in Art and Life," *Saturday Night*, 24 September 1927, 1–2;
    "Gene" LeVerne Devore, letter to the editor, *Globe*, 14 September 1927, 4;
    H. I. MacDonald, letter to the editor, *Globe*, 16 September 1927, 4; Honi
    Soit [pseud.] letter to the editor, *Evening Telegram*, 17 September 1927, 24;
    and Lawren Harris and H.K. Gordon, "The Nudes at the CNE," in *The
    Canadian Forum* 8 no. 85 (October 1927), 392.

30 "Box Office Rush at 'Ex' Art Gallery Not Due to Nude Art, Says Official,"
    Toronto Daily Star, 3 September 1927, 19 and "Line up Crowds Art Gallery
    Many Pictures Are Sold," *Evening Telegram*, 6 September 1927, 21.

31 Sybille Pantazzi, "Foreign Art at the Canadian National Exhibition, 1905–
    1938," *National Gallery of Canada Bulletin* 22 (1973).

32 "Those Pictures in the Nude," *Toronto Daily Star*, 10 September 1927, 6. See
    also An Artist's Daughter [pseud.] letter to the editor, *Globe*, 15 September
    1927, 14.

33 Another Woman [pseud.] letter to the editor, *Globe*, 13 September 1927, 6.
    See also the response by Thomas C. Rumney, letter to the editor, *Globe*, 15

September 1927, 14. "Public Display – Unusual Interest in 'Art,'" *Evening Telegram*, 2 September 1927, 24.

34 In the 1920s, the committees involved in art selection made a conscious effort to improve the quality of both the foreign and the domestic art shown in their Gallery, and to make the art show of interest to the public generally. CNEA, Minutes of the Canadian National Exhibition Graphic and Applied Arts Committee Minutes, 28 October 1926. The need for a new Gallery was described by the Ontario Society of Artists as "most urgent." See Ontario Society of Artists, President's Annual Report, 1927–8, and *Toronto Daily Star*, 7 September 1927, 1.

35 CNEA, Minutes of the Meeting of the Fine Arts Committee, 28 October 1926. The motion to attempt to sell more Canadian art was originally passed in 1919. CNEA, Minutes of the Meeting of the Fine Arts Committee, 30 May 1919.

36 CNEA, Annual Report 1927.

37 One of Them [pseud.] letter to the editor, *Toronto Daily Star*, 8 September 1927, 6; and "New Highway Through Exhibition Means Wrecking of Art Gallery," *Toronto Daily Star*, 7 September 1927, 1.

38 CNEA, Annual Report of the Canadian National Exhibition, 1928 and CNEA, The Annual Meeting of the Canadian National Exhibition, 22 February 1928.

39 Griselda Pollock, "Beholding Art History: Vision, Place, and Power," in *Vision and Textuality*, ed. Stephen Melville, and Bill Readings (Durham, NC: Duke University Press, 1995), 50.

40 *Toronto Daily Star*, 27 August 1927, 1. On the complex interplay of identities on the fairgrounds, see Walden, *Becoming Modern in Toronto*, chapter 4.

41 Art Lover [pseud.], letter to the editor, *Toronto Daily Star*, 29 August 1927, 6.

42 "The Nude in Art and Life," *Saturday Night*, 24 September 1928, 1–2.

43 Robert Rydell, *All the World's a Fair: Visions of Empire at American International Expositions, 1876–1916* (Chicago: University of Chicago Press, 1984), 2.

44 CNEA, *The Official Catalogue of the Canadian National Exhibition, 1927* and CNEA, The Annual Meeting of the Canadian National Exhibition, 22 February 1928.

45 A Woman [pseud.] letter to the editor, *Globe*, 9 September 1927, 4.

46 Art galleries were important institutions that reflected cultural standards and had been reordered in the late nineteenth-century as spaces where middle-class ideals and values could be transmitted to other classes. Walden, *Becoming Modern in Toronto*, 239–42. See also Bennett, *The Birth of the Museum*, 28. On the construction of the CNE's art galleries, see Walden, *Becoming Modern in Toronto*, 242 and 287–8 and Pantazzi, "Foreign Art at the Canadian National Exhibition," 1–3.

47 Walden, *Becoming Modern in Toronto*, 287–8.

48 Bennett, *The Birth of the Museum*, 3.

49 Norman Harris, "'Circus' Pictures at Exhibition People Say Nudes Poor Taste," *Evening Telegram*, 3 September 1927, 8.

50 "Those Pictures of the Nude at the Exhibition Art Gallery," *Evening Telegram*, 27 August 1927, 21.

51 Editorial, *Globe*, 10 September 1927, 14.

52 D. McTavish, letter to the editor, *Globe*, 30 August 1927, 4.

53 "Public Display Unusual Interest in 'Art'" *Evening Telegram*, 2 September 1927, 24.

54 Walden, *Becoming Modern in Toronto*, 245.

55 Editorial, *Globe*, 10 September 1927, 14.

56 *Globe*, 15 September 1927, 14.

57 "Women State Protest Over 'Nudes' At Fair," *Toronto Daily Star*, 9 September 1927, 22.

58 An Artist's Daughter [pseud.] letter to the editor, *Globe*, 15 September 1927, 4.

59 Characterologist [pseud.] letter to the editor, *Toronto Daily Star*, 25 September 1927, 6.

60 Letter to the editor, *Globe*, 12 September 1927, 4.

61 School Marm [pseud.] letter to the editor, *Evening Telegram*, 10 September 1927, 16. See also Harper, *Painting in Canada*, 232.

62 "Women State Protest Over 'Nudes' At Fair," *Toronto Daily Star*, 9 September 1927, 22.

63 On women, respectability, art, and exhibition culture in the nineteenth century, see E.A. Heamann, *The Inglorious Arts of Peace: Exhibitions in Canadian Society During the Nineteenth Century* (Toronto: University of Toronto Press, 1999), 263–4.

64 Bennett, *The Birth of the Museum*, 28–30.

65 Lynne Marks, *Roller Rinks and Revivals: Religion, Leisure, and Identity in Late-Nineteenth-Century Small-Town Ontario* (Toronto: University of Toronto Press, 1996), chapter 4.

66 Walden, *Becoming Modern in Toronto*, 154, 157–8. For earlier incarnations of this dynamic at exhibitions, including the C.N.E, see Heaman, *The Inglorious Arts of Peace*, 262–4. For an exploration into the history of looking in a different Canadian context, see Lianne McTavish, "Learning to See in New Brunswick, 1862–1929," *Canadian Historical Review* 87 no. 4 (December 2006), 553–81.

67 In advertisements for the midway throughout the 1920s, the CNE suggested that the midway had been cleaned up by using the line "nothing to offend." See, for example, the advertisement from the *Evening Telegram*, 31 August

1920, 17. On the carnival menace, see Tina Loo and Carolyn Strange, "The Travelling Show Menace: Contested Regulation in Turn-of-the-Century Ontario," *Law and Society Review* 29, no. 4 (1995), 639–67.

68 "New Novel Features to Help 49th CNE," *Toronto Daily Star*, 27 August 1927, 28.

69 Auditor's Reports show the receipts from them midway as estimated to be worth $69,000 to $81,000 for the CNE. This would not include what the contracted shows themselves would make. Johnny J. Jones stated that the CNE receipts for the company were expected to be worth over $100,000. CNEA Auditor's Report, Midway File and *Billboard*, 25 January 1919 and 6 September 1919.

70 See the advertisement in *Globe*, 2 September 1927, 2 For more on the politics of the midway, see, for example, Robert Bogdan, *Freak Show: Presenting Human Oddities for Amusement and Profit* (Chicago: University of Chicago Press, 1988); Rachel Adams, *Sideshow U.S.A.: Freaks and the American Cultural Imagination* (Chicago: University of Chicago Press, 2001); Heamann, *The Inglorious Arts of Peace*, 269; Walden, *Becoming Modern in Toronto*, 269–74; Robert Rydell, *World of Fairs: The Century-of-Progress Expositions* (Chicago: University of Chicago Press, 1993), 135–46; and Stencell, *Girl Show*.

71 Walden, *Becoming Modern in Toronto*, 270.

72 To view the painting, which was advertised in the *Globe*, one paid the fee and entered a darkened tent where the painting was hung at the far end. The Jones Exposition described *Stella* as "the world's most perfectly formed woman." *Stella* is mentioned in advertisements and reports on Johnny J. Jones in *Billboard Magazine*. See, for example, *Billboard*, 25 January 1919, 75 and 5 July 1919, 67. The Johnny J. Jones Exposition had most of the contracts for the CNE midway throughout the 1920s as they were contracted from 1919 and 1920 and from 1923 to 1927. On which company was awarded the midway contract during the 1920s, see CNEA, Midway File.

73 Walden, *Becoming Modern in Toronto*, 278–9.

74 Stenographer [pseud.], letter to the editor, *Globe*, 17 September 1927, 4.

75 D. McTavish, letter to the editor, *Globe*, 30 August 1927, 4; A Mother [pseud.], letter to the editor, *Globe*, 8 September 1927, 4; and Father [pseud.], letter to the editor, *Evening Telegram*, 27 August 1927, 21.

76 Jas. W. Hird, letter to the editor, *Globe*, 16 September 1927, 4.

77 Rentoul Castell, letter to the editor, *Globe*, 22 September 1927, 4.

78 An Artist's Daughter, [pseud.] letter to the editor, *Globe*, 15 September 1927, 14.

79 Bennett, *The Birth of the Museum*, 1.

80 Berger, *Ways of Seeing*, 9.

81 H. Paulin, letter to the editor, *Toronto Daily Star,* 17 September 1927, 6; and The Observer [pseud.], "Modern Art and the Old Puritanism," *Toronto Daily Star,* 22 September 1927, 6.

82 "Why Make Vulgarity and Divine Thing?" *Toronto Daily Star,* 8 September 1927, 16.

83 Alice Hulmer, letter to the editor, *Globe,* 22 September 1927, 4.

84 John C. Read, letter to the editor, *Globe,* 15 September 1927, 14.

85 H. Paulin, letter to the editor, *Toronto Daily Star,* 17 September 1927, 6; and (Rev.) A.W. Shepherd, letter to the editor, *Globe,* 27 September 1927, 4.

86 Comacchio, *The Dominion of Youth,* 32.

87 Alice Humler, letter to the editor, *Globe,* 22 September 1927, 4.

88 Another Woman, [pseud.] letter to the editor, *Globe,* 13 September 1927, 6.

89 R.H. McD., letter to the editor, *Globe,* 16 September 1927, 4.

90 J.W. Jones, letter to the editor, *Globe,* 22 September 1927, 4. The point that people should be less concerned about the art and more concerned about their daughters was brought up in other letters. See also A Lover of Real Art [pseud.] *Toronto Daily Star,* 13 September 1927, 6.

91 "Flapper Age Now between 30 and 50, Says Alma Gluck," *Vancouver Sun,* 31 May 1927, 2.

92 The idea of the "public woman" as prostitute did not mean that women were excluded from participating in public life during the nineteenth century. Women participated in reform efforts and in public celebrations like parades, bazaars, and fairs as both contributors and spectators. However, respectable women's participation in public was carefully controlled and regulated in order to maintain their claim to being a "Lady." On women's participation in the public sphere in the nineteenth century, see Ian Radforth, *Royal Spectacle: The 1860 Visit of the Prince of Wales to Canada and the United States* (Toronto: University of Toronto Press, 2004), 116–20, 150–63; E.A. Heamann, *The Inglorious Arts of Peace: Exhibitions in Canadian Society During the Nineteenth Century* (Toronto: University of Toronto Press, 1999), 268–9; Cecilia Morgan, *Public Men and Virtuous Women: The Gendered Languages of Religion and Politics in Upper Canada, 1791–1850* (Toronto: University of Toronto Press, 1996), 196, 202–15; Walden, *Becoming Modern in Toronto,* passim; Prentice *et al, Canadian Women,* chapter 7; and Bonnie Huskins, "The Ceremonial Space of Women: Public Processions in Victorian Saint John and Halifax," in *Separate Spheres: Women's Worlds in the 19th-Century Maritimes,* ed. Janet Guildford and Suzanne Morton (Fredericton: Acadiensis Press, 1994), 145–59.

93 Warsh, "Smoke and Mirrors," 183–221; Robert A. Campbell, *Sit Down and Drink Your Beer: Regulating Vancouver's Beer Parlours, 1925–1954* (Toronto: University of Toronto Press, 2001); and Rudy, *The Freedom to Smoke,* chapter 6.

94 "Art's Art in Gallery, Nudes are Fine Art," *Toronto Daily Star*, 14 September 1927, 2; "Paintings to Remain in 'Ex' Art Gallery," *Evening Telegram*, 30 August 1927, 21; and "'Nudes' Not Banned," *Evening Telegram*, 14 September 1927, 23.

95 A Husband and Father, [pseud.] letter to the editor, *Evening Telegram*, 19 September 1927, 24.

96 Berger, *Ways of Seeing*, 46.

97 School Marm [pseud.] letter to the editor, *Evening Telegram*, 10 September 1927, 16. See also Harper, *Painting in Canada*, 232.

98 A Daughter [pseud.], letter to the editor, *Evening Telegram*, 2 September 1927, 24.

99 Alice Humler, letter to the editor, *Evening Telegram*, 17 September 1927, 18.

100 Lynda Nead, "Strip: Moving Bodies the 1890s," *Early Popular Visual Culture* 3, no. 2 (September 2005): 144–5.

101 *Globe*, 10 September 1927, 14.

102 Nead, "Strip," 139.

103 Nead, "Strip," 136.

104 Morris, *Embattled Shadows*, 3.

105 Archives of Ontario, File RG 56-1-1-1, British Films, 1926–1932, Letter From L.C. Serrios to J.D. Monteith, February 2, 1928.

106 "Premier Back in Ottawa," *Toronto Telegram*, 31 December 1927, 17.

6 Modern Girls and Machines

1 F. Scott Fitzgerald, *The Great Gatsby* (New York: Scribner, 1925, reprinted with preface and notes by Matthew J. Bruccoli, New York: Scribner Books, 1995), 15. Citations are to the Scribner 1995 edition.

2 See explanatory note by Bruccoli, 208.

3 de Grazia, "Introduction," 4.

4 For more on the shifts in patterns of consumption and their impact on Canadian retailers, see Belisle, *Retail Nation*, 36–44.

5 Archives of Ontario, RG 56-1-1-1, British Films, 1926–1932, Memo to Hon. J.D. Monteith, Provincial Secretary from J.C. Boylen, Acting Chairman; RG 56-1-2-121, *Annual Report, 1922–23*; Thompson with Seager, *Canada: 1922–1939*, 176; Valance S.J. Patriarche, "The Cinema of To-Day," in *Dalhousie Review* 7, no. 4 (January 1928): 419; and Rebecca Coulter, "Teen-Agers in Edmonton, 1921–1931" (PhD diss., University of Alberta, 1987), 125.

6 Berger, *Ways of Seeing*.

7 Cynthia Comacchio, "Mechanomorphosis: Science, Management, and 'Human Machinery' in Industrial Canada, 1900–45," *Labour/Le Travail* 41 (Spring 1998): 35–67, especially 49.

8 Tinkler and Warsh, "Feminine Modernity in Interwar Britain and North America," 126.

9 Jean Baudrillard, "The Finest Consumer Object: The Body," in *The Body: A Reader*, Mariam Fraser and Monica Greco, eds., (New York: Routledge, 1995), 277.

10 Thorstein Veblen, *Theory of the Leisure Class: An Economic Study of Institutions* (New York [1912], 1972).

11 Abigail Solomon-Godeau, "The Other Side of Venus: The Visual Economy of Feminine Display," in *The Sex of Things: Gender and Consumption in Historical Perspective*, Victoria de Grazia with Ellen Furlough, eds., (Berkeley: University of California Press, 1996), 113.

12 Marchand, *Advertising the American Dream*, 104–5.

13 See, for example, the Fisher Body adverts that appeared in successive months in 1928 and 1929. *Saturday Night*, 15 December 1928, 13; 9 February 1929, 9; and 12 January 1929, 9.

14 Conor, *The Spectacular Modern Woman*, 113.

15 *Maclean's*, 15 July 1929.

16 "It's A Girl," *Saturday Night*, 15 February 1928, 1.

17 David Nye, *American Technological Sublime* (Cambridge, MA: The MIT Press, 1996).

18 *Maclean's*, 15 April 1926, 30.

19 See, for example, the advertisement in *Maclean's*, 15 July 1929, 27.

20 John M. Lyle, "Address by John M. Lyle, 22 February 1929 at the Art Gallery of Toronto," in *Documents in Canadian Architecture*, Geoffrey Simmins, ed. (Peterborough: Broadview Press, 1992), 155.

21 Patriarche, "The Cinema of To-Day," 419.

22 Sherrie A. Innes, "The Feminine En-Gendering of Film Consumption and Film Technology in Popular Girls' Serial Novels, 1914–1931," *Journal of Popular Culture* 29, no. 3 (Winter 1995),173. On the technological developments, see Gerald Graham, *Canadian Film Technology, 1896–1986* (Newark: University of Delaware Press, 1989).

23 *Chatelaine*, June 1929.

24 *Saturday Night*, 17 July 1920, 7.

25 See, for example, the advertisements that appeared in *Maclean's*, 1 June 1926, 33; and *Saturday Night*, 27 August 1927, 28.

26 Significantly, however, this did not temper the discursive construction of women as flighty, distracted, or just plain bad drivers acting behind the wheel as they did at the department store counter.

27 Kristin Ross, *Fast Cars, Clean Bodies: Decolonization and the Reordering of French Culture* (Cambridge: M.I.T. Press, 1995), 38. Emphasis in the original.

28 *Saturday Night*, 17 July 1920, 3.

29 Archives of Ontario, RG 56-1-2-124, *Annual Report 1928*. That the American-
ness of film culture should be a point of concern is unsurprising given the
context of English-Canadian cultural nationalism at the time, which was
honed in on, in filmmaking. In Canada, the focus on the early period for film
has been studied most rewardingly in terms of the Canadian film industry and
American-Canadian cultural/political relations. See Morris, *Embattled Shadows*;
Gerald Mast, *A Short History of the Movies* (Toronto: MacMillan, 1992); George
Melnyk, *One Hundred Years of Canadian Cinema* (Toronto: University of
Toronto Press, 2004); Ted Magder, *Canada's Hollywood: The Canadian State
and Feature Films* (Toronto: University of Toronto Press, 1993); and David
Clandfield, *Canadian Film* (Toronto: Oxford University Press, 1987).

30 *Hush*, 27 September 1928, 8, 12.

31 *Maclean's*, 1 January 1926, 35; 1 June 1926, 33; and 1 May 1929, 39.

32 See, for example, *Saturday Night*, 24 April 1920, 21; 4 June 1927, 22;
Maclean's, 15 March 1924, 60; 15 November 1925, 57; and *Chatelaine*,
January 1929.

33 On car ownership, see James Dykes, *Canada's Automotive Industry* (Toronto:
McGraw-Hill, 1970), 31; John de Bondt, *Canada On Wheels: A Portfolio of
Early Canadian Cars* (Toronto: Oberon Press, 1970), 7–8; and Levine, *The
Devil in Babylon*, 233–4. Levine argues that by the late 1920s cars were a necessity. He cites the famous American *Middletown* study by Robert and
Helen Lynd. The Lynds performed research on cultural and social trends
in Muncie, Indiana, in 1924–5. They found that people were willing to for-
go food in order to save for a car, and that more working-class families had
cars than bathtubs.

34 Nathan Miller, *New World Coming: the 1920s and the Making of Modern America*
(New York: Scribner, 2003), 192.

35 Interview with Jean C., November 1981 quoted in Coulter, "Teen-Agers in
Edmonton," 128.

36 Comacchio, *The Dominion of Youth*, chapter 3. See also Beth Bailey, *From
Front Porch to Back Seat: Courtship in Twentieth-Century America* (Baltimore:
Johns Hopkins University Press, 1988).

37 Chambers, *Misconceptions*, 72–5.

38 Patriarche, "The Cinema of To-Day," 30.

39 *Hush*, 22 December 1927, 9.

40 On nineteenth-century concerns in Canada, see Mitchinson, *The Nature of
Their Bodies*, 60–1.

41 Prentice, *et al, Canadian Women*, 167.

42 On sex education in schools, see Christabelle Laura Sethna, "The Facts of
Life: The Sex Instruction of Ontario Public School Children, 1900–1950"
(Ph.D. dissertation, University of Toronto, 1995), 124–5.

43 University of Waterloo Archives, Doris Lewis Rare Book Room, E1339, *Healthy, Happy Womanhood*, (Toronto: Canada Social Hygiene Council), reprinted by permission of the American Social Hygiene Association, no date, 1920s.

44 Sethna, "The Facts of Life," 124. The Ontario Women's Christian Temperance Movement employed Beall until 1912 when he joined the Ontario Board of Education and lectured with them until the early 1930s. Sethna, "The Facts of Life," 71–2.

45 Archives of Ontario, RG 56-3 File 2.69 Restricted Feature Files, 1918–1971.

46 Archives of Ontario, File RG 56-1-1-4, Censorship File, 1911–1921, Letter from Samuel M. Meher to Peter Smith, Provincial Treasurer, 16 January 1920; and AO, RG 56-3, Censorship File, Letter for Chief Censor, Ontario Motion Picture Bureau from Gordon Bates, Canadian Social Hygiene Council, 23 December 1921.

47 See, for example, *Globe*, 28 May 1927, 5; *Saturday Night* 8 October 1927, 1; 15 October 1927, 20; 15 October 1927, 12.

48 Stephen Davies, "'Reckless Walking Must Be Discouraged': The Automobile Revolution and the Shaping of Modern Urban Canada to 1930," *Urban History Review* 18, no. 2 (October 1989): 123–38.

49 Comacchio, *The Dominion of Youth*, 31.

50 Heidi Kenaga, "Making the 'Studio Girl': The Hollywood Studio Club and Industry Regulation of Female Labour," *Film History* 18, no. 2 (2006): 130; Strange, *Toronto's Girl Problem*, 59; Peiss, *Cheap Amusements*, 180; and Cathy L. James, "'Not Merely for the Sake of an Evening's Entertainment': The Educational Uses of Theatre in Toronto's Settlement Houses, 1910–1930," *History of Education Quarterly* 38, no. 3 (Autumn, 1998): 295.

51 "The Problem of the Missing Girl," *Chatelaine*, March 1929; and Trevor Maguire, "Something Wrong Somewhere," *The Woman Worker*, March 1927, 6–8 reprinted in Hobbs and Sangster, *The Woman Worker*, 195–9.

52 Peiss, *Hope in a Jar*, 129, 141.

53 Canada, *House of Commons Debates*, (27 May 1920), p. 2811 (Mr. P.F. Casgrain, MP).

54 Archives of Ontario, RG 56-1-1-4, Censorship File, 1911–1921, Report on the Conference of the Censor Boards of Canada, 4 November 1921 (Conference was from November 1–3, 1921), 3.

55 Shelley Stamp Lindsey, "Toronto's 'Girl Workers': The Female Body and Industrial Efficiency in *Her Own Fault*," *Cinemas: Journal of Film Studies* 6, no. 1 (fall, 1995): 81–99.

56 *Catholic Register*, 18 August 1921, 4.

57 *Saturday Night*, 31 July 1920.

58 Patriarche, "The Cinema of To-Day," 420.

59 *Vancouver Sun*, 23 May 1927.

60 Initially, the injunction stopped Valentino from any employment. Under appeal the contract's clause that stopped him from "any other business of any kind or class whatsoever" was removed. *New York Times*, 20 January 1923, 13.

61 On this period in Valentino's life, see Norman A. Mackenzie, *The Magic of Rudolph Valentino*, (London: Research Publishing Company, 1974, 61–5; and Irving Shulman, *Valentino*, (New York: Simon and Schuster, 1967), 223–44.

62 Mackenzie, *The Magic of Rudolph Valentino*, 63–4; and Shulman, *Valentino*, 223–4.

63 Mackenzie, *The Magic of Rudolph Valentino*, 61–5; and Shulman, *Valentino*, 223–30. This promise was most likely just a way to garner publicity. Given the fact that Valentino had no movie opportunities at the time since he had left his studio, and a court injunction stopped him from working for others, Valentino was not looking for a new leading lady. For an example of the advertisements, see *Globe*, 16 April 1923, 2.

64 *Globe*, 16 April 1923, 2.

65 Joseph M. Mauro, *Thunder Bay: A History*, Thunder Bay: Lehto Printers Ltd., 1981, 299. Niblock's parents had lived in Port Arthur, Ontario before relocating to Toronto.

66 The Murray Kay store advertised after Niblock's early appearances that they would be issuing only one thousand tickets for each of her appearances given the overwhelming demand. On her appearances at the Murray Kay store, see *Globe*, 13 December 1923, 15; 14 December 1923, 14; and 19 December 1923, 14. On her involvement with the Shriners, see *Globe*, 11 December 1923, 12.

67 "Crippled Children will Reap Benefit," *Globe*, 13 December 1923, 14.

68 *New York Times*, 29 November 1923, 30.

69 "Toronto's Beauty Best in America," *Globe*, 29 November 1923, 1.

70 "This Too, Was Once 'Un-American,'" *New York Times*, 30 November 1923, 14.

71 *Victoria Daily Times* reported that Claudia Ross won a contest in Columbus, Ohio over hundreds of women because of "the freshness and naturalness of her beauty, absence of make-up and of an attempt to pose." See *Victoria Daily Times*, 6 May 1927, 2.

72 *Globe*, 13 December 1923, 15.

73 David O. Selznick, "Rudolph Valentino and his 88 American Beauties," 1923.

74 For a contemporary example, see Anne Elizabeth Wilson, "The Problem of the Missing Girl," *Chatelaine* March 1929, 8–9, 58–9. For the Canadian

context, see Valverde, *The Age of Light, Soap and Water,* chapter 4; and Strange, *Toronto's Girl Problem,* 96–102.

75 On these contests see, for example, *Manitoba Free Press,* 3 May 1927, 21; *Regina Leader,* 25 April 1927, 10; and *Victoria Times,* 14 May 1927, 12; *Victoria Times,* 18 April 1927, 9; 11 May 1927, 11; 18 May 1927, 1; 21 May 1927, 3; 11 June 1927, 1; *Vancouver Sun,* 14 May 1927, 1; and 13 June 1927, 5.

76 See, for example, the newspaper coverage from 26–7 June in the *Ottawa Citizen.*

77 Morduant Hall, "Tillie, the Spinner of Yarns," *New York Times,* 7 June 1927.

78 Ryan, "The Projection of a New Womanhood," 366–85; and Higashi, *Virgins, Vamps, and Flappers,* chapter 5.

79 *Toronto Daily Star,* 19 September 1927, 33.

80 Dance Collection Danse, (hereafter DCD) Karen Rennie's interview with Gail Grant, 16 July 1991. In the early 1930s, while dancing at Radio City Music Hall in New York City, Edith Grant had here name changed to Gail Grant by her fellow dancers who thought that Edith did not sound theatrical enough. Later when she married, she used the name Gail Grant Ryan, although Gail Grant remained her stage name. DCD, Karen Rennie's interview with Gail Grant, 8 February 1992; and Lawrence Adams's interview with Nancy Caldwell, 16 August 1989.

81 "Final Prize List and Rules in 'Miss Victoria' Beauty Contest are Issued To-Day," *Victoria Times,* 19 April 1927, 7.

82 DCD, Rennie's interview with Gail Grant, 16 July 1991.

83 *Victoria Times,* 18 May 1927, 1; and 21 May 1927, 3.

84 "Miss Canada Draws Vanderbilt's Praise," *Victoria Times,* 26 May 1927, 9; and "Marriage Proposals Most Exciting of Miss Canada's Trip," *Victoria Times,* 31 May 1927, 5.

85 "Beauty Queen to Get Try-Out at Hollywood," *Victoria Times,* 18 April 1927, 9.

86 There are a few exceptions of women who made brief forays into Hollywood acting careers, but none achieved the fame and fortune promised by pageant organizers. "Adrienne Truex, Newest Film Beauty, Comes From Texas," *Victoria Times,* 3 June 1927, 14; and Deford, *There She Is,* 131–2.

87 Carolyn Kitch, *The Girl on the Magazine Cover: The Origins of Visual Stereotypes in American Mass Media* (Chapel Hill: University of North Carolina Press, 2001), 131.

88 "Expression Is Essence of Beauty, Writes Coffin," *Victoria Daily Times,* 21 May 1927.

89 Deford, *There She Is.*

90 DCD, Karen Rennie's interview with Gail Grant, 2 June 1991.

91 DCD, Rennie's interview with Gail Grant, 2 June 1991; and 16 July 1991.

92 DCD, Gail Grant's scrapbook.
93 DCD, Lawrence Adams's interview with Gail Grant, 8 October 1990.
94 Archives of Ontario, RG 56-1-1-1, British Films, 1926–1932.
95 Jean Graham, "At Five O'Clock," *Saturday Night,* 25 August 1928, 35.

Conclusion

1 "Champions of Modern Girl Lose," *The Halifax Herald,* 5 May 1927.
2 Katrina Srigley, "Clothing Stories: Consumption, Identity, and Desire in Depression-Era Toronto," in *Journal of Women's History* 19, no. 1 (2007): 82–104.
3 Thomas Thorner with Thor Frohn-Nielson, *"A Country Nourished on Self-Doubt": Documents in Post-Confederation Canada* 2nd edition (Toronto: Broadview Press, 2003), 264.

Bibliography

Primary Sources

Archival Sources

Library and Archives of Canada
   John Wentworth Russell fonds
Archives of Ontario
   Ontario Board of Censors
   Office Attorney General Files
Other Depositories
   City of Toronto Archives
   Dance Collection Danse Archives
   Canadian National Exhibition Archives
   University of Waterloo Archives

Selected Books and Published Material

Allan, Maud. *My Life and Dancing*. London: Everett and Co., 1908.
Arvidson, Linda. *When Movies Were Young*. New York: Benjamin Bloom [1925] 1968.
Clark, C.S. *Of Toronto the Good*. Montreal: The Toronto Publishing Company, 1898; Coles Canadian Collection, 1970.
Division of Industrial Hygiene. *Health Confessions of Business Women by Business Women*. Provincial Board of Health, 1923.
Fitzgerald, F. Scott. *The Great Gatsby*. New York: Penguin, [1926] 1950.
– *Bernice Bobs Her Hair and Other Stories*. New York: Signet Classics, 1996.

Hobbs, Margaret, and Joan Sangster, eds. *The Woman Worker, 1926–1929.*
   St. John's: Canadian Committee on Labour History, 1999.
Kellerman, Annette. *Physical Beauty – How to Keep It: Annette Kellerman Illustrated.*
   New York: George H. Doras, 1918.
King, William Lyon Mackenzie. *The Mackenzie King Diaries, 1893–1931.*
   Transcript. Toronto, 1973.
Nystrom, Paul H. *Economics of Fashion.* New York: Ronald Press, 1928.
Simmons, Geoffrey, ed. *Documents in Canadian Architecture.* Peterborough:
   Broadview Press, 1992.
Montgomery, Lucy Maud. *Anne of Green Gables.* New York: Seal Books Edition
   [1908] 1996.
Murphy, Emily. *The Black Candle.* Toronto: Thomas Allen, 1922; reprinted Coles
   Canadiana Collection, 1973.
Read, D. and R. Hann, eds. *The Great War and Canadian Society: An Oral History.*
   Toronto: Hogtown Press, 1978.
Thomas, W.I. *The Unadjusted Girl with cases and standpoint for behaviour analysis.*
   Boston: Little, Brown and Co, 1923.

Film

David O. Selznick. *Rudolph Valentino and his 88 American Beauties.* 1923.

Secondary Sources

Unpublished Sources

Coulter, Rebecca. "Teen-Agers in Edmonton, 1921–1931." Ph.D. diss.,
   University of Alberta, 1987.
Gentile, Patrizia. "Searching for 'Miss Civil Service' and 'Mr. Civil Service':
   Gender Anxiety, Beauty Contests and Fruit Machines in the Canadian Civil
   Service, 1950–1973." Master's thesis, Carleton University, 1996.
– "Queen of the Maple Leaf: A History of Beauty Contests in Twentieth
   Century Canada," Ph.D. diss., Queen's University, 2006.
Milligan, Ian. "Embracing the 'Big History' Shift: Social Historians and Digital
   History (or 'how I learned to stop worrying and love the n-gram')." Paper de-
   livered at the Cultural Historiographies conference, Guelph, Ontario, March
   2012.
Wolfe, Deborah Sue. "Beauty as Vocation: Women and Beauty Contests in
   America." Ph.D. diss., Columbia University, 1994.

Published Secondary Sources

Adorno, Theodor W. and Max Horkheimer. "The Culture Industry:
Enlightenment as Mass Deception," in *Dialectics of Enlightenment*, 120–67.
New York and London: Verso [1944], 1972.

Anderson, Benedict. *Imagined Communities: Reflections on the Origin and Spread of
Nationalism.* London: Verso, 1983.

Anderson, Kay. *Vancouver's Chinatown: Racial Discourse in Canada, 1875–1980.*
Montreal and Kingston: McGill-Queen's University Press, 1995.

Andrews, Maggie and Mary M. Talbot. *All the World and Her Husband: Women in
Twentieth-Century Consumer Culture.* London and New York: Cassell, 2000.

Arnup, Katherine. *Education for Motherhood: Advice for Mothers in Twentieth-
Century Canada.* Toronto: University of Toronto Press, 1994.

Avery, Donald. *Reluctant Host: Canada's Response to Immigrant Workers, 1896–1994.*
Toronto: McClelland and Stewart, 1995.

Ayukawa, Midge. "Japanese Pioneer Women: Fighting Racism and Rearing the
Next Generation," in *Sisters or Strangers? Immigrant, Ethnic, and Racialized
Women in Canadian History,* edited by Marlene Epp, Franca Iacovetta and
Frances Swyripa, 233–47. Toronto: University of Toronto Press, 2004.

Azoulay, Dan. *Hearts and Minds: Canadian Romance at the Dawn of the Modern Era,
1900–1930.* Calgary: University of Calgary Press, 2011.

Bacchi, Carol Lee. *Liberation Deferred? The Ideas of the English Canadian Suffragists,
1877–1918.* Toronto: University of Toronto Press, 1982.

Backhouse Constance. *Colour-Coded: A Legal History of Racism in Canada, 1900–
1950.* Toronto: University of Toronto Press, 1999.

– *Carnal Crimes: Sexual Assault Law in Canada, 1900–1975.* Toronto: The Osgoode
Society for Canadian Legal History, University of Toronto Press, 2008.

Bailey, Beth L. *From Front Porch to Back Seat: Courtship in Twentieth-Century
America.* Baltimore: Johns Hopkins University Press, 1988.

Banet-Weiser, Sarah. *The Most Beautiful Girl in the World: Beauty Pageants and
National Identity.* Berkeley: University of California Press, 1999.

Banner, Lois. *American Beauty.* New York: Alfred A. Knopf, 1983.

Banta, Martha. *Imaging American Women: Ideas and Ideals in Cultural History.* New
York: Columbia University Press, 1987.

Bartky, Sandra Lee. *Femininity and Domination: Studies in the Phenomenology of
Oppression.* New York: Routledge, 1990.

– "Suffering to Be Beautiful." In *Gender Struggles: Practical Approaches to
Contemporary Feminism,* edited by Constance L. Mui and Julien S. Murphy,
244–5. Lanham, MD: Rowman and Littlefield Publishers Inc., 2002.

Baskerville, Peter. *A Silent Revolution? Gender and Wealth in English Canada, 1860–1930.* Montreal and Kingston: McGill-Queen's University Press, 2008.

Baudrillard, Jean. "The Finest Consumer Object: The Body." In *The Body: A Reader,* edited by Mariam Fraser and Monica Greco, 277–82. New York: Routledge, 1995.

Beetham, Margaret. *A Magazine of Her Own? Domesticity and Desire in the Woman's Magazine, 1800–1914.* New York: Routledge, 1996.

Belisle, Donica. "Toward a Canadian Consumer History." *Labour/Le Travail* 52, no. 2 (Fall 2003): 181–206.

– *Retail Nation: Department Stores and the Making of Modern Canada.* Vancouver: University of British Columbia Press, 2011.

– "Crazy for Bargains: Inventing the Irrational Female Shopper in Modernizing English Canada." *Canadian Historical Review* 92, no. 4 (December 2011): 581–606.

Bennett, Tony. *The Birth of the Museum: History, Theory, Politics.* New York: Routledge, 1995.

Berger, Carl. "The True North Strong and Free." In *Nationalism in Canada,* edited by Peter Russell, 3–26. Toronto: McGraw-Hill Ryerson Ltd., 1966.

– *The Writing of Canadian History: Aspects of English-Canadian Historical Writing since 1900.* 2nd ed. Toronto: University of Toronto Press, 1986.

Berger, John. *Ways of Seeing.* Toronto: Macmillan, 1972.

Bivans, Ann Marie. *Miss America: In Pursuit of the Crown.* New York: Mastermedia, 1991.

Bogdan, Robert. *Freak Show: Presenting Human Oddities for Amusement and Profit.* Chicago: University of Chicago Press, 1988.

Bordo, Susan. *Unbearable Weight: Feminism, Western Culture, and the Body.* Berkeley: University of California Press, 1993.

Bowlby, Rachel. *Just Looking: Consumer Culture in Dreiser, Gissing, and Zola.* London: Methuen, 1985.

Brookes, Barbara. "'The Glands of Destiny': Hygiene, Hormones and English Women Doctors in the First Half of the 20th Century." *Canadian Bulletin of Medical History* 21, no. 1 (2006): 49–67.

Brookfield, Tarah. "Modelling the UN's Mission in Semi-Formal Wear: Edmonton's 'Miss United Nations' Pageants of the 1960s." In *Contesting Bodies and Nation in Canadian History,* edited by Patrizia Gentile and Jane Nicholas. Toronto: University of Toronto Press, 2013.

Brumberg, Joan Jacobs. *The Body Project: An Intimate History of American Girls.* New York: Random House, 1997.

Buck-Morss, Susan. *The Dialectics of Seeing: Walter Benjamin and the Arcades Project.* Cambridge, MA: MIT Press, 1989.

Buckley, Suzann and Janice Dickin McGinnis. "Venereal Disease and Public Health Reform in Canada." *Canadian Historical Review* 63, no. 3 (September 1982): 337–54.

Campbell, Robert A. *Sit Down and Drink Your Beer: Regulating Vancouver's Beer Parlours, 1925–1954.* Toronto: University of Toronto Press, 2001.

Canning, Kathleen. *Gender History in Practice: Historical Perspectives on Bodies, Class and Citizenship.* Ithaca: Cornell University Press, 2006.

Carr, Angela. *Toronto Architect Edmund Burke: Redefining Canadian Architecture.* Montreal and Kingston: McGill-Queen's University Press, 1995.

Carstairs, Catherine. *Jailed for Possession: Illegal Drug Use, Regulation, and Power in Canada, 1920–1961.* Toronto: University of Toronto Press, 2006.

Chambers, Lori. *Misconceptions: Unmarried Motherhood and the Ontario Children of Unmarried Parents Act, 1921–1969.* Toronto: Osgoode Society for Canadian Legal History, University of Toronto Press, 2007.

Chicago, Judy and Edward Lucie-Smith. *Women and Art: Contested Territory.* New York: Watson-Guptill Publications, 1999.

Chow, Karen. "Popular Sexual Knowledges and Women's Agency in 1920s England: Marie Stopes's 'Married Love' and E.M. Hull's 'The Sheik.'" *Feminist Review* 63 (Autumn 1999): 64–87.

Clark, T.J. *The Painting of Modern Life: Paris in the Art of Manet and His Followers.* New York: Knopf, 1985.

Clarke, David B., Marcus A. Doel, and Kate M.L. Housiaux, "General Introduction." In *The Consumption Reader,* edited by David B. Clarke, Marcus A. Doel, and Kate M.L. Housiaux, 1–23. New York and London: Routledge, 2003.

Cleverdon, Catherine. *The Woman Suffrage Movement in Canada.* Toronto: University of Toronto Press, 1970.

Cohen, Colleen Ballerino, Richard Wilk, and Beverly Stoltje. *Beauty Queens on the Global Stage: Gender, Contests, and Power.* New York: Routledge, 1996.

Cohen, Ronny H. "Tut and the 20s: 'The Egyptian Look.'" *Art in America* (March/April 1979), 97.

Coleman, Daniel. *White Civility: The Literary Project of English Canada.* Toronto: University of Toronto Press, 2008.

Colpitts, George, "The Domesticated Body and the Industrialized Woman's Fur Coat in Canada in the Interwar Period." In *Contesting Bodies and Nation in Canadian History,* edited by Patrizia Gentile and Jane Nicholas. Toronto: University of Toronto Press, 2013.

Comacchio, Cynthia. *Nations Are Built of Babies: Saving Ontario's Mothers and Children, 1900–1940.* Montreal and Kingston: McGill-Queen's University Press, 1993.

– "Dancing to Perdition: Adolescence and Leisure in Interwar English-Canada." *Journal of Canadian Studies* 32, no. 3 (Fall 1997): 5–35.

- "'A Postscript for Father': Defining A New Fatherhood in Interwar Canada." *Canadian Historical Review* 78, no. 3 (September 1997): 385–408.
- "Mechanomorphosis: Science, Management, and 'Human Machinery' in Industrial Canada, 1900–1945." *Labour/Le travail* 41 (1998): 35–67.
- *The Infinite Bonds of Family: Domesticity in Canada, 1850–1940.* Toronto: University of Toronto Press, 1999.
- *The Dominion of Youth: Adolescence and the Making of Modern Canada, 1920–1950.* Waterloo, ON: Wilfrid Laurier University Press, 2006.
Comiskey, Carolyn. "Cosmetic Surgery in Paris in 1926: The Case of the Amputated Leg." *Journal of Women's History* 16, no. 3 (Fall 2004): 30–54.
Comiskey, Carolyn Ward. "'I Will Kill Myself … If I Have to Keep My Fat Calves!': Legs and Cosmetic Surgery in Paris in 1926." In *Body Parts: Critical Explorations in Corporeality*, edited by Christopher E. Forth and Ivan Crozier, 247–63. Lanham, MD: Lexington Books, 2005.
Conor, Liz. *The Spectacular Modern Woman: Feminine Visibility in the 1920s.* Bloomington and Indianapolis: Indiana University Press, 2004.
- "'Blackfella Missus Too Much Proud': Techniques of Appearing, Femininity, and Race in Australian Modernity." In *The Modern Girl Around the World: Consumption, Modernity, Globalization*, edited by Alys Eve Weinbaum, Lynn M. Thomas, Priti Ramamurthy, Uta G. Poiger, Madeleine Y. Dong, and Tani E. Barlow, 220–39. Durham and London: Duke University Press, 2008.
Conrad, Margaret and Alvin Finkel. *History of the Canadian Peoples: 1867 to the Present*, Vol. 2, 3rd ed. Toronto: Addison, Wesley, Longman, 2002.
Cook, Sharon Anne. "'Liberation Sticks' or 'Coffin Nails'? Representations of the Working Woman and Cigarette Smoking in Canada, 1919–1939." *Canadian Bulletin of Medical History* 24, no. 2 (2007): 367–401.
- *Sex, Lies and Cigarettes: Canadian Women, Smoking, and Visual Culture, 1880–2000.* Montreal and Kingston: McGill-Queen's University Press, 2012.
Cott, Nancy. *The Grounding of Modern Feminism.* New Haven: Yale, 1997.
Cranfield John and Kris Inwood. "The Great Transformation: A Long-Run Perspective On Physical Well-Being in Canada." *Economics and Human Biology* 5 (2007): 204–28.
Crow, Thomas. "Modernism and Mass Culture in the Visual Arts." In *Modernism and Modernity: The Vancouver Conference Papers*, edited by Benjamin H.D. Buchloh, Serge Guilbaut, and David Solkin, 215–64. Halifax: Press of the Nova Scotia College of Art and Design, 1983.
Crowley, Terry. *Agnes Macphail and the Politics of Equality.* Toronto: James Lorimer, 1990.
Cruikshank, Ken and Nancy B. Bouchier. "Dirty Spaces: Environment, the State, and Recreational Swimming in Hamilton Harbour, 1870-1946." *Sport History Review* 29, no. 1 (1998): 1–20.

Cutherbert Brandt, Gail, Naomi Black, Paula Bourne, and Magda Fahrni. *Canadian Women: A History*, 3rd ed. Toronto: Nelson, 2011.

Damon-Moore, Helen. *Magazines for the Millions: Gender and Commerce in the Ladies' Home Journal and Saturday Evening Post, 1880–1910.* New York: State University of New York Press, 1994.

Darian-Smith, Kate and Sara Willis. "From Queen of Agriculture to Miss Showgirl: Embodying Rurality in Twentieth-Century Australia." *Journal of Australian Studies* 71, (2001): 17–32.

Davidoff, Lenore and Catherine Hall. *Family Fortunes: Men and Women of the English Middle Class, 1780–1850.* London: Hutchinson, 1987.

Davies, Stephen. "'Wreckless Walking Must Be Discouraged': The Automobile Revolution and the Shaping of Modern Urban Canada to 1930." *Urban History Review* 18, no. 2 (October 1989): 123–38.

Dawn, Leslie. *National Visions, National Blindness: Canadian Art and Identities in the 1920s.* Vancouver: University of British Columbia Press, 2006.

de Bondt, John. *Canada On Wheels: A Portfolio of Early Canadian Cars.* Toronto: Oberon Press, 1970.

de Grazie, Victoria with Ellen Furlough, ed. *The Sex of Things: Consumption in Historical Perspective.* Berkeley: University of California Press, 1996.

Deford, Frank. *There She Is: The Life and Times of Miss America.* New York: Viking, 1971.

Douglas, Ann. *Terrible Honesty: Mongrel Manhattan in the 1920s.* New York: Farrar, Straus, and Giroux, 1995.

Dua, Enakshi. "Racializing Imperial Canada: Indian Women and the Making of Ethnic Communities." In *Sisters or Strangers? Immigrant, Ethnic, and Racialized Women in Canadian History,* edited by Marlene Epp, Franca Iacovetta and Frances Swyripa, 71–88. Toronto: University of Toronto Press, 2004.

Dubinsky, Karen. *Improper Advances: Rape and Heterosexual Conflict in Ontario, 1880–1929.* Chicago: University of Chicago Press, 1993.

Duval, Paul. *Canadian Impressionism.* Toronto: McClelland and Stewart, 1990.

Dykes, James. *Canada's Automotive Industry.* Toronto: McGraw-Hill, 1970.

Erdman, Andrew L. *Blue Vaudeville: Sex, Morals, and the Mass Marketing of Amusement, 1895–1915.* Jefferson, NC: McFarland & Company, Inc., 2004.

Fawcett, "Romance, Glamour and the Exotic: Femininity and Fashion in Britain in the 1900s." In *New Woman Hybridities: Femininity, Feminism, and International Consumer Culture, 1880–1930,* edited by Ann Heilman and Margaret Beetham, 145–157. New York: Routledge, 2004.

Featherstone, Mike. "The Body in Consumer Culture." *Theory, Culture and Society* 1, no. 2 (September 1982): 18–33.

Felski, Rita. *The Gender of Modernity.* Cambridge, MA: Harvard University Press, 1995.

Fiamengo, Janice. "Rediscovering Our Foremothers Again: Racial Ideas of Canada's Early Feminists, 1885-1945." *Essays on Canadian Writing* 75 (2002): 85–112.

– *The Woman's Page: Journalism and Rhetoric in Early Canada.* Toronto: University of Toronto Press, 2008.

Filey, Mike. *I Remember Sunnyside: The Rise and Fall of a Magical Era.* Toronto: Brownstone Press, 1981.

Fischer, Lucy. *Designing Women: Cinema, Art Deco and the Female Form.* New York: Columbia University Press, 2003.

Forbes, Ernest. "The Ideas of Carol Bacchi and the Suffragists of Halifax." *Atlantis* 10, no. 2 (Spring 1985): 199–226.

Forth, Christopher. *Masculinity in the Modern West: Gender, Civilization, and the Body.* New York: Palgrave Macmillan, 2008.

Foss, Brian. "Living Landscape." In *Edwin Holgate,* edited by Rosalind Pepall and Brian Foss. Montreal: Museum of Fine Arts, 2005.

Foucault, Michel. "Technologies of the Self." In *Technologies of the Self: A Seminar with Michel Foucault* edited by Luther H. Martin, Huck Gutman, and Patrick A. Hutton. Amherst: University of Massachusetts Press, 1988.

Foucault, Michel. *Discipline and Punish: The Birth of the Prison.* New York: Vintage, 1995.

Francis, Daniel. *The Imaginary Indian: The Image of the Indian in Canadian Culture.* Vancouver: Arsenal Pulp Press, 1992.

Friedan, Betty. *The Feminine Mystique.* New York: W.W. Norton and Company, 2001 [1963].

Fussell, Paul. *The Great War and Modern Memory.* London: Oxford University Press, 1975.

Ganeva, Mila. *Women in Weimar Fashion: Discourses and Displays in German Culture, 1918–1933.* Rochester: Camden House, 2008.

Geller, Peter. *Northern Exposures: Photographing and Filming the Canadian North, 1920–45.* Vancouver: University of British Columbia Press, 2004.

Gentile, Patrizia and Jane Nicholas, eds. *Contesting Bodies and Nation in Canadian History.* Toronto: University of Toronto Press, 2013.

Glyn, Anthony. *Elinor Glyn: A Biography.* New York: Doubleday & Company, Inc., 1955.

Goss, David. "The Fairest Girl." *Beaver* 83, no. 1 (February/March 2003): 29–32.

Grosz, Elizabeth. *Volatile Bodies: Toward a Corporeal Feminism.* Indianapolis: Indiana University Press, 1994.

Hamlin, Kimberly A. "Bathing Suits and Backlash: The First Miss American Pageants, 1921-1927." In *There She Is, Miss America: The Politics of Sex, Beauty, and Race in America's Most Famous Pageant,* edited by Elwood Watson and Darcy Martin, 27–51. New York: Palgrave Macmillan, 2004.

Hansen Atchison, Devon. "Shades of Change." In *Consuming Modernity: Changing Gendered Behaviours and Consumerism, 1919–1940*, edited by Cheryl Krasnick Warsh and Dan Malleck. Vancouver: University of British Columbia Press, 2013.

Hansen, Miriam. *Babel and Babylon: Spectatorship in American Silent Film.* Cambridge, MA: Harvard University Press, 1994.

Harper, J. Russell. *Painting In Canada: A History*, 2nd ed. Toronto: University of Toronto Press, 1977.

Harris, Richard. *Creeping Conformity: How Canada Became Suburban, 1900–1960.* Toronto: University of Toronto Press, 2004.

Heamann, E.A. *The Inglorious Arts of Peace: Exhibitions in Canadian Society During the Nineteenth Century.* Toronto: University of Toronto Press, 1999.

Henry, Wade A. "Imagining the Great White Mother and the Great King: Aboriginal Tradition and Royal Representation at the 'Great Pow-wow' of 1901." *Journal of the Canadian Historical Association* n.s. 11, 2000: 87–108.

Higashi, Sumiko. *Virgins, Vamps and Flappers: The American Silent Movie Heroine.* Montreal: Eden Press Women's Publications, Inc., 1978.

Hirschbein, Laura Davidow. "The Flapper and the Fogey: Representations of Gender and Age in the 1920s." *Journal of Family History* 26, no. 1 (January 2001): 112–37.

Hjartarson, Paul. "'Virgin Land,' the Settler-Invader Subject, and Cultural Nationalism: Gendered Landscape in the Cultural Construction of Canadian National Identity." In *Gender and Landscape: Renegotiating Morality and Space*, edited by Lorraine Dowler, Josephine Carubia, and Bonj Szczygiel, 203–20. New York and London: Routledge, 2005.

Hollows, Joanne. *Feminism, Femininity, and Popular Culture.* Manchester: Manchester University Press, 2000.

Houston, Susan E. "'A little steam, a little sizzle, a little sleaze': English-Language Tabloids in the Interwar Period." *Papers of the Bibliographical Society of Canada* 40, no. 1 (Spring 2002): 37–59.

Huskins, Bonnie. "The Ceremonial Space of Women: Public Processions in Victorian Saint John and Halifax." In *Separate Spheres: Women's Worlds in the 19th-Century Maritimes*, edited by Janet Guildford and Suzanne Morton, 145–59. Fredericton: Acadiensis Press, 1994.

Huyssen, Andreas. *After the Great Divide: Modernism, Mass Culture, Postmodernism.* Bloomington and Indianapolis: Indiana University Press, 1986.

Iacovetta, Franca and Mariana Valverde, eds. *Gender Conflicts: New Essays in Women's History.* Toronto: University of Toronto Press, 1992.

Innes, Sherrie A. "The Feminine En-Gendering of Film Consumption and Film Technology in Popular Girls' Serial Novels, 1914–1931." *Journal of Popular Culture* 29, no. 3 (Winter 1995): 169–82.

Irvine, Dean. *Editing Modernity: Women and Little-Magazine Cultures in Canada 1916–1956.* Toronto: University of Toronto Press, 2008.

James, Cathy L. "'Not Merely for the Sake of an Evenings Entertainment': The Educational Uses of Theatre in Toronto's Settlement Houses, 1910–1930." *History of Education Quarterly* 38, no. 3 (Autumn 1998): 287–311.

Jasen, Patricia. *Wild Things: Nature, Culture, and Tourism in Ontario, 1790–1914.* Toronto: University of Toronto Press, 1995.

Jay, Martin. "Scopic Regimes of Modernity." In *Vision and Visuality*, edited by Hal Foster, 3–23. Seattle: Bay Press, 1988.

Jessup, Lynda. "Bushwackers in the Gallery: Antimodernism and the Group of Seven." In *Antimodernism and the Artistic Experience*, edited by Lynda Jessup, 130–52. Toronto: University of Toronto Press, 2001.

Jimenez, Margarita and Laura Mulvey. "The Spectacle is Vulnerable: Miss World, 1970." In *Visual and Other Pleasures*, edited by Laura Mulvey, 3–5. London: MacMillan Press Ltd, 1989.

Johnston, Russell. *Selling Themselves: The Emergence of Canadian Advertising.* Toronto: University of Toronto Press, 2001.

Jones, Jennifer. "The Beauty Queen As Sacrificial Victim." *Theatre History Studies* 18, (June 1998): 99–106.

Kalman, Harold. *A History of Canadian Architecture*, vol. 2. Toronto: Oxford University Press, 1994.

Kaprielian-Churchill, Isabel. "*Odars* and 'Others': Intermarriage and the Retention of Armeian Ethnic Identity," In *Sisters or Strangers? Immigrant, Ethnic, and Racialized Women in Canadian History*, edited by Marlene Epp, Franca Iacovetta and Frances Swyripa, 248–265. Toronto: University of Toronto Press, 2004.

Kasson, John. *Amusing the Millions: Coney Island at the Turn of the Century.* New York: Hill & Wang, 1978.

Kealy, Linda. *Enlisting Women for the Cause: Women, Labour, and the Left in Canada, 1890–1920.* Toronto: University of Toronto Press, 1998.

Kelcey, Barbara E. "Dress Reform in Nineteenth Century Canada." In *Fashion: A Canadian Perspective*, edited by Alexandra Palmer, 229–48. Toronto: University of Toronto Press, 2004.

Kenaga, Heidi. "Making the 'Studio Girl': Hollywood Studio Club and Industry Regulation of Female Labour." *Film History* 18, no. 2 (2006): 129–39.

Kidd, Bruce. *The Struggle for Canadian Sport.* Toronto: University of Toronto Press, 1996.

Kitch, Carolyn. *The Girl on the Magazine Cover: The Origins of Visual Stereotypes in American Mass Media.* Chapel Hill: University of North Carolina Press, 2001.

Korinek, Valerie. *Roughing It in the Suburbs: Reading Chatelaine Magazine in the Fifties and Sixties.* Toronto: University of Toronto Press, 2000.

Kossuth, Robert S. "Dangerous Waters: Victorian Decorum, Swimmer Safety, and the Establishment of Public Bathing Facilities in London (Canada)." *International Journal of the History of Sport* 22, no. 5 (September 2005): 796–815.

Lang, Marjory. *Women Who Made the News: Female Journalists in Canada, 1880–1945.* Montreal and Kingston: McGill-Queen's University Press, 1999.

Latham, Angela J. *Posing a Threat: Flappers, Chorus Girls, and Other Brazen Performers of the 1920s.* Hanover, NH: University of New England Press, 2000.

Lears, T.J. Jackson. *No Place of Grace: Antimodernism and the Transformation of American Culture, 1880–1920.* Chicago: University of Chicago Press, 1981.

– "From Salvation to Self-Realization." In *The Culture of Consumption*, edited by Richard Wightman Fox and T.J. Jackson Lears, 1–38. New York: Pantheon Books, 1983.

– *Fables of Abundance: A Cultural History of Advertising in America.* New York: Basic Books, 1994.

Leavitt, Sarah A. *From Catharine Beecher to Martha Stewart: A Cultural History of Domestic Advice.* Chapel Hill and London: The University of North Carolina Press, 2002.

Leeds Craig, Maxine. *Ain't I a Beauty Queen? Black Women, Beauty and the Politics of Race.* New York: Oxford University Press, 2002.

LeGates, Marlene. *Making Waves: A History of Feminism in Western Society.* Toronto: Copp Clark, 1996.

Lenskyj, Helen. *Out of Bounds: Women, Sport and Sexuality.* Toronto: Women's Press, 1986.

Lenton-Young, Gerald. "Variety Theatre." In *Early Stages: Theatre in Ontario, 1800–1914*, edited by Ann Saddlemyer, 166–213. Toronto: University of Toronto Press, 1990.

Levine, Allen. *The Devil in Babylon: Fear of Progress and the Birth of Modern Life.* Toronto: McClelland and Stewart, 2005.

Little, Margaret. *No Car, No Radio, No Liquor Permit: The Moral Regulation of Single Mothers in Ontario, 1920–1997.* Don Mills: Oxford University Press, 1998.

Loo, Tina and Carolyn Strange. "The Travelling Show Menace: Contested Regulation in Turn-of-the-Century Ontario." *Law and Society Review* 29, no. 4 (1995): 639–67.

Loo, Tina. "Making a Modern Wilderness: Conserving Wildlife in Twentieth-Century Canada." *Canadian Historical Review* 82, no. 1 (March 2001): 92–121.

López, Rick A. "The India Bonita Contest of 1921 and the Ethnicization of Mexican National Culture." *Hispanic American Historical Review* 82, no. 2 (2002): 291–328.

Lowe, Margaret. *Looking Good: College Women and Body Image, 1875–1930.* Baltimore, MD: Johns Hopkins University Press, 2003.

Mackenzie, Norman A. *The Magic of Rudolph Valentino*. London: The Research Publishing Co., 1974.

Macmillan, Margaret. *Paris 1919: Six Months that Changed the World*. Toronto: Random House, 2001.

MacTavish, Newton. *The Fine Arts in Canada*. Toronto: Macmillian Co., 1925.

Marchand, Roland. *Advertising the American Dream: Making Way for Modernity, 1920–1940*. Berkeley: University of California Press, 1985.

Mar, Lisa Rose. "The Tale of Lin Tee: Madness, Family Violence, and Lindsay's Anti-Chinese Riot of 1919." In *Sisters or Strangers? Immigrant, Ethnic, and Racialized Women in Canadian History*, edited by Marlene Epp, Franca Iacovetta and Frances Swyripa, 108–32. Toronto: University of Toronto Press, 2004.

– "Beyond Being Others: Chinese Canadians as National History." *BC Studies* 156 (Winter 2007–2008): 13–34.

Marks, Lynne. *Roller Rinks and Revivals: Religion, Leisure, and Identity in Late-Nineteenth-Century Small-Town Ontario*. Toronto: University of Toronto Press, 1996.

Mauro, Joseph M. *Thunder Bay: A History*. Thunder Bay: Lehto Printers Ltd., 1981.

McClintock, Anne. *Imperial Leather: Race, Gender, and Sexuality in the Colonial Contest*. New York: Routledge, 1995.

McKay, Ian. *The Quest of the Folk: Antimodernism and Cultural Selection in Twentieth-Century Nova Scotia*. Montreal and Kingston: McGill-Queen's University Press, 1994.

McKenzie, Kirsten. "Being Modern on a Slender Income: 'Picture Show' and 'Photoplayer' in early 1920s Sydney." *Journal of Women's History* 22, No. 4 (Winter 2010): 114–36.

McLaren, Angus. *Our Own Master Race: Eugenics in Canada, 1885–1945*. Toronto: McClelland and Stewart, 1990.

McLaren, Angus and Arlene Tigar McLaren. *The Bedroom and the State: The Changing Practices and Politics of Contraception and Abortion in Canada, 1880–1997*. Don Mills: Oxford University Press, 1997 [1986].

McMaster, Lindsey. *Working Girls in the West: Representations of Wage-Earning Women*. Vancouver: University of British Columbia Press, 2008.

McPherson, Kathryn. "'The Case of the Kissing Nurse': Femininity, Sexuality, and Canadian Nursing, 1900–1970." In *Gendered Pasts: Historical Essays in Femininity and Masculinity in Canada* edited by Kathryn McPherson, Cecilia Morgan, and Nancy M. Forestell, 179–98. Don Mills: Oxford University Press, 1999.

McRobbie, Angela. *Feminism and Youth Culture: From Jackie to Just Seventeen*. London: Macmillan, 1987.

Mellen, Peter. *The Group of Seven.* Toronto: McClelland and Stewart, 1970.

Melman, Billie. *Women and the Popular Imagination in the Twenties: Flappers and Nymphs.* London: Macmillan Press, 1988.

Miller, Ian Hugh Maclean. *Our Glory and Our Grief: Torontonians and the Great War.* Toronto: University of Toronto Press, 2002.

Miller, J.R. *Shingwauk's Vision: A History of Native Residential Schools.* Toronto: University of Toronto Press, 1996.

Miller, Muriel. *Famous Canadian Artists.* Peterborough: Woodland Publishing, 1983.

Miller, Nathan. *New World Coming: The 1920s and the Making of Modern America.* New York: Schribner, 2003.

Mitchinson, Wendy. *The Nature of Their Bodies: Women and Their Doctors in Victoria Canada.* Toronto: University of Toronto Press, 1991.

Monod, David. *Store Wars: Shopkeepers and the Culture of Mass Marketing, 1890–1939.* Toronto: University of Toronto Press, 1996.

Morgan, Ceclia. *Public Men and Virtuous Women: The Gendered Languages of Religion and Politics in Upper Canada, 1791–1850.* Toronto: University of Toronto Press, 2006.

- *"A Happy Holiday": English Canadians and Transatlantic Tourism, 1870–1930.* Toronto: University of Toronto Press, 2008.

Morris, Jerrold. *The Nude in Canadian Painting.* Toronto: New Press, 1972.

Morris, Peter. *Embattled Shadows: A History of Canadian Cinema, 1985–1939.* Montreal and Kingston: McGill-Queen's University Press, 1978.

Morton, Suzanne. *Ideal Surroundings: Domestic Life in a Working-Class Suburb in the 1920s.* Toronto: University of Toronto Press, 1995.

Myers, Tamara. *Caught: Montreal's Modern Girls and the Law, 1869–1945.* Toronto: University of Toronto Press, 2006.

Nasgaard, Roald. *The Mystic North: Symbolist Landscape Painting in Northern Europe and North America, 1890–1940.* Toronto: University of Toronto Press, 1984.

Nead, Lynda. *The Female Nude: Art, Obscenity and Sexuality.* New York: Routledge, 1992.

- "Paintings, Films, and Fast Cars: A Case Study of Hubert von Herkomer." *Art History* 25, no. 2 (April 2002): 240–55.

- "Strip! Moving Bodies in the 1890s." *Early Popular Visual Culture* 3, no. 2 (September 2005): 135–50.

Needham, Gerald. "Manet, 'Olympia' and Pornographic Photography." In *Woman as Sex Object: Studies in Erotic Art, 1730–1970,* edited by Thomas B. Hess and Linda Nochlin, 80–9. London: Allen Lane, 1972.

Nelles, H.V. *The Art of Nation-Building: Pageantry and Spectacle at Quebec's Tercentenary.* Toronto: University of Toronto Press, 1999.

Newman, Karen. "Directing Traffic: Subjects, Objects, and the Politics of Exchange." *Differences* 2, no. 2 (1990): 41–54.

Nicholas, Jane. "Gendering the Jubilee: Gender and Modernity in the Diamond Jubilee of Confederation Celebrations, 1927." *Canadian Historical Review* 90, no. 2 (June 2009): 247–74.

– "Representing the Modern Man: Beauty Culture and Masculinity in Early Twentieth Century Canada." In *Canadian Men and Masculinities: Historical and Contemporary Perspectives*, edited by Wayne Martino and Christopher Greig. Toronto: Canadian Scholars' Press, 2012.

Ohmann, Richard. *Selling Culture: Magazines, Markets, and the Class at the Turn of the Century*. London and New York: Verso, 1998.

Opp, James. *The Lord for the Body: Religion, Medicine, and Protestant Faith Healing in Canada, 1880-1930*. Montreal and Kingston: McGill-Queen's University Press, 2007.

Osborne, Brian. "The Iconography of Nationhood in Canadian Art." In *The Iconography of Landscape: Essays on the Symbolic Representation, Design and Use of Past Environments*, edited by David Cosgrove and Stephen Daniels, 162–78. Cambridge: Cambridge University Press, 1988.

Ostrey, Aleck. *Nutrition Policy in Canada, 1870–1939*. Vancouver: University of British Columbia Press, 2006.

Palmer, Bryan. *Working Class Experience: The Rise and Reconstitution of Canadian Labour, 1800–1980*. Toronto, Butterworth, 1983.

Pang, Henry. "Miss America: An American Ideal, 1921-1969." *Journal of Popular Culture* 2, no. 4 (1969): 687–96.

Pantazzi, Sybille. "Foreign Art at the Canadian National Exhibition, 1905-1938." *National Gallery of Canada Bulletin* 22 (1973).

Parr, Joy. *The Gender of Breadwinners: Women, Men and Change in Two Industrial Towns, 1880–1950*. Toronto: University of Toronto Press, 1990.

– *Domestic Goods: The Material, The Moral, and the Economic in the Postwar Years*. Toronto: University of Toronto Press, 1999.

Peiss, Kathy. *Cheap Amusements: Working Women and Leisure in Turn-of-the-Century New York*. Philadelphia: Temple University Press, 1986.

– "Making Up, Making Over: Cosmetics, Consumer Culture, and Women's Identity." In *The Sex of Things Consumption in Historical Perspective*, edited by Victoria de Grazie, with Ellen Furlough, 311–36. Berkeley: University of California Press, 1996.

– *Hope in a Jar: The Making of America's Beauty Culture*. New York: Metropolitan Books, 1998.

– "Girls Lean Back Everywhere." In *The Modern Girl Around the World*, edited by Alys Weinbaum, et al., 347–53. Durham, NC: Duke University Press, 2008.

Pendergast, Tom. *Creating the Modern Man: American Magazines and Consumer Culture, 1900–1950.* Columbia and London: University of Missouri Press, 2000.

Pennington, Doris. *Agnes Macphail: Reformer: Canada's First Female MP.* Toronto: Simon and Pierre, 1989.

Perry, Adele. *On the Edge of Empire: Gender, Race, and the Making of British Columbia, 1849–1871.* Toronto: University of Toronto Press, 2001.

Pett, L.B. "The Canadian weight-height survey," *Human Biology* 28 (1956): 177–88.

Phillips, Ruth B. "Performing the Native Woman: Primitivism and Mimicry in Early Twentieth-Century Visual Culture." In *Antimodernism and the Artistic Experience: Policing the Boundaries of Modernity*, edited by Lynda Jessup, 26–49. Toronto: University of Toronto Press, 2001.

Pickles, Katie. "The Old and New on Parade: Mimesis, Queen Victoria, and Carnival Queens on Victoria Day in Interwar Victoria." In *Contact Zones: Aboriginal and Settler Women in Canada's Colonial Past*, edited by Katie Pickles and Myra Rutherdale, 272–91. Vancouver: University of British Columbia Press, 2005.

Pollock, Griselda. *Visions and Difference: Feminism, Femininity, and Histories of Art.* New York: Methune, 1988.

– "Beholding Art History: Vision, Place, and Power." In *Vision and Textuality*, edited by Stephen Melville and Bill Readings, 48–67. Durham, NC: Duke University Press, 1995.

Prentice, Alison, Paula Bourne, Gail Cuthbert Brandt, Beth Light, Wendy Mitchinson, and Naomi Black. *Canadian Women: A History* 2nd ed. Toronto: Harcourt Brace, 1996.

Radforth, Ian. "Performance, Politics, and Representation: Aboriginal People and the 1860 Royal Tour of Canada." *Canadian Historical Review* 84, no. 1 (March 2003): 1–32.

– *Royal Spectacle: The 1860 Visit of the Prince of Wales to Canada and the United States.* Toronto: University of Toronto Press, 2004.

Ramamurthy, Priti. "All-Consuming Nationalism: The Indian Modern Girl in the 1920s and 1930s." In *The Modern Girl Around the World*, edited by Alys Weinbaum, et al., 147–73. Durham: University of North Carolina Press, 2008.

Rennie, Karen. *Moon Magic: Gail Grant and the 1920s Dance in Regina.* Toronto: Dance Collection Danse, 1992.

Regular, Keith. "On Public Display." *Alberta History* 34, no. 1 (Winter 1986): 1–10.

Riverol, A.R. *Live From Atlantic City: The History of the Miss America Pageant Before, After and in Spite of Television.* Bowling Green, OH: Bowling Green State University Popular Press, 1992.

Roberts, Mary Louise. *Civilization Without Sexes: Reconstructing Gender in Postwar France, 1917–1927*. New York: Columbia University Press, 1994.

Robertson, Jennifer. "Japan's First Cyborg? Miss Nippon, Eugenics, and Wartime Technologies of Beauty, Body, and Blood." *Body and Society* 7, no. 1 (2001): 1–34.

Rockwell, Norman. *My Adventures as an Illustrator*. New York: Doubleday and Company Inc., 1960.

Ross, Kristin. *Fast Cars, Clean Bodies: Decolonization and the Reordering of French Culture*. Cambridge: MIT Press, 1995.

Rubin, Gayle. "The Traffic In Women: Notes on the 'Political Economy' of Sex." In *Feminist Theory: A Reader*, edited by Wendy Kolmar and Frances Bartkowski, 228–44. Mountain View, CA: Mayfield Publishing Company, 2000.

Rudy, Jarrett. *The Freedom to Smoke: Tobacco Consumption and Identity*. Montreal and Kingston: McGill-Queen's University Press, 2006.

Rutherford, Paul. "Made in America: The Problem of Mass Culture in Canada." In *The Beaver Bites Back: American Popular Culture in Canada*, edited by David H. Flaherty and Frank E. Manning, 260–80. Montreal and Kingston: McGill-Queen's University Press, 1993.

Ryan, Louise. "Locating the Flapper in Rural Irish Society: The Irish Provincial Press and the Modern Woman in the 1920s." In *New Women Hybridities: Femininity, Feminism, and International Consumer Culture, 1880–1930*, edited by Ann Heilman and Margaret Beetham, 90–101. New York: Routledge, 2004.

Ryan, Mary P. "The Projection of a New Womanhood: The Movie Moderns in the 1920s." In *The Projection of a New Womanhood: The Movie Moderns in the 1920s*, edited by William G. Shade and Jean E. Friedman. Boston: Allyn and Bacon, 1976.

Rydell, Robert. *All the World's a Fair: Visions of Empire and American International Expositions, 1876–1916*. Chicago: University of Chicago Press, 1984.

Said, Edward. *Orientalism*. New York: Vintage Books, 1978.

Sangster, Joan. "The 1907 Bell Telephone Strike: Organizing Women Workers." *Labour/Le Travail* 3 (1978): 109–30.

– *Dreams of Equality: Women on the Canadian Left, 1920–1950*. Toronto: McClelland and Stewart, 1989.

– *Earning Respect: The Lives of Working Women in Small Town Ontario, 1920–1960*. Toronto: University of Toronto Press, 1995.

– *Regulating Girls and Women: Sexuality, Family, and the Law in Ontario, 1920–1960*. Don Mills: Oxford University Press, 2001.

Sato, Barbara. *The New Japanese Woman: Modernity, Media and Women in Interwar Japan*. Durham and London: Duke University Press, 2003.

– "Contesting Consumerisms in Mass Women's Magazines." In *The Modern Girl
   Around the World*, edited by Alys Weinbaum, et al., 263–87. Durham:
   University of North Carolina Press, 2008.
Scanlon, Jennifer. *Inarticulate Longings: The Ladies' Home Journal, Gender and the
   Promise of Consumer Culture*. New York and London: Routledge, 1995.
Schneirov, Matthew. *The Dream of a New Social Order: Popular Magazines in
   America, 1893–1914*. New York: Columbia University Press, 1994.
Schwartz, Vanessa R. "Walter Benjamin for Historians." *American Historical
   Review* 106, no. 5 (December 2001): 1721–43.
Scott, Joan Wallach. *Gender and the Politics of History*. New York: Columbia
   University Press, 1988.
Shantz, Mary Ann. "Citizenship Embodied and the Body as Spectacle: Nudist
   Pageants in Postwar Canada." In *Contesting Bodies and Nation in Canadian
   History*, edited by Patrizia Gentile and Jane Nicholas. Toronto: University of
   Toronto Press, 2013.
Shissler, A. Holly. "Beauty is Nothing to be Ashamed of: Beauty Contests as
   Tools of Women's Liberation in Early Republican Turkey." *Comparative Studies
   of South Asia, Africa and the Middle East* 21, no. 1 (2004): 107–22.
Shteir, Rachel. *Striptease: The Untold History of the Girlie Show*. New York: Oxford
   University Press, 2004.
Shulman, Irving. *Valentino*. London: Leslie Frewin, [1967] 1968.
Silverberg, Miriam. "The Modern Girl as Militant." In *Recreating Japanese Women,
   1600–1945*, edited by Gail Bernstein, 239–66. Berkeley: University of
   California Press, 1991.
Slater, Don. *Consumer Culture and Modernity*. Cambridge: Polity, 1999.
Sluis, Ageeth. "BATACLANISMO! Or, How Female Deco Bodies Transformed
   Postrevolutionary Mexico City." *The Americas* 68, no. 4 (April 2010): 469–99.
Smart, Judith. "Feminists, flappers, and Miss Australia: contesting the meanings
   of citizenship, femininity and the nation in the 1920s." *Journal of Australian
   Studies* 71 (2001) 1–16.
Smith, Alison. *The Victorian Nude: Sexuality, Morality and Art*. Manchester:
   Manchester University Press, 1996.
Søland, Brigitte. *Becoming Modern: Young Women and the Reconstruction of
   Womanhood in the 1920s*. Princeton and Oxford: Princeton University Press,
   2000.
Solomon-Godeau, Abigail. "The Legs of the Countess." *October* 39 (Winter
   1986): 65–108.
– "The Other Side of Venus: The Visual Economy of Feminine Display." In *The
   Sex of Things: Gender and Consumption in Historical Perspective*, edited by Victoria

de Grazia with Ellen Furlough, 113–50. Berkeley: University of California Press, 1996.

Srigley, Katrina. "Clothing Stories: Consumption, Identity, and Desire in Depression-Era Toronto." *Journal of Women's History* 19, no. 1 (2007): 82–104.

Stamp Lindsey, Shelley. "Toronto's 'Girl Workers': The Female Body and Industrial Efficiency in *Her Own Fault.*" *Cinemas: Journal of Film Studies* 6, no. 1 (Fall 1995): 81–99.

Stearns, Peter N. *Fat History: Bodies and Beauty in the Modern West.* New York: New York University Press, 2002.

Steedman, Carolyn Kay. *Landscape for a Good Woman.* New Brunswick, NJ: Rutgers University Press, 1987.

Steedman, Mercedes. *Angels of the Workplace: Women and the Construction of Gender Relations in the Canadian Clothing Industry, 1890–1940.* Toronto: McClelland and Stewart, 1997.

Steele, Valerie. *Fashion and Eroticism: Ideals of Feminine Beauty from the Victorian Era to the Jazz Age.* New York, Oxford University Press, 1985.

Stencell, A.W. *Girl Show: Into the Canvas World of Bump and Grind.* Toronto: ECW Press, 1999.

Stern, Bat-Sheva Margalit. "Who's the Fairest of Them All? Women, Womanhood, and Ethnicity in Zionist Eretz Isael." *Nasham: A Journal of Jewish Women's Studies and Gender Issues* 11, no. 1 (Spring 2006): 142–63.

Stewart, Mary Lynn. *Dressing the Modern Frenchwomen: Marketing Haute Couture, 1919–1939.* Baltimore: Johns Hopkins University Press, 2008.

Stratton, Jon. *The Desirable Body: Cultural Fetishism and the Erotics of Consumption.* Manchester: Manchester University Press, 1996.

Strange, Carolyn. *Toronto's Girl Problem: The Perils and Pleasures of the City, 1800–1930.* Toronto: University of Toronto Press, 1995.

Strange, Carolyn and Tina Loo. *Making Good: Law and Moral Regulation in Canada, 1867–1939.* Toronto: University of Toronto Press, 1997.

Strong-Boag, Veronica. *The Parliament of Women: The National Council of Women of Canada, 1893–1929.* Ottawa: National Museum, 1976.

– *The New Day Recalled: Lives of Girls and Women in English-Canada, 1919–1939.* Toronto: Copp, Clark, Pitman, 1988.

Strong-Boag Veronica and Carole Gerson. *Paddling Her Own Canoe: The Times and Texts of E. Pauline Johnson Tekahionwake.* Toronto: University of Toronto Press, 2000.

Studlar, Gaylyn. "'The Perfect Lover'? Valentino and Ethnic Masculinity in the 1920s." In *The Silent Film Reader,* edited by Lee Grievson and Peter Krämer, 290–304. New York: Routledge, 2004.

Susman, Warren, I. "'Personality' and the Making of Twentieth-Century Culture." In *New Directions in American Intellectual History*, edited by John Higham and Paul K. Conkin, 212–26. Baltimore: Johns Hopkins University Press, 1979.

Sutherland, Fraser. *The Monthly Epic: A History of Canadian Magazines 1789–1989*. Markham, ON: Fitzhenry and Whiteside, 1989.

Thompson, John Herd with Allen Seager. *Canada 1922–1939: Decades of Discord.* Toronto: McClelland and Stewart, 1985.

Tinkler Penny and Cheryl Krasnick Warsh. "Feminine Modernity in Interwar Britain and North America: Corsets, Cars, and Cigarettes." *Journal of Women's History* 20, no. 3 (2008): 113–43.

Tippet, Maria. *Making Culture: English-Canadian Institutions and the Arts Before the Massey Commission.* Toronto: University of Toronto Press, 1990.

Valverde, Mariana. "The Love of Finery: Fashion and the Fallen Woman in Nineteenth Century Social Discourse." *Victorian Studies* 32, no. 2 (Winter 1989): 167–88.

– *The Age of Light, Soap, and Water: Moral Reform in English-Canada, 1885–1925.* Toronto: McClelland and Stewart, 1991.

Vance, Jonathan. *Death So Noble: Memory, Meaning and the First World War.* Vancouver: University of British Columbia Press, 1997.

Veblen, Thorstein. *Theory of the Leisure Class: An Economic Study of Institutions.* New York [1912], 1972.

Vipond, Mary. "Canadian Nationalism and the Plight of Canadian Magazines in the 1920s." *Canadian Historical Review* 58, no. 1 (March 1977): 43–63.

– "The Image of Women in Mass Circulation Magazines in the 1920s." In *The Neglected Majority*, edited by Susan Mann Trofimenkoff and Alison Prentice, 116–124. Toronto: McClelland and Stewart, 1977.

Walden, Keith. *Becoming Modern in Toronto: The Industrial Exhibition and the Shaping of a Late Victorian Culture.* Toronto: University of Toronto Press, 1997.

Walker, James W. St. G. *"Race," Rights and the Law in the Supreme Court of Canada.* Waterloo: Wilfrid Laurier University Press, 1997.

Walsh, Margaret. "The Democratization of Fashion: The Emergence of the Women's Dress Pattern Industry." *Journal of American History* 66, no. 2 (September 1979): 299–313.

Ward, Peter. *White Canada Forever: Popular Attitudes and Public Policy Towards Orientals in British Columbia.* Montreal and Kingston: McGill-Queen's University Press, 1978.

Warsh, Cheryl Krasnick. "Smoke and Mirrors: Gender Representations in North American Tobacco and Alcohol Advertisements Before 1950." *Histoire sociale/ Social History* 31, no. 62 (1999): 183–222.

Watson, Elwood and Darcy Martin, eds. *There She Is, Miss America: The Politics of Sex, Beauty, and Race in America's Most Famous Pageant.* New York: Palgrave Macmillan, 2004.

Weinbaum, Alys Eve. "Racial Masquerade: Consumption and Contestation of American Modernity." In *The Modern Girl Around the World: Consumption, Modernity, Globalization,* edited by Alys Eve Weinbaum, et al., 120–46. Durham and London: Duke University Press, 2008.

Weinbaum, Alys Eve, Lynn M. Thomas, Priti Ramamurthy, Uta G. Poiger, Madeleine Y. Dong, and Tani E. Barlow, eds. *The Modern Girl Around the World: Consumption, Modernity, Globalization.* Durham and London: Duke University Press, 2008.

Weinbaum, Alys Eve, Lynn M. Thomas, Priti Ramamurthy, Uta G. Poiger, Madeleine Y. Dong, and Tani E. Barlow, "The Modern Girl as Heuristic Device: Collaboration, Connective Comparison, Multidirectional Citation." In *The Modern Girl Around the World: Consumption, Modernity, Globalization,* edited by Alys Eve Weinbaum, et al., 1–24. Durham and London: Duke University Press, 2008.

White, Randall. *Too Good To Be True: Toronto in the 1920s.* Toronto: Dundurn, 1993.

Wolf, Naomi. *The Beauty Myth: How Images of Beauty are Used Against Women.* New York: Vintage, 1991.

Wright, Cynthia. "'Feminine Trifles of Vast Importance': Writing Gender into the History of Consumption." In *Gender Conflicts: New Essays in Women's History,* edited by Franca Iacovetta and Mariana Valverde, 229–60. Toronto: University of Toronto Press, 1992.

– "Rewriting the Modern: Reflections of Race, Nation, and the Death of a Department Story." *Histoire sociale/Social History* 33, no. 65 (2000): 153–67.

Index

flappers, 76, 87, *89,* 90; "Confessions of a Flapper," 97; aging and, 40, 47, 176–7; cars and, 192; depiction of, in film and print media, 23, 28, 48–50, *96,* 97, 104, 118; perceived as moral threat, 95–7, *96,* 98, 104
Ford Models A and T, gendering of, 190
Francis, Daniel, 118

Garden, Mary, 85
gender history: and working girls, 7–8
gender relations, shifting, 97, 106
gendering of cars, 187–94
Gentile, Patrizia, 124, 146
Gibson Girl, 5, 74, 123
Gibson, Charles Dana, 5
"girl," use of word, 10–11
"Girl of Tomorrow, The," 97
Girl Power, 10
Globe (newspaper), 28, 104; on beauty pageants, 131, 132–3, 145, 146–7, 202; on CNE art exhibit, 167, 168
Gluck, Alma, 176, 177
Glyn, Elinor, 41, 143
Gold, Peggy (Miss Nanaimo), 208
Gompers, Samuel (AFL), 128
Gorman, Margaret (Miss America 1921), 128, 208
Grable, Betty, 53
Grant, Edith (Miss Regina 1927), 205–6, *207,* 208, 209, *209*
Gray, Sylvia, 71, 213
Great Gatsby, The (F. Scott Fitzgerald), 184
Grip (graphic art firm), 161
grooming in public, 74–6, 77
Grosz, Elizabeth, 8–9

Group of Seven, 13, 16, 158–61. *See also* antimodernism; cultural nationalism; nationhood and race
Grrls, 10

Haines, Fred S., 161, 163
hair removal, 50, 73, *75,* 115
hair, bobbed, 48–50; "Bernice Bobs Her Hair" (F. Scott Fitzgerald), 118; "Pokey and Her Flapper-Masher Bob," 49–50; in modern art, 157; reactions to, 82; as statement, 48–9; workplace reactions to, 48
hair, grey, 50
Halifax Herald, 211
Hansen, Miriam, 104
Harris, Lawren, 153
health, 83, 139, 186; in advertising, 195–6; cosmetics and, 80; Modern Girls and, 37, 101; of the nation, 14, 26, 84, 95, 97–8, 111, 116; sexual, 195–6. *See also* discipline of the female body
heterosexual choice, 120
heterosexual competition, 43, 133, 212
heterosexuality: in advertising, 54, 189, 203; anxieties about Modern Girls', 87, 103–4, 108; in movies, 196; restrictions on Modern Girls', 107–8
Hill, Earle, 205
Hirschbein, Laura Davidow, 47
Hjaratarson, Paul, 159
Hollywood: beauty pageants and, 199, 203–7, 206; lure of, 196–7, 203
Hollywood films, 103, 118; government intervention and, 197. *See also* Valentino, Rudolph
Hopper, Edna Wallace, 85

Studies in Gender and History

General editors: Franca Iacovetta and Karen Dubinsky